India and Japan

Strategic Studies

As India navigates its way from the margins of global politics to its very centre, the Strategic Studies Series will take a comprehensive look at relations and issues in South Asia and beyond, spanning political, economic and socio-cultural realms. The aim is to explore the relationship between politics and the multiple dimensions of power. Defining strategic studies in its broadest sense, it will focus on contemporary trends in India and the region, using historical narrative where required to provide context, and will include both theoretical and policy-oriented writings directed towards fostering rigorous scholarship. This series will comprise research monographs and edited volumes that will appeal to a wide audience of students as well as the worldwide community of South Asian scholars and practitioners.

Series Editor

Harsh V. Pant is Vice President for Studies and Foreign Policy at Observer Research Foundation, New Delhi and Professor of International Relations with King's India Institute at King's College London.

Other Books from the Series

Chris Ogden (ed.), *New South Asian Security: Six Core Relations Underpinning Regional Security*

Harsh V. Pant (ed.), *Afghanistan's Regional Dilemmas: South Asia and Beyond*

Harsh V. Pant, *Indian Foreign Policy: An Overview*

Yogesh Joshi and Frank O'Donnell, *India in Nuclear Asia: Evolution of Regional Forces, Perceptions, and Policies*

T. V. Paul (ed.), *The China–India Rivalry in the Globalisation Era*

E. Sridharan (ed.), *Eastward Ho? India's Relations with the Indo-Pacific*

Šumit Ganguly and Dinshaw Mistry (eds), *Enduring and Emerging Issues in South Asian Security*

India and Japan
A Natural Partnership in the Indo-Pacific

Edited by

Harsh V. Pant
Madhuchanda Ghosh

Orient BlackSwan

INDIA AND JAPAN: A NATURAL PARTNERSHIP IN THE INDO-PACIFIC

ORIENT BLACKSWAN PRIVATE LIMITED

Registered Office
3-6-752 Himayatnagar, Hyderabad 500 029, Telangana, India
e-mail: centraloffice@orientblackswan.com

Other Offices
Bengaluru, Chennai, Guwahati,
Hyderabad, Kolkata, Mumbai,
New Delhi, Noida, Patna

First published by Orient Blackswan Private Limited 2024

ISBN 978-93-5442-797-8

041153

Typeset in
ITC Berkeley 10/12.5
by Manmohan Kumar, Delhi

Printed in India at
Avantika Printers Private Limited, New Delhi 110 020

Published by
Orient Blackswan Private Limited
3-6-752 Himayatnagar, Hyderabad 500 029, Telangana, India
e-mail: info@orientblackswan.com

For sale only in India, Pakistan, Nepal, Bhutan, Bangladesh, Sri Lanka and the Maldives.

Contents

Tables and Figures

Tables

Figures

Abbreviations

AAF	Afghan Air Force
AAGC	Asia–Africa Growth Corridor
ACD	Asian Cooperation Dialogue
ACSA	Acquisition and Cross-Servicing Agreement
ADIZ	Air Defense Identification Zone
ADMM-Plus	ASEAN Defense Ministers' Meeting Plus
AEP	Act East Policy
AGEs	anti-governmental elements
AI	artificial intelligence
AIIB	Asian Infrastructure Investment Bank
ALP	Afghan Local Police
ANA	Afghan National Army
ANI	Andaman and Nicobar Islands
ANP	Afghan National Police
ANSF	Afghan National Security Force
AOIP	ASEAN Outlook on the Indo-Pacific
APEC	Asia-Pacific Economic Cooperation
ARF	ASEAN Regional Forum
ASEAN	Association of Southeast Asian Nations
ATLA	Acquisition, Technology and Logistic Agency
BDN	Blue Dot Network
BIMSTEC	Bay of Bengal Initiative for Multi-Sectoral Technical and Economic Cooperation
BJP	Bhartiya Janata Party
BPM	Business Process Management
BRI	Belt and Road Initiative
CARs	Central Asian Republics
CBIC	Chennai–Bengaluru Industrial Corridor
CCP	Chinese Communist Party

CEPA	Comprehensive Economic Partnership Agreement
CNPC	China National Petroleum Corporation
CPEC	China–Pakistan Economic Corridor
CPTPP	Comprehensive and Progressive Agreement for Trans-Pacific Partnership
DBP	Defense Buildup Program
DFC	Dedicated Freight Corridor
DFCCIL	Dedicated Freight Corridor Corporation of India Limited
DIPP	Department of Industrial Policy and Promotion
DMIC	Delhi–Mumbai Industrial Corridor
DMICDC	DMIC Development Corporation
DRDO	Defence Research and Development Organisation
EAMF	Expanded ASEAN Maritime Forum
EAS	East Asia Summit
EMS	electronic manufacturing services
EPA	Economic Partnership Agreement
EPQI	Expanded Partnership for Quality Infrastructure
EWEC	East–West Economic Corridor
FDI	foreign direct investment
FIEO	Federation of Indian Export Organisations
FOIP	Free and Open Indo-Pacific (Strategy)
FTAs	Free Trade Agreements
GDP	gross domestic product
GSOMIA	General Security of Military Information Agreement
GST	Goods and Services Tax
HA/DR	humanitarian assistance and disaster relief
HIG	Hizb-e Islami Gulbuddin
HLAG	high-level advisory group
HSR	high-speed railway
IBC	Insolvency and Bankruptcy Code
ICT	Information and Communications Technology
IGHQ	Imperial General Headquarters
INA	Indian National Army
INDOPACOM	Indo-Pacific command
IONS	Indian Ocean Naval Symposium
IOR	Indian Ocean Region

IORA	Indian Ocean Rim Association
IPOI	Indo-Pacific Oceans Initiative
IRGC	Islamic Revolutionary Guard Corps
ISAF	International Security Assistance Force
ISI	Inter-Services Intelligence
ISIS	Islamic State of Iraq and Syria
ISKP	Islamic State Khorasan Province
JAI	Japan-America-India
JBIC	Japan Bank for International Cooperation
JETRO	Japan External Trade Organization
JICA	Japan International Cooperation Agency
JIMEX	Japan-India Maritime Exercise
JIT	Japan Industrial Townships
JMSDF	Japan Maritime Self-Defence Force
JNPT	Jawaharlal Nehru Port
JSG	Joint Study Group
JUSE	Union of Japanese Scientists and Engineers
LDB	Logistics Data Bank
LEMOA	Logistics Exchange Memorandum of Agreement
LOTFA	Law and Order Trust Fund
LTTE	Liberation Tigers of Tamil Eelam
MAHSR	Mumbai–Ahmedabad High-Speed Railway
MEA	Ministry of External Affairs
MeitY	Ministry of Electronics and Information Technology
METI	Ministry of Economy, Trade and Industry
MNRE	Ministry of New and Renewable Energy
MoC	Memorandum of Cooperation
MOU	Memorandum of Understanding
MSDF	Maritime Self Defense Force
MSRI	Maritime Silk Road Initiative
NA	Northern Alliance
NDB	New Development Bank
NDS	National Directorate of Security
NDS	National Defence Strategy
NICDC	National Industrial Corridor Development Corporation
NPT	Nuclear Non-Proliferation Treaty
NSS	National Security Strategy

NTPC	National Thermal Power Corporation
OBOR	One Belt One Road
ODA	Official Development Assistance
OECD	Organization for Economic Co-operation and Development
OIC	Organisation of Islamic Cooperation
PACOM	Pacific Command
PLA	People's Liberation Army
PLAN	People's Liberation of Army Navy
PLI	Production-linked Incentive
PPP	public–private partnership
PRC	People's Republic of China
PTAs	Preferential Trade Agreements
Quad/QSD	Quadrilateral Security Dialogue
RCEP	Regional Comprehensive Economic Partnership
ReCAAP	Regional Cooperation Agreement on Combating Piracy and Armed Robbery against Ships in Asia
RFID	radio frequency identification
RIMPAC	Rim of Pacific
RSM	Resolute Support Mission
SAARC	South Asian Association for Regional Cooperation
SARS	Severe Acute Respiratory Syndrome
SBI	State Bank of India
SCO	Shanghai Cooperation Organisation
SCRI	Supply Chain Resilience Initiative
SDF	Self-Defense Forces
SDGs	Sustainable Development Goals
SIGAR	Special Inspector General for Afghanistan Reconstruction
SIMBEX	Singapore-India Maritime Bilateral Exercises
SLOCs	sea lines of communication
STEP	Special Terms for Economic Development Partnership
SUVs	sport utility vehicles
TPP	Trans-Pacific Partnership
TQM	total quality management
TSD	Trilateral Strategic Dialogue
UIDAI	Unique Identification Authority of India
UNAMA	United Nations Assistance Mission in Afghanistan

UNCLOS	United Nations Convention on the Law of the Sea
UNDP	United Nations Development Programme
WASH	water, sanitation and hygiene
WMDs	weapons of mass destruction
WPNS	Western Pacific Naval Symposium
WWII	World War II

one

Introduction

Harsh V. Pant and Madhuchanda Ghosh

In the 21st century, the Indo-Pacific region has emerged as a new theatre of strategic and economic competition in the world. The Indo-Pacific refers to the Western Pacific and the Indian Ocean regions as an interconnected geopolitical and economic space. Major international and regional powers, for instance, Pacific actors such as Japan and the United States, Pacific Rim actors in the South China Sea and the Western Pacific, and India in the Indian Ocean[1] are projecting their soft and hard power and forging partnerships amongst themselves in maritime trade as well as Humanitarian Assistance and Disaster Relief (HADR) exercises.

India and Japan have always been two critical anchors in the very conceptualisation of the Indo-Pacific.[2] The concept itself was first introduced by Japan's former Prime Minister Shinzo Abe. In his 2007 address to the Indian Parliament, Abe floated the idea of the 'confluence of the Indian and the Pacific Oceans' as the 'seas of freedom and prosperity'.[3] During his second term as the prime minister, Abe expanded the concept and talked about a 'quadrilateral initiative', the 'Arc of Freedom and Prosperity', Asia's 'democratic security diamond' and a 'Free and Open Indo-Pacific' (FOIP) connecting the two oceans—the Indian and the Pacific—and the two continents—Asia and Africa.[4] All these conceptualisations refer to India as a key partner of Japan in the Indo-Pacific region.

The strategic salience of the Indo-Pacific concept appears to stem from the fact that India has emerged as a central regional actor with a growing presence in Southeast and East Asia.[5] Moreover, the great dependence of international trade and energy flows on the sea lines of communication (SLOCs) between the Pacific and the Indian Oceans is another factor behind the world's growing focus on the region. A major reason for the structural shift to the Indo-Pacific region has been the rise of China as a comprehensive international power. China today seeks to carve out a new Sino-centric world order facilitated by its Belt and Road Initiative (BRI) and underpinned by an aggressive pursuit of territorial claims. The shift can also be attributed to the relative decline of the US's influence in Asia in recent years.

With the emerging structural changes, the parameters of Japan and India's foreign policies are undergoing significant transformation. Japan appears to be emerging as a 'normal state'. This has been evident from the former Abe administration's endeavour to restore Japan's position as a 'normal' country by receding from its post-World War II pacifist constitutional orientation. India on the other hand is growing its strategic profile by expanding its naval influence beyond the Indian Ocean and by forging strategic links with the major powers in the region and beyond.

Significantly, since the dawn of the new millennium, India's relationship with Japan has evolved from a global partnership to a 'Special Strategic and Global Partnership'.[6] This indicates the steady expansion of the scope and nature of their relationship. The present-day warmth and cordiality reached through a substantial progress in India–Japan relations stand in stark contrast to the mutual indifference of the past when the Cold War in Asia cast a shadow on the bilateral relationship.

Strategic Divide in Cold War Asia

Positioned at opposite ends of the Asian geopolitical spectrum, the political will to develop a robust relationship was grossly lacking on both sides. The leaderships of both Japan and India found it hard to look for congruence of interests and comprehend each other's security compulsions. On the economic front, the divergence was marked by Japan's free-market economy and its remarkable growth from the 1960s to the 1980s as opposed to India's inward-looking mixed economic model. The pressures of strategic and geopolitical imperatives during the Cold War contributed to the divergence in foreign policy objectives between India and Japan. While Japan was reluctant to deepen its engagement with a pro-Soviet India, India perceived Japan as toeing the American line on regional and global issues and lacking its own independent political and diplomatic standpoint. In short, it was a saga of missed opportunities because of the adverse geostrategic and geopolitical scenario caused by the Cold War.

Growing Synergy in Post-Cold War Asia

The structural changes in post-Cold War Asia have given Japan and India much more strategic manoeuvrability. India's economic liberalisation has helped the country broaden its relations with most of the major powers in the world, including the US and Japan. India–Japan relations have undergone unprecedented transformation during the tenures of the Japanese premiers Junichiro Koizumi and Shinzo Abe, which have contributed to building a robust strategic relationship between the two countries.

Koizumi Era

In a major commitment to India's economic growth, Japanese Prime Minister Junichiro Koizumi announced Japan's support to India's flagship infrastructural project, the Delhi–Mumbai freight and industrial corridors.[7] In April 2005, Koizumi's India visit led to the creation of the India–Japan Joint Study Group (JSG), with the objective of suggesting measures to expand trade and improve economic relations between the two countries. In 2006, the JSG recommended developing an Economic Partnership Agreement (EPA)/Comprehensive Economic Partnership Agreement (CEPA).[8] Subsequently, during then Prime Minister Manmohan Singh's visit to Tokyo in October 2010, the two countries signed a Joint Declaration on the conclusion of the CEPA. In February 2011, Japan's Foreign Minister Seiji Maehara and India's Commerce and Industry Minister Anand Sharma signed the CEPA in Tokyo.[9]

The CEPA aimed to eliminate tariffs on 90 per cent of Japanese exports to India and 97 per cent of Indian exports to Japan. The bilateral trade, estimated at a meagre USD 3.5 billion in 1990, rose to USD 14.6 billion in 2010. After CEPA, India's exports witnessed growth from 2011. It peaked at USD 7.3 billion in 2013. According to the Ministry of Commerce, India's exports to Japan stood at USD 4.5 billion in 2019–20 and imports from Japan at USD 12.43 billion. In 2020, the trade balance widened to USD 7.91 billion in favour of Japan.[10]

Abe Era

During his two tenures as Japan's premier, Koizumi's successor Shinzo Abe further encouraged this growing friendship between the two countries.

Abe was perhaps Japan's most Indophile prime minister. The Abe era led to Tokyo's massive infrastructural investment in India. During the meeting between Prime Minister Narendra Modi and his then Japanese counterpart Abe in September 2014, Japan declared 3.5 trillion yen of public and private investment and financing, including Official Development Assistance (ODA), into India in the next five years to finance appropriate public and private projects of mutual interest.[11]

The breakthroughs achieved in Japan–India relations during the Abe period included a Special Strategic Partnership between Tokyo and New Delhi, a mechanism of an annual prime ministerial-level summit as well as an Acquisition and Cross-Servicing Agreement (ACSA).[12] The ACSA allows India and Japan to share resources such as food and fuel between Japan' s Self-Defense Forces and the Indian military. It grants Japan access to Indian naval facilities in the Andaman and Nicobar Islands and allows India access to Japan's naval facilities in Djibouti. Interestingly, Abe himself moved the Indo-Japan civil nuclear partnership through Japan's legislature, the National Diet. This pact was Japan's first with a non-NPT nation. During Modi's visit to Japan in 2016, India and Japan signed the 'Agreement for Cooperation in Peaceful Uses of Nuclear Energy'.[13] The two sides signed agreements on manufacturing skill development in India, cooperation in space, earth sciences, agriculture, forestry and fisheries, transport and urban development.

It may be recalled that Modi and Abe also developed a close personal relationship during this time. During the 2017 summit, Modi hosted Abe in Ahmedabad with great fanfare, including a road-show, visits to historical sites and a traditional Gujarati dinner.[14] Reciprocating this gesture, Abe welcomed Modi informally in his holiday home overlooking the iconic Mount Fuji, where the two leaders held informal talks. Abe also hosted Modi at a personal villa near Lake Kawaguchi in Yamanashi for a private dinner.[15] Modi happens to be the only foreign political leader to have received such a personal welcome from Abe.

During the Indian Prime Minister's October 2018 visit to Japan, New Delhi and Tokyo signed a new Memorandum of Cooperation on healthcare to pursue the synergies between India's Ayushman Bharat Digital Mission and Japan's Asia Health and Wellbeing Initiative.[16] This was aimed at pursuing mutual cooperation in various fields, such as honing the skills of doctors in key emerging areas as well as providing technical training for Indian nurses studying in Japanese caregiving facilities. Japan is also keen on Ayurveda which it envisions incorporating in its healthcare system to bring a new dimension to the sector.

Emerging Contours of India–Japan Relations in Post-Covid Asia

Relations between India and Japan have continued to grow further in the post-Abe political landscape of Japan as well. Japanese Premier Yoshihide Suga made it clear in his very first remark after being elected to his new post by the Parliament in September 2020 that his dispensation would be towards a 'continuity cabinet' to further advance all the policies followed by his predecessor Abe.[17]

Going by a press release issued by India's Ministry of External Affairs (MEA) on 25 September 2020, after Prime Minister Modi telephonically congratulated Suga on his taking over as Japan's premier, the two top leaders agreed to strengthen the India–Japan Special Strategic and Global Partnership.[18] They concurred that the New Delhi–Tokyo partnership is more relevant in today's times given the global challenges, including the COVID-19 pandemic. Both emphasised the economic architecture of a free, open and inclusive Indo-Pacific region.

In recent years, Japan has helped in India's effort to achieve Sustainable Development Goals (SDGs) set forward by the UN. Japan has made public and private effort in India in the fields of healthcare, WASH (water, sanitation and hygiene), environment and women's empowerment.[19] In this context, it needs to be noted that in the UN SDG Summit 2023, Prime Minister Fumio Kishida expressed his government's determination to strongly lead the international community's efforts to achieve the SDGs.[20] The Kishida government has been advocating focus on the concept of human security as the key to achieving the SDGs related to 'human dignity'[21] and at the SDG summit, the Japanese premier emphasised that Japan will continue to contribute towards the achievement of the SDGs related to this concept.[22] In the G7 Hiroshima Summit held in May 2023 too, Japan, as the G7 Presidency, led the expression of the G7's commitment to accelerate the comprehensive implementation of the SDGs.

Limited access to clean water, sanitation and hygiene (SDG 6) is usually linked to poverty (SDG 1) and hunger (SDG 2). Human health in India is adversely affected by a growing scarcity of clean water and an increasing contamination of the water system. WASH is the foundation for preventing infectious diseases as the COVID-19 pandemic has demonstrated to the world. Japanese water treatment solution provider Daiki is laying the groundwork for a world-class water resource recovery system in India using its Daiki Axis Johkasou technology to treat and reuse water bodies at a local level.[23] The Kishida government has aligned the health sector policy of the Japan International Cooperation Agency (JICA) with the Indian government's programmes towards building an Atmanirbhar (self-reliant) and Ayushman (healthy) Bharat by focusing on collaborative healthcare projects in India through ODA loans, grant aid and technical cooperation projects. JICA's support is based on need-based priorities and is in line with SDG 3 which aims to 'Ensure healthy lives and promote well-being for all at all ages'.[24] The Kishida government has also partnered with the Indian Ministry of New and Renewable Energy (MNRE) to accelerate climate-resilient development, net-zero emissions and post-COVID green recovery in 10 states across the country by extending USD 5.16 million in climate grant to the United Nations Development Programme (UNDP).[25]

Seeking solutions to environmental problems in India has become a priority and the Indian government has been promoting the 'Clean India' mission. Air pollution is a serious problem, and there is major concern about its harmful effects on the health of citizens. To address this, the Embassy of Japan in India launched 'Japan's Blue Sky Initiatives' in 2018 to promote cooperation in controlling India's air pollution through the use of Japanese knowledge and technology. 'Japan's Blue Sky Initiatives' comprise a list of efforts implemented by Japanese companies in India to improve air quality. It includes, for instance, introducing an intelligent transport system to improve the efficiency of car travel and reduce the emission of air pollutants from automobiles; developing, selling, and disseminating environmentally conscious next-generation cars to effectively control harmful emissions; developing and disseminating the use of solar pump systems for irrigation that use high-efficiency motors which can reduce the emission of air pollutants from conventional diesel pumps; making effective use of ethanol and plastics in agricultural waste to reduce the amount incinerated by conventional burning, thus reducing the resulting emission of air pollutants; expanding metro ridership and promoting a modal shift to reduce emission from automobiles.[26]

The Kishida government has driven forward initiatives for gender equality and women's empowerment in Japan. Between 2012 and 2023, the number of women workers increased by approximately 3.7 million and the number of female executives rose 5.8 times.[27] These results have come from concerted efforts among the public and private sectors to promote women's empowerment as one of the pillars of Japan's growth strategy. The Kishida administration has also positioned 'women's economic empowerment' at the core of its concept of the 'New Form of Capitalism', to resolve issues such as correcting the pay gap, promoting re-skilling and eradicating violence against women.[28] To this end, the Japanese government hosted a summit of the G7 nations on gender equality and women's empowerment. In India, Japan is promoting women's empowerment through its direct involvement in various field projects. As the former Japanese Ambassador Kenji Hiramatsu noted, 'I would like to add that Japanese companies in India are indispensable partners in the social advancement of women. To take a couple of examples, Reliance Nippon Life Insurance is hiring more than 3,500 women as Life Planning Officers in their 150 branch offices, offering customers face-to-face consultations and services.... Yakult Danone India is famous for their "Yakult Ladies" who visit customers by riding a scooter every day and deliver their healthy products.'[29]

New Dynamics in Indo-Japanese Economic Cooperation

Japan has been working with India to bolster its economy after COVID-19. Japan Bank for International Cooperation (JBIC) signed loan agreements (totaling INR 11,000 crore) with the State Bank of India (SBI) and National Thermal Power Corporation (NTPC) in October 2020 to boost India's automobile and solar power generation sectors.[30] The Ministry of Economy, Trade and Industry (METI) is working with the Ministry of Commerce and Industry to increase the competitiveness of Indian industries. Japan has been providing India with oxygen generators and helping to equip hospitals with ICUs as well as infection prevention and management facilities. Japan has also contributed towards the enhancement of telemedicine using digital technology in numerous villages across India.

In September 2020, the Commerce/Trade Ministers of Japan and India (and Australia) concurred to launch a new initiative for resilient supply chains in the Indo-Pacific region. Japan External Trade Organization (JETRO) has begun implementing the 'Program for Strengthening Overseas

Supply Chains'[31] and has already adopted two projects from India on rare earth and automobile keyless entry parts under this programme.

The atmosphere is thus very conducive for India–Japan relations to flourish in future. Former Japanese Ambassador to India Kenji Hiramatsu said, 'a strong India is in Japan's best interest and for that, we must provide even more support'.[32] In the wake of the COVID-19 outbreak, Japan provided India extensive assistance to fight the pandemic.[33] Japan's assistance has ranged from 50 billion yen (about INR 7,500 crore) budget support and 1 billion yen (about INR 150 crore) grant assistance through international organisations such as UNDP, United Nations Children's Fund (UNICEF), United Nations High Commissioner for Refugees (UNHCR) and The International Federation of Red Cross and Red Crescent Societies (IFRC).

Expanding Cooperation in Defence and Technology

The growing convergence of Indo-Japanese interests has resulted in the two nations' military cooperation expanding rapidly in recent years. Defence ties between India and Japan have grown considerably even though the Japanese bureaucracy has reportedly been dragging its feet in sharing defence equipment and technology. Today, Japan is one of India's closest friends and biggest investors.[34] Japan has involvement in virtually every large infrastructure and developmental project in India. Japan's top three carriers, NTT Docomo, KDDI and SoftBank Corp, rolled out their 5G services in 2020. Japan is keen on India's inclusion in the Comprehensive and Progressive Agreement for Trans-Pacific Partnership (CPTPP), the Regional Comprehensive Economic Partnership (RCEP) and the Blue Dot Network (BDN) driven by the US, Australia and Japan. The Joint Working Group on Information and Communications Technology (ICT), established in January 2014, has been making good progress.

Connectivity

Connectivity is getting a lot of focus in India–Japan relations today. The two states are spearheading the Asia Africa Growth Corridor.[35] They are committed to pursue joint connectivity and infrastructure projects in the Indo-Pacific area. In 2021, Japan issued its first ODA to the Andaman and Nicobar Islands situated at the mouth of the Malacca Strait.[36] Japan has also been conducting road connectivity projects in India's northeastern states such as Meghalaya, Mizoram, Assam and Tripura that border Bangladesh and Myanmar. It is expected that these efforts will lead to India's internal development and link the country more substantively to Southeast Asia.

Way Forward

In the emerging geopolitical landscape, a convergence of New Delhi's Act East Policy (AEP) and Tokyo's Free and Open Indo-Pacific Strategy is evident from the expanding bilateral cooperation between the two countries.[37] Both states have reasons to support the establishment of a rules-based order in the Indo-Pacific, safeguard the maritime commons stretching from the Indian Ocean Region (IOR) to the Pacific and contribute toward maintaining the regional balance of power. India's AEP, in consonance with Japan's FOIP, has made the idea of building trilateral and quadrilateral frameworks of cooperation central to foreign policy vis-à-vis the Indo-Pacific. Moreover, India and Japan's 'natural partnership' is a unique amalgamation. This natural partnership has immense potential for collaborative research not only in the domains of academics, linguistics, natural and social sciences but also in the unique values held by the two countries. It is now high time for Tokyo and New Delhi to aspire to move beyond the current knowledge exchanges and instead implement a holistic approach towards understanding each other more deeply. Strategically, an India–Japan partnership has immense potential in knowledge-sharing that needs greater involvement and collaboration between Indian and Japanese universities. In this regard, there is a crucial need for holistic Area Studies programmes in both countries that focus on the counterpart nation. The Japanese way of life has many commonalities with the Indian way of life—a deeper collaboration in this sphere would bolster this unique bonhomie. It is likely that the India–Japan partnership in tackling global menaces related to climate change in the dawn of the Asian Century will bring wider regional and global consensus rather than conflicts.

Driven by economic complementarities, high-powered diplomacy and shared geopolitical concerns, the India–Japan relationship is emerging as one of the strongest partnerships in Asia. As Prime Minister Modi has stated, this relationship can exercise 'a profound influence on shaping the course of Asia and our interlinked ocean regions'.[38] The bilateral and regional foreign policy goals and ambitions of India and Japan in the Indo-Pacific are clearly laid out in the 'India-Japan Vision 2025',[39] and the two states are working on translating this vision into tangible deliverables as indicated in their efforts to institutionalise the different dimensions of the bilateral relationship by undertaking several initiatives. For instance, the CEPA and the civilian nuclear deal aim at enhancing the bilateral cooperation on economic and energy issues respectively, while the 2+2 Dialogue as well as the wide range of joint initiatives in the area of defense cooperation like the Annual Defence Ministerial Dialogue and the ACSA focus on bolstering the strategic partnership. As the two major Indo-Pacific states, India and Japan's foreign policy goals to expand the framework of cooperation has translated into working together in the minilateral and multilateral forums, including the Japan-Australia-India trilateral Supply Chain Resilience Initiative (SCRI), the Japan-America-India trilateral (JAI), the Quadrilateral Security Dialogue (Quad/QSD), the Indian Ocean Rim Association (IORA) to name a few. Japan's engagement with India's Northeastern region and the Andaman and Nicobar Islands, which are India's key strategic outposts in the IOR, also reflect Tokyo's intent to perceive India as an important partner in the Indo-Pacific region. Though the bilateral relationship is seeing an unprecedented positive transformation, some constraining factors have been affecting the dynamism of this strategic partnership. Divergent perspectives of the two on the nuclear issue had been a major irritant in the bilateral relationship for decades,[40] but the two states have been able to converge on this to an extent as evident in the conclusion of the historic civil nuclear agreement.

There are other retarding factors which remain to be overcome before there can be a comprehensive and sustainable regime of cooperation between the two states. For instance, bilateral trade volume has remained low despite efforts at institutionalising the economic partnership through initiatives like the CEPA. This is because bilateral trade is adversely affected by the absence of a diversified trade structure and the range of commodities traded between the two countries has remained very narrow. Though India has gained significance as an investment destination for Japanese investors over the last decade, in terms of Japan's total outward FDI flows, India's share continues to lag behind that of other competing economies like China, Indonesia and Thailand. The poor infrastructure in India, especially in the transport and power sectors; issues concerning trade facilitation; and the complex taxation system have been impeding factors that have discouraged Japanese firms from investing in India in a big way. Moreover, several factors affect services exports from India to Japan, such as linguistic barriers, lengthy visa procedures, etc. While the economic partnership continues to be negatively impacted by such factors, Japan's security partnership with India has also confronted domestic constraints. In spite of the 2014 Peace and Security Legislation,[41] Japan's defense capability is constitutionally limited. Article 9 of the Japanese Constitution[42] remains a hindrance to expanding Japan's defense cooperation with other Indo-Pacific states including India, and there is an ongoing debate within Japan as to how far the government can go in this regard. From Abe to Kishida, policy makers have been exploring ways to make the most of what little space is available to them. While the Indo-Pacific construct assumes key importance in the policy designs of the two states, given its geostrategic dimensions, India and Japan need to work on ameliorating the existing domestic constraints to accomplish the full potential of their 'Special Strategic and Global Partnership' and realise the foreign policy goals laid out in the India-Japan Vision Statement 2025. The India–Japan partnership aims to move beyond mere cost–benefit analysis in the dynamism of international affairs and shape regional, national and international peace and security in the broader Indo-Pacific region. Common strategic interests and concerns rightly propelled Abe to call Japan and India 'natural allies' and it is in that spirit that ties between the two nations have continued to grow and evolve.

A Brief Overview of This Book

This volume attempts to critically assess the evolution of India–Japan relations with a particular focus on the growing shift in power in the Indo-Pacific region. It brings together a cross-generational group of scholars and analysts from both countries who examine various aspects of this key bilateral relationship, the growing partnership at the regional level, continuing obstacles to fully cementing the ties and concrete policies that the two sides can undertake for strengthening India–Japan relations.

In Chapter 2, 'India and Japan in the Indo-Pacific Era', Purnendra Jain analyses how mutual perceptions of the two nations have evolved and argues that the ties that bind Japan and India tightly today are based on Japan's changed perception of India. A Japan that was once neutral and even disinterested in India, neglecting the country despite New Delhi's attempt to woo Tokyo, is now deeply engaged with India.

In Chapter 3, 'Emerging Contours of India–Japan Strategic Partnership', Raj Kumar Kothari probes the growing strategic convergence between the two states in the rapidly changing Indo-Pacific strategic landscape. He underscores that the emerging post-COVID regional strategic realities are likely to push the two nations even closer and would further deepen interdependence and cooperation between them.

Chapter 4, 'The China Factor in India–Japan Relations' by Harsh V. Pant and Shashank Mattoo, delves deeper into the emergent 'China factor' in bolstering India–Japan relations. The authors argue that consolidating diplomatic efforts in the Quad, expanding the scope of cooperation to Third World countries as well as greater alignment in the domain of technology are critical developments in India and Japan's expanding engagement which demonstrate Tokyo and New Delhi's strategic balancing vis-à-vis China. However, challenges remain in the underperformance of the Asia Africa Growth Corridor (AAGC), divergences in realms of domestic economic environments and defense technology. The authors suggest that India's deepening strategic divide with China can be traced in tandem with the rapid growth in their strategic profiles and the regional ambitions of both the countries, stimulated by sustained border clashes and China's naval expansion in the IOR. They also examine the economic convergences between India and Japan by taking stock of the economic complementarity between New Delhi and Tokyo.

In Chapter 5, 'The Indo-Japanese Pivot to Asia: New Opportunities and Challenges', Madhuchanda Ghosh analyses the new phase in Indo-Japanese relations by exploring the variables shaping the emerging contours of the bilateral ties. The chapter examines the growing convergence between the two states in the rapidly changing Indo-Pacific strategic landscape. It also examines the constraints in the bilateral relationship which the two states need to work on for building a robust, comprehensive and sustainable relationship in the Asian Century.

Chapters 6 ('Partnerships in a Multi-aligned World: Quad in the Indo-Pacific' by Shubhrajeet Konwer), 8 ('India, Japan and the US: Shaping Strategic Discourse in the Indo-Pacific' by Sayantan Haldar) and 11 ('Institutionalising the Indo-Pacific: Japan–India Cooperation over Regional Multilateralism' by Kei Koga) examine Japan and India's expanding engagement in the emerging regional mini-lateral frameworks and reflect on the intricacies of the efforts of institutionalisation of the Indo-Pacific. Their analyses underscore the need to securitise the Indo-Pacific region manifested in terms of regional initiatives, such as the Quad/QSD, the JAI Trilateral Meeting, the Australia–India–Japan trilateralism and the Malabar exercises.

In Chapter 7, 'Securing the Indo-Pacific: Cooperation of Two Maritime Resident Powers', Joshy M. Paul argues that to assert itself in the IOR, Japan needs to build a credible partnership with India which is a 'resident power' in the IOR. He examines Japan's maritime security calculations and the centrality of India in Tokyo's evolving maritime security strategy towards the IOR. Chapter 9, 'Japan–India Security Cooperation amidst Regional Flux', by Satoru Nagao too provides an audit of India and Japan's regional maritime security cooperation and connectivity in the Indo-Pacific. Nagao posits that Japan and India together can play a key role in enhancing regional security in the IOR and the South China Sea and argues that the rise of India will help ease the role of the US and Japan in the IOR. He suggests that India and Japan can cooperate to fulfill several strategic objectives which include managing China in the South China Sea as well as along the India–China border.

In Chapter 10, 'Japan–India Economic Partnership in an Evolving Strategic Context', Makoto Kojima focuses on the economic ties between Japan and India and how the changing strategic calculus of the two nations is adding a new sense of urgency to further cementing the economic dimension of their engagement. Even the outbreak of COVID-19 added new momentum to their economic ties as they seek to reduce their reliance on Sino-centred supply chains for their strategic materials. He examines how India's emerging economic partnership with Japan will expand the East Asian supply chain to India. Kojima also takes note of the growth in Japanese FDI into India and the 'Make in India' initiative which has the potential to transform India into a new Asian production network.

In Chapter 12, 'Afghanistan after the US Withdrawal: New Avenues for Japan–India Cooperation', Kenta Aoki traces the potential areas of cooperation between India and Japan in Afghanistan. He looks into the rising influence of China, Russia and Iran in Afghanistan and argues that the international community should complement the peace process in the country. The chapter underscores the importance of the Chabahar Port and the need for cooperation globally, and particularly between India and Japan, to ensure peace and development in Afghanistan.

In Chapter 13, 'Remembering the War: Japan's Commemoration of the Battle of Imphal and Kohima', Ryohei Kasai examines Japan's historical connection with, and growing engagement in, India's northeastern region and the strategic importance of the Northeast as a gateway to the Indo-Pacific.

Conclusion

This volume is an attempt to bring together some of the most important thinkers in India and Japan to reflect upon the state of this very important bilateral relationship. And as the perspectives from Japan and India in this volume underscore, this bilateral relationship has indeed been going from strength to strength but it nevertheless requires constant investment from the top leaderships and bureaucracies of both nations. With increasing challenges in the Indo-Pacific, the need for like-minded nations to work together is becoming all the more necessary. India and Japan have led the way in shaping the Indo-Pacific discourse over the last decade. It is important for the two countries to take the lead in shaping the evolving strategic realities by not only nurturing their ties but also reaching out to other nations who have a similar regional and global outlook. New Delhi and Tokyo have a special responsibility in this regard as the Indo-Pacific region undergoes a dramatic transformation.

Notes and References

1. David Scott, 'India and the Indo-Pacific Discourse', in Harsh V. Pant, ed., *New Directions in India's Foreign Policy: Theory and Praxis* (Cambridge University Press, 2019), pp. 195–214.
2. Harsh V. Pant and Kashish Parpiani, *America and the Indo-Pacific: Trump and Beyond* (London: Routledge, 2021).
3. Ministry of Foreign Affairs of Japan, '"Confluence of the Two Seas": Speech by H. E. Mr. Abe Shinzo, Prime Minister of Japan at the Parliament of the Republic of India', 22 August 2007, available at http://www.mofa.go.jp/region/asia-paci/pmv0708/speech-2.html, accessed on 19 July 2023.
4. See Ministry of Foreign Affairs of Japan, 'Remarks by Mr. Nobuo Kishi, State Minister for Foreign Affairs at the Indian Ocean Conference 2016', 2 September

2016, available at https://www.mofa.go.jp/mofaj/files/000185853.pdf, accessed on 11 July 2023. However, the new diplomatic policy was called 'Free and Open India and Pacific Strategy' in this speech. Also see Ministry of Foreign Affairs of Japan, *Diplomatic Bluebook 2017* (June 2017).

5. Harsh V. Pant and Anant S. Mann, 'The Indo-Pacific: From Theory to Practice', in Pratnashree Basu, ed., *Brass Tacks: Unpacking the Indo-Pacific Template* (New Delhi: ORF and Global Policy Journal, 2021), pp. 12–18; Rory Medcalf, 'The Indo Pacific: What's in a Name?', *Brookings Institution*, 25 October 2013, available at https://www.brookings.edu/articles/the-indo-pacific-whats-in-a-name/, accessed on 11 July 2023.

6. Ministry of Foreign Affairs of Japan, 'Japan and India Vision 2025 Special Strategic and Global Partnership: Working Together for Peace and Prosperity of the Indo-Pacific Region and the World', 12 December 2015, available at https://www.mofa.go.jp/s_sa/sw/in/page3e_000432.html, accessed on 11 July 2023.

7. Embassy of Japan in India, 'Commencement of the Feasibility Study on the Development of Multimodal, High-Axle Load Dedicated Freight Corridors for Delhi-Mumbai and Delhi-Howrah Rail Routes with Computerized Control', 9 June 2006, available at https://www.in.emb-japan.go.jp/Press_Releases_Tokyo/Press_Releases_Tokyo35.html, accessed on 11 July 2023.

8. Ministry of Foreign Affairs of Japan, 'Report of the India-Japan Joint Study Group', June 2006, p. 113, available at https://www.mofa.go.jp/region/asia-paci/india/report0606.pdf, accessed on 5 August 2023.

9. Ministry of Foreign Affairs of Japan, 'Signing of the Comprehensive Economic Partnership Agreement between Japan and the Republic of India (IJCEPA) and Meeting between Mr. Seiji Maehara, Minister for Foreign Affairs, and H. E. Mr. Anand Sharma, Minister of Commerce and Industry of the Republic of India', 16 February 2011, available at https://www.mofa.go.jp/announce/announce/2011/2/0216_01.html, accessed on 11 July 2023.

10. Amiti Sen, 'CEPA Review: India Wants Pact Revision; Japan Proposes Corrections within Existing Framework', *The Hindu Business Line*, 26 February 2021, available at https://www.thehindubusinessline.com/economy/cepa-review-india-wants-pact-revision-japan-proposes-corrections-within-existing-framework/article33942744.ece, accessed on 11 July 2023.

11. Ajay Kaul, 'Japan to Give $35 Billion to India for Infra Projects', 1 September 2014, *Business Today*, available at https://www.businesstoday.in/latest/economy-politics/story/narendra-modi-japan-india-infra-projects-136280-2014-09-01, accessed on 11 July 2023.

12. Sanjay Pulipaka, 'India-Japan Strategic Partnership and the Multipower Order', *The Economic Times*, 5 November 2018, available at https://economictimes.indiatimes.com/blogs/et-commentary/india-japan-strategic-partnership-and-the-multipowerorder/, accessed on 11 July 2023.

13. Ministry of External Affairs (Government of India), 'The Entry into Force of India-Japan Agreement for Cooperation in the Peaceful Uses of Nuclear Energy', 20 July 2017, available at https://mea.gov.in/press-releases.htm?dtl/28678/The_entry_into_force_of_IndiaJapan_Agreement_for_Cooperation_in_the_Peaceful_Uses_of_Nuclear_Energy#:~:text=The%20India%2DJapan%20Agreement%20for,of%20diplomatic%20notes%20between%20Dr.&text=Kenji%20Hiramatsu%2C%20Ambassador%20of%20Japan,the%20Prime%20Minister%20to%20Japan, accessed on 11 July 2023.

14. *The Times of India*, 'PM Modi and Shinzo Abe Hold Grand Roadshow in Ahmedabad: Key Developments', 13 September 2017, available at https://timesofindia.indiatimes.com/india/pm-modi-and-shinzo-abe-hold-grand-roadshow-in-ahmedabad-key-developments/articleshow/60498490.cms, accessed on 11 July 2023.

15. Kyodo News, 'Japan PM Abe Invites Modi to Resort near Mt. Fuji', 28 October 2018, available at https://english.kyodonews.net/news/2018/10/71d8b456da29-japan-pm-abe-invites-modi-to-resort-near-mt-fuji.html, accessed on 11 July 2023.

16. Ministry of External Affairs (Government of India), 'India-Japan Vision Statement', 29 October 2018, available at https://www.mea.gov.in/bilateral-documents.htm?dtl/30543/IndiaJapan_Vision_Statement, accessed on 11 July 2023.

17. Ryotaro Nakamaru, 'Suga Becomes Japan PM, Forms Continuity Cabinet as Abe Era Ends', Kyodo News, 17 September 2020, available at https://english.kyodonews.net/news/2020/09/e728ad6b92a7-suga-to-take-office-as-japan-pm-amid-virus-economic-woes.html, accessed on 11 July 2023.

18. Ministry of External Affairs (Government of India), 'Phone Call between Prime Minister Shri Narendra Modi and H. E. Suga Yoshihide, Prime Minister of Japan', 25 September 2020, available at https://mea.gov.in/press-releases.htm?dtl/33058/Phone+call+between+Prime+Minister+Shri+Narendra+Modi+and+HE+SUGA+Yoshihide+Prime+Minister+of+Japan, accessed on 11 July 2023.

19. Japan International Cooperation Agency, 'World Water Day: JICA Facilitates Availability of Clean Drinking Water' 22 March 2020, available at https://www.jica.go.jp/Resource/india/english/office/topics/press200322.html, accessed on 11 July 2023.

20. Ministry of Foreign Affairs of Japan, 'Statement by H.E. Mr. KISHIDA Fumio, Prime Minister of Japan, at the SDG Summit, 19 September 2023', available at https://www.mofa.go.jp/files/100555630.pdf, accessed on 26 October 2023.

21. Ibid.

22. Ibid.

23. Keerthana Kantharaj, 'Here is How India & Japan Re-Use Wastewater Using Johkasou Technology', CEO Insights Asia, available at https://www.ceoinsightsasia.com/business-inside/here-is-how-india-japan-reuse-wastewater-using-johkasou-technology-nwid-9458.html, accessed on 26 October 2023.

24. JICA, 'JICA Assisted Health Sector Projects in India', available at https://www.jica.go.jp/Resource/india/english/office/others/c8h0vm00004cesxi-att/brochure_26.pdf, p.5, accessed on 26 October 2023.

25. Vishwa Mohan, 'IMD joins hands with Japan government and UNDP to accelerate climate actions', *The Times of India*, 11 August 2022, available at https://timesofindia.indiatimes.com/india/imd-joins-hands-with-japan-government-and-undp-to-accelerate-climate-actions/articleshow/93505952.cms, accessed on 26 October 2023.

26. Embassy of Japan in India, 'Japan's Blue Sky Initiatives', available at https://www.in.emb-japan.go.jp/files/000387586.pdf, accessed on 31 October 2023.

27. Ogura Masanobu (Minister in charge of Women's Empowerment and Minister of State for Gender Equality), 'Minister's Message on International Women's Day 2023', Gender Equality Bureau Cabinet Office, available at https://www.gender.go.jp/english_contents/international/un/iwd/iwd_2023.html, accessed on 26 October 2023.

28. Ibid.

29. 'Japan renews commitment to work on women empowerment in India', *Business Standard*, 6 March 2019, available at https://www.business-standard.com/article/news-ani/japan-renews-commitment-to-work-on-women-empowerment-in-india-119030600038_1.html, accessed on 26 October 2023.

30. Gaurav Noronha, 'JBIC Signs Loan Agreements Totaling Rs 11,000 crore to support Indian Industry', *The Economic Times*, 29 October 2020, available at https://economictimes.indiatimes.com/news/economy/finance/jbic-signs-loan-agreements-totaling-rs-11000-crore-to-support-indian-industry/articleshow/78928228.cms?from=mdr, accessed on 11 July 2023.

31. Dipanjan Roy Chaudhary, 'India-Japan-Australia Decide to Launch Resilient Supply Chain Initiative in the Indo-Pacific Region', *The Economic Times*, 2 September 2020, available at https://economictimes.indiatimes.com/news/economy/foreign-trade/india-japan-australia-decide-to-launch-resilient-supply-chain-initiative-in-the-indo-pacific-region/articleshow/77870346.cms?from=mdr, accessed on 11 July 2023.

32. Pramit Pal Chaudhuri, 'Defense, Connectivity Key in PM Narendra Modi's Japan Visit', *Hindustan Times*, 23 October 2018, available at https://www.hindustantimes.com/india-news/defence-connectivity-key-in-pm-narendra-modi-s-japan-visit/story-PWKXTDWWRRFVqTNVzQcV0J.html, accessed on 11 July 2023.

33. Sidhant Sibal, 'Japanese envoy calls RCEP's offer to India as observer 'exceptional'; Sees Malabar exercise with four forces next year', WION, 24 November 2020, available at https://www.wionews.com/india-news/japanese-envoy-calls-rceps-offer-to-india-as-observer-exceptional-sees-malabar-exercise-with-four-forces-next-year-345152, accessed on 11 January 2024.

34. Harsh V. Pant and Pratnashree Basu, 'A "fab" way to conduct India-Japan tech diplomacy', *The Hindu*, 19 August 2023, available at https://www.thehindu.com/opinion/op-ed/a-fab-way-to-conduct-india-japan-tech-diplomacy/article67210701.ece, accessed on 4 February 2024.

35. Frank-Jurgen Richter, 'The alternative to Chinese debt for Africa from Japan and India', *Nikkei Asia*, 23 November 2018, available at https://asia.nikkei.com/Opinion/The-alternative-to-Chinese-debt-for-Africa-from-Japan-and-India, accessed on 11 July 2023.

36. Ken Moriyasu, 'Japan sends first-ever aid to Indian islands at the mouth of Malacca', *Nikkei Asia*, 7 April 2021, available at https://asia.nikkei.com/Politics/International-relations/Indo-Pacific/Japan-sends-first-ever-aid-to-Indian-islands-at-mouth-of-Malacca, accessed on 11 July 2023.

37. ANI News, 'India's Act East policy, Japan's vision for Indo-Pacific converge at northeast: Japanese envoy', 15 February 2021, available at https://www.aninews.in/news/world/asia/indias-act-east-policy-japans-vision-for-indo-pacific-converge-at-north-east-japanese-envoy20210215141345/, accessed on 11 July 2023.

38. Ministry of External Affairs (Government of India), 'Media Statement by Prime Minister with Japanese Prime Minister in New Delhi', 12 December 2015, available at https://www.mea.gov.in/Speeches-Statements.htm?dtl/26175/Media+Statement+by+Prime+Minister+with+Japanese+Prime+Minister+in+New+DelhiDecember+12+2015#:~:text=No%20friend%20will%20matter%20more,ocean%20regions%20more%20than%20ours, accessed on 12 September 2023.

39. Ministry of External Affairs (Government of India), 'Joint Statement on India and Japan Vision 2025: Special Strategic and Global Partnership Working Together for Peace and Prosperity of the Indo-Pacific Region and the World', 12 December 2015, available at https://www.mea.gov.in/bilateral-documents.htm?dtl/26176/Joint_Statement_on_India_and_Japan_Vision_2025_Special_Strategic_and_Global_Partnership_Working_Together_for_Peace_and_Prosperity_of_the_IndoPacific_R, accessed on 11 January 2024.

40. For a detailed analysis see Madhuchanda Ghosh, 'India and Japan's Growing Synergy: From a Political to a Strategic Focus', *Asian Survey*, vol. 48, no. 2, pp. 293–296.

41. See Ministry of Foreign Affairs of Japan, 'Japan's Security Policy', available at https://www.mofa.go.jp/fp/nsp/page1we_000084.html, accessed on 11 January 2024.

42. See Prime Minister of Japan and His Cabinet, 'The Constitution of Japan', available at https://japan.kantei.go.jp/constitution_and_government_of_japan/constitution_e.html, accessed on 11 January 2024.

PART I

PERSPECTIVES FROM INDIA

two

India and Japan in the Indo-Pacific Era

Evolution of Mutual Perceptions and Bilateral Relations

PURNENDRA JAIN

India–Japan relations are now multi-dimensional and significantly deeper than what they were for much of the post-World War II period. The long-held perception of India as a 'distant nation' began to shift in the early 2000s once Japan signalled that India was an important country to foster engagement with. Early signs of change in Japan's views of India came about by a prime ministerial visit to India in the early 2000s, a couple of years after a fall-out following India's 1998 nuclear testing which Japan condemned strongly and openly. But Japan's positive views on India further intensified with Prime Minister Shinzo Abe's visit to India in 2007 and since then, the bilateral relationship has been soaring high with the two nations now recognising each other as special strategic and global partners in the Indo-Pacific strategic landscape.

The current close ties between the two nations are likely to continue mainly because of convergence in their strategic outlook in a new geopolitical and geoeconomic environment where India is considered a critical regional player. In this chapter I argue that the ties that bind Japan and India tightly today are based on Japan's changed perception of India. A Japan that was once neutral or even at times disinterested in India, despite New Delhi's attempts to woo Tokyo, is now deeply engaged with India.

To pursue the argument above, I organise this chapter under the following sections. First, I outline the two countries' brief enthusiasm for each other in the 1950s, followed by Japan's low-level engagement with India during the Cold War and post-Cold War periods for close to four decades, bringing evidence for this through both Japanese- and English-language printed sources. The second section discusses Japan's fledgling interest in India post the 1998 nuclear tests, starting with the visit of Prime Minister Yoshiro Mori in 2000, and explains the circumstances leading to this visit. In the third section, Prime Minister Abe's catalytic effect on lifting the relationship to a new height is underlined. Japan's increasing interest in India, both at government and non-government levels, is presented through numerous institutional architectures and growing Japanese business interest in India. Here we note significant growth in the military or defence fields while economic ties remain underdeveloped. The factors for such interest include changing external circumstances and increasingly positive views of India at broader levels, which will be explained by the growth in academic and popular publications on their relationships, opinion poll results and other relevant reports. The fourth and final section will discuss Japan's view of India since Abe's retirement in 2020 and what lies ahead.

In each of the four sections outlined above, India's perceptions of Japan will also be briefly discussed. Based on available evidence it is safe to conclude that India's views of Japan have generally been positive, as is evident through the continued engagement with Japan, despite New Delhi's occasional disappointment and frustration with Japan's treatment of India. Now those elements of annoyance and feelings of disappointment have largely dissipated and Japan consistently ranks high in India's perception. The relationship today stands on firm ground. However, it would not be advisable for either country to take the current relationship for granted as external and domestic circumstances do change and interests can diverge if the relationship is not nurtured and regularly renewed.

A Short Golden Period Followed by Prolonged Low-key Engagement

Relations between post-war Japan and post-Independence India began on a highly positive note. Unlike Japan's other Asian neighbours, neither India nor Japan held mutual grievances from previous encounters and India did not press Japan for war reparations. The positive historical legacy led to immense bilateral goodwill in the post-war period. India invited Japan to the first Asian Games held in New Delhi in 1951 while Japan was still under Allied occupation. India supported Japan's membership of the Colombo Plan in the face of initial objections by Australia and

New Zealand.[1] New Delhi strongly supported Japan's participation in the Afro-Asian Conference held in Bandung, Indonesia in 1955. Japan's Prime Minister Nobusuke Kishi and his Indian counterpart Prime Minister Jawaharlal Nehru received huge welcomes during their respective visits to New Delhi and Tokyo in 1957. This was preceded by a Japan visit by India's Vice President Dr Sarvepalli Radhakrishnan in 1956 and followed by India's finance minister Morarji Desai's visit to Japan in 1960, and Japanese Prime Minister Hayato Ikeda's visit to India in 1961, all of which indicated interest in each other at high levels.

India's regional peace and cooperation initiatives were reported in a positive light in Japanese newspapers, and public opinion polls in Japan placed Prime Minister Nehru as the most respected and most-liked Indian leader.[2] India supplied some key raw materials (such as iron ore) for Japan's industrialisation and became the first recipient of Japan's Official Development Assistance (ODA) loans, commonly known as yen loans, in 1958. India's rather long-held positive image in Japan (both pre-war and post-war) was captured in two major Japanese books, and one even characterised the 1950s as an 'India boom' period in Japan.[3] Japan's business communities were equally excited at the prospect of a huge market like India at a time when prospects for other markets such as China and Southeast Asia did not look bright. On the Indian side, P. A. Narasimha Murthy's writings outlined a detailed history of India–Japan relations in a comprehensive fashion with an overall friendly and mutually positive perception of each other in the early post-war years.[4]

The warmth and cordiality between the two countries did not last long as Japan's perception of India began to shift because New Delhi's worldview, foreign policy objectives and actions did not match with those of Japan's. This happened both because of India's economic and strategic unattractiveness as well as Japan shifting its focus elsewhere. Japan was tightly tied with the US via the bilateral security treaty of 1960 while India championed the Third World and actively engaged in the Non-Aligned Movement. The bilateral relationship between India and Japan during this period did not rupture but the two nations drifted apart and disillusion ensued. India's image in Japan as a 'peaceful' nation suffered hugely with the wars with China in 1962 and with Pakistan in 1965. India was likewise disenchanted with Japan's neutrality when it sought Japan's support in the abovementioned wars.[5] An eminent scholar of India's foreign policy characterised the relationship of the time as 'somnambulant'.[6]

As the bilateral relationship took a nosedive from the mid-1960s and Japan's interest in India dissipated, New Delhi was disappointed. While Japan poured billions of dollars in trade, investment and aid into East and Southeast Asia in the 1970s and 1980s, India received only a minuscule share even though India fulfilled the criteria of being a democracy and having development challenges such as poverty, which should have made it particularly eligible for a larger share of Japan's official aid. Japan willingly invested heavily in Communist China in the 1980s, while democratic India remained on the sidelines of Japan's economic outreach in Asia, despite New Delhi's appeal to Tokyo. Academics, opinion makers, political leaders and diplomats in India sought closer cooperation from Japan, but Japan's response remained cool.[7] However, one strong link that kept the two nations connected was Tokyo's continued ODA to India throughout this period and this link has been, and still is, a great connector in the bilateral relationship. Relations seemed to improve a little in the early 1990s when at the time of India's dire economic circumstances, Japan came to India's rescue through various financial packages.[8]

It is hard to find systematic surveys and public opinion poll results of perceptions of each other during this period; perhaps such polls were not conducted. Based on a quick scan of academic writings and literature both in Japanese and English, it is safe to deduce that Japan did not regard India as an attractive partner for developing a close and comprehensive relationship. Strategically, India was outside of the US camp and had embraced the Soviet Union, and thus was perceived to be on the other side in the strategic dichotomy of Cold War politics. Eminent Japanese scholar Takashi Inoguchi encapsulated this growing estrangement between Tokyo and New Delhi by noting that India had the 'largest sized embassy in Moscow, even though India's diplomatic corps was exceptionally small,' and that Japan had 'its largest embassy in Washington, D.C., giving the impression that Japan's diplomacy consisted of the United States and its smallish derivatives'.[9] Economically, Japanese recognised little potential in India's autarky with a highly regulated and socialist-type economy, where economic growth remained very low and which lacked the resources and markets that matched Japan's economic needs. With more attractive investment and trade destinations in East and Southeast Asia, Japan did not need to pay much attention to India, which was generally regarded as 'distant' and 'difficult'. A quick literature survey of the relationship of the time makes it amply clear that there was low bilateral interaction between the two, with only India periodically making approaches towards Japan. Takako Hirose characterised this period as 'the dark age' in the Japan–India relationship.[10] Marie Izuyama mentions India's 'marginalisation' in Japan's regional vision in this period.[11] Murthy's view is slightly more positive, recognising that the relationship did not break, and aid initiatives continued to serve as a connection, even if it was weak.[12]

Under the leadership of Yasuhiro Nakasone (1982–87) and Rajiv Gandhi (1984–89) in the mid-1980s, there came the promise of a 'new era' with 'winds of change', in response to Gandhi's initiatives to open up the Indian economy.[13] But that too proved short-lived, with a politically unstable period in India following the Gandhi government. Economic liberalisation in the early 1990s saw India more upbeat under the Narasimha Rao government (1991–96), with Manmohan Singh as India's finance minister. Yet post Rao, another period of political instability followed; three prime ministers from different political parties over three years signalled India's uncertain political and policy environment. In the early years after the end of the Cold War and the weakening of India's ties with the former Soviet Union (Russia) in the early 1990s, Japan's official attitude towards India remained unchanged.[14] Japan's concerns about India's bureaucratic labyrinth, lack of infrastructure, and absence of long-term policy continued as before. Takenori Horimoto, a specialist in India–Japan relations, commented that 'Japan and India have long been out of sync, their mutual interests coinciding only rarely.[15]

Japan saw no economic or geopolitical compulsions to revise its position on India and proceeded as if the Cold War strategic logic prevailed on the sub-continent. Toru Ito noted that India's interest in Japan following the end of the Cold War and the economic liberalisation programme pursued by the Rao government in the early 1990s could have launched the bilateral relationship at least in the economic field to a new height, but Japan was simply not interested at the time. Tokyo instead focused on China, South Korea and Southeast Asia, and India's nuclear testings in 1998 finally brought the relationship to its lowest point. Ito calls this the 'lost decade' in Japan–India relationship.[16] Japan responded severely to the nuclear tests with economic measures, diplomatic sanctions and the freezing of its new aid to India. Even as late as 1998, Japanese Ambassador to India Hiroshi Hirabayashi confirmed in an interview published on 12 July 1998 in *The Indian Express* that the nuclear tests were one major reason for deterioration of the relationship, but he also pointed out that the Indian economy needed accelerated reform and significant improvement in the environment for investors, and suggested that India scrap red-tapism, bureaucratic harassment and delays.[17]

India–Japan Relations: Post 1998 Nuclear Tests

The events of 1998 were a huge shock to Japan. The neglected, distant but largely amicable bilateral relationship of previous years plummeted with Japan's actively indignant response to nuclear testing by India, which did not expect such harsh criticism from Japan. But winds began to blow in the right direction again around late 1998 when Tokyo began to soften its disposition and move in a new, more cordial direction with Prime Minister Yoshiro Mori's visit to India in 2000, reciprocated by Prime Minister Atal Bihari Vajpayee's visit to Japan in 2001.[18] The Manmohan Singh government that replaced the BJP's Vajpayee government in 2004 was as enthusiastic as its predecessor to strengthen Japan ties. The process of mending the half-burnt bridge continued under Junichiro Koizumi (2001–06), but accelerated with a truly new enthusiasm when Shinzo Abe became Japan's Prime Minister in 2006. His 'Confluence of the Two Seas' speech to the Indian Parliament, on his visit to India in 2007, became one of the most cited speeches by a Japanese prime minister. Even after Abe's Liberal Democratic Party (LDP) lost power in 2009, the newly elected Democratic Party of Japan (DPJ) continued a substantial engagement with India and even achieved some notable landmarks. For example, the two nations signed a comprehensive and economic partnership agreement in 2011, and they held their first ever naval bilateral exercise in 2012.

The role of Prime Minister Singh (2004–14) was no doubt very valuable in promoting and strengthening this bilateral relationship, but Narendra Modi's coming to power in 2014 injected new energy into this relationship. Modi's deep interest in Japan, his recognition of Japan as a valuable regional partner for India, and his close personal ties with Prime Minister Abe had developed even before Modi became prime minister.[19] Abe, who was already India-inclined, grew even more enthusiastic. Not only Abe and his government, but also the Japanese media and other stakeholders in Japan generally responded well to Modi's rise in India and to his policy towards Japan. Without going into fine details, in the next section, we shall briefly outline some of the key developments in India–Japan relations in recent years and examine the factors behind the upward trajectory in bilateral ties.

Key Indicators of Strengthening Ties

This section lists some selected indicators that point to the gradual strengthening of India–Japan ties through both the pre-Modi and the Modi periods. The improvement observed in various areas of cooperation shows that bilateral ties have increased gradually in small steps rather than in leaps and bounds.

Trade and Investment

This area of bilateral ties has seen slight improvement, but remains significantly underdeveloped. Despite a Comprehensive Economic Partnership Agreement (CEPA) signed in 2011, trade volumes have not increased sizeably. Indeed, trade stagnated during 2012–13 at USD 18.5 billion. Since 2014, it began going down and in 2018–19 stood at USD 17.63 billion. Moreover, India's exports to Japan have fallen, creating a huge trade imbalance. In 2018–19, India's exports to Japan reached only USD 4.86 billion, much lower than the figures in the pre-Modi era, while Japan exported USD 12.77 billion worth of goods to India, creating more than USD 8 billion trade surplus in favour of Japan. The huge trade surplus against India continues even though bilateral trade has crossed the USD 20 billion mark set decades ago as a target.[20] Japanese direct investment in India has increased since 2008, but only erratically. From 2000 until mid-2019, total Japanese investments in India were USD 30.746 billion.[21] The number of Japanese companies operating in India has seen a steady rise—from 1,229 in 2015 to 1,454 in 2019. Significantly though, growth in the number of companies has not translated into considerable increased investment.[22] Under a 2015 Modi-Abe initiative, 12 Japanese industrial townships in nine Indian states have been set up with support from the Japan External Trade Organization.[23] India's 'Make in India' and 'Skill India' initiatives seem to have made only a small difference to Japan–India trade and investment ties. The pace and scale of development in the bilateral economic relationship have yet to take off in a significant way and the pandemic that hit India's economy hard contributed to the sluggish growth.[24] However, this may change post-pandemic due to Japan's aim to diversify its trade and investment away from China as India becomes an attractive destination. Two other areas in bilateral ties have, however, grown rapidly in recent years: Japan's aid projects in India, and more significantly, defence and security ties.

Aid Connection

Japan's ODA remained an unbroken link between Japan and India throughout the post-war period and ever since. Support towards India continued even when Japan turned its attention to China in the 1980s and 1990s with significant amounts of aid while also maintaining substantial flows to Southeast Asian nations. Even when Tokyo imposed economic sanctions on India in 1998 following the nuclear tests, it affected only new flows of aid while funding of projects already underway continued. Further, with the end of soft loans in 2008 and all aid projects to China in late 2018, Japan has substantially increased both the amount of ODA and the number of projects in India, even though Japan's overall ODA budget has shrunk. In 2015 and 2016, net yen loan disbursements to India increased substantially, with almost a 50 per cent increase in 2016 from 2014.[25] Calculations vary between the amount committed and disbursed, but loans to India increased significantly in 2021–22, as reported by the Indian Embassy in Tokyo.[26] Japan's aid to India is largely for infrastructure projects through the loan programme; grant aid and technical assistance are miniscule.[27] Japan's ODA financing of the bullet train project, which is to run from Mumbai to Ahmedabad, is a standout and strategically significant scheme.[28] Japan has never before given a country such a huge soft loan on generous terms for a single project, which symbolises Japan's deep interest in India's development and Abe's trust in India as a critical partner in his Indo-Pacific vision.[29] Most infrastructure projects in India have a strategic edge to them.[30] Japan's aid to development projects in India's Northeast or to the Andaman and Nicobar Islands have a military-strategic connotation. Locations of both these areas are strategically vital. India has for the first time accepted foreign assistance for the development of these regions, thus confirming its trust in Japan.

Defence and Security Cooperation

Of all areas, this field is the newest and most intense and distinctive in the current evolution of the bilateral relationship between India and Japan.[31] Prime ministerial summits and joint statements of the last decade have repeatedly highlighted the common security concerns of the two nations, especially those related to maritime management, including piracy and freedom of navigation. The two nations have also institutionalised their security partnerships through the Japan–India Comprehensive Security Dialogue in 2001; the Joint Statement towards a Japan–India Strategic and Global Partnership in 2006; the Joint Declaration on Security Cooperation between Japan and India in 2008; and the bilateral 2+2 Dialogue, upgraded to the ministerial level with the first meeting occurring in 2019 The two nations also signed an Acquisition and Cross-Servicing Agreement (ACSA) in 2020, allowing a reciprocal provision of supplies and services between the two armed forces.

Furthermore, high-level exchanges are in place between Japan's Acquisition, Technology and Logistics Agency and the Indian Department of Defence Production, alongside active interactions between defence industries of the two countries. At the Japan–India Summit Meeting in December 2015, the two sides signed the bilateral agreement on Transfer of Defence Equipment and Technology, and on Security Measures for the Protection of Classified Military Information, further deepening their strategic ties. Defence chiefs of the two nations now visit each other regularly and hold talks on matters of mutual concern, alongside an annual defence ministerial dialogue.[32]

India and Japan also conduct operational-level activities. The Japan Ground Self-Defense Force and the Indian Army held their first bilateral exercise in 2018. The Japan Air Self-Defense Force and the Indian Air Force also conducted their first exercise 'Shinyuu Maitri-18' in 2018. Both these exercises were conducted again in 2019 and in subsequent years, making them annual drills. The Japan Maritime Self-Defense Force and the Indian Navy have been conducting naval exercises known as the Japan India Maritime Exercise (JIMEX) since 2012, the seventh edition of which was conducted in July 2023 in India. In June 2021 alone, they conducted two exercises: one in the Indian Ocean and the other in the East China Sea.[33] K. Tamari has analysed the process of transformation from 'confrontation to cooperation' in detail.[34]

Factors Driving the Deepening Ties and Growing Interest

The China factor is the most obvious driver of India's improving relationship with Japan, as is further examined in this volume by Harsh V. Pant and Shashank Mattoo (see Chapter 4, 'The China Factor in India–Japan Relations'). Pant and Mattoo cite writings by Japanese analysts such as Takenori Horimoto and Hidetaka Yoshimatsu on the impact of China on India–Japan relations.[35] Koizumi's India visit in April 2005 came in the background of deteriorating Japan–China relations. The joint statement issued by the Indian and Japanese prime ministers on this visit emphasised the importance of the India–Japan partnership in a 'new Asian era' and the 'strategic orientation' of the nations' global partnership. Here 'strategic' was a significant addition that symbolised the nature of their converging interests.

The United States has played no less important a role in anchoring Japan to India. Mori's trip to India in 2000 followed Bill Clinton's visit to India earlier that year (22 years after Jimmy Carter's visit in 1978) and this indicated a thawing of the US and Japan's frosty relationship with India.[36] Natsuyo Ishibashi argues that Japan has been interested in seeing India aligned with US foreign policy objectives.[37] In fact, Japan–India analysis also got traction with third country scholars, beyond India and Japan-based researchers, beginning a completely new trend signifying the importance of Japan–India relations in a global context.[38] With increasing numbers of Indian IT professionals employed in Japan, India–Japan relations have also become a subject of analysis from political economy perspectives.[39] Handbooks on domestic and foreign policies of Japan and India also carry analyses of India–Japan relations.[40] In Japan, although the discussion remained rather concentrated among area studies scholars, there is now greater interest in India beyond India and South Asia specialists.[41] Overall, interest in India is rising in Japan as is evident from the growing number of publications on India in Japan, signifying the importance of this bilateral relationship both in regional and global contexts.[42] The Japanese Ministry of Foreign Affairs (MOFA) has conducted irregular public opinion polls in India to gauge India's perceptions of Japan. In a 2009 public opinion poll, 76 per cent of those polled in India believed that relations were excellent or good and they were highly appreciative of Japan's role in the world, and recognised Japan's aid and investment in India;[43] 94 per cent valued Japan as a peace-loving nation and 85 per cent valued Japan's ODA to India. Interestingly, Japan ranked as the most reliable partner (46 per cent) with Russia in number two (23 per cent) and America number three (14 per cent).[44] The latest 2022 poll results show an upward trajectory with 70 per cent of Indian respondents regarding Japan as 'very friendly' or 'somewhat friendly'.[45] In another poll too, a 2019 Pew survey, India was seen positively in Japan: 58 per cent held a favourable view of India, while only 24 per cent expressed unfavourable views.[46] Very few in these videos see India as a modern democratic state, although some do think Indians are good at mathematics.[47] The Japan–India Association publishes a range of magazines and materials highlighting India–Japan connections and developments.[48] The Association has been given an even higher profile by first appointing former prime minister Shinzo Abe to replace Mori, and after Abe's assassination in July 2022, appointing another former prime minister and Abe's confidant Yoshihide Suga as the head of the Association. Akitaka Saiki, a former Japanese ambassador to India, currently serves as the Association's president.[49] The war in Ukraine since early 2022 has brought Japan and India on different pages in terms of their strategic thinking and responses to Russia.

While Japan's expectations of India keep rising, India finds itself in a difficult situation because of various reasons. The bullet train project which was launched with much fanfare as a flagship infrastructure project has hit several bottlenecks and some expect a five-year delay in its completion and significant escalation in cost, which of course is not to Japan's liking.[50]

With Abe gone, it is not clear who India's cheerleaders are at the top political levels in Japan. Japan, under Prime Minister Kishida, is now paying more attention to Australia and the UK, both allies of the US, and there seems to be a little less emphasis on India. Under Suga, Tokyo also refocused on Southeast Asia as his visit to two Southeast Asian nations—Indonesia and Vietnam—soon after taking office would suggest. Japan's current priority is to find a balance between maintaining a solid attachment with its security provider, the US, and managing relations with its immediate neighbour China, a competitor and rival of the US. How New Delhi's strategic approach supports Japan's overall foreign policy aims will largely determine India's place in Japan's foreign policy outlook. Thus, for the bilateral relationship to maintain its momentum, it is necessary for New Delhi to keep a close eye on Tokyo's strategic thinking and make sure that India remains a strategic and economic attraction for Japan.

Notes and References

1. Hiroaki Shiga, 'Role of Japan in the Evolution of India's Aid Policy', in Jin Sato and Yasutami Shimomura, eds, *Rise of Development Donors in Asia: Emerging Donors and Japan's Impact* (London: Routledge, 2012).
2. Kohei Okata, ed., *Nihon to Indo* [Japan and India] (Tokyo: Sanseido, 1978), p. 201.
3. Okata, ed., *Nihon to Indo*; Toshio Yamazaki and Mitsuru Takahashi, eds, *Nihon to Indo: Koryu no Rekishi* [Japan and India: A History of their Relationship] (Tokyo: Sanseido, 1993), p. 218.
4. P. A. Narasimha Murthy, *India and Japan: Dimensions of their Relations: Historical and Political* (New Delhi: ABC Publishing House, 1986) and Murthy, *India and Japan: Dimensions of their Relations: Economic and Cultural* (New Delhi: Lancers Books, 1993).
5. Savitri Vishwanathan, *Indo wa Nihon kara toi kuni ka?* [Is India too far from Japan?] (Kyoto: Kokusai Nihon Bunka Kenkyu Centaa, 1993).
6. V. P. Dutt, *India's Foreign Policy in a Changing World* (New Delhi: Vikas Publishing House, 1999), p. 319.
7. Vishwanathan, *Indo wa Nihon kara toi kuni ka?*; see essays in the monthly journal *Seminar*, vol. 397 (September 1992), especially 'Wooing Japan: A Symposium on Developing a Fruitful Relationship'; Purnendra Jain and Maureen Todhunter, 'India and Japan: Newly Tempering Relations', in Purnendra C. Jain, ed., *Distant Asian Neighbours: Japan and South Asia* (New Delhi: Sterling Publishers, 1996).
8. Purnendra Jain, 'Twin Peaks: Japan's Economic Aid to India in the 1950s and 2010s', JICA-R1 Working Paper, no. 139 (February 2017), p. 21, available at https://www.jica.go.jp/Resource/jica-ri/publication/workingpaper/l75nbg0000054lpc-att/JICA-RI_WP_No.139.pdf, accessed on 18 July 2023.
9. Takashi Inoguchi, 'Japanese Foreign Policy as an "Asian" Country', in Lam Peng Er and Purnendra Jain, eds, *Japan's Foreign Policy in the Twenty-first Century: Continuity and Change* (Lanham: Lexington Books, 2020), p. 62.
10. Takako Hirose, 'Japan in Dilemma: The Search for a Horizontal Japan-South Asia Relationship', in Purnendra C. Jain, ed., *Distant Asian Neighbours: Japan and South Asia* (New Delhi: Sterling Publishers, 1996), pp. 41–44.

11. Marie Izuyama, 'India, China, and Japan's Policy of Asian Regionalism', in Kanti Bajpai, Selina Ho and Manjari Chatterjee Miller, eds, *Routledge Handbook of China–India Relations* (London: Routledge, 2020).

12. Murthy, *India and Japan: Dimension of their Relations: Economic and Cultural*, p. 335.

13. Kamlendra Kanwar, ed., *India-Japan: Towards a New Era* (New Delhi: USBPD, 1992).

14. Purnendra Jain, 'India's Calculus of Japan's Foreign Policy in Pacific Asia', in Takashi Inoguchi, ed., *Japan's Asian Policy: Revival and Response* (New York: Palgrave Macmillan, 2002).

15. Takenori Horimoto, 'Synchronizing Japan–India Relations', *Japan Quarterly*, vol. 40, no. 1 (January 1993), p. 34, available at https://search.proquest.com/docview/1304282633/fulltextPDF/7CD3CC193A3D4E3FPQ/1?accountid=8203, accessed on 20 July 2023.

16. Toru Ito, *Indo gaiko ni okeru Nihon no shuhenka* [Japan's marginalisation in India's foreign policy], in Takenori Horimoto, ed., *Gendai Nichiin kankei nyumon* [Introduction to Contemporary Japan–India Relations] (Tokyo: Tokyo University Press), p. 94.

17. *The Indian Express*, 12 July 1998, from the author's personal archive.

18. The author makes this observation based on the press clippings in his personal archive. The above observation about 1998–99 is based on reports suggesting positive directions in the relationship, following a lot of convincing by India.

19. Purnendra Jain, 'A New High', in Yamini Chowdhury and Anusua Diya Chowdhury, eds, *Modi and the World: The Ringside View Inside Out* (New Delhi: Bloomsbury, 2016).

20. Embassy of India in Tokyo, 'India-Japan Commercial Relations', available at https://www.indembassy-tokyo.gov.in/eoityo_pages/NjA, accessed 12 August 2023.

21. Ibid.

22. Figures provided by Gaimusho (Ministry of Foreign Affairs of Japan) to author in November 2019; see Japanese Embassy in India, 'Japan-India Relations', available at https://www.mofa.go.jp/region/asia-paci/india/data.html, accessed on 2 July 2021.

23. *Progress Report of the Japan Industrial Townships (JITs) in India <Japanese Side>* (Ministry of Economy, Trade and Industry (METI) Japan, February 2021), available at https://www.meti.go.jp/press/2020/03/20210315002/20210315002-1.pdf, accessed on 18 July 2023.

24. Vrishti Beniwal, Eric Martin, Dhwani Pandya and Shruti Srivastava, 'India Supercharged Its Economy 30 Years Ago, COVID-19 Unraveled It in Months', *The Japan Times*, 8 July 2021, available at https://www.japantimes.co.jp/

news/2021/07/08/business/economy-business/india-economy-covid-19/, accessed on 18 July 2023.

25. Figures provided to the author in November 2019 by the Southwest Asia Division of the Japan Ministry of Foreign Affairs.

26. Indian Embassy in Tokyo, 'India-Japan Bilateral Economic Relations', available at https://www.indembassy-tokyo.gov.in/eoityo_pages/NjQw#:~:text=Japan%20is%20the%20largest%20bilateral,related%20to%20basic%20human%20needs, accessed 16 August 2023.

27. JICA, 'Operations and Activities in India, 2020-2021', p. 8, available at https://www.jica.go.jp/Resource/india/english/office/others/c8h0vm00004cesxi-att/brochure_24.pdf, accessed 16 August 2023.

28. Purnendra Jain, 'Japan's Foreign Aid and "Quality" Infrastructure Projects: The Case of the Bullet Train in India', JICA-RI Working Paper, no. 184 (March 2019), available at https://www.jica.go.jp/Resource/jica-ri/publication/workingpaper/l75nbg0000153t43-att/JICA_RI_WP_No.184.pdf, accessed on 18 July 2023.

29. This assessment consistently figured in my conversations with my interlocutors in Japan in 2018–20.

30. Purnendra Jain, 'Japan's development assistance to India: A strategic edge?' Japan Forum, vol. 33, no. 2 (2021), available at https://doi.org/10.1080/09555803.2018.1530283, accessed on 11 January 2024.

31. Madhuchanda Ghosh, 'India and Japan's Growing Synergy: From a Political to a Strategic Focus', *Asian Survey*, vol. 48, no. 2 (2008), pp. 282–302.

32. Press Information Bureau of the Government of India, 'Joint Press Statement on the India-Japan Annual Defence Ministerial Dialogue', 20 August 2018, available at https://pib.gov.in/newsite/PrintRelease.aspx?relid=181975, accessed on 18 July 2023.

33. Ministry of Foreign Affairs of Japan, 'Agreement between the Government of Japan and the Government of the Republic of India for Cooperation in the Peaceful Uses of Nuclear Energy', available at https://www.mofa.go.jp/mofaj/files/000202920.pdf, accessed on 25 July 2019.

34. K. Tamari, 'Kaku mondai o meguru tairitsu kara kyoryoku e no tenkai' [Nuclear issues: Transformation from confrontation to cooperation], in T. Horimoto (ed.), *Gendai Nichi'In kankei nyumon* [Introduction to contemporary Japan–India relations] (Tokyo: Tokyo University Press, 2017).

35. Arpita Mathur, *India-Japan Relations: Drivers, Trends and Prospects* (Singapore: S. Rajaratnam School of International Studies, 2012); Purnendra Jain, 'Twin Peaks: Japan's Economic Aid to India in the 1950s and 2010s', JICA-RI Working Paper, no. 139 (February 2017), p. 21, available at https://www.jica.go.jp/Resource/jica-ri/publication/workingpaper/l75nbg0000054lpc-att/JICA-RI_WP_No.139.pdf, accessed on 18 July 2023; Emi Mifune, 'Rising

China and Japan-India Relations, in Takenori Horimoto, ed., *Introduction to Contemporary Japan-India Relations* (in Japanese) (Tokyo: University of Tokyo Press, 2017).

36. See chapters by Satoru Nagao, Tomoko Kiyota and Michael Kugelman in Shihoko Goto, ed., *The Rebalance within Asia: The Evaluation of Japan-India Relations* (Washington, D.C.: Wilson Center, 2014), available at http://www.wilsoncenter.org/publication/the-rebalance-within-asiathe-evolution-japan-india-relations, accessed on 18 July 2023.

37. Such India-based analysts include Brahma Chellaney, C. Raja Mohan, Harsh Pant and Dhruva Jaishankar, to list a few. Around the mid-2010s, Tokyo University Press, for example, published six volumes covering Indian society, politics, economy, and culture and religion, indicating a growing interest on the subject of India among the academic community in Japan. Many books of general nature on India also began to pop up in bookstores in the 2010s, a phenomenon previously unseen in Japan.

38. See for example, Victoria Tuke, 'Japan's Foreign Policy towards India: A Neoclassical Realist Analysis of the Foreign Making System', PhD thesis (University of Warwick, 2011).

39. For example, Rohan Mukherjee and Anthony Yazaki, eds, *Poised for Partnership. Deepening India-Japan Relations in the Asian Century* (New Delhi: Oxford University Press, 2016); Rajesh Basrur and Sumita Kutty, eds, *India and Japan: Assessing the Strategic Partnership* (Singapore: Palgrave Pivot, 2018).

40. One such example is Rohan Mukherjee, 'Japan's Strategic Outreach to India and the Prospects of a Japan–India Alliance', *International Affairs,* vol. 94, no. 4 (2018), available at DOI: 10.1093/ia/iiy030, accessed on 21 July 2023.

41. The Japanese Institute of International Affairs established a research cluster to study the concept of Indo-Pacific and India became a central subject of analysis in these discussions.

42. Ministry of Foreign Affairs of Japan, 'India's Public Perceptions about Japan', March 2000, available at http://www.mofa.go.jp/region/asia-paci/india/survey/2000/index.html, accessed on 21 July 2023.

43. Center for Media Studies (Commissioned by the Ministry of Foreign Affairs of Japan), 'Public Opinion Poll on Japan in India' (16 February to 17 March 2013), available at https://www.mofa.go.jp/files/000006651.pdf, accessed on 21 July 2023.

44. Ministry of Foreign Affairs of Japan, 'Opinion Poll: Image of Japan in India' (November 2016), available at https://www.mofa.go.jp/files/000209503.pdf, accessed on 21 July 2023.

45. BBC World Service, 'Views of China and India Slide While UK's Ratings Climb: Global Poll', pp. 9, 13, available at https://globescan.com/wp-content/uploads/2013/05/2013_country_rating_poll_bbc_globescan.pdf, accessed on 21 July 2023.

46. Ask Japanese, 'Ask Japanese about INDIA: What Japanese think of India and Indians', video, available at https://www.youtube.com/watch?v=takUOnUeN3A, accessed on 21 July 2023.

47. Takenori Horimoto, 'Japan-India Rapprochement and Its Future Issues,' Japan's Diplomacy Series, Japan Digital Library (The Japan Institute of International Affairs, 2015), available at https://www2.jiia.or.jp/en/pdf/digital_library/japan_s_diplomacy/160411_Takenori_Horimoto.pdf, accessed on 11 January 2024.

48. The Japanese edition of this book is *Saigo no Chotaikoku Indo* (Nikkei BP, 2017).

49. See a new book on Abe's importance to the India–Japan relations: Sanjaya Baru (ed.), *The Importance of Shinzo Abe: India, Japan and the Indo-Pacific* (New Delhi: Harper Collins, 2023).

50. Press Trust of India, 'Want India to 'commit more' to Quad: Japanese Deputy Defence Minister', *The Week* (25 December 2020), available at https://www.theweek.in/news/world/2020/12/25/want-india-to-commit-more-to-quad-japanese-deputy-defence-minister.html, accessed on 21 July 2023.

three

Emerging Contours of India–Japan Strategic Partnership

Raj Kumar Kothari

The core aim of this chapter is to undertake a study of the strategic, political and economic aspects of India–Japan bilateral relations as they have evolved in the present century. An attempt has been made to identify issues of common concern that could be worked on to strengthen ties and to highlight the challenges and opportunities that India and Japan have been confronting in the process of enhancing their strategic partnership. Considering the fact that China's rise is one of the major concerns to both, this chapter takes into account the shifting power dynamics in Asia that pushes both sides to come closer. The moot point is to analyse and comprehend: is the bilateral relationship that has started shaping up in recent years—after a long period of benign neglect—just a balancing act in response to China's ascendance in the region or is there actually enough substance in and a strong foundation beneath the ties to carry forward the relationship in future? The chapter attempts to answer this question using a qualitative research methodology backed by historical and analytical approaches.

Introduction

At the dawn of the 21st century, Japan crafted a new strategic policy framework with India as a newfound partner. During the Cold War years, Japan was mostly interested in developing and sustaining a strategic partnership with the United States only. The primary goal of the US–Japan strategic partnership treaty was to contain the spread of communism. While Japan extended strategic and logistical support to the US to realise this objective, the US had to protect Japan by providing defense from perceptible threats from its two neighbours, namely, North Korea and China. With the end of the Cold War, India and Japan both made efforts to reappraise the potential of their relations and this brought the two closer. The following section will trace the trends in India–Japan bilateral relations from a historical perspective. The latter sections will focus on the circumstances and ground realities that brought India and Japan closer and catalysed a strategic partnership, and delineate the various challenges posed by China's rise in the region.

India–Japan Relations from a Historical Perspective

The victory of Japan over Czarist Russia in 1905 led to the rise of nationalist movements in Asia against the colonial powers.[1] This development produced great excitement in India and people associated with the Indian National Congress were rejuvenated to fight against the British colonial masters. When the Indian freedom struggle entered a crucial phase in the 1930s, many students from India started going to Japan for seeking higher education and industrial training. The Indian nationalist movement was considerably influenced by Japan through assistance in education and industrial development.[2]

Trade links between India and Japan date back to the late 19th and early 20th centuries, with Japan exporting cotton crepe, cotton yarn, knitwear, silk, buttons, celluloid bangles, bags, fans, toys, purses, umbrellas, wood products, glassware, soap, paper and other materials to India and importing raw cotton, rubber, ivory, sheepskin, tapioca, pepper, and other goods from India. Several Indian merchants connected with the match trade were also based in Japan. Research by Takashi Oishi, cited in Rajamohan, Rahut and Jacob, indicates that Japanese investment in Indian match factories existed as early as 1927, and Japanese foreign investment existed in India from the early 1900s.[3] In 1937, Japan's import from India were worth USD 69.5 million and its exports to India were around USD 72.5 million.[4] These figures show that trade and commerce between India and Japan at that point of history were significant.

Cultural ties between India and Japan goes back to the 6th century AD when Buddhism made its way to Japan via China and Korea. During the summer of 1916, Rabindranath Tagore spent about four months in Japan, where during a lecture at the Keio Gijuku University he stated:

> ...the welcome which flowed towards me, with such outburst of sincerity, was owing to the fact that Japan felt the nearness of India to herself, and realised that her own heart has room to expand beyond her boundaries and the boundaries of the modern time.[5]

Earlier, Swami Vivekananda, after his visit to Japan in 1893, had expressed great hope for better relations between India and Japan.[6] These historical instances indicate the eagerness on the part of the two countries to come closer to each other. Following the establishment of diplomatic relations in 1952, India and Japan signed a cultural agreement in 1956 that came into force the following year. Cultural exchange between the two sides got another major boost in the 1980s when the Japanese local governments became involved in exchange activities with their Indian counterparts. Japan Month was celebrated in India from October to November 1987. Subsequently, the Festival of India was celebrated in April 1988 in Japan through which traditional Indian performing arts became popular among the Japanese.

Despite the existing complementarity between India and Japan in political and economic fields, for a long time, at least till the late 1980s, the two countries maintained distance from each other. Relations worsened during the Second World War when India and Japanese troops fought against each other. But after the war, when India expressed dissatisfaction with the war trials of Japanese officials, Japan appreciated the support. Radha Binod Pal, one of three Asian judges appointed to the International Military Tribunal for the Far East—the 'Tokyo Trials' of Japanese war crimes committed during the Second World War—was the only one who submitted a judgment which insisted that all the defendants were not guilty.[7] This, added to the fact that India also waived all reparation claims against Japan, was greatly appreciated by civil societies in Japan.

In the post-war years, both India and Japan became extremely busy with different aspects of nation-building. While Japan was trying to emerge from the war and rebuild its economy, India was beginning to gain a foothold as an independent country, largely focusing on national reconstruction. Later, during the Cold War years too, relations between India and Japan did not pick up due to ideological differences that prevented them from nurturing warm ties. India and Japan adopted different approaches towards international politics and management of the domestic economy. As Kanti Bajpai puts it: '...India and Japan do not have a deep history of cooperation and closeness in the modern period.'[8] India distanced herself from Japan due to Tokyo being a camp follower of the United States. Japan, on the other hand, perceived India as a chaotic, dysfunctional and poor country.

Post-Cold War Trends

With the introduction of the economic liberalisation programme in India in the early 1990s, combined with an expansion of strategic vision (with regard to Asia and subsequent strategic proximity to the United States and other powers) as well as the adoption of the Look East Policy in 1991, Tokyo started paying more attention towards New Delhi. Japan's Prime Minister Toshiki Kaifu visited India in 1991 which provided a big boost to Indo-Japan relations. According to Sanjana Joshi, during this period, there was a 'growing Japanese consciousness of the importance of a "re-association" with Asia not only in economic terms, but also increasingly in political and strategic terms.'[9]

India and Japan thus began sharing a special relationship with a common propensity to seek peaceful resolution of conflicts and greater economic and strategic engagements in the Asian continent. However, when India conducted nuclear tests in 1998, this evolving relationship got temporarily derailed. Japan suspended all political exchanges with India and even economic assistance was frozen for a few years.[10] But this was resolved in less than two years' time, when Japan's Prime Minister Yoshiro Mori undertook a five-day visit to New Delhi in August 2000, heralding a new phase in the relationship and promising to work towards developing a global partnership. While during the Cold War years bilateral ties between India and Japan were confined to limited cultural and economic exchanges, in the 21st century, it widened to cover a broad range of subjects. In the economic field, bilateral ties have expanded and include trade, joint ventures, technical collaboration, R&D cooperation, and others. Politically and strategically, India and Japan are engaged in issues such as nuclear disarmament, energy security, maritime security, climate change, terrorism, piracy, UN reforms, and other topics of regional and global importance.[11]

India–Japan Cultural Relations

The Japan Foundation opened its office in New Delhi in January 1994 and it has been actively engaged in cultural exchanges between the two countries ever since. Japan has also been extending cultural grants to aid research institutes, universities and cultural faculties to promote Japanese culture in India. Through the UNESCO–Japan Funds-in-Trust for the Preservation of World Cultural Heritage, Japan has been helping with the preservation and restoration of Buddhist monuments in Sanchi and Satdhara.[12] In September 2014, during his official visit to Japan, Prime Minister Narendra Modi expressed his deepest gratitude towards Japan, stating: 'I am…touched by the warmth and enthusiasm that I have experienced in meeting with a wide cross-section of people here….I am excited by the boundless possibilities for our cooperation.'[13] However, it needs to be stated that despite having congruent interests, India and Japan's mutual appreciation has been confined largely to the societal and cultural domains. There exists tremendous potential in the fields of political, strategic and economic relations, which we shall delve into in the next two sections.

India–Japan Economic Relations

Due to a variety of reasons, including India's big and growing market and its resources, Tokyo's interest in New Delhi has been on the rise in recent years. The signing of the historic India–Japan Comprehensive Economic Partnership Agreement (CEPA) and its implementation from August 2011 has accelerated trade and commerce between the two nations. During Prime Minister Narendra Modi's visit to Japan in September 2014, Prime Minister Shinzo Abe pledged 3.5 trillion yen in investment in India's public and private sectors over five subsequent years.[14]

Total trade between India and Japan in 2012–13 was around USD 18.61 billion. It was only about 1 per cent of Japan's global trade.[15]

Table 3.1 India–Japan Trade between 2011–18 (in USD billion)

	2011–12	2012–13	2013–14	2014–15	2015–16	2016–17	2017–18
India's export to Japan	6.33	6.10	6.81	5.38	4.66	3.85	4.73
India's import from Japan	11.99	12.41	9.48	10.13	9.85	9.75	10.97
India–Japan bilateral trade	18.32	18.51	16.29	15.51	14.51	13.60	15.71

Source: India–Japan Economic Relations, Embassy of India, Tokyo, Japan, available at https://mea.gov.in/Portal/ForeignRelation/India-Japan_Bilateral_Relations_March_2023.pdf, accessed on 19 September 2023.

It is important to note that trade volume between New Delhi and Tokyo continues to grow, reaching 21.96 billion USD in 2022–23, although there still remains a huge imbalance. In the same year, 2022–23, India's export to Japan was around USD 5.46 billion, whereas import from Japan was around USD 16.49 billion.[16] During the last two decades, there has been a tangible improvement in India–Japan bilateral economic relations after years of stagnation. But even then, compared with China–Japan trade, the volume of trade between India and Japan is quite low. As listed in Table 3.1, Japan's bilateral trade with India totalled USD 15.71 billion during 2017–18. Imports to India from Japan during this period were USD 10.97 billion and exports from India were USD 4.73 billion. Since petroleum products form a big share in this bilateral trade, fluctuations of oil prices affect the bilateral trade volume as well.

On the whole, imports from Japan constituted 2.35 per cent of India's total imports; and India's exports to Japan were 1.46 per cent of India's total exports in FY 2021–22. India's primary exports to Japan are petroleum products, chemical elements/compounds, fish and fish preparations, non-metallic mineral ware, metalliferous ores and scrap; clothing and accessories, iron and steel products, textile yarn/fabrics, and machinery.[17] India's primary imports from Japan are machinery, iron and steel products, electronic goods, transport equipment, organic chemicals, etc.[18]

The Federation of Indian Export Organisations (FIEO) has argued that India should export value-added products to Japan in order to utilise its full potential. According to S. K. Saraf, President of FIEO,

> The current export [in 2019] does not reflect the true potential of trade between India and Japan. The untapped export potential for Japan is more than $3 billion in sectors such as pharmaceuticals, gems & jewellery, marine products, rice, bovine meat, knitted T-shirts, ferro silicon, aluminium.[19]

Due to the investment-friendly policies introduced by the Government of India, the country has been ranked as one of the most attractive investment destinations in recent years, as per the survey report of Japan Bank for International Cooperation (JBIC) in 2022.[20] The survey ranks India as the most promising country, pushing China down to the second place in the list of most attractive investment destinations. In recent years, Japanese Foreign Direct Investment (FDI) into India has increased considerably, though the volume remains small compared to Japan's total outward FDI. In the financial years 2015–16, 2016–17, and 2017–18, Japan's FDI into India has been USD 2.61 billion, USD 4.7 billion and USD 1.6 billion respectively. Japan ranks fifth among the top investors in India. Since 2000, Japan's FDI into India has been in the fields of automobiles, electrical equipment, telecommunications, chemicals, insurance and pharmaceuticals.[21] The flow of FDI in India during 2021–22 stood at USD 1.49 billion. The moot point however is that on the whole, Japan's investment in India is very small compared to its total outward FDI.[22]

The number of Japanese companies registered in India increased by 5.2 per cent in 2018 compared to the previous year, 2017. As of June 2022, the total number reached 1,439.[23] According to the joint survey conducted by the Embassy of Japan in India and the Japan External Trade Organization (JETRO), as of October 2022, manufacturing firms account for half of the total numbers.[24] Similarly, the number of Indian companies in Japan has also been on the rise, with the number now crossing 100. India's investment in Japan in the first quarter of 2018 was around USD 385 million with total investment crossing USD 1 billion.[25]

Official Development Assistance (ODA) from Japan

Since the late 1950s, Japan has been providing bilateral loans and grants to India. Japanese ODA has aided priority sectors like power and transportation, environmental projects, and projects related to basic human needs.

Some Examples and Possibilities of Economic Cooperation

It is expected that Japan and India will also immensely benefit from closer economic and developmental partnerships in areas such as energy, water supply and irrigation, health, environment, technology, and people-to-people exchanges. Already the two have partnered on projects in the strategically sensitive regions of Andaman and Nicobar Islands and India's Northeast. India has signed a contract with NEC Corporation of Japan to install an undersea cable from Chennai to the Andaman and Nicobar Islands. Besides, Japan is also involved in road connectivity projects linking the states in India's Northeast to ASEAN countries.[26]

In recent years, Japan has been facing a serious demographic challenge because of its rapidly ageing and shrinking population. There has been a labour crunch in blue-collar industries. High-tech companies are facing a critical shortage of IT workers and engineers that could be filled by opening the doors to highly skilled IT talents from India. In contrast, India has an expansive population, and it is a significant challenge to provide adequate jobs for the ever-growing skilled workforce.[27] Thus, through closer understanding and cooperation, challenges faced by both sides could be mitigated.

Cooperation in the Energy Sector

As per the India–Japan Joint Statement of December 2006, both sides agreed to promote energy cooperation in the energy sector in a comprehensive manner.[28] In December 2019, the Union Cabinet chaired by Prime Minister Modi approved the signing of a Memorandum of Understanding between the Central Electricity Authority of India and Japan for cooperation to improve efficiency and environmental impact through sustainable and low-carbon supply of electricity.[29] This aimed to provide a framework to address issues and barriers in the area of thermal power development by means of training programmes and knowledge-sharing activities. The energy sector is one of the important areas where there is tremendous potential for India and Japan to work together.

Strategic Partnership and the Indo-Pacific

The strategic partnership between India and Japan must be discussed against the backdrop of the profound changes that are taking place at the global level in general and at the East Asian regional level in particular. There is a broad consensus in both countries that the interests and concerns of India and Japan converge at one point.[30] In fact, the current nature of strategic partnership between India and Japan will largely determine the peace, security and prosperity of East Asia in the coming years and decades. It is worthwhile to mention in this context that India and Japan both share land and maritime boundaries with China, and therefore there is a need for strong strategic and maritime cooperation between New Delhi and Tokyo in order to counter China's assertiveness in military and strategic fields. Moreover, India and Japan heavily depend on overseas resources and trade for their respective economic development.

At the very beginning of the 21st century, the two countries expressed the desire to take their bilateral relationship to a qualitatively new level. During a landmark visit of Yoshiro Mori, the then Prime Minister of Japan, to New Delhi in August 2000, India and Japan mooted the idea of a 'Global Partnership in the 21st Century'.[31] Thereafter, the eight-fold initiative agreed upon during Prime Minister Junichiro Koizumi's visit to India in 2005 laid the foundation of a global partnership between the two sides.[32] Prime Minister Manmohan Singh's visit to Japan in December the following year created the much-needed institutional mechanism to take the partnership forward. A joint statement was released on the occasion which focused on the need to strengthen strategic and global partnership between India and Japan.[33]

The strategic partnership encompasses wide-ranging bilateral and multilateral issues, including defence cooperation. India looks towards Japan to aid the promotion of New Delhi's interests in East Asia and Japan considers New Delhi a close political partner in dealing with East Asian security issues. The US, Japan and India have a shared interest in establishing an open and inclusive regional architecture in Asia at a time when a variety of new forums and institutions are taking shape. The three countries have thus been coordinating closely to ensure that Asia retains an open regionalism. US President Donald Trump during his visit to India in February 2020 talked about revitalising the Quadrilateral Security Dialogue (Quad[34]), consisting of the US, India,

Japan and Australia, to ensure a free and open Indo-Pacific.[35] India and Japan held their 2+2 foreign and defence ministerial meeting on 30 November 2019.[36] Significantly, Japan is only the second country after the US with which India has such a high-level 2+2 dialogue. The joint statement released after the 2019 meeting highlighted that such dialogue 'will further enhance the strategic depth of bilateral security and defence cooperation.'[37] The trilateral cooperation between Japan, India and the US, or the quadrilateral dialogue that includes these three countries as well as Australia, should however not be seen as a counter to China, but rather as a stabilising factor in broader regional dynamics.

It is important to note that while the United States' Indo-Pacific strategy emphasises the containment of a rising China, India and Japan share a more inclusive approach which includes engaging regional neighbours in matters relating to security and development. Engagement efforts such as the Asia-Africa Growth Corridor, joint infrastructure projects in Indian Ocean littorals and sub-regional cooperation frameworks promote not only viable development assistance but also act as an alternative to China's BRI (Belt and Road Initiative), which is fast gaining ground.[38]

India and Japan reaffirmed their support for ASEAN's outlook on the Indo-Pacific adopted at the 34th ASEAN Summit in Bangkok in June 2019.[39] A synergy was thus found between India's 'Indo-Pacific Oceans Initiative', Japan's 'Vientiane Vision 2.0', and ASEAN's outlook on the Indo-Pacific region. Besides, Tokyo and New Delhi have also been engaged in joint infrastructure development projects in the Indian Ocean Region that coincides with ASEAN's strategic and economic objectives. Together India, Japan and the ASEAN are focusing on maritime cooperation, connectivity, sustainable development and economic activities like trade and commerce in the Indo-Pacific.[40]

Kanti Bajpai raises a fundamental and vital question with regard to China's rise: What should be India and Japan's strategy to counter China, which will probably become the biggest power on earth by 2030?[41] Geographically, India and Japan are China's neighbours. Both have unresolved territorial quarrels and a history of conflict and rivalry with China. If India and Japan were to go along with China, it would mean accepting East Asia and South Asia as within the Chinese sphere of influence. Thus, it is obvious that neither India nor Japan will agree to be Beijing's junior partners in order to receive security guarantee in return. Besides, India and Japan would not be interested in curtailing their relations with the US either. In this situation, the Quad remains the best possible scenario for India, Japan, the US and Australia.

Bajpai further argues that there is little that India and Japan can do to prevent the Eurasian heartland from being dominated by China in association with Russia. In the words of Bajpai:

> ...India is cut off from the great landmass of Eurasia by Pakistan, Afghanistan and Himalayas. Japan stands off shore. What they can do is to build a coalition in Southeast Asia as well as [with] Australia, New Zealand and the Pacific Island states to counter Chinese power and influence in maritime area...the past decade has shown that India and Japan have the incentive to come together.[42]

India and Japan have also started to explore various other joint infrastructure projects in the Indo-Pacific subregions of the Bay of Bengal and Mekong.[43] Changing geopolitical realities have brought about a renewed attention to the Bay of Bengal and BIMSTEC (Bay of Bengal Initiative for Multi-Sectoral Technical and Economic Cooperation), which caters to the Indo-Pacific and a wide Indian Ocean community that New Delhi espouses. Thus, a strong India–Japan relationship will play an important role in the emerging Asian security architecture and will contribute to the peace, stability and prosperity of Asia and in turn, the world.

One of the important features of Japan's foreign policy in recent years has been its gradual but steady rise as an independent player in the arena of international relations. For a long time, in the post-war years, Japan's security was solely dependent upon the US. A few factors, according to Rajamohan and others,[44] have led to a change in Japan's foreign policy: First, the US has expressed that it would like to see Japan take up a greater share of the responsibilities under their bilateral security treaty;[45] second, the rise of China and the lack of transparency on its part on military preparedness, in conventional and non-conventional fields, have compelled Japan to consider strengthening its defence and security establishments to counter any threat on an urgent basis; and third, Japan has realised over the years that economic might alone is insufficient to earn respect from the world community, and has thus encouraged developments to strengthen defence capabilities. With its new and revised foreign policy, Japan has started taking an independent stand on its foreign and security matters.

Conclusion

Right from the late 1940s till date, India–Japan relations have not moved in a unilinear direction, and have been marked by ups and downs. The relationship has gone through various stages from an initial warmth to estrangement during the Cold War, followed by the further rupture caused by India's nuclear tests of 1998, and finally culminating in the present phase of intimacy.

As outlined in this chapter, India–Japan bilateral engagements failed to deepen during the Cold War years because their strategic and defence interests did not coincide due to various regional and extra-regional factors, particularly the foreign policy approach of the US at that point of time. A window of opportunities started opening up in the post-Cold War years, particularly with the demise of the Soviet Union. Over the years, the rise of China factor played an important role that brought New Delhi and Tokyo on the same boat. Improved Indo-US relations which subsequently resulted in the development of a strategic partnership also paved the way for closer ties between India and Japan.

Today, India and Japan share a global vision of peace, stability and shared prosperity, based on sustainable development. Partnership between the two is marked by shared democratic values, commitment to human rights, pluralism, an open society and the rule of law. The global partnership between New Delhi and Tokyo reflects a broad convergence of their long-term political, economic and strategic interests, aspirations, objectives and concerns. In fact, India and Japan view each other as responsible partners, capable of responding to global challenges jointly. A strong, prosperous and dynamic India is therefore in the interest of Japan, and vice versa.

India and Japan have a shared vision for the Indo-Pacific region and a strong commitment to multilateralism. The two have forged a strategic partnership and chalked out long-term plans to deepen and strengthen bilateral relations. The present study reveals that though the rise of China and the resultant power shift in Asia is bringing India and Japan closer, the relationship itself has been growing steadily since the very beginning of this century. Maintaining the balance of power vis-à-vis China is thus not the only factor that brings India and Japan nearer. Functional needs, interdependence and the prospects of mutual gains have also been of immense significance in fostering bilateral ties. This chapter predicts that under the changed circumstances, particularly the rise of China, India–Japan bilateral political and strategic relations shall continue to improve in the coming years and that economic ties between them are likely to be further strengthened in view of current trends and future prospects. The international system is undergoing a major transition with the weakening of the US-led liberal order which is being increasingly challenged by China's hegemonic rise. In view of evolving power relations in the Asia Pacific region, both New Delhi and Tokyo are gearing up to play an important role in designing the future security architecture of Asia in a cooperative framework.

India–Japan bilateral relations in the field of trade and commerce have been improving steadily over the last few years. The two sides are moving towards a strategic global partnership—the 'Japan and India Vision 2025 Special Strategic and Global Partnership Working Together for Peace and Prosperity on the Indo-Pacific and the World'—which signals a broad convergence of their long-term political and strategic goals. This shows that India's rise as an important power in Asia and the world is in the interest of Japan and vice versa.

Notes and References

1. 'Russo-Japanese War', Brittanica, available at https://www.britannica.com/event/Russo-Japanese-War, accessed on 18 September 2023.
2. Arpita Mathur, *India-Japan Relations: Drivers, Trends and Prospects*, RSIS Monograph No. 23 (S. Rajaratnam School of International Studies, Nanyang Technological University, 2012), p. 4.
3. P. G. Rajamohan, Dil Bahadur Rahut and Jabin T. Jacob, 'Changing Paradigm of Indo-Japan Relations: Opportunities and Challenges', Working Paper no. 212 (Indian Council for Research on International Economic Relations, New Delhi, April 2008), pp. 2–3, available at https://core.ac.uk/download/pdf/6256622.pdf, accessed on 24 July 2023.
4. Ibid.
5. Rabindranath Tagore, *The Spirit of Japan* (Tokyo: Indo-Japanese Association, 1916), p.5, available at http://www.gutenberg.org/files/33131/33131-h/33131-h.htm, accessed on 24 July 2023.
6. Sanjay Baru, 'Vivekananda went to Japan in 1893. He was fascinated by its army, tunnels, match factories', *The Print*, 10 August 2023, available at https://theprint.in/pageturner/excerpt/vivekananda-went-to-japan-in-1893-he-

was-fascinated-by-its-army-tunnels-match-factories/1708352/, accessed on 19 January 2024.

7. Norimitsu Onishi, 'Decades After War Trials, Japan Still Honors a Dissenting Judge', *The New York Times*, 31 August 2007, available at https://www.nytimes.com/2007/08/31/world/asia/31memo.html, accessed on 24 July 2023.

8. Kanti Bajpai, 'India and Japan: Strategic Partners for the 21st Century', *India and Japan: Growing Partnership and Opportunities for Co-operation* (Centre for Public Policy Research, Kochi, August 2019), p. 3.

9. Sanjana Joshi, 'Prospect for Security Cooperation Between India and Japan', *Strategic Analyses*, vol. 25, no. 2 (2001), pp. 185–196.

10. Rajamohan, Rahut and Jacob, 'Changing Paradigm of Indo-Japan Relations', pp. 3–4.

11. Rajaram Panda, 'Changing Dynamics of India-Japan Relations: Future Trends', p.1, available at https://src-h.slav.hokudai.ac.jp/rp/publications/no06/01_Panda.pdf, accessed on 25 July 2023.

12. Ministry of External Affairs, Government of India, 'India-Japan Relations', available at https://www.mea.gov.in/Portal/ForeignRelation/India-Japan_Relations.pdf, accessed on 23 September 2023.

13. 'Remarks by Prime Minister at the Joint Press Briefing with Prime Minister Shinzo Abe of Japan', available at https://www.narendramodi.in/asm/remarks-by-prime-minister-at-the-joint-press-briefing-with-prime-minister-shinzo-abe-of-japan-6526 accessed on September 23, 2023.

14. 'PM Narendra Modi's Japan Visit: 10 Key Takeaways', *The Economic Times*, 2 September 2014, available at https://economictimes.indiatimes.com/news/politics-and-nation/pm-narendra-modis-japan-visit-10-key-takeaways/articleshow/41524126.cms?from=mdr, accessed on 19 September 2023.

15. Ministry of External Affairs, Government of India, 'India-Japan Relations Background', available at https://www.mea.gov.in/Portal/ForeignRelation/Japan_January_2014.pdf , accessed on 19 January 2024.

16. Data by Department of Commerce, Government of India. See Embassy of India, 'India–Japan Commercial Relations', available at https://www.indembassy-tokyo.gov.in/eoityo_pages/NjA, accessed on 19 September 2023.

17. Ministry of External Affairs, India, 'India-Japan Bilateral Relations', available at https://mea.gov.in/Portal/ForeignRelation/India-Japan_Bilateral_Relations_March_2023.pdf, accessed on 31 August 2023.

18. Ministry of External Affairs, India, 'India-Japan Relations', available at https://mea.gov.in/Portal/ForeignRelation/India_japanBilateral_Brief_September_2019.pdf, accessed on 19 September 2023.

19. Kirtika Suneja, 'Exporters body keen on value added exports to Japan', *The Economic Times*, 18 October 2019, available at https://economictimes.indiatimes.

com/news/economy/foreign-trade/exporters-body-keen-on-value-added-exports-to-japan/articleshow/71655260.cms?from=mdr, accessed on 28 July 2023.

20. Japanese Bank for International Cooperation, 'FY 2022 JBIC Survey (34th) Report on Overseas Business Operations by Japanese Manufacturing Companies', available at https://www.jbic.go.jp/en/information/press/press-2022/1216-017128.html, accessed on 22 September 2023.

21. India-Japan Bilateral Economic relations, Embassy of India, Tokyo, available at https://www.indembassy-tokyo.gov.in/eoityo_pages/NjQw, accessed on 19 January 2024.

22. Rezaul H. Laskar, 'Japanese Foreign Minister Seeks Improvement of Investment Environment in India', *Hindustan Times*, 28 July 2023, available at https://www.hindustantimes.com/india-news/japan-urges-india-to-improve-investment-environment-highlighting-tax-and-infrastructure-challenges-101690552130708.html, accessed on 23 September 2023.

23. Atul Ranjan, 'Japanese firms operating in India increased by over 5% in 2018', *The Japan Times*, 25 December 2018, available at https://www.japantimes.co.jp/news/2018/12/25/business/japanese-firms-operating-india-increase-5-2018/, accessed on 22 January 2024.

24. Ministry of External Affairs, India, 'India-Japan Bilateral Relations', available at https://www.mea.gov.in/Portal/ForeignRelation/Japan_- Bilateral_Brief_MEA_Website_Oct_2023.pdf, accessed on 22 January 2024.

25. 'Business Council – Japan', CCI India, available at https://www.cciindia.org/japan.html, accessed on 22 January 2024.

26. Tan Ming Hui and Nazia Hussain, 'Japan-India: An Indigenous Indo-Pacific Axis', *The Diplomat*, 18 March 2020, available at https://thediplomat.com/2020/03/japan-india-an-indigenous-indo-pacific-axis/, accessed on 28 July 2023.

27. Hui and Hussain, 'Japan-India: An Indigenous Indo-Pacific Axis'.

28. Ministry of External Affairs, Government of India, 'Joint Statement Towards India–Japan Strategic and Global Partnership', 15 December 2006, available at https://mea.gov.in/bilateral-documents.htm?dtl/6368/Joint+Statement+Towards+IndiaJapan+Strategic+and+Global+Partnership, accessed on 28 July 2023.

29. 'Cabinet Approves MoU between India and Japan Coal Energy Centre for Cooperation in the Field of Supply of Electricity', *Business Standard*, 12 December 2019, available at https://www.business-standard.com/article/news-cm/cabinet-approves-mou-between-india-and-japan-coal-energy-centre-for-cooperation-in-the-field-of-supply-of-electricity-119121200195_1.html, accessed on 28 July 2023.

30. Debasis Bhattacharya, 'India-Japan Strategic Partnership: Growing Convergence', Vivekananda International Foundation, 10 May 2022, available at

https://www.vifindia.org/2022/may/10/india-japan-strategic-partnership-growing-convergence%20%20%20%20, accessed on 23 September 2023.

31. Ministry of External Affairs, Government of India, 'Joint Statement Towards India-Japan Strategic and Global Partnership', 15 December 2006, available at https://mea.gov.in/bilateral-documents.htm?dtl/6368/Joint+Statement+Towards+IndiaJapan+Strategic+and+Global+Partnership#:~:text=The%20two%20leaders%20welcome%20the%20Joint%20Statement%20issued%20following%20talks,prosperity%20in%20Asia%20and%20in, accessed on 28 July 2023.

32. Ministry of Foreign Affairs of Japan, 'Japan-India Joint Declaration', 10 December 2001, available at https://www.mofa.go.jp/region/asia-paci/india/joint0112.html, accessed on 28 July 2023.

33. Ministry of External Affairs, Government of India, 'Joint Statement Towards India-Japan Strategic and Global Partnership', 15 December 2006, available at https://mea.gov.in/bilateral-documents.htm?dtl/6368/Joint+Statement+Towards+IndiaJapan+Strategic+and+Global+Partnership#:~:text=The%20two%20leaders%20welcome%20the%20Joint%20Statement%20issued%20following%20talks,prosperity%20in%20Asia%20and%20in, accessed on 28 July 2023.

34. The Quad is an economic and security dialogue among Australia, India, Japan and the US that began in 2007 and was revived in 2017 after a ten-year gap.

35. Hui and Hussain, 'Japan-India: An Indigenous Indo-Pacific Axis'.

36. Minister for Foreign Affairs of Japan, Toshimitsu Motegi, Minister of Defense of Japan, Taro Kono, External Affairs Minister of India, Subrahmanyam Jaishankar, and Defence Minister of India, Rajnath Singh met on 30 November 2019 in New Delhi for the first Japan–India 2+2 Foreign and Defence Ministerial Meeting. It was affirmed that this dialogue will further enhance the strategic depth of bilateral security and defence cooperation. Acknowledging emerging security challenges, the Ministers reiterated their commitment to advancing bilateral security cooperation based on the 2008 Joint Declaration on Security Cooperation and the 2009 Action Plan to Advance Security Cooperation. Recalling that the two sides had a shared vision of a free, open, inclusive and rules-based Indo-Pacific region in which the principles of sovereignty and territorial integrity are ensured, and all countries enjoy freedom of navigation and overflight, the Ministers emphasised that further strengthening of bilateral cooperation was in mutual interest of both countries and would also help in furthering the cause of the peace, security and prosperity in the Indo-Pacific region. For more details, refer to 'Joint Statement: First Japan-India 2+2 Foreign and Defence Ministerial Meeting', available at https://www.mofa.go.jp/files/000544338.pdf, accessed on 28 July 2023.

37. Ibid.

38. Ibid.

39. '34th ASEAN Summit in Bangkok highlights June 2019 "ASEAN Today"', 25 June 2019, The ASEAN Secretariat, available at https://asean.org/34th-asean-summit-in-bangkok-highlights-june-2019-asean-today/, accessed on 28 July 2023.

40. Hui and Hussain, 'Japan-India: An Indigenous Indo-Pacific Axis'.

41. Bajpai, 'India and Japan: Strategic Partners for the 21st Century'.

42. Ibid.

43. Hui and Hussain, 'Japan-India: An Indigenous Indo-Pacific Axis'.

44. Rajamohan, Rahut and Jacob, 'Changing Paradigm of Indo-Japan Relations', p. 1.

45. The security treaty between the US and Japan was signed on 8 September 1951 in San Francisco, California. The treaty came into force on 28 April 1952. One of the important articles of the treaty was Japan allowing the US to promote its military presence in the Far East. Further, Japan was prohibited from providing foreign powers any military bases or military-related rights without the consent of the US.

four

The China Factor in India–Japan Relations

Harsh V. Pant and Shashank Mattoo

The spectre of conflict and strategic competition has begun to haunt the Indo-Pacific in earnest. In the South China Sea, Southeast Asian nations like Vietnam and Indonesia have nervously watched increasing Chinese incursions into their territorial waters. Further north, the disputed Senkaku/Diaoyu Islands have emerged as a significant regional fault line with Chinese vessels making their presence felt, much to the discomfiture of Japan. Further, at the time of writing of this chapter, Indian and Chinese troops remain locked in a deadly confrontation in the Himalayan heights that has dominated headlines and significantly impacted bilateral relations.

As the full scale of China's economic and military power is brought to bear on the region, India and Japan have grown ever closer in an attempt to balance the scales of power. This relationship, while undoubtedly forged in crisis and in the desire to unite against a common competitor, has grown beyond a simple deterrent and now encompasses a confluence of interests across a range of economic, multilateral and security matters. In the first section, this chapter provides a brief account of China's economic and military rise from the 1980s till the present. In doing so, we also cover the beginnings of strategic competition between India, Japan and China. The second section traces the evolution of the Indo-Japanese economic and strategic partnership in the face of an increasingly assertive China. The final section looks to the future of the relationship between India and Japan and points both to potential roadblocks and the unexplored avenues of cooperation.

Enter the Dragon

As has become a truism to assert in strategic circles, China's meteoric rise to economic and military power has few parallels in history. Former Czech

President Vaclav Havel captured the global mood best when he mused that 'things have happened so fast that we haven't yet had time to be astonished'.[1] Upon taking charge from Chairman Mao and his successors (popularly known as the Gang of Four), Deng Xiaoping, a liberalising Communist Party veteran, saw the writing on the wall.[2] China's centrally planned economy, administered by the gargantuan bureaucratic machine that is the Chinese Communist Party (CCP), was failing. In 1978, China accounted for less than 1 per cent of global trade,[3] possessed a per capita income of just USD 850 and suffered from low productivity growth.[4] Over the next few decades, China engaged in a series of reforms that jump-started economic growth. Once it began, the Chinese economic juggernaut ran strong for several decades and, in 2013, China's per capita income stood at USD 7,080 and total foreign trade volumes, at USD 3 trillion, grew to 143 times its 1978 levels.[5] With greater economic growth and spending capacity came a sea change in China's confidence and perception of its interests. The 1993 Guidelines on military strategy ended China's traditional focus on fighting invasions in homeland territory to 'territorial disputes along China's periphery and Taiwan's unification'.[6] The United States' crushing victory over Iraq in the Gulf War caused the People's Liberation Army (PLA) to sit up and take notice.[7] Top military authorities conferred and concluded that the future belonged to high-technology warfare which China was unequipped for.[8] Since then, China's military has moved from strength to strength. China's breakneck economic growth rates allowed every Chinese leader after Jiang Zemin to funnel money into China's defence budget with outlays increasing sevenfold between 1998 and 2018.[9] China now possesses the world's largest army and navy (by ship numbers), a vast Strategic Support Force that handles technological warfare and a growing global footprint as China offers military support as part of its Belt and Road Program.[10] At the 19th National Congress of the CCP, President Xi Jinping made clear that China's intention was to have its military become a 'world class force' that would be capable of winning global conflicts by 2049.[11]

India and Japan, China's neighbours and one-time supporters of its meteoric rise, have watched China's power grow with increasing disquiet. With Japan, the deterioration in relations with China comes from three primary sources: China's growing security interests, Japan's alliance with the US and the complicated history wars waged by both powers.[12] Firstly, China's rise has greatly expanded its perception of its national security interests and its confidence and ability in securing those interests. China's limited military interests in the region and its focus on economic growth during the decades of its rise meant that, for the most part, relations with Japan and India remained manageable and cordial.[13] For Japan, relations with China began to deteriorate in the 1990s as Japan's economy came to a screeching halt while China's was only just beginning to experience breakneck growth rates; this effectively shifted the economic balance of power in the relationship and reduced China's erstwhile dependency on Japanese investment.[14] Starting from the 1990s, China's use of its increasing military and economic clout to intimidate opponents in Taiwan and in the South China Sea elicited a sea change in Japanese thinking about China as policymakers gradually became reluctant realists regarding the threat posed by their western neighbour.[15] Matters were not helped by Chinese Foreign Minister Yang Jiechi's reaction to ASEAN and US criticism of these actions during a 2010 ASEAN Summit where he bluntly stated that 'China is a big country, and other countries are small countries, and that's just a fact'.[16] Throughout the 2010s, Sino-Japanese relations went from bad to worse as both sides clashed over everything from the disputed Senkaku/Diaoyu Islands to China's fortification of islands in the South China Sea.[17] China's actions, coupled with the political rise of Japan's hawkish conservatives led by long-time Prime Minister Shinzo Abe, have only aggravated tensions between the East Asian giants.

Secondly, part of Beijing's threat perception of Japan comes from its alliance with the US. While the US alliance was once seen by Chinese strategic elites as a useful check on possible Japanese militarism, Japan has now transformed from a protege to a partner in US actions.[18] In line with US policy, it has termed Taiwan a 'common sphere of interest',[19] has actively participated in checking Chinese actions in the South and East China Sea. Further, during Abe's tenure, Japan made strides towards becoming a 'normal nation' as many in Japanese politics urged for an urgent rethink of the island nation's commitment to pacifism; this is a move that has been met with approval in Washington.[20] For Beijing, a Japan with stronger security capabilities is one that can take on a greater security burden in the region and play a larger role in the now central aim of US's grand strategy in Asia: balancing China's power. Thirdly, there is the perennial problem of East Asia's history wars, which centre around Japan's atrocities against

China in the 20th century.[21] While Japan fired the first shot through attempts by numerous conservative groups to whitewash history, China has allowed the issue to gain staying power.[22] Shaken by the Tiananmen Square protests of 1989, the CCP embarked on a campaign of patriotic education, which played up China's victimhood at the hands of Japanese militarism.[23] Veteran Asia watcher Richard McGregor observed that this decision cemented strong anti-Japanese sentiment among the Chinese populace that has made the possibility of a rapprochement difficult for fear of pushback from the public.[24]

As possibly the only other continental power capable of balancing China's growing influence, India has also had to deal with the strategic flux that has come to characterise the current moment in Asian geopolitics. Tensions between these two powers stem from several sources: the rise of both nations in a short span of time, unresolved boundary disputes, China's bonhomie with Pakistan and the power differential that exists between the two countries.[25] China's rapid expansion in military capability, seen through its buildup of military assets and infrastructure on its border with India and through Chinese naval projection in the Indian Ocean region on matters ranging from intelligence gathering to counter-piracy operations, has been met with disquiet in India.[26] Matters are not helped by the fact that China has actively worked to thwart India's foreign policy goals by opposing its bid to join multilateral fora like the UN Security Council, the Nuclear Suppliers Group and the Missile Control Technology Regime.[27] To New Delhi, this has been as clear a sign as any that Beijing does not look upon India's rise favourably. Further, China's closeness to Pakistan has meant that it has acted against Indian interests on issues ranging from China–Pakistan Economic Corridor (CPEC) projects in the disputed territory in Kashmir to blocking Indian attempts to blacklist terrorists like Masood Azhar. Finally, disputes over the unsettled border and resulting territorial claims have acted as a cloud hanging over the bilateral relationship.[28] Numerous attempts to resolve territorial claims and reduce tensions have foundered, leaving misunderstandings and resentment to fester. After a confrontation in the alpine heights of the Himalayas in April 2020 caused the first casualties on its border with China in more than four decades, Indian strategic elites had to rapidly adjust their threat perception of China and call for a more robust policy of internal and external balancing.[29]

India and Japan Grow Closer

Indian and Japanese concerns regarding China centre around the same key issues: anxiety over territorial sovereignty, fears for the future of free and open navigation on the high seas, China's desire to challenge the status quo in the region through an expanding maritime and military footprint and the need for economic growth to help close the power differential with China.[30] Add to this a shared belief in democracy, economic liberalism and a rules-based international order, and one has the makings of a strong bilateral partnership. Relations were derailed temporarily after India's 1998 nuclear tests but found solid ground again in 2000 following Prime Minister Yoshiro Mori's visit to India.[31] However, it was only during Junichiro Koizumi's tenure that relations with India expanded significantly in the economic and strategic domains.[32] The noted Japanese South Asian affairs expert Takenori Horimoto suggests that the massive anti-Japan protests in China in 2005 jolted Tokyo into the realisation that banking excessively on China for economic growth was unwise and this prompted a more concerted outreach to India.[33] In 2006, both powers established a Joint Strategic and Global Dialogue and followed it up in 2007 with the Foreign Ministers' Strategic Dialogue.[34] 2007 also saw Shinzo Abe articulate his vision for a closer relationship between both countries with his 'Confluence of the Two Seas' speech in front of India's Parliament.[35] In 2008, both powers signed the Joint Declaration on Security Cooperation.[36] Despite this emerging closeness, both sides were at pains to point out that their partnership was not aimed at countering Chinese influence. While official documents from both countries' defence ministries during this period highlight growing concern about Chinese military acquisitions, New Delhi and Tokyo did not wish to overtly antagonise Beijing.[37] For example, India stayed away from the Quad after its first iteration in 2007, slowed the pace of its expanding defence ties with the United States and maintained a studied silence when, in 2013, China declared an Air Defense Identification Zone (ADIZ) in the Indo-Pacific that encroached on territories held by Japan and Korea.[38] In Japan, the 2009 election of the maverick pro-China Prime Minister Yukio Hatoyama signalled a shift towards a more conciliatory policy towards China.[39]

However, Shinzo Abe's return to power in 2012 and Narendra Modi's election in 2014 spelled the beginning of an Indo-Japanese relationship that actively worked to build a strong deterrent to China in the region.

During the 2000s and early 2010s, both sides practised a policy of hedging that has, since 2013, acquired all the characteristics of a balancing strategy against China.[40] This was made especially clear by Abe in a 2012 article[41] entitled 'Asia's Democratic Security Diamond' where he detailed his concerns over the South China Sea becoming 'Lake Beijing' and tensions over the Senkaku Islands.[42] In light of this, he reiterated his earlier support for an Indo-Japanese relationship that could 'shoulder more responsibility as guardians of navigational freedom across the Pacific and Indian Oceans'.[43] Horimoto opines that 'dealing with China with its remarkable economic growth and new status as a major military power has become the top priority for both countries.'[44] Today, Horimoto's assertion that 'hedging policies in relation to China' are 'a major factor in the Japan–India rapprochement' is one few would dispute.[45] For our purposes here, we shall divide the deepening partnership between the two countries since 2014 into two sections: economic and strategic.

Economic Balancing

Since the early 2000s, the economic relationship between the two nations has deepened considerably as Japan looks for new markets and India searches for investments and high technology. In 2003, India became the largest recipient of the Japanese Official Development Assistance (ODA) and soon after, an Indo-Japanese Joint Study Group was established to look into the expansion of economic ties.[46] This eventually led to the negotiation of the Comprehensive Economic Partnership Agreement (CEPA) in 2011 that sought to liberalise trade by broadly eliminating tariffs, providing for intellectual property protections and creating a favourable environment for businesses to thrive.[47] As competition with China heats up, the Indo-Japanese economic relationship aims to achieve a number of strategic goals. Firstly, Japan has invested much into India's economic growth in an effort to aid its internal balancing against China and to boost its own flagging growth. Secondly, India and Japan have a common interest in using their economic heft in Southeast Asia to counter China's growing presence in the region.

Sustained economic growth is an absolute strategic imperative for the Indo-Japanese economic relationship given the resource gap when compared to the Chinese economic juggernaut. Firstly, the economic partnership has presided over the induction of record levels of Japanese investment into the Indian economy. In a 2014 summit, Abe and Modi announced the India–Japan Investment Promotion Partnership which envisioned a mammoth USD 33.61 billion investment into the Indian economy over a period of five years.[48] Japan also pledged to double the number of Japanese companies operating in India by 2019.[49] During a 2022 visit to India, Japanese Prime Minister Fumio Kishida promised to invest USD 42 billion (5 trillion yen) in India. Japan also pledged to double the number of Japanese companies operating in India by 2019.[50] In the two decades since Mori's breakthrough 2000 visit, FDI has surged to a total value of USD 34.1 billion.[51] Headline-making investment levels aside, the last few years have seen a targeted and institutionalised effort to build a strong Indo-Japanese economic partnership. The year 2019 saw the launch of the India-Japan Industrial Competitiveness Partnership that aims to boost India's economic development through the 'utilization of industrial zones to promote foreign direct investment, lowering cost of logistics, and facilitating smooth governmental procedures'.[52] Further, Invest India's flagship Japan Plus initiative has ushered in streamlined and simplified business processes for Japanese businesses looking to establish a presence in India.[53]

Japan and India have also worked to expand the former's economic presence in India through Japan Industrial Townships (JIT). These townships, built exclusively for use by Japanese companies, combine advanced infrastructure and facilities with streamlined bureaucratic approval systems in order to enhance Japan's economic footprint in India.[54] As of 2020, 12 JITs have been set up across the country with a 13th scheduled to open in Assam.[55] Added to this, Japan has also taken a keen interest in India's plan to increase domestic manufacturing. The Japan-India Make in India Special Finance Facility has made USD 12 billion available in economic assistance to support manufacturing in the JITs.[56] India's push to build an economically vital skilled workforce through its Skill India programme has also found Japanese support. New Delhi and Tokyo have collaborated on the creation of Japan-India Institutes for Manufacturing, which aim to train '30,000 Indians to Japanese-style manufacturing skills and practices over the next 10 years' and '300,000 Indian students in Japan, especially in the IT sector'.[57]

The partnership has devoted much effort towards improving India's domestic infrastructure which remains a significant roadblock to more investment and economic growth. Between 2002 and 2011, the Japan

International Cooperation Agency devoted 25 per cent of its spending in India to transportation, with money going towards investments in roads, railways and ports.[58] Some prominent examples of projects that received Japanese support are the Delhi and Bangalore metros, Mumbai–Delhi Freight Corridor and the high speed rail link between Mumbai and Ahmedabad.[59] Existing infrastructure has also received an upgrade with a notable example being Japan International Cooperation Agency's investment in decreasing congestion at the Chennai Port.[60] Japan has also thrown its weight behind an overhaul of India's notoriously unreliable power infrastructure. In Andhra Pradesh, Maharashtra and West Bengal, investments in renewable power and rural electrification have found significant success.[61] Japan's focus on infrastructure has also been vital to India's plans to boost economic growth and enhance its strategic presence in its traditionally underdeveloped and strategically vital Northeastern provinces. Although Japan has invested in India's Northeast since the 1980s, it has stepped up its commitment in recent years and in 2014, unveiled a USD 854 million low-interest loan to build 1,200 kilometres of road in the region.[62] During recent high-level meetings of the Act East Forum, both powers indicated a desire to expand collaboration in the Northeast to skill development, hydropower and sustainable development.[63] Once again, India's troubled relationship with China on boundary issues has driven cooperation with Japan. Disputes over territory meant that few nations or private bodies were willing to invest in India's Northeast, lest they invoke Beijing's displeasure.[64] However, Japan's decision to stand squarely behind the Indian government on territorial disputes and to commit resources to enhance connectivity in the region allows greater opportunities for economic growth and strategic mobility for India.[65] Japan's offer to build power plants on the Andaman and Nicobar Islands is also significant. Given the islands' proximity to the strategically vital Strait of Malacca, a Japanese-built power plant and the potentially reliable power supply that comes with it has the potential to reinforce India's existing defence capabilities.[66] India's solicitation of Japanese aid in this linchpin of regional security, which is likely to be a theatre for competition with China, is a marker of the trust New Delhi and Tokyo have come to share.[67]

Finally, Indo-Japanese economic cooperation has also aimed to diversify global supply chains in a bid to improve resilience and reduce dependence on China. In September 2020, Japan, India and Australia hammered out the details of a trade understanding, christened the Supply Chain Resilience Initiative (SCRI).[68] Each of the three parties to the SCRI has clashed with China politically over the course of the last few years with lasting negative economic consequences, given China's critical leverage in global supply chains and willingness to use the same in order to achieve political goals. While negotiators continue to fine-tune the terms and sectoral focus of the SCRI, preliminary discussions point towards closer cooperation in industries like steel, petroleum and petrochemicals and automotives.[69] Further, Japan's government made headlines in 2020 when it offered substantial economic subsidies to Japanese companies in China if they moved operations back home or to Southeast Asia.[70] India's later inclusion in this programme showed that both powers had tipped their hand and were committed to their economic balancing vis-a-vis China.[71]

Besides this, the two countries are also actively engaged in the Quad's efforts on supply chain security while economic security has become a fixture of India–Japan bilateral meetings.

Defence and Strategic Balancing

Horimoto notes that while economic ties 'were certainly one of the major factors in the Japan-India rapprochement, an even bigger factor was security policy to cope with China as the top priority in common.'[72] For India, Japan's willingness to utilise its advanced economic and industrial base to support key strategic projects in India and sensitive regions like Southeast Asia, its advocacy of concepts like the Free and Open Indo-Pacific and desire to build up its military capabilities makes it a critical strategic partner.[73] For Japan, India's potential to stand as China's only real rival on the continent drives its desire to bring the South Asian power on side.[74] While India strives to contain Chinese influence in the Indian Ocean, in Central Asia and upon neighbours like Bhutan and Nepal, Japan can push to constrain China in the South and East China Sea. The Indo-Japanese strategic relationship, which has deepened at considerable speed since 2014, has come a long way since the days of Atal Bihari Vajpayee and Yoshiro Mori. A telling indication of this was the Vision 2025 document, released in 2015 when Shinzo Abe visited New Delhi, that acted as a blueprint for future strategic cooperation and ran the gamut from freedom of navigation in the Indo-Pacific and sharing of defence technology to joint development of next generation technologies like 5G and IoT.[75] We shall consider each of the avenues for cooperation over the next few pages.

To begin with, the centrepiece of the Indo-Japanese strategic relationship is their joint vision of a Free and Open Indo-Pacific (FOIP), supported militarily by the Quad. Originally championed by Japan, the FOIP envisions an Indo-Pacific regional order characterised by an adherence to international law, a commitment to settling disputes peacefully and freedom of navigation for all parties.[76] This FOIP vision found many takers in Washington, especially in the Trump administration, and has gradually been adopted by New Delhi and Canberra.[77] The Quad, first proposed by Japan's Shinzo Abe in 2006, acts primarily to operationalise and implement such a vision. While leaders of the Quad members have taken great pains in the past to sell the regional grouping as a coalition of like-minded democracies focused on a range of issues, the grouping's activities have raised questions about whether its main purpose is to balance against China.[78] To counter this claim, the Quad engagement has seen leaders discuss subjects as diverse as democracy in Myanmar, the COVID-19 pandemic and North Korean denuclearisation.[79] However, the fate of the Quad has been intimately tied to the members' relationship with China. While the story varies depending on whom one asks, the failure of the first edition of the Quad in 2007 revolved centrally around Indian and Australian reluctance to more directly confront China.[80] The grouping's revival and more overt focus on regional security in 2017 was no accident and reflected a changed strategic landscape wherein all parties had grown more wary of China's growing use of military and economic might to secure its interests in the region.[81] For its part, Beijing has always viewed the FOIP and groupings like the Quad as attempts to contain Chinese influence and played a key role in ensuring the untimely demise of the first edition of the Quad.[82] From its support for the Partnership for Quality Infrastructure, which is a thinly veiled competitor to China's BRI, to its provision of vast quantities of COVID-19 vaccines, the Quad serves Indo-Japanese interests by articulating joint values, providing a platform for cooperation, appealing to other regional players and curtailing potential coercive action from China.[83]

A shared disquiet over China's rise and the rise of groupings like the Quad have also catalysed a long overdue institutionalisation of the diplomatic and defence partnership between the two powers. On the diplomatic front, 2019 saw Japan become among the first countries with which India instituted a ministerial 2+2 dialogue.[84] Tacked onto this are the Defence Ministerial Dialogue and the Defence Policy Dialogue. India and Japan also launched the Act East Forum, managed by the foreign ministries of both powers, which aims to find common ground between India's Act East Policy and Japan's Free and Open Indo-Pacific vision.[85] On the defence side of the equation, Japan was made a permanent participant of the hitherto bilateral naval Malabar Exercises between the United States and India in 2015.[86] This development came on the heels of several years of steadily deepening naval ties; both sides had exercised together for the first time in 2007 and established an official bilateral exercise in 2011.[87] Air and ground forces also held joint exercises for the first time soon after; these have since become annual features.[88] From anti-submarine training to joint counter-terrorism exercises, Indian and Japanese defence forces now cooperate across the board. Both sides also concluded the landmark Acquisition and Cross-Servicing Agreement (ACSA) in 2020, a military logistics treaty that enables sharing of supplies and services. Indian ships traversing the high seas in East Asia can now refuel at Japanese bases with India returning the favour for Japanese ships in the Indian Ocean.[89] Much like the Chinese navy in the Indian Ocean, the Indian Navy can also operate more freely in the Western Pacific on matters ranging from regional security to humanitarian assistance.[90] Fortuitously, India's push to indigenise defence manufacturing capabilities coincided with Japan's repeal of its Cold War-era ban on arms exports which resulted in a 2015 Agreement on defence technology sharing.[91] In 2017, representatives from both sides met in Tokyo for the first dialogue on defence industry cooperation.[92] Finally, in response to the rapid evolution of new-age technologies and their potentially transformative impact on warfare, cooperative research agreements encompassing unmanned ground vehicles and robotics have been concluded.[93]

However, both powers understand that bilateral cooperation can only go so far to ensure that their balancing policy towards China is successful. As such, third countries and multilateral forums have taken on special significance to the two powers. The use of trilateral talks with Australia and the United States, which took off in 2015, broadened cooperation on issues ranging from regional security to humanitarian relief and arguably helped smooth the way to bolder and more ambitious initiatives like the Quad.[94] In Southeast Asia, India and Japan have also invested much effort in wooing strategically vital countries like Vietnam and Myanmar.

For the former, both India and Japan have agreed to provide assistance in the domain of maritime security, in the form of patrol boats and radar technology, given Vietnam's familiarity with and opposition to China's domineering activities in the South China Sea.[95] Vietnam's importance to the balancing strategy against China was made clear when the newly anointed Yoshihide Suga chose the Southeast heavyweight for his first foreign visit as Prime Minister. Hanoi benefited immensely from Japan's aforementioned subsidy plan aimed at relocating Japanese businesses outside China given that over half the companies involved chose Vietnam as their base of operations. To sweeten the pot, Tokyo also offered Hanoi an in-principle agreement to provide military technology. Indonesia, another country that has recently clashed with China over territorial disputes in the South China Sea, has also been at the receiving end of Japanese largesse as the latter announced a number of new infrastructure projects and low-interest loans.[96] In China-friendly Myanmar, Japanese and Indian companies have stepped up investment levels to the tune of billions of dollars while the governments of the two countries have pledged similar amounts to infrastructural development and oil and gas projects.[97] In recent years, India and Japan have warily watched Sri Lanka's growing economic reliance on China. Japan's willingness to collaborate with India on the development of Trincomalee Port is intended to halt Sri Lanka's drift towards China and also turn Trincomalee into a highly visible advertisement for the Indo-Japanese development model.[98] This billion-dollar PR move is especially significant given the allegations of debt-trap diplomacy that have hung like a cloud over the China-built Hambantota Port. The two countries collaborated closely to ease Sri Lanka's ongoing economic and debt crisis.[99] Outside of Southeast Asia, both parties have tried to challenge China's BRI in Africa and appeal to third countries through the Asia-Africa Growth Corridor (AAGC).[100] The AAGC, launched in 2017, rests on four main pillars: 'development of cooperative projects, quality infrastructure and institutional connectivity, capacity building and skilling and people to people partnerships.'[101]

The balancing against China also relies on the skillful management of multilateral forums to counter the latter's influence. During Prime Minister Manmohan Singh's visit to Tokyo in 2006, both sides agreed to cooperate 'in multilateral forums like the UN, SAARC, EAS and ARF'.[102] China's rising influence across a range of geographies and institutions in tandem with the relative decline of American power necessitates a comprehensive Indo-Japanese multilateral strategy. The 2017 formation of the India-Japan Dialogue on ASEAN affairs highlighted a commitment to formulating a joint policy towards the multilateral body. Further, the India-ASEAN Action Plan 2021–25 lays out India's ambition to expand its partnership with the multilateral forum on trade, investment, maritime security and border defence.[103] Both sides also agreed to work together on exchanging best practices on emerging technologies like artificial intelligence (AI) and machine learning.[104] While India's role in balancing China through ASEAN forums is fairly new, Japan has worked to reduce the latter's influence since 2005.[105] China and Japan clashed over India's proposed inclusion in the East Asia Summit given Japanese fears, shared by Singapore and Indonesia, that the absence of a balancing power like India would greatly strengthen China's hand.[106] Japan has also been a longtime supporter of India's bid for a permanent seat on the UN Security Council which, if achieved, would help strengthen the position of friendly powers like India, Japan and Germany in the Council, dilute Chinese influence, and ensure more diverse representation in international institutions. Both India and Japan have donated generously to the African Development Bank in an attempt to boost their footprint in the region; further, Japan has just concluded an agreement to provide USD 638 million to the Abidjan-based body.[107]

The final front of the Indo-Japanese strategic balancing against China lies in the high technology sector. From chipmaking and 5G to AI and quantum computing, China's desire to build itself into a 'world-class power' will depend considerably on the ability of its economic juggernaut to acquire a competitive technological advantage. China's recent announcement of a mammoth USD 1.4 trillion plan to invest in high technology and its abrasive confrontations with other nations when questioned over widespread intellectual property rights theft, the use of AI for mass surveillance and the security of its 5G networks have pushed India and Japan to band together.[108] To begin with, both powers removed a long-standing irritant in the bilateral relationship by formalising a Civil Nuclear Agreement in 2016. Later, in 2018, a Digital Partnership agreement helped formalise 'cooperation on AI technologies between top research institutes like Japan's AIST and India's IIT Hyderabad, as well as government agencies like Japan's METI and India's NITI Aayog.'[109] A Joint Working Group on 5G technology was set up soon after to coordinate policy.[110] Additionally, Japan's interest in establishing a Japan–India Internet of Things (IoT) initiative is both a proactive and smart policy given that the economic value of IoT is estimated to be USD 11.1 trillion by 2025.[111]

Finally, in 2019, both sides launched the India-Japan Space Dialogue which cemented plans of information exchange and joint development of space policy.[112] And more recently, in 2023, India's Cabinet approved a memorandum of understanding on semiconductor supply chains with Japan.[113]

Challenges

While the Indo-Japanese policy of balancing against China has made real gains, it is likely to come up against several bumps on the road in the years to come.

Firstly, much of the efficacy of the balancing policy will depend on the efficacy of bilateral cooperation in third countries. Early indicators are not entirely encouraging. After its announcement with great fanfare in 2017, the Asia-Africa Growth Corridor has underperformed. Several bilateral meetings later, the AAGC has found little to no mention in joint statements and has not featured on the agendas of leaders from either side. Takuya Taniguchi puts the AAGC's failure down to an outsized focus on how the initiative played with the media rather than on hammering out a detailed and workable policy that clearly divided responsibilities between the two governments.[114] Neither side has since pushed to get the ball rolling and the AAGC has been quietly and ignominiously shelved.[115] Meanwhile, a joint railway line slated for construction in Iran has also run into trouble. Indian media reported that the project has been plagued by cost overruns to the tune of USD 2 billion.[116] While third-country projects, especially in infrastructure, are likely to suffer teething troubles, New Delhi and Tokyo would be well served to learn from these early setbacks. The Japan International Cooperation Agency (JICA) has indicated that it would like to work with India on projects in third countries.[117] The new Bay of Bengal–Northeast India Industrial Value Chain Concept, which was unveiled by Prime Minister Fumio Kishida during his March 2023 visit to India, aims to bolster Indo-Japanese cooperation with Bangladesh.[118]

Secondly, India's business environment will need to undergo sea changes if Japan is to play an effective role in India's internal strengthening.

Japan's government went so far as to intercede on behalf of Japanese companies after the outbreak of the COVID-19 pandemic and requested their Indian counterparts to improve logistics, reduce customs duties and loosen stringent labour laws.[119] Matters are not helped by India's gridlocked contract enforcement regime, opaque tax laws, inadequate infrastructure and byzantine bureaucratic regulations.[120] This has repercussions for Indo-Japanese balancing policy against China. To begin with, a complicated regulatory environment will only serve to dampen India's growth prospects and in so doing, will undermine the internal balancing necessary for India to close the gap with China. Secondly, it may render closer integration between the Indian and Japanese economies difficult. Rajesh Mehta and Anand Mishra, in an article for the *Financial Express*, find that burdensome red tape remains an impediment to Japanese business in India.[121] This has a direct impact of the Indo-Japanese balancing policy. Despite consistently figuring among India's largest sources of foreign investment, Japan is only India's 12th largest trading partner with volumes totalling USD 17.63 billion in 2018–19.[122] By contrast, China is India's largest trading partner with a total bilateral trade value of around USD 87 billion, almost five times more than Indo-Japanese trade.[123] Without closer economic ties, an Indo-Japanese balancing policy cannot hope to remain a credible deterrent to China. Finally, India's well-known economic weaknesses can have sizeable strategic implications; this was on display for all to see when India refused to join the Regional Comprehensive Economic Partnership (RCEP). The Indian government chose to safeguard domestic interests in agriculture and manufacturing and admitted, on a global stage, that its economy was unprepared to face the cold winds of global economic competition. Regardless of its reasons for doing so, New Delhi's decision to pass on the largest trade bloc in the world today has undermined Japan's influence and has worried a number of ASEAN countries who had counted on India's presence to balance China.[124] Former diplomat and commentator Kishore Mahbubani, who termed this New Delhi's Brexit moment, scathingly commented that 'India will come to realize that "Look East" and "Act East" policies will mean absolutely nothing if it does not join RCEP'.[125]

Thirdly, defence technology is likely to remain an irritant in the relationship for the foreseeable future. The protracted, and ultimately unsuccessful, negotiations over the US-2I maritime rescue aircraft are emblematic of the larger problems that New Delhi and Tokyo will have to work through. Proposals to purchase the aircraft, designed by Japan's ShinMaywa Industries, found political support from Prime Minister Narendra Modi during his 2014 visit to Japan. Tussles over pricing, offset clauses and technology transfers have delayed the sale despite numerous attempts to clinch a final agreement and as of this writing, matters remain deadlocked.[126] Analysts speculate that Japan's bruising experience with India's notoriously hidebound defence procurement system was behind the refusal of two Japanese companies to respond to the Indian Navy's Request for Information on the Soryu class submarines.[127] However, as Titli Basu points out, Japan's concerns over technology transfers and local building requirements were not India-specific and marred negotiations with Australia as well over the Soryu submarines. Given that Japan only repealed its ban on arms exports in 2014,[128] Japan's defence exports industry is also relatively inexperienced and only won its first major contract in August 2020.[129] It has since concluded another pact with Indonesia.[130] India's massive market and still-nascent indigenous defence industry make it an attractive customer for Japan's advanced defence sector. While India must shed its labyrinthine defence procurement rules, Japan's maturing defence exports providers must meet India halfway in the interests of the wider Indo-Japanese balancing policy against China.

In his 2006 book *Utsukushii Kuni e (Towards a Beautiful Country)*, Shinzo Abe wrote that 'it would not be a surprise if in another 10 years, Japan–India relations overtake Japan–US and Japan–China relations.'[131] Today, as US power in Asia recedes while China's star rises, India and Japan find themselves in an international system undergoing its greatest upheaval since the end of the Cold War. The challenges posed by the still-nascent fourth industrial revolution, the onset of climate change and the proliferation of new-age security challenges will sorely test and vex all nations. Both powers have attempted to find their footing in this new reality and have found the going easier when relying on each other. India and Japan have chosen to navigate these rough waters by building an all-weather partnership that runs the gamut from joint security concerns to high technology development and economic cooperation. In an era characterised by flux and uncertainty, the Indo-Japanese partnership is emerging as an island of stability in an ocean of churn and chaos. Abe's dream may yet become reality.

Notes and References

1. Sam Roggeveen, 'China, America and the Thucydides Trap: An Interview with Graham Allison', *The Interpreter* (The Lowy Institute, 2017), available at https://www.lowyinstitute.org/the-interpreter/china-america-thucydides-trap-interview-graham-allison, accessed on 31 July 2023.

2. George Magnus, *Red Flags: Why Xi's China is in Danger* (Yale University Press, 2018).

3. Xiaojun Li, 'China's Geoeconomic Strategy: China as a Trading Superpower', in Nicholas Kitchen, ed., IDEAS reports – Special Reports, SR012. LSE IDEAS, (The London School of Economics and Political Science, 2012), available at https://eprints.lse.ac.uk/44204/1/China%27s%20Geoeconomic%20Strategy%20_China%20as%20a%20Trading%20Superpower%20%28LSERO%29.pdf, accessed on 31 July 2023.

4. Magnus, *Red Flags*, p. 32.

5. Ibid.

6. Taylor Fravel, *Active Defence: China's Military Strategy Since 1949* (Princeton University Press, 2020).

7. Fravel, *Active Defence.*

8. Ibid.

9. Ibid.

10. Ibid.

11. Ibid.

12. Richard McGregor, *Asia's Reckoning: China, Japan, and the Fate of U.S. Power in the Pacific Century* (Penguin Random House, 2018).

13. McGregor, *Asia's Reckoning.*

14. Ibid., p. 184.

15. Ibid.

16. Ibid., p. 303.

17. Ibid.

18. Ibid.

19. Wu Xinbo, 'The End of the Silver Lining: A Chinese View of the U.S.–Japanese Alliance', *The Washington Quarterly,* vol. 29, no. 1 (2005), pp. 119–130.

20. Ibid.

21. Ibid.

22. Ibid.

23. McGregor, *Asia's Reckoning,* p. 197.

24. Ibid.

25. Harsh Pant and Yogesh Joshi, *The US Pivot and Indian Foreign Policy* (Palgrave Macmillan, 2016).

26. Joshua White, 'China's Indian Ocean Ambitions: Investment, Influence, and Military Advantage', *Global China* (The Brookings Institution, 2020).

27. Pant and Joshi, *The US Pivot.*

28. Ibid.

29. Takenori Horimoto, *Toward the World's Third Great Power: India's Pursuit of Strategic Autonomy* (Iwanami Shoten, 2015).

30. Horimoto, *Toward the World's Third Great Power.*

31. Ibid., p. 4.

32. Ibid., p. 5.

33. Ibid.

34. Ibid.

35. Ibid., p. 6.

36. Ibid.

37. Ibid., p. 7.

38. Hidetaka Yoshimatsu, 'Partnership against the Rising Dragon? Japan's Foreign Policy towards India', *The Pacific Review*, vol. 33, no. 3–4 (2019), pp. 608 –634.

39. Ibid., p. 612.

40. Ibid.

41. Shinzo Abe, 'Asia's Democratic Security Diamond', Project Syndicate, 27 December 2012, available at https://www.project-syndicate.org/magazine/a-strategic-alliance-for-japan-and-india-by-shinzo-abe, accessed on 1 August 2023.

42. Ibid., p. 614.

43. Ibid., p. 617.

44. Horimoto, *Toward the World's Third Great Power,* p. 7.

45. Ibid.

46. Pant and Joshi, *The US Pivot.*

47. Horimoto, *Toward the World's Third Great Power,* p. 7.

48. Kirtika Suneja, 'Look Forward to Japan's Participation in PLI Schemes: DPIIT Secretary', *The Economic Times*, 12 March 2021, available at https://economictimes.indiatimes.com/news/economy/policy/tokyos-sops-to-companies-indias-pli-schemes-to-help-attract-japanese-investment-dpiit-secretary/articleshow/81462972.cms?from=mdr, accessed on 23 August 2023.

49. James Przystup and Thomas Lynch, *India-Japan Strategic Cooperation and Implications for U.S. Strategy in the Indo-Asia-Pacific Region* (National Defence University Press, 2017), available at https://ndupress.ndu.edu/Portals/68/Documents/stratperspective/inss/Strategic-Perspetives-24.pdf?ver=2017-03-14-123654-447, accessed on 23 August 2023.

50. 'Japan PM Kishida announces $42 billion investment in India', *Reuters*, 19 March 2022, available at https://www.reuters.com/world/india/japan-pm-kishida-announces-42-billion-investment-india-2022-03-19/, accessed on 12 January 2024.

51. Przystup and Lynch, *India-Japan Strategic Cooperation.*

52. Devika Chawla and Seerat Kohli, 'Why is India the best place for Japanese investments in the post Covid-19 world', Invest India, 18 May 2020, available at https://www.investindia.gov.in/siru/why-india-best-place-japanese-investments-post-covid-19-world, accessed on 12 January 2024.

53. 'Japanese Investments in India—Overview & Opportunities', Invest India, available at https://www.investindia.gov.in/country/japan-plus#:~:text=An%20%E2%80%9CIndia%2DJapan%20Digital%20Partnership,on%20%E2%80%9CDigital%20ICT%20Technologies%E2%80%9D, accessed on 23 August 2023.

54. Celine Pajon and Isabelle Saint-Mezard, 'The India-Japan Economic Partnership: A Politically Driven Process', *Asie.Visions*, no. 100 (September 2018).

55. Pajon and Saint-Mezard, 'The India-Japan Economic Partnership'.

56. Dipanjan Chaudhury, 'Japan's $12 Billion "Make In India" Fund To Push Investments'. *The Economic Times*, 14 December 2015, available at https://economictimes.indiatimes.com/news/economy/finance/japans-12-billion-make-in-india-fund-to-push-investments/articleshow/50154789.cms?from=mdr, accessed on 23 August 2023.

57. 'Japan-India Institute for Manufacturing to Create 30,000 Skilled Manpower for India, Gets ISO Certification', *The Financial Express*, 5 November 2018, available at https://www.financialexpress.com/auto/car-news/japan-india-institute-for-manufacturing-to-create-30000-skilled-manpower-for-india-gets-iso-certification/1373175/, accessed on 23 August 2023.

58. Przystup and Lynch, *India-Japan Strategic Cooperation*, p. 13.

59. Ibid.

60. Japan International Cooperation Agency (JICA), 'The Project On Improvement of Chennai Port Operation: Final Report', September 2016, available at https://openjicareport.jica.go.jp/pdf/12269890.pdf, accessed on 12 January 2024.

61. Przystup and Lynch, *India-Japan Strategic Cooperation*, p. 14.

62. Ibid., p. 15.

63. Dipanjan Chaudhury, 'Indo-Pacific Partnership: India-Japan Explore New Projects for Northeast', *The Economic Times*, 28 January 2021, available at https://economictimes.indiatimes.com/news/economy/foreign-trade/indo-pacific-partnership-india-japan-explore-new-projects-for-northeast/articleshow/80512236.cms?from=mdr, accessed on 23 August 2023.

64. Przystup and Lynch, *India-Japan Strategic Cooperation*, p. 16.

65. Ibid., p. 14.

66. Ibid., p. 16.

67. Dipanjan Chaudhury, 'Japan Extends Aid for Andaman Infrastructure Project to Bolster Indo-Pacific Partnership', *The Economic Times*, 26 March 2021, available at https://economictimes.indiatimes.com/news/economy/infrastructure/

japan-extends-aid-for-andaman-infra-project-to-bolster-indo-pacific-partnership/articleshow/81709068.cms, accessed on 23 August 2023.

68. Abhijnan Rej, 'India and Japan Sign Military Logistics Agreement for All to See', *The Diplomat*, 12 September 2020, available at https://thediplomat.com/2020/09/india-and-japan-sign-military-logistics-agreement-for-all-to-see/, accessed on 23 August 2023.

69. 'Key Areas to be Focused under India-Japan-Australia Supply Chain Initiative', *Business Standard*, 6 November 2020, available at https://www.business-standard.com/article/economy-policy/key-areas-to-be-focused-under-india-japan-australia-supply-chain-initiative-120110601741_1.html, accessed on 23 August 2023.

70. 'Japan Govt to Pay at Least $536 Million for Companies to Leave China', *Business Standard*, 20 July 2020, available at https://www.business-standard.com/article/international/japan-govt-to-pay-at-least-536-million-for-companies-to-leave-china-120072000004_1.html, accessed on 23 August 2023.

71. Takako Gakuto, 'Japan Adds India and Bangladesh to "China Exit" Subsidy Destinations', *Nikkei Asia*, 4 September 2020, available at https://asia.nikkei.com/Economy/Japan-adds-India-and-Bangladesh-to-China-exit-subsidy-destinations, accessed on 23 August 2023.

72. Horimoto, *Toward the World's Third Great Power,* p. 9.

73. Ibid.

74. Ibid.

75. Ibid.

76. Benjamin Rimland and Patrick Buchan, *Defining the Diamond: The Past, Present, and Future of the Quadrilateral Security Dialogue* (Center for Strategic and International Studies, 2020), available at https://www.csis.org/analysis/defining-diamond-past-present-and-future-quadrilateral-security-dialogue, accessed on 23 August 2023.

77. Rimland and Buchan, *Defining the Diamond,* p. 2.

78. Ibid., p. 3.

79. Ibid.

80. Ibid.

81. Ibid., p. 4.

82. Iain Marlow, 'What Is the Quad and Should China Fear It?', *Bloomberg*, 26 March 2021, available at https://www.bloomberg.com/news/articles/2021-03-26/what-is-the-quad-and-should-china-fear-it-quicktake, accessed 23 August 2023.

83. Marlow, 'What Is the Quad and Should China Fear It?'.

84. Rajesh Basrur and Sumitha Narayanan Kutty, 'Modi's India and Japan: Nested Strategic Partnerships', *International Politics*, vol. 59 (2021), available at https://link.springer.com/article/10.1057/s41311-021-00288-2#citeas, accessed on 23 August 2023.

85. Basrur and Kutty, 'Modi's India and Japan: Nested Strategic Partnerships'.

86. Przystup and Lynch, *India-Japan Strategic Cooperation*, p. 21.

87. Ibid.

88. Ibid., p. 22.

89. Joshy Paul, 'India–Japan Maritime Security Cooperation: Secondary States' Soft Balancing in the Indo-Pacific', *Maritime Affairs: Journal of the National Maritime Foundation of India*, vol. 15, no. 2 (2019), pp. 59–77.

90. Ibid.

91. G. V. C. Naidu and Ishida Yasuyuki, 'India–Japan Defence Ties: Building a Strategic Partnership', *Strategic Analysis*, vol. 43, no. 1 (2019), pp. 13–27.

92. Ibid.

93. Satoru Nagao, 'The Rise of India and Japan-America-India Defence Technology Cooperation', *ORF*, 11 February 2020, available at https://www.orfonline.org/expert-speak/the-rise-of-india-and-japan-america-india-defence-technology-cooperation-61272/, accessed on 23 August 2023.

94. Yoshimatsu, 'Partnership against the Rising Dragon?', p. 619.

95. Ibid.

96. Shashank Mattoo, 'Suga Starts Strongly', *ORF*, 12 December 2020, available at https://www.orfonline.org/expert-speak/suga-starts-strongly/, accessed on 23 August 2023.

97. Sayo Sasaki, 'Japan, Fearing Impact on Businesses and Benefits for China, Faces Myanmar Balancing Act', *The Japan Times*, 11 February 2021, available at https://www.japantimes.co.jp/news/2021/02/11/national/japan-balancing-act-myanmar/, accessed on 23 August 2023. *See also* Huma Siddiqui, 'Neighbourhood First: India to Invest USD 6 Bn for Setting Up a Petroleum Refinery in Myanmar,' *The Financial Express*, 6 October 2020, available at https://www.financialexpress.com/defence/neighbourhood-first-india-to-invest-usd-6-bn-for-setting-up-a-petroleum-refinery-in-myanmar/2099145/, accessed on 23 August 2023.

98. Jagannath Panda, ed., *Scaling India-Japan Cooperation in Indo-Pacific and Beyond 2025: Corridors, Connectivity and Contours* (New Delhi: IDSA, 2020).

99. Suhasini Haidar, 'India-Japan look to restart trilateral cooperation with Sri Lanka, but with caution', *The Hindu*, 10 August 2023, available at https://www.thehindu.com/news/national/india-japan-look-to-restart-trilateral-cooperation-with-sri-lanka-but-with-caution/article67180586.ece, accessed on 12 January 2024.

100. Takuya Taniguchi, 'Should We Forget about the Asia-Africa Growth Corridor?', *Lettres du Centre Asie*, no. 87 (Ifri: 2020).

101. Ibid.

102. Pant and Joshi, *The US Pivot*.

103. Joe Devanesan, 'India, Japan Look to ASEAN to Tighten Continental Cybersecurity Co-op', *Tech Wire Asia*, 26 October 2020, available at https://

techwireasia.com/2020/10/india-japan-look-to-asean-to-tighten-continental-cybersecurity-co-op/, accessed on 24 August 2023.

104. Ibid.

105. Chien-Peng Chung, 'China and Japan in "ASEAN Plus" Multilateral Arrangements', *Asian Survey*, vol. 53, no. 5 (2013), pp. 801–824.

106. Ibid.

107. 'Japan Agrees $668 Million Loan to African Development Bank Fund', *Nippon*, 17 February 2021, available at https://www.nippon.com/en/news/reu20210217KBN2AH16V/, accessed on 24 August 2023; 'India', African Development Bank, available at https://www.afdb.org/en/countries/non-regional-member-countries/india, accessed on 24 August 2023.

108. 'China's Got a New Plan to Overtake the U.S. in Tech', *Bloomberg News*, 21 May 2020, available at https://www.bloomberg.com/news/articles/2020-05-20/china-has-a-new-1-4-trillion-plan-to-overtake-the-u-s-in-tech, accessed on 12 January 2024.

109. Shashank Mattoo and Ratnadeep Chakraborty, *A New Partnership for the Digital 21st Century*, ORF Issue Brief No. 132 (March 2021), available at https://www.orfonline.org/research/a-new-partnership-for-the-digital-21st-century-japan-india-and-france/, accessed on 24 August 2023.

110. Ibid.

111. Ministry of External Affairs, Government of India, 'Joint Statement on India and Japan Vision 2025: Special Strategic and Global Partnership Working Together for Peace and Prosperity of the Indo-Pacific Region and the World', 12 December 2015, available at https://www.mea.gov.in/bilateral-documents.htm?dtl/26176/Joint_Statement_on_India_and_Japan_Vision_2025_Special_Strategic_and_Global_Partnership_Working_Together_for_Peace_and_Prosperity_of_the_IndoPacific_R, accessed on 24 August 2023; James Manyika et al., *The Internet of Things: Mapping the Value Beyond the Hype* (McKinsey Global Institute, 2015), available at https://www.mckinsey.com/~/media/McKinsey/Industries/Technology%20Media%20and%20Telecommunications/High%20Tech/Our%20Insights/The%20Internet%20of%20Things%20The%20value%20of%20digitizing%20the%20physical%20world/The-Internet-of-things-Mapping-the-value-beyond-the-hype.pdf, accessed on 24 August 2023.

112. Ministry of External Affairs, GoI, 'Joint Statement on India and Japan Vision 2025'.

113. 'Cabinet approves Memorandum of Cooperation between India and Japan on Japan-India Semiconductor Supply Chain Partnership', PIB Delhi, 25 October 2023, available at https://pib.gov.in/PressReleaseIframePage.aspx?PRID=1970784, accessed on 12 January 2024.

114. Taniguchi, 'Should We Forget about the Asia-Africa Growth Corridor?'.

115. Ibid.

116. Sandeep Dikshit, 'India's Strategic Rail Projects with Japan, Iran in Trouble', *Tribune India*, 15 July 2020, available at https://www.tribuneindia.com/news/nation/indias-strategic-rail-projects-with-japan-iran-in-trouble-112932, accessed on 24 August 2023.

117. Shashank Mattoo, 'Japan interested in partnering with India to build infra abroad: JICA India chief', *Mint*, 11 October 2023, available at https://www.livemint.com/economy/japan-interested-in-partnering-with-india-for-infra-building-abroad-11697046286467.html, accessed on 12 January 2024.

118. Rezaul Laskar, 'Japan to help build industrial value chain linking B'desh port, India's northeast', *Hindustan Times*, 19 May 2023, available at https://www.hindustantimes.com/india-news/japan-aims-to-create-new-industrial-value-chain-in-india-s-northeast-and-bangladesh-using-matarbari-sea-port-says-ambassador-101684424595739.html, accessed on 28 October 2023.

119. Amiti Sen, 'Japan Concerned over Fate of its Companies in India', *Hindu Businessline*, 18 May 2020, available at https://www.thehindubusinessline.com/economy/japan-concerned-over-fate-of-its-companies-in-india/article31615569.ece, accessed on 24 August 2023.

120. 'Ease of Doing Business in India', *The World Bank*, available at https://archive.doingbusiness.org/en/data/exploreeconomies/india, accessed on 24 August 2023.

121. Rajesh Mehta and Anand Mishra, 'India – Japan Are Top Strategic Partners but the Sub-Optimal Economic Relationship Needs Fixing,' *The Financial Express*, 7 August 2020, available at https://www.financialexpress.com/economy/india-japan-are-top-strategic-partners-but-the-sub-optimal-economic-relationship-needs-fixing/2047745/, accessed on 24 August 2023.

122. Ministry of External Affairs, Government of India. 'Brief Note on India-Japan Bilateral Relations', February 2020, available at https://www.mea.gov.in/Portal/ForeignRelation/India-Japan_Bilateral_Brief_feb_2020.pdf, accessed on 24 August 2023.

123. Ananth Krishnan, 'India's Trade with China Falls in 2020, Deficit a Five-year Low', *The Hindu,* 15 January 2021, available at https://www.thehindu.com/business/Economy/indias-trade-with-china-falls-in-2020-deficit-at-five-year-low/article33581648.ece#:~:text=Two%2Dway%20trade%20in%202020,the%20lowest%20figure%20since%202016, accessed on 24 August 2023.

124. Takenori Horimoto, 'Indo-Pacific Order and Japan–India Relations in the Midst of COVID-19', *Journal of Asian Economic Integration,* vol. 2, no. 2 (2020).

125. Ibid.

126. Titli Basu, 'A Review of India-Japan Defence Technology Cooperation', IDSA Comment (Manohar Parrikar Institute for Defence Studies and Analyses, 2018), available at https://idsa.in/idsacomments/india-japan-defence-technology-cooperation-tbasu-310818, accessed on 24 August 2023.

127. Ibid.

128. Ibid.

129. Mike Yeo, 'Japan Secures First-Ever Major Defense Export with Philippine Radar Order', *Defense News*, 28 August 2020, available at https://www.defensenews.com/global/asia-pacific/2020/08/28/japan-secures-first-ever-defense-export-with-philippine-radar-order/, accessed on 24 August 2023.

130. Junko Horiuchi, 'Japan Signs Deal to Export Defense Equipment to Indonesia', *Kyodo News*, 30 March 2021, available at https://english.kyodonews.net/news/2021/03/57f983dc7f10-japan-to-reach-deal-with-indonesia-on-defense-equipment-exports.html, accessed on 24 August 2023.

131. Shinzo Abe, *Utsukushii Kuni e* [*Towards a Beautiful Country*] (Bunshun Shinso, 2006).

five

The Indo-Japanese Pivot to Asia

New Opportunities and Challenges

MADHUCHANDA GHOSH

In the emerging geopolitical scenario in Asia, few relationships among the major powers have undergone such a remarkable turnaround as that between Japan and India. Japan's Civil Nuclear Agreement with India, its permanent membership in the Indo-US Malabar exercises and Tokyo's massive infrastructure investment in India inter alia have transformed the low-intensity Indo-Japanese relationship into one of the fastest growing bilateral relations, acquiring new strategic and economic dimensions. The coronavirus pandemic and the ensuing geopolitical and geoeconomic uncertainties have pushed the two nations even closer. This chapter analyses the new phase in Indo-Japanese relations and explores the variables shaping the emerging contours of their bilateral ties. It examines the growing convergence between the two states in the rapidly changing Indo-Pacific strategic landscape. The chapter is organised into three sections. The first section examines the several multilayered factors shaping the Indo-Japanese strategic partnership and looks into issues on which the foreign policy perspectives of the two states are converging, with a particular focus on the Indo-Pacific regional construct, including enhancing maritime security and connectivity, growing synergies with ASEAN, strategic convergence with the United States and balancing of China's expanding military and strategic influence. The second section examines the obstacles towards fully cementing the ties which are particularly evident in the domain of bilateral economic engagement and the two countries' divergent perceptions on collaborating vis-à-vis the regional multilateral mechanism, the Regional Comprehensive Economic Partnership (RCEP). The third and final section offers concluding remarks.

In the changing post-Cold War Asian strategic environment, Japan and India are growing closer. For decades, the two states could not develop the bilateral relationship, which remained low-profile because of their different approaches towards international politics during the Cold War era. Structural changes in the post-Cold War period in Asia allowed Japan and India greater strategic manoeuvrability. For instance, the reduction of the US troops, marked by the closure of America's largest overseas military base located in the Philippines in 1992, affected the strategic balance in Asia, and this induced Japan to venture into a search for like-minded strategic partners. In this context, India's growing importance in America's Asia policy also influenced Tokyo's perception of India as a potential like-minded partner in Asia. The Asian geostrategic environment is in a state of dramatic flux as evident from the rise of new power centres, formation of new strategic partnerships and military arrangements. China's rise and its ambition to carve out a new Sino-centric order is causing a major structural shift in the regional strategic landscape by increasingly challenging US primacy. The COVID-19 pandemic disrupting the world's supply chain has illustrated how critical China is to the health of the global economy.

As the Sino-US trade war intensifies, Sino-Russian bonhomie is growing along strategic lines. The US–China strategic rivalry, escalating tensions in the South China Sea, North Korea's launching ballistic missiles in clear violation of the UNSC resolutions and emerging critical non-traditional security challenges (the COVID-19 outbreak being the latest one) are some of the unprecedented developments that are shaping the contours of Japan's relations with India. In the changing security architecture in Asia, the focus of Indo-Japanese relations has moved from the political towards the strategic, since both countries share core strategic interests, whether over their heavy dependence on West Asian oil, the safety of the sea lanes in the Indian Ocean Region (IOR) or the growing power disequilibrium in Asia. With these emerging structural changes in the Asian strategic environment, the parameters of Japan and India's foreign policies are undergoing significant changes: While India is growing its strategic profile by expanding its naval influence beyond the Indian Ocean and by forging strategic links with the major powers in the region and throughout the world, Japan appears to be emerging as a 'normal state'[1] with growing political and military potentiality as evident from the former Abe government's endeavour to restore Japan's position to 'normal' by receding from its pacifist constitutional orientation.

Unlike its relations with other Asian states, most of which had a tumultuous past with Japan, Japan's relationship with India is marked by a positive historical legacy. Apart from spiritual and cultural linkages through Buddhism as well as other intellectual exchanges, Japan's assistance to Subhas Chandra Bose, one of the key nationalist leaders of India during India's independence movement, continues to shape popular Indian perceptions about Japan. In the early years of the post-war period, a positive image of India was built with Japan's appreciation of Justice Radhabinod Pal's dissenting judgement at the Tokyo International Military Tribunal for the Far East in 1948. Despite this positive historical legacy, the political will to deepen Indo-Japanese bilateral ties was absent in both countries for decades. This was the case because, especially during the Cold War era, India had devised a non-aligned strategy to avoid embroilment in bipolar rivalry while Japan was aligned with and dependent on the United States. As Sumit Ganguly points out, this non-aligned stance was, in essence, a foreign policy strategy designed so that India could pursue its own interests free from external domination.[2] While India's Cold War strategic posture, which was marked by its overtures towards the Soviet Union, precluded it from cultivating close ties with the US's allies, Japan was reluctant to deepen its engagement with India because of its pro-Soviet leanings. In short, it was a saga of missed opportunities because of the Cold War strategic and geopolitical compulsions. Since the 2000s the sustained engagement and concerted efforts of the leadership of Japan and India have laid the foundation for a growing partnership between the two states.

Japan and India's Converging Interests in the Emerging Indo-Pacific Strategic Landscape

The 'Indo-Pacific' construct, which conceives the Western Pacific and the Indian Ocean as an interconnected geopolitical and geoeconomic space, has assumed key importance in the geopolitics of 21st-century Asia. The strategic salience of the Indo-Pacific concept appears to stem from two factors. First, India has emerged as a central regional actor since the 2000s with growing strategic presence in Southeast and East Asia. The major powers in the region including the US, Japan, Australia and many of the ASEAN countries are deepening their political, strategic and economic engagement with India. Moreover, Beijing's aggressive diplomacy and its growing military assertiveness are not confined to East Asia but extends into the Indian Ocean. The concept of the Indo-Pacific thus encapsulates the emerging geopolitical theatre much more clearly than the Asia Pacific which leaves out India.[3] The second factor stems from the Indo-Pacific region's growing strategic importance because of the great dependence of international trade on the sea lines of communication (SLOCs) between the Pacific and the Indian Oceans. The security of and access to the SLOCs are a significant factor in the formation of strategic partnerships among the central regional actors. The converging and competing interests of the three major Asian powers—China, India and Japan—have driven them to articulate different strategic frameworks in the region as indicated in Japan's 'Confluence of the Two Seas' idea, China's Maritime Silk Road Initiative (MSRI) and India's Act East Policy (AEP).[4]

India's Act East Policy, which is the foundational element of its 'free, open and inclusive' vision[5] for the Indo-Pacific region, appears to converge with Japan's Free and Open Indo-Pacific strategy (FOIP), based on their shared values of upholding the rule of law; giving importance to international law, in particular the United Nations Convention on the Law of the Sea (UNCLOS); freedom of navigation and overflight; peaceful resolution of disputes without resorting to threat or use of force; and unimpeded lawful commerce in international waters.[6] The former Japanese premier Shinzo Abe's floating the idea of 'Confluence of the Indian and the Pacific Oceans', in his 2007 address to the Indian Parliament, as the 'dynamic coupling of seas of freedom and prosperity',[7] indicated the growing importance of the Indian Ocean in Japan's foreign policy calculus. Abe's further expanding the concept, during his second term as prime minister, by talking about a 'Free and Open Indo-Pacific' maritime space[8]—which calls for connecting the two oceans, the Indian and the Pacific, and the two continents Asia and Africa—indicates Japan's intent to expand its strategic influence and maritime engagement in this region. Pointing to the Indian Ocean's resurgence as a critical waterway in the global maritime landscape, Abe noted India's importance as a net security provider in the region and proposed that India and Japan could together play a critical role in bolstering maritime security while maintaining the regional status quo.[9]

Japan's changing perception on India's expanding role in the domain of regional maritime security seems to be shaped by the fact that the Indian Navy has assumed critical importance in conducting anti-piracy operations in the Indian Ocean, where many Japanese ships have been targets of pirate attacks. In one significant incident in November 1999, the Indian Coast Guard and Navy rescued the Japanese vessel MV *Alondra Rainbow*. Pirates had hijacked the Japanese oil cargo from the South China Sea. The ramifications of this successful rescue were immense, showing to the world, including Japan, that India could be a stabilising force in the rapidly deteriorating regional security environment. Japan's important strategic conceptualisations, like the 'Confluence of the Two Seas', the 'Quadrilateral Initiative', the 'Arc of Freedom and Prosperity', Asia's 'Democratic Security Diamond' and the FOIP, all refer to India as a key partner of Japan in the region.

Tokyo's intent to deepen its maritime security cooperation with New Delhi also appears to be driven by the fact that India is strategically located in the Indo-Pacific region: it sits astride two 'choke points' for global oil supply—the Strait of Hormuz to its west and the Strait of Malacca to its east. These sea lines constitute the routes for the passage of approximately one-third of international trade and half of the world's crude oil resources. The main trade routes from Europe and the Persian Gulf to Japan and other East Asian countries are through these maritime choke points. For instance, over 80 per cent of Japan's oil cargo from the Persian Gulf is transported through the Malaccan Strait, the main passage between the Indian Ocean and the South China Sea. Thus, India's strategic location and its expanding role in enhancing SLOCs security, including in the Malacca Strait, makes India strategically vital to Japan. A growing interest on both sides to deepen their cooperation on the issues of peace and stability, maritime security, freedom of navigation and development of the Indo-Pacific region is evident from the joint statements. While the 2017 joint statement focused on devising an integrated Indo-Pacific strategy,[10] the October 2018 joint statement reiterated their 'unwavering commitment' 'to working together towards a free and open Indo-Pacific'.[11]

The foundation of the improved bilateral engagement between Tokyo and New Delhi has been based on a new dimension of mutual 'strategic and security interests'.[12] As David Brewster notes, there has been a strong conceptual support heralded by the strategic communities of Japan and India towards the expanding security relationship between the two states.[13] Since the institutionalisation of a bilateral security dialogue, India and Japan have been deepening their maritime security cooperation. It is significant to note that in 2012, Tokyo and New Delhi began holding joint naval exercises called the Japan-India Maritime Exercise (JIMEX), the first of which was held in the Pacific, and the second in the Bay of Bengal in 2013. The revival of the JIMEX in October 2018, after a lapse of five years, indicates the growing concern of the two states with regard to threats to freedom of navigation and respect for a rules-based order in the region. According to Kumagai Naoki, a Japanese diplomat, the JIMEX-18 reflects the shared strategic vision of the two states vis-à-vis enhancing maritime security and promoting freedom of navigation in the region.[14] The Indo-Japanese strategic relations received a new boost in November 2019 when the bilateral mechanism of the 2+2 Dialogue was elevated to the ministerial level.[15] For the first time since its initiation in 2010, Foreign and Defense Ministers of the two states led the delegations of this Dialogue. It needs to be noted that Japan and Australia[16] are the only two countries besides the US with which India has such a high-level 2+2 Dialogue.

Bilateral mechanisms as the 2+2 Dialogue, Annual Defence Ministerial Dialogue, India-Japan Act East Forum and the new Acquisition and Cross-Servicing Agreement (ACSA) are likely to deepen the strategic depth of the bilateral security and defense cooperation between India and Japan. ACSA would enhance the security engagement between the two countries whereby India could have access to Japan's naval facility in Djibouti and Japan could gain access to Indian facilities in the Andaman and Nicobar Islands (ANI).[17] The Andaman and Nicobar Islands, situated in the western approaches to the Malacca Strait, constitute India's key strategic outpost in the IOR. The strategic advantage that the Andamans provide to India is the ability to exercise surveillance and monitor the world's most strategic trade route with high traffic, that is, the Malacca Strait. This seems to have played a major part in Japan's growing interest to engage with India in infrastructural upgradation of the ANI. For instance, Japan is developing basic infrastructure such as reliable power and communications in the islands and laying an optic fibre cable across the Bay of Bengal. Japan's NEC Corporation has been contracted to install an undersea cable from Chennai to the ANI. This will support India's planned build-up of naval and air assets in the islands and possibly contribute towards an undersea surveillance system to monitor submarines.

Apart from investing in developmental projects in the ANI, Tokyo is also involved in connectivity projects in India's Northeastern region. Infrastructural upgradation of the Northeast is vital for New Delhi as it will build a connectivity continuum that will help strengthen India's linkages with the Indo-Pacific region, especially the ASEAN countries including the South China Sea. With India's Northeastern region emerging as a pivot area of New Delhi's AEP, India and Japan have agreed to deepen their cooperation in enhancing connectivity in the region. For instance, in 2017, the two states set up the India-Japan Act East Forum with the aim of providing a platform for bilateral collaboration focusing on the 'economic modernization'[18] of the Northeast under the rubric of India's AEP and Japan's FOIP. Japan's growing engagement in that part of India is reflected through its immediate investment of about 205.784 billion yen (USD 1.8 billion) towards infrastructure and manufacturing projects.[19] It needs to be noted that this initiative of India-Japan Act East Forum, with representation from India's Northeastern states, comes in the backdrop of Chinese troops making repeated incursions into India's Northeastern territory.[20]

New Delhi welcoming Japanese investments in boosting connectivity in the ANI and the Northeast is quite symbolic. It indicates that New Delhi perceives Tokyo as a key strategic partner whom India is prepared to trust when it comes to its strategically sensitive border regions where New Delhi has not allowed other countries to invest. Apart from collaborating with New Delhi in connectivity projects within India, Japan is also keen on partnering with India in enhancing strategic connectivity within and among the critical maritime regions for bolstering economic linkages. This is particularly reflected in their joint infrastructure and connectivity project, the Asia-Africa Growth Corridor (AAGC), which involves building a sea corridor linking eastern and southern Africa with India and East Asia. An important component of the Vision Statement of the 13th Summit, the AAGC converges with India's development cooperation with Africa and the AEP, and Japan's FOIP and Expanded Partnership for Quality Infrastructure (EPQI) for 'realizing a free and open Indo-Pacific'.[21] Horimoto Takenori pointed out that Japan and India's bid to actively engage the African Development Bank and several African countries in the AAGC project in the planning and implementation stages indicates the inclusive nature of the project, which is in stark contrast with China's unilateral connectivity projects.[22] India and Japan's intent to partner in the AAGC seems to be a part of Tokyo and New Delhi's soft-balancing vis-à-vis Beijing's grand strategic design of establishing a Sino-centric regional order through the Belt and Road Initiative (BRI).[23] As Harsh Pant and Ritika Passi have noted, India's response to the BRI is marked by heightened security concerns as New Delhi perceives with apprehension China's efforts to gain geopolitical leverage in the region through its unilateral strategic moves.[24]

China's Expanding Military Influence Pushing India and Japan Closer

The strategic rationale behind India's bolstering relations with Japan is reflected in its endeavour to engage with Japan in two areas of its core national interests: economy and security, and also to cope with a rising China. As Harsh Pant and Yogesh Joshi have noted, tensions between India and China are driven by several factors: the rise of both nations in a short span of time, unresolved border disputes, increasing strategic competition exacerbated by the growing power disequilibrium, Beijing's strong ties with India's arch-rival Pakistan and the power differential that exists between New Delhi and Beijing.[25] India and Japan have reasons to be concerned about China's geostrategic ambitions and increasing military preponderance across the Pacific and the Indian Oceans. As Brahma Chellaney noted more than a decade ago, '[i]n the emerging Asia, the two non-Western democracies, India and Japan, look like natural allies as China drives them closer'.[26] China's bid for maritime primacy in the Indo-Pacific region has security implications for both Japan and India, who are alerted by Beijing's growing emphasis on naval power projection and anti-ship ballistic missiles. Further, China's emerging blue-water navy, backed by comprehensive national and maritime power, is affecting the strategic balance in the Indo-Pacific maritime landscape. Patrick Cronin notes that the balance of naval power is particularly favourable to China in its near seas where shore-based missiles and aircraft can support the People's Liberation of Army Navy's (PLAN) fleet.[27] Horimoto Takenori argues that India and Japan should deepen cooperation in the Indo-Pacific region in the light of the escalation of the strategic competition between China and the US.[28]

As India and Japan deepen maritime security cooperation in the Indo-Pacific, China's rapidly growing military and strategic influence is being monitored closely by the two states. New Delhi's worries about security appear to stem from the apprehension that under China's ambitious MSRI connectivity project, the acquisition and construction of ports could serve a dual purpose.[29] The commercial ports could be used as military facilities for the Chinese navy to help mitigate China's geographical disadvantages in the region and expand PLAN's footprint in the Indian Ocean Region (IOR) and in this context, Asian affairs analyst Shihoko Goto opines that China is capitalising on the lack of US strategic focus in the IOR.[30] The MSRI appears to be the reincarnation of the 'String of Pearls' strategy[31] which focuses on building bases in the IOR in order to expand naval power and secure the Strait of Malacca from potential blockade during war. Beijing's establishment of a military base in Djibouti in 2017 appears to be the first step in what is likely to become a network of Chinese bases across the IOR. The military base in Djibouti provides China with a rudimentary power-projection that is bolstered by its access to ports in Pakistan, Sri Lanka, Bangladesh and Myanmar. Researcher Joshua White is of the opinion that Pakistan, as China's key strategic partner, is likely to play a critical role in enhancing Beijing's military assertiveness in the South Asian region.[32] It must be noted that under the MSRI project, China's economic assistance to the smaller states reflects predatory loan practices, a lack of social or environmental assessments, and it has entangled some littoral states in Chinese strategic objectives and debt trap diplomacy. For instance, Cambodia's bilateral public debt with China is close to USD 5 billion.[33] Sri Lanka had to lease out the Beijing-funded Hambantota port on its southern coast to China, in a bid to ease the debt burden it had accumulated with Beijing.[34]

Tokyo's concerns about the MSRI seem to relate mostly to its energy vulnerability and the risk that the MSRI could be employed to limit or block energy shipments to East Asia. This concern was particularly reflected in the comments of Akitaka Saiki, the former Vice Minister for Foreign Affairs, who viewed that Japan sees no difference regarding security issues in the Indian Ocean, Pacific Ocean, South or East China Seas.[35]

The growing presence of Chinese nuclear submarines in the IOR is another cause of security concern for India. PLAN's expanding footprint in the IOR seems to have propelled New Delhi to accelerate the modernisation of the Indian naval forces. And for this, New Delhi is increasingly seeking cooperation from Japan and the US. For example, the Modi government is exploring the possibility of working with Japan in building submarines[36] and has sought technology share from the US for India's next aircraft carrier.[37]

China's growing military assertiveness has been a primary factor behind Tokyo's heightening anxiety regarding security. Japanese domestic politics is increasingly being influenced by the ruling Liberal Democratic Party's endeavour towards bolstering national security and restoring Japan's position as a 'normal' country by receding from its earlier pacifist constitutional orientation. The Abe administration set the trend which is being followed by the subsequent governments. For instance, the current Kishida government, soon after its formation, swiftly approved and began work on three vital security-related documents: the National Security

Strategy (NSS 2022), the National Defence Strategy (NDS 2022) and the Defense Buildup Program (DBP). While the DBP lays down the procedures for procuring equipment necessary for implementing Japan's defense strategy,[38] the NDS 2022 outlines Japan's national security strategy.[39] The NSS 2022 delineates Japan's long-term security policy for the next decade,[40] following the previous NSS developed by the Abe government.

The Kishida government came into power amid Japan's hardening threat perceptions vis-à-vis China. Fumio Kishida, who replaced Yoshihide Suga on 4 October 2021, had in his election campaign a major focus on how to build a more assertive foreign policy platform, especially vis-à-vis China, which played a significant role in his electoral triumph. The three security-related documents indicate a major shift in practice in the country's post-war defense paradigm, while maintaining the basic principle—the *Senshu Boei* (Exclusively Defense Oriented Policy)—followed since 1954, when the Self-Defense Forces came into being. In this context it needs to be noted that a paradigm shift in Japan's post-war defense strategy has been to create the *hangeki noryoku* (capability to counterstrike). While the Kishida government's security strategy is largely shaped by the erstwhile Abe government's strategic posture, there has been a significant departure in threat perception, particularly from Abe's conciliatory policy towards Russia which was aimed at helping resolve the territorial dispute between the two states over the Kurile Islands, to the present hawkish stance on Russia after the invasion of Ukraine. A shift in the Kishida government's threat perception vis-à-vis China has also been noted, for instance in the 2013 NSS in which China was described as a 'source of concern for the international community, including Japan.' The 2022 NSS presents a stronger view of China as 'a serious source of concern for Japan and the international community, and the greatest challenge [...] ever posed'.

The sharp deterioration in Sino-Japanese relations seems to have propelled the Kishida government to approve the first update to the country's official security strategy in nine years, announcing a doubling of the amount earmarked for Japan's military spending in the next five years with 2 per cent of the GDP by 2027. This marks a significant departure from the decades-long precedent on spending constraints in defense. The Kishida government also declared its intention to procure Tomahawk, the long-range missile from the US.[41] In August 2023, the Kishida government asked for a record 7.7 trillion yen (USD 52.67 billion) in spending for the 2024 fiscal year as part of its plan to boost military spending by 43 trillion yen over five years.[42] Amid Beijing's growing tensions with Tokyo and Delhi, it is not hard to comprehend why the issue of the 'free and open Indo-Pacific' was the main agenda of Kishida's March 2023 visit to India. India's concern over Beijing's naval power projection in the South China Sea and East China Sea was clearly indicated by Prime Minister Modi during his May 2023 visit to Japan. In an interview with the leading Japanese daily *Yomiuri Shimbun*, PM Modi addressed China's military expansion in the South China Sea and the East China Sea and said that India is committed to protecting its sovereignty and integrity while promoting peaceful resolution of maritime disputes.[43]

The revival of the Quadrilateral initiative, the Quad 2.0,[44] in 2017 is one of the most crucial military and diplomatic dimensions of the pursuit of congruent strategies of these states in tackling emerging traditional and non-traditional challenges in the Indo-Pacific, including China's growing military assertiveness in the region. In this context, it needs to be noted that the idea of the quadrilateral dialogue of cooperation was first mooted by Abe in his book, *Utsukushii kuni e* (*Towards a Beautiful Country*). In the book, Abe says, 'It is of crucial importance to Japan's national interest that it further strengthen ties with India', adding, 'It would not be a surprise if in another 10 years, Japan-India relations overtake Japan-US and Japan-China relations'.[45]

Beijing's expanding military influence and the increasing assertiveness of its land reclamation and territorial claims in disputed areas in the South and East China Seas over the past decade have been a key driver of the strengthening alignment among the Quad members.[46] A rules-based regional order based on ASEAN centrality and backed by the Quad's strategic weight will be significant in terms of presenting a tangible alternative to China's drive for building a Sino-centric order through its unilateralist regional forays into South Asia, Southeast and East Asia.

Synergies with ASEAN

Apart from bilateral mechanisms, the existing regional multilateral mechanisms, particularly the ASEAN, provide crucial platforms for India and Japan to engage collectively on transnational security challenges and capacity-building through the ASEAN Defense Ministers' Meeting Plus (ADMM-Plus), the ASEAN Regional Forum (ARF) and the Expanded ASEAN Maritime Forum (EAMF). Located at the geographic centre of the

Indo-Pacific, the ASEAN remains at the core of the Indo-Pacific approach of both Japan and India. For instance, in the first 2+2 Ministerial Dialogue in November 2019, India and Japan reaffirmed their support for the ASEAN and noted that the ASEAN Outlook on the Indo-Pacific (AOIP),[47] Japan's Vientiane Vision 2.0 and India's Indo-Pacific Oceans Initiative (IPOI) have overlapping interests in striving for an Indo-Pacific region that is inclusive and open to all countries in the region.

The ASEAN is likely to assume critical significance in managing Indo-Pacific affairs given that Southeast Asia is rising as a key geopolitical theatre where the 'freeness' and 'openness' of the Indo-Pacific will be tested. As China locks horns with its neighbours Indonesia, Vietnam, Philippines, Brunei, Malaysia and Taiwan over the control of the three sets of islands and rocks in the South China Sea, and with Japan over competing claims to the Senkaku/Diaoyu Islands in the East China Sea, these strategic waterways are emerging as global flashpoints. These ensuing tensions in the East and South China Seas also impinge on India's economic and strategic interests in the region. Moreover, China's aggressive behaviour in Hong Kong is on the rise.[48] In the era of 'America First' and China's rising military assertiveness in the Indo-Pacific region, many of the Southeast Asian states, as Joshua Kurlantzick notes, are trying to clearly integrate India into Southeast Asia as a forceful counterweight to China and hedge against a declining United States.[49] The key ASEAN states favouring India's entry into the Regional Comprehensive Economic Partnership (RCEP) indicates this emerging trend. However, India's opting out of RCEP has been a setback for ASEAN.

It is noteworthy that specific Southeast Asian states are seeking to diversify their strategic partnerships beyond a binary choice between Washington and Beijing. For instance, Singapore has built robust maritime security ties with both India and Japan, and the three are working closely within the regional initiative, the Regional Cooperation Agreement on Combating Piracy and Armed Robbery against Ships in Asia (ReCAAP). Another instance is New Delhi and Tokyo building a trilateral framework of cooperation with Vietnam. India and Japan are also engaged in multiple infrastructural development projects with specific ASEAN states, such as the India–Myanmar–Thailand Trilateral Highway and the Bay of Bengal Industrial Growth Belt which will enhance subregional connectivity. Both India and Japan have strategic partnerships with ASEAN and key ASEAN states have the potential to emerge as critical maritime partners of India and Japan in the Indo-Pacific region, particularly on the issue of SLOC security, given that many of the ASEAN states are heavily dependent on SLOCs for maritime trade and economic prosperity.

The US Factor in India–Japan Strategic Convergence

While both India and Japan are deepening their strategic engagement with the ASEAN states through bilateral, minilateral and multilateral frameworks of cooperation, they are also keen on bolstering their strategic cooperation with the US in the Indo-Pacific. A convergence of the New Delhi's AEP, Washington's Indo-Pacific strategy and Tokyo's FOIP could be perceived in the expanding trilateral cooperation, which was abbreviated by Prime Minister Modi as 'JAI' (as an acronym for Japan, America and India), a word which also stands for 'victory'. Upgrading the JAI dialogue to a summit-level meeting in 2018 was a significant development in the emerging US–India–Japan relations which indicates the strategic intent of the three states to bolster such a minilateral initiative. It is significant to note that in July 2018, the US designated India as a major defence partner and enhanced defence trade- and technology-sharing with India to a level commensurate with that of its closest allies and partners.[50] The next year, the US Senate passed a legislative provision that brought India on par with America's NATO allies for increasing defence cooperation.[51] As a close US ally, Japan's changing perception of India has been shaped by the warming of Indo-US ties, including Tokyo's perception vis-à-vis the initiation of the trilateral dialogue. For instance, noting the US Secretary of State Hillary Clinton's proposal for a US–Japan–India trilateral in her speech on Asia on 12 January 2010,[52] Abe opined that the proposed trilateral would provide an opportunity to begin the process of operationalising regional cooperation across the Pacific and the Indian Oceans as a seamless construct, along with engaging the ASEAN particularly in the domain of maritime security, humanitarian assistance and disaster relief (HA/DR), counter-piracy and counter-terrorism.[53] The US has been encouraging India and Japan to come closer as it endeavours to maintain the strategic balance in Asia.

The 2014 Tokyo Declaration gave a new fillip to the India–US–Japan security engagement when New Delhi and Tokyo agreed to hold regular maritime exercises, attaching importance to Japan's 'continued participation' in the Malabar exercises. While Japan's participation in the Malabar drills held in 2007, 2009 and 2014 was in the capacity of an invited observer, the October 2015 Malabar exercise marked a major turning point with Japan's inclusion as a permanent participant.[54] India's decision to include Japan as a permanent member in the Malabar exercise, which was traditionally a bilateral Indo-US exercise, demonstrates that Japan has assumed a key importance in India's Indo-Pacific strategy.

Emerging Non-traditional Security Challenges: Common Strategic Concerns

Apart from the ensuing traditional security challenges, India and Japan face non-traditional security challenges that are posing a serious threat to regional security in the Indo-Pacific. Perhaps the most critical non-traditional security challenge which shook both the states and the world at large is the COVID-19 pandemic. The COVID-19 and its predecessor, the SARS (Severe Acute Respiratory Syndrome) coronavirus epidemic, both originating from China, caused a major security concern. A fallout of the COVID-19 pandemic seems to be Tokyo and New Delhi's growing reluctance to deepen their economic engagement with Beijing. For instance, in April 2020, the Indian government modified its FDI policy to include China in the list of countries where any investment would need the government's approval.[55] Moreover, the pandemic—which deepened India's employment crisis from bad to worse—seemingly pushed the Indian government to take a new look at an old solution: self-reliance. The Indian government is now aiming at helping companies get more focused on Indian consumers as opposed to exports, while also using the potentially vast market to lure foreign firms to set up operations in the country and employ Indians.[56] Moreover, there is a growing trend among the leading economic powers, such as the US, the EU, Australia, Japan and others, to decouple their economies from the China-dominated global supply chain and they are looking to diversify their interests.[57] The coronavirus outbreak demonstrated to the world that over-reliance on China with regard to supply chains and large-scale production could cripple the global economy. Japan announced a corpus of USD 2.2 billion to help Japanese firms decouple from China and relocate their supply chain network elsewhere.[58] India is the only other country in the world that has a similar potential to transform itself into a global manufacturing powerhouse. The Indian government's actions such as the 'Make in India' initiative, building industrial corridors, de-licensing industries, and inviting foreign direct investments for massive infrastructural upgradation indicate efforts to project India as a new global manufacturing hub. Such efforts are likely to intensify with the growing sentiment among the world's leading economic powers to reduce their dependence on the China-dominated global supply chain in the post-pandemic era.

India's vaccine diplomacy has been taken positively by many countries across the globe, generating a lot of goodwill for New Delhi. It has considerably facilitated an improvement of India's image vis-a-vis its smaller neighbours, negating much of the criticism India faced for being a big power. As Sudha Ramachandran notes, India's vaccine diplomacy is helping it to 'polish' its image and shed the perception of India being a 'big brother', and in turn also counter-balancing China's considerable sway among the South Asian and Indian Ocean littoral states.[59] Moreover, New Delhi's vaccine diplomacy, as Shashi Tharoor notes, has been a boon to the country's aspirations to be recognised as a global power.[60] India's soft power has been growing significantly through healthcare exports which could go a long way in bolstering India's position in the global order. The Canadian premier, Justin Trudeau, reportedly stated that the world's victory over COVID-19 would be 'because of India's tremendous pharmaceutical capacity'.[61] Japan could be a critical partner of India in scaling up the aid and assistance sufficiently, with regard to the cooperation drive vis-à-vis distribution of vaccines.

While preventing and tackling such global health emergencies have been prioritised as issues of core strategic interest by both India and Japan, the need to address security challenges, such as sea piracy, terrorism and proliferation of weapons have also been highlighted in the joint statements. In the November 2019 2+2 Ministerial Dialogue, for example, New Delhi and Tokyo called upon all countries to take resolute action in rooting out terrorist safe havens and infrastructure.[62] Both India and Japan are located in a security environment that is plagued by burgeoning terrorist networks, terrorist activities and proliferation of weapons of mass destruction (WMDs). India continues to be one of the worst-hit countries in the world, suffering from countless terrorist incidents. Japan has also experienced terrorism in the brutal killings of Japanese citizens by the Islamic State of Iraq and Syria (ISIS).[63] The sarin gas attack in the Tokyo subway in 1995 cannot be brushed aside as an isolated act of terrorism, given that terrorist networks in Japan's vicinity, especially in some of the countries in Southeast Asia such as Thailand and Indonesia, are burgeoning. India, which is more experienced in dealing with terrorism, therefore makes a good counter-terrorism partner to Japan.

In this context, it is important to note that nuclear terrorism is an issue of critical security concern for Tokyo as demonstrated by the fact that Japan's first nuclear reactor to restart after the Fukushima Daiichi meltdown was shut down in March 2020 after failing to meet anti-terrorism requirements.[64] New Delhi has offered training and related support to Tokyo's terrorism-focused intelligence collection unit. Besides terrorism, India and Japan have also underscored the grave security challenge posed by the problem of arms proliferation. What needs to be seriously taken note of is that the problem of proliferation of WMDs stretches from the east to the west of Asia, as is evident from the nuclear nexus between North Korea, Iran and Pakistan. Unless the problem of clandestine proliferation is tackled, the region is not going to reap a dividend of peace simply from the dismantling of North Korea's nuclear weapons programme.

Areas of Divergence in the Emerging India–Japan Relations

Languishing Trade Relations

Grandiose conceptualisations of 'strategic' relations lose meaning without a robust economic engagement. Stagnation of bilateral trade is one of the veritable hindrances towards building a strong India–Japan strategic partnership. While India has been the largest recipient of Japanese Official Development Assistance (ODA) loans since 2003, its trade relations with Japan have been languishing. Though the two states confirmed a shared commitment in the 2007 joint statement to raise the bilateral trade volume to USD 20 billion within the next three years, the target has not been achieved even after more than a decade. Compared to Japan's thriving trade with China which recorded an approximate volume of USD 317 billion in 2018,[65] its trade with India stood at a meagre USD 17.6 billion.[66] The Sino-Indian trade volume figured at USD 95.7 billion in 2018.[67] One retarding factor adversely affecting the bilateral trade seems to be the absence of a diversified trade structure. The range of commodities traded between the two countries has remained very narrow. Export products from India to Japan are mainly gems, jewellery, iron, manganese ore, and marine products. Japanese export items to India have been confined mainly to machinery, transport equipment, iron and steel products and electrical goods. Poor infrastructure in India, especially in the transport and power sectors, ground-level hassles like unpredictability of tax regulations and procedural delays are other impeding factors affecting bilateral trade.

While the sluggish growth in trade relations continues to be an obstacle in the comprehensive development of bilateral ties, it is noteworthy that Japanese foreign direct investments are on the rise. Japan has emerged as the third largest investor in India. Japanese investment constituted 8 per cent of the total FDI in India with a cumulative investment of USD 26 billion during the period 2000 to 2017.[68] Japan's strong intent to invest in India's infrastructural advancement is particularly evident in the Delhi–Mumbai Industrial Corridor (DMIC), an ambitious USD 90 billion project. One of the largest connectivity projects in the world, it is a 1,500 kilometre-long industrial corridor connecting New Delhi with Mumbai, along with the Dedicated Freight Corridor (DFC), a high-speed rail link. Again, the high-speed rail corridor project (the Shinkansen bullet train) connecting Mumbai and Ahmedabad is another high-visibility flagship project showcasing Japan's technical and financial assistance to India.

Perhaps the main discomfiting feature of Indo-Japanese economic engagement is that it is largely ODA-based rather than FDI-based. However, in the wake of the Sino-US trade war and the spread of COVID-19 from China, India could witness a new wave of investments from Japanese investors who intend to pull out of China. As Taga Masayuki pointed out, India offers one of the largest and fastest-growing consumer markets in the world for foreign investments which no Japanese companies can ignore in the long term.[69] India and Japan need to give optimum focus to potential economic complementarities and opportunities. These include focusing on the synergy between Japan's technological expertise and capital and India's huge infrastructural and energy needs; Japan's rapidly ageing and shrinking population alongside the growing need for workers and India's huge reservoir of highly skilled workers below the age of 25; and India's software skills and Japan's manufacturing techniques. Japan is a superpower in hi-tech products, making around a fourth of the world's production. The information and technology agreement between India and Japan could go a long way in enhancing India's strength in the domain of emerging technologies such as artificial intelligence and machine learning.[70]

Apart from the continued obstacles to their bilateral economic engagement, India and Japan have foreign policy divergences on issues of regional economic cooperation as well, particularly on the RCEP, which we discuss in the following section.

Contrasting Perspectives on RCEP

Since the initiation of the dialogue on the institutionalisation of the RCEP, India had expressed its keenness to participate in this regional trade bloc as revealed through its active participation in all the RCEP ministerial meetings during the seven-year period of negotiations. The RCEP is conceptualised to be the world's largest trading bloc, covering half of the global population. India's withdrawal from the RCEP in 2019 has undermined that objective. Though the official reason given for opting out was that India's key concerns about agriculture and domestic industry were not addressed by the RCEP,[71] the actual reason behind New Delhi's pulling out seems to be China. China has been practising large-scale dumping in India for years. At a time of slowing domestic economic growth, particularly in the post-COVID global economic scenario, India's entry into the RCEP could exacerbate the country's problems by opening the floodgates to the entry of Chinese goods. India cannot become more competitive without curbing China's dumping practices.

While the Indian government has serious reservations about joining the RCEP, Japan as a flag-bearer of free trade has strongly promoted this trading bloc. Being an export-driven economy, Japan is keen on the RCEP, which is the world's biggest free-trade pact, as it would help boost the country's exports. However, Japan does not desire the RCEP without India. This was particularly reflected when Japanese trade minister Kajiyama Hiroshi reportedly stated Japan's willingness to take the lead to help resolve 'outstanding issues' so that India can rejoin the RCEP.[72] Tokyo's keenness to ensure India's entry into the RCEP seems to stem from the concern that India's absence might facilitate an augmentation of Beijing's influence in the world's largest trading bloc.

Conclusion

There is no doubt that the nature of Indo-Japanese relations has been transformed in unprecedented ways over the past two decades. New Delhi perceives Japan as a like-minded partner that can assist in the growth of its strategic and economic profile, both in the region and internationally. While Japan's foreign policy, including its FOIP, continues to be firmly anchored to its alliance with the US, its moves to bolster its strategic relationship with India and deepen the bilateral maritime engagement in the Indo-Pacific are shaping the emerging contours of Tokyo's Asia Policy. This clearly indicates that Tokyo has started taking a wider and more active diplomatic course in the 21st century which is likely to further widen and expand in the post-COVID world, with Japan's new premier Yoshihide Suga following his predecessor Abe's strategic intent to diversify Japan's strategic and economic interests in the region.

A number of trends will determine the future pattern of India–Japan relations and the scope of their strategic partnership. First, both Japan and India value the freedom of the high seas for their economic prosperity. Given the deteriorating security environment in the Indo-Pacific region, they are likely to intensify their ongoing maritime security cooperation and deepen their engagement with the Quad 2.0. Second, to enhance regional connectivity and balance against China's BRI, India and Japan would look towards further expanding the scope of their trilateral engagements with the US and also with Australia. Through the US-led Blue Dot Network (BDN) and the AAGC, the two states could play a critical role in connecting the economic growth poles in the strategic sub-regions of the Indo-Pacific by advancing regional infrastructure, connectivity and capacity-building. Third, in the post-COVID era, India would be a critical partner to Japan and the US in deepening their engagement with the Indian Ocean Rim Association (IORA), at a time when Beijing is increasing its focus on rebuilding its relations with IOR countries that are critical to the BRI through soft-power promotion. Fourth, apart from obstacles in bilateral economic relations and divergences in regional economic engagement, as evident in the case of the RCEP, there would also be differences over how close India would like to get to the US. New Delhi's foreign policy towards both the US and China is marked by strategic flexibility. Although India has partnered with Japan in regional initiatives and mechanisms in which the US figures as a key actor, India is also a member of China-led initiatives such as the Shanghai Cooperation Organisation (SCO), the Asian Infrastructure Investment Bank (AIIB), New Development Bank (NDB) and the China–Russia–India trilateral dialogue. India is also a member of the BRICS, which brings together Brazil, Russia, India, China and South Africa. All these indicate that, as Ian Hall notes, New Delhi is pursuing a multi-alignment strategy.[73] New Delhi seems to aim at reaping maximum benefits from its relations with the US, Japan, China and Russia.

In the fluid and complex regional geostrategic scenario in Asia, Japan perceives India as a key partner. Strategically, Tokyo and New Delhi share several regional and global objectives such as ensuring maritime security, freedom of navigation, terrorism, non-proliferation and balancing against China's growing military assertiveness in the Indo-Pacific region. The extent to which Japan's strategic ties with India are transformed will have a decisive impact on the political, economic and military balance of power in post-COVID Asia.

Notes and References

1. 'Normal state' here refers to a state that sees military power as a necessary and central feature of its overall national capabilities.
2. Sumit Ganguly, 'India's Foreign Policy Grows Up', *World Policy Journal*, vol. 20, no. 4 (Winter 2003/04), p. 1.
3. Rory Medcalf, 'Reimagining Asia: From Asia-Pacific to Indo-Pacific', *Asan Forum*, 26 June 2015, available at http://www.theasanforum.org/reimagining-asia-from-asia-pacific-to-indo-pacific, accessed on 25 August 2023; Aparna Pande and Satoru Nagao, 'Whose Indo-Pacific?' *The American Interest*, 3 August 2018, available at https://www.the-american-interest.com/2018/08/03/whose-indo-pacific, accessed on 25 August 2023.
4. Madhuchanda Ghosh, 'India's Strategic Convergence with Japan in the Changing Indo-Pacific Geopolitical Landscape,' *Asia Pacific Bulletin*, vol. 392, 16 August 2017, available at https://www.eastwestcenter.org/publications/indias-strategic-convergence-japan-in-the-changing-indo-pacific-geopolitical-landscape, accessed on 28 August 2023.
5. Ministry of External Affairs, Government of India, 'Prime Minister's Keynote Address at Shangri La Dialogue', 1 June 2018, available at https://www.mea.gov.in/Speeches-Statements.htm?dtl/29943/Prime+Ministers+Keynote+Address+at+Shangri+La+Dialogue+June+01+2018, accessed on 28 August 2023.
6. Ministry of Foreign Affairs of Japan, 'Japan-India Vision Statement', 29 October 2018, available at https://www.mofa.go.jp/files/000413507.pdf, accessed on 28 August 2023.
7. Ministry of Foreign Affairs of Japan, 'Confluence of the Two Seas', Speech by H.E. Mr. Abe Shinzo, Prime Minister of Japan at the Parliament of the Republic of India, 22 August 2007. http://www.mofa.go.jp/region/asia-paci/pmv0708/speech-2.html, accessed on 28 August 2023.

8. The term 'Free and Open Indo-Pacific Strategy' was used by Prime Minister Shinzo Abe for the first time at the sixth Tokyo International Conference of African Development (TICAD VI), held in Kenya in August 2016. For further details, see 'Address by Prime Minister Shinzo Abe at the Opening Session of the Sixth Tokyo International Conference on African Development (TICAD VI)', 27 August 2016, available at https://www.mofa.go.jp/afr/af2/page4e_000496.html, accessed on 28 August 2023.

9. Author's interview with Shinzo Abe, the then former prime minister of Japan, Tokyo, 21 October 2011.

10. Ministry of External Affairs, Government of India, 'India-Japan Joint Statement during Visit of Prime Minister of Japan to India', 14 September 2017, available at https://www.mea.gov.in/bilateral-documents.htm?dtl/28946/IndiaJapan+Joint+Statement+during+visit+of+Prime+Minister+of+Japan+to+India+September+14+2017, accessed on 28 August 2023.

11. Ministry of External Affairs, GoI, 'India-Japan Vision Statement'.

12. Madhuchanda Ghosh, 'India and Japan's Growing Synergy: From a Political to a Strategic Focus', *Asian Survey*, vol. 48, no. 2 (2008), p. 283.

13. David Brewster, 'The India-Japan Security Relationship: An Enduring Security Partnership?', *Asian Security*, vol. 6, no. 2 (2010), p. 116.

14. Author's interview with Kumagai Naoki, Political Minister, Embassy of Japan, New Delhi, 5 March 2019.

15. Lt Gen. Prakash Katoch, 'First India-Japan 2+2 Dialogue', *Indian Defence Review*, 12 December 2019, available at http://www.indiandefencereview.com/news/first-india-japan-22-dialogue/, accessed on 31 August 2023.

16. Shubhajit Roy, 'India, Australia upgrade strategic talks to Minister level, as with US, Japan', *The Indian Express,* 5 June 2020.

17. Aman Thakker and Elliot Silverberg, 'India and Japan Eye the Dragon in the Room', *Foreign Policy*, 20 November 2019, available at https://foreignpolicy.com/2019/11/20/china-war-navy-india-japan-eye-dragon-in-the-room/#cookie_message_anchor, accessed on 31 August 2023.

18. Ministry of External Affairs, Government of India, 'Launch of India–Japan Act East Forum', 5 December 2017, available at https://www.mea.gov.in/press-releases.htm?dtl/29154/Launch_of_IndiaJapan_Act_East_Forum, accessed on 31 August 2023.

19. Press Information Bureau, Government of India, 'Japan to invest Rs 13,000 cr in Northeast', 12 June 2019, available at http://pib.gov.in/newsite/PrintRelease.aspx?relid=190376, accessed on 31 August 2023.

20. Snehesh Alex Philip, 'India-China border tensions flare up again as soldiers get into scuffles in Ladakh, Sikkim', *The Print,* 10 May 2020, available at https://theprint.in/defence/india-china-border-tensions-flare-up-again-as-soldiers-get-into-scuffles-in-ladakh-sikkim/418429/, accessed on 31 August 2023.

21. 'Asia Africa Growth Corridor: Partnership for Sustainable and Innovative Development: A Vision Document', 22–26 May 2017, available at http://ris.org.in/vision-document-asia-africa-growth-corridor-partnership-sustainable-and-innovative-development, accessed on 31 August 2023.

22. Author's interview with Horimoto Takenori, Visiting Professor, Gifu Women's University, Japan, 11 January 2020.

23. Rajesh Basrur and Sumitha Narayanan Kutty, 'Modi's India and Japan: Nested Strategic Partnerships', *International Politics*, vol. 59 (2022), p. 7.

24. Harsh V. Pant and Ritika Passi, 'India's Response to China's Belt and Road Initiative: A Policy in Motion', *Asia Policy*, vol. 24, no. 1, pp. 88–95.

25. Harsh Pant and Yogesh Joshi, *The US Pivot and India's Foreign Policy* (Palgrave Macmillan, 2016).

26. Brahma Chellaney, *Asian Juggernaut: The Rise of China, India and Japan* (New Delhi: Harper Collins India, 2006), p. 221.

27. Patrick M. Cronin, 'China's Bid for Maritime Primacy in the Indo-Pacific', *The Maritime Executive*, 3 March 2020.

28. Horimoto Takenori, 'Indo-Pacific Order and Japan–India Relations in the Midst of COVID-19', *Journal of Asian Economic Integration*, vol. 2, no. 2, pp. 140–158.

29. Amitendu Palit, 'The Maritime Silk Road Initiative (MSRI): Why India is Worried, What China Can Do', *Global Policy,* 31 May 2017, available at https://www.globalpolicyjournal.com/blog/31/05/2017/maritime-silk-road-initiative-msri-why-india-worried-what-china-can-do, accessed on 31 August 2023.

30. Author's research interview with Shihoko Goto, Director of Asia Program of Wilson Center, Washington D.C., 6 July 2022, conducted during Fulbright Research Program at the Asia Center, Harvard University.

31. Bill Gertz, 'China Builds up Strategic Sea Lanes', *Washington Times*, 18 January 2005.

32. Author's research interview with Joshua White, Professor at School of Advanced International Studies, John Hopkins University, Washington D.C., 6 July 2022, during Fulbright Research Program at the Asia Center, Harvard University.

33. Kim Kong Heng and Veasna Var, 'Cambodia and the issue of Chinese Debt trap', *International Policy Digest*, 20 May 2019.

34. Maria Abi-Habib, 'How China Got Sri Lanka to Cough up a Port', *The New York Times*, 25 June 2018, available at https://www.nytimes.com/2018/06/25/world/asia/china-sri-lanka-port.html, accessed on 31 August 2023.

35. Akitaka Saiki, 'Maritime security issues in the region cannot be separated: Japan's Vice Minister', *ORF*, 6 September 2015, available at http://www.orfonline.org/research/maritime-security-issues-in-the-region-cannot-be-separated-japans-vice-minister/, accessed on 31 August 2023.

36. Isabel Reynolds, Iain Marlow and N. C. Bipindra, 'Abe-Modi bromance may not overcome hurdles to submarine sale', *The Economic Times*, 12 July 2018.

37. Ashley J. Tellis, 'Making Waves: Aiding India's Next Generation Aircraft Carrier', Carnegie Endowment for International Peace, 22 April 2015.

38. Ministry of Defence, Japan, 'Defence Buildup Program', 16 December 2022, available at https://www.mod.go.jp/j/policy/agenda/guideline/plan/pdf/program_en.pdf, accessed on 20 October 2023.

39. Ministry of Defence, Japan, 'National Defense Strategy', 16 December 2022, available at https://www.mod.go.jp/j/policy/agenda/guideline/strategy/pdf/strategy_en.pdf, accessed on 14 October 2023.

40. Ministry of Foreign Affairs of Japan, 'National Security Strategy', 16 December 2022, available at https://www.mofa.go.jp/fp/nsp/page1we_000081.html, accessed on 24 October 2023.

41. Ben Dooley and Hisako Ueno, 'Japan moves to double military spending with a wary eye on China', *The New York Times*, 16 December 2022, available at https://www.nytimes.com/2022/12/16/world/asia/japan-national-security-strategy.html, accessed on 16 October 2023.

42. Sakura Murakami, 'Japan makes record defense spending request amid tension with China', *Reuters*, 31 August 2023, available at https://www.reuters.com/business/aerospace-defense/japan-makes-record-defence-spending-request-amid-tension-with-china-2023-08-31/, accessed on 12 January 2024.

43. 'At G7 Summit in Japan, PM Modi's sharp take on China's aggression in the Indo-Pacific', *India Today*, 20 May 2023, available at https://www.indiatoday.in/india/story/g7-summit-japan-pm-modi-china-aggression-indo-pacific-2381841-2023-05-20, accessed on 20 October 2023.

44. Patrick Gerard Buchan and Benjamin Rimland, 'Defining the Diamond: The Past, Present and Future of Quadrilateral Security Dialogue', CSIS, 16 March 2020, available at https://www.csis.org/analysis/defining-diamond-past-present-and-future-quadrilateral-security-dialogue, accessed on 31 August 2023.

45. Shinzo Abe, *Utsukushii kuni e* [*Towards a Beautiful Country*] (Tokyo: Bungei Shunju, 2006).

46. Andrew Shearer and Jesse Barker Gale, 'The Quadrilateral Security Dialogue and the Maritime Silk Road Initiative', *Asia Maritime Transparency Initiative*, 4 April 2018, available at https://amti.csis.org/quadrilateral-security-dialogue-maritime-silk-road/, accessed on 31 August 2023.

47. Simon Tay and Jessica Wau, 'The Indo-Pacific Outlook: A New Lens for ASEAN', *East Asia Forum*, 20 April 2020, available at https://www.eastasiaforum.org/2020/04/20/the-indo-pacific-outlook-a-new-lens-for-asean/, accessed on 31 August 2023.

48. Helier Cheung and Roland Hughes, 'Why are there protests in Hongkong? All the context you need', *BBC News*, 21 May 2020, available at https://www.bbc.com/news/world-asia-china-48607723, accessed on 31 August 2023.

49. Joshua Kurlantzick, 'Southeast Asia Seeks New Partners in the Era of America First', Council on Foreign Relations, 14 March 2018, available at https://www.cfr.org/blog/southeast-asia-seeks-new-partners-era-america-first, accessed on 31 August 2023.

50. 'US elevates India's defence trade status to Nato-level allies, Delhi welcomes move', *The Indian Express*, 31 July 2018, available at https://indianexpress.com/article/india/us-india-defence-trade-status-to-nato-level-5284516/, accessed on 31 August 2023.

51. 'U.S. Senate passes legislative provision to give India NATO ally-like status', *The Hindu*, 2 July 2019, available at https://www.thehindu.com/news/international/us-senate-passes-legislative-provision-to-give-india-nato-ally-like-status/article28263010.ece, accessed on 31 August 2023.

52. Hillary Rodham Clinton, 'Remarks on Regional Architecture in Asia: Principles and Priorities', U.S. Department of State, Archived Content, 12 January 2010, available at https://2009-2017.state.gov/secretary/20092013clinton/rm/2010/01/135090.htm, accessed on 8 September 2023.

53. Author's interview with Shinzo Abe, the then former prime minister of Japan, Tokyo, 21 October 2011.

54. B. J. Miller, 'Japan Makes Three: India, U.S. Trilateralize Malabar Drills', *World Politics Review*, August 11, 2015.

55. 'Govt approval must for all FDIs from neighbouring countries including China', *The Times of India*, 18 April 2020.

56. Bill Spindle and Rajesh Roy, 'India's Coronavirus Crisis Spurs a New Look at Self-Reliance', *The Wall Street Journal*, 17 May 2020, available at https://www.wsj.com/articles/indias-coronavirus-crisis-spurs-a-new-look-at-self-reliance-11589724001, accessed on 31 August 2023.

57. Keith Johnson and Robbie Gramer, 'The Great Decoupling', *Foreign Policy*, 14 May 2020, available at https://foreignpolicy.com/2020/05/14/china-us-pandemic-economy-tensions-trump-coronavirus-covid-new-cold-war-economics-the-great-decoupling/, accessed on 8 September 2023.

58. Mercy Kuo, 'Japan prods firms to leave China, affecting ties with Beijing and Washington', *The Japan Times*, 8 May 2020.

59. Sudha Ramachandran, 'India's Vaccine Diplomacy: A Potent Card?', *The Diplomat*, 26 January 2021, available at https://thediplomat.com/2021/01/indias-vaccine-diplomacy-a-potent-card/, accessed on 31 August 2023.

60. Shashi Tharoor, 'India's smart vaccine diplomacy', *Japan Times*, 15 March 2021, available at https://www.japantimes.co.jp/opinion/2021/03/15/

commentary/world-commentary/india-smart-vaccine-diplomacy/, accessed on 31 August 2023.

61. Dipanjan Roy Chaudhury, 'Canadian PM's outreach to India: Justin Trudeau dials PM Modi for vaccines', *The Economic Times*, 11 February 2021, available at https://economictimes.indiatimes.com/news/politics-and-nation/canadian-pms-outreach-to-india-justin-trudeau-dials-pm-modi-for-vaccines/articleshow/80794704.cms?from=mdr, accessed on 31 August 2023.

62. Dipanjan Roy Chaudhury, 'India, Japan favour strong action against terror infrastructure and terror financing', *The Economic Times*, 30 November 2019.

63. Martin Fackler, 'Departing from Japan's Pacifism. Shinzo Abe Vows Revenge for Killings', *The New York Times*, 1 February 2015, available at https://www.nytimes.com/2015/02/02/world/departing-from-countrys-pacifism-japanese-premier-vows-revenge-for-killings.html, accessed on 29 November 2023.

64. Kotaro Fukuoka, 'Japan shuts nuclear reactor over anti-terrorism shortfalls', *Nikkei Asian Review*, 17 March 2020, available at https://asia.nikkei.com/Business/Energy/Japan-shuts-nuclear-reactor-over-anti-terrorism-shortfalls, accessed on 31 August 2023.

65. John West, 'The China-Japan Economic Relationship Is Getting Stronger', *Brink News*, 20 January 2020, available at https://www.brinknews.com/the-china-japan-economic-relationship-is-getting-stronger/, accessed on 8 September 2023.

66. Embassy of India, Japan, 'India–Japan Commercial Relations', available at https://www.indembassy-tokyo.gov.in/eoityo_pages/NjA, accessed on 31 August 2023.

67. 'India China bilateral trade make steady growth in 2019', *DD News*, 1 January 2020, available at http://ddnews.gov.in/business/india-china-bilateral-trade%C2%A0continue%C2%A0-make-steady-growth, accessed on 31 August 2023.

68. 'Japan's investments in India have not been without pitfalls', *The Asian Age*, 16 April 2019.

69. Author's interview with Taga Masayuki, Consul General of Japan in Kolkata, 15 May 2020.

70. S. Ronendra Singh and Amiti Sen, 'India and Japan sign MoU to enhance cooperation in ICT, including 5G tech', *The Hindu Businessline*, 15 January 2021.

71. 'Experts laud decision to avoid RCEP, say it will protect industry, farmers', *Business Standard*, 4 November 2019.

72. Brahma Chellaney, 'RCEP without India isn't to Japan's liking', *Japan Times*, 17 December 2019.

73. Ian Hall, 'Multi-alignment and Indian Foreign Policy under Narendra Modi', *The Commonwealth Journal of International Affairs*, vol. 106, no. 3 (2016), pp. 271–286.

six

Partnerships in a Multi-aligned World

Quad in the Indo-Pacific

SHUBHRAJEET KONWER

> Officials from India's Ministry of External Affairs, Australia's Department of Foreign Affairs, Japan's Ministry of Foreign Affairs and United States' Department of State met in Manila on November 12, 2017 for consultations on issues of common interest in the Indo-Pacific region. The discussions focused on cooperation based on their converging vision and values for promotion of peace, stability and prosperity in an increasingly interconnected region that they share with each other and with other partners. They agreed that a free, open, prosperous and inclusive Indo-Pacific region serves the long-term interests of all countries in the region and of the world at large.
>
> Ministry of External Affairs, Government of India, 'India-Australia-Japan-U.S. Consultations on Indo-Pacific (November 12, 2017)'.

The importance of the Quad—the quadrilateral security dialogue between Australia, India, Japan and the United States—lies in the fact that it symbolises a confluence of nations having common strategic goals, but this 'coming together' of nations is also based on camaraderie based on shared democratic values. However, achieving common goals will be far from easy as the Quad makes further inroads into the Indo-Pacific region. While the Quad countries seem to be 'somewhat' guided by the goal of containing China in this region, structural conditions dictate that each state will not only have to pool resources together but will also have to be individually more prepared to deal with any eventuality. This Indo-Pacific region, though resource-rich and strategically important, also consists of some countries where the virtues of Western liberal democracy are not strictly entertained. These countries of the Indo-Pacific region too have their own needs as well as their limitations when it comes to choosing alliances and partnerships.

The ongoing 'special military operation' by Russia in Ukraine (February 2022), together with the persisting tensions between Washington and Beijing, has significant ramifications for the global community. It is evident that multi-aligned interactions have grown more prevalent in the context of a dynamic global order. While the US and its 'core partners' have been largely acting in unison and have condemned Russia's actions, India, despite being close to the West, has been reluctant to do so. However, Beijing has emerged as one of Moscow's ardent supporters. But despite strained relationships with Western nations, China continues to be a substantial economic partner of the West. Hence, it is imperative to examine the significance of multilateral frameworks in such an 'anarchical'[1] setting.

The Joint Statement of the Hiroshima Quad Summit (2023) did not include a condemnation of Russia's activities in Ukraine or any acknowledgment of the increasing assertiveness of China in East Asia.[2] It shows that the Quad countries are also careful not to tinker with the state of affairs in the Indo-Pacific. Achieving more credible 'goals' is still in its early stages, reflecting the reality that cooperation among the four member states, particularly on 'hard' diplomatic and security issues, is still weak. In light of the fluidity of global politics and the multiplicity of competing interests, the Quad countries must fortify their existing strategic bilateral ties while also establishing a system of institutions to discourage and control the greater threat, especially China's. The Quad's ability to affect political and security matters in the Indo-Pacific area will be put to the test in the years ahead.

This innocuous statement by the Government of India, cited at the beginning of this chapter,[3] essentially confirms that the four democratic countries—the US, Japan, Australia and India—are looking to protect common interests in the Indo-Pacific region. However, this is not the first time these countries have expressed their desire to have a commonality of goals in the Indo-Pacific region. At the bilateral level, these countries have often expressed the need for greater stability in the Indo-Pacific, but have been alarmed by the growing presence of China in the region. Scholars like J. Mearsheimer have argued that the central feature of international politics in the 21st century will be the 'intense security competition' between China and the United States.[4] In the changed geopolitical environment, it is clear that given the 'rise of China' and the 'pivot' to the region by the US,[5] there will be tension and constraints on the strategies adopted by middle powers like Australia, Japan and India, who will have to tread the tightrope carefully. While the role of the big players will obviously matter, the response of major Southeast Asian states such as Indonesia and Vietnam will also be important.[6] This chapter elucidates the constraints associated with alliances and partnerships within a multi-aligned hierarchical world. The initial section of this analysis will explore the strategic environment of the Indo-Pacific region. The second section will examine the significance of alliances within a world characterised by multiple alignments, with particular emphasis on the role played by the Quadrilateral Security Dialogue (Quad) in the Indo-Pacific region. The third section will underscore the constraints and shortcomings of the Quad within a world that embraces multiple alignments. Lastly, the concluding section will provide a summary of the key findings and implications derived from this examination.

Indo-Pacific and the Quad: Contested Region, Contested Concept

The 'Indo-Pacific' is a profoundly geopolitical and geoeconomic concept.[7] David Scott argues that the term 'Indo-Pacific' refers to Pacific actors like Japan and the United States interacting with India in the Indian Ocean, and India interacting with other Pacific Rim actors in the South China Sea and the South and Western Pacific.[8] According to K. He, from a realist perspective, the 'Indo-Pacific concept is mainly understood as a balancing strategy'; from a liberal paradigm, it is seen as a 'new institutional setting, which aims to facilitate cooperation among states across the Pacific and the Indian Oceans'; and from a constructivist perspective, it is seen as a 'new ideational construct based on shared values and a common identity in the region.'[9] Thus, Indo-Pacific as a concept, as well as a region, continues to be debated from different quarters. While recognising the importance of regional organisations such as ASEAN, the Quad is dedicated to preserving and developing Indo-Pacific stability and to upholding the international order based on the rule of law.[10] Nonetheless, it is critical to recognise the Quad's geopolitical undercurrents, since each of the four nations engaged has its own security concerns. For some countries, the Quad is seen as a 'strategy', while for others it is a grouping for availing new economic opportunities. For the United States, the Indo-Pacific is a strategy which is 'an ironclad and enduring commitment' to a region that spans the Pacific Ocean to the Indian subcontinent.[11] From India's perspective, the Indo-Pacific is a vast region which starts 'from the shores of Africa to that of the Americas' and 'Southeast Asia is at its centre'.[12] Beijing on the other hand thinks that the concept of Indo-Pacific 'will dissipate like ocean foam.'[13] Thus, the Indo-Pacific region is geographically too expansive and politically too complex to be understood from a single dominant viewpoint which would be acceptable to all. Furthermore, there is significant divergence in the way the Quad countries perceive threat to the stability of the Indo-Pacific region both collectively and individually. Competing and overlapping regional initiatives with visions such as that of the 'Asia-Pacific' or rival institution-building in the region can be linked with the rise of China.[14] There is no doubt that the key concern of the Quad countries is the growing presence of China in the ASEAN region.

Quad in a Multi-aligned World

The importance of alliances and partnerships in a multi-aligned world is rather contested. According to Hans Morgenthau, the issue of alliances is a 'matter not of principle but of expediency' and calculations are made by states in a manner so that 'the burden of the commitments resulting from the alliance is likely to outweigh the advantages to be expected.'[15] Stephen Walt sees alliances arising as a response to a 'threat' which is a combination of capabilities (power) and intent (both motivations and perceptions).[16] While alliances signal to other nations that the allies share certain interests and so are likely to coordinate their actions in the future,[17] there is no consensus as to whether formation of alliances is indeed an effective policy for inducing deterrence and promoting peace.[18] This prompts a crucial inquiry into the objectives that states want to accomplish by their engagement in the Quad, especially within the context of the Indo-Pacific region.

For regional and global powers, the world order is being shaped by the size and density of their strategic partnership[19] which enables nations to be active stakeholders. The rise of China has had a ripple effect on relations between the major democratic countries. The Joint Statement of Australia-Japan-United States Defence Ministers Meeting in 2018 stressed that:

> The ministers affirmed the importance of the Indo-Pacific region, and the key role Australia, Japan, and the United States play in upholding a free, prosperous, inclusive, and open international order. The ministers articulated the shared principles of respect for sovereignty, promotion of free and fair trade and investment, and adherence to international rules and norms. The ministers reaffirmed their strong support for ASEAN and its central role in the regional architecture.[20]

The gravity of the Quad is reflected in the relations between its members; its role cannot be judged in isolation. Though it is a bureaucratic-level foreign-ministry-led dialogue process[21] complemented by bilateral and trilateral partnerships in different fields, the Quad seeks to achieve something substantially more: the containment of China. The US's 'pivot to Asia' which was 'committed to security, prosperity and human rights in the Asia-Pacific'[22] has been much scrutinised and has in turn pushed forward the idea of the Quad as a dialogue process. But the need for such a dialogue can also be easily linked to the rise of China in the Indo-Pacific region.

Defense ties between the four countries have also strengthened collectively, as well as at the bilateral level. The India–US Malabar series of naval exercises which started in 1992 has subsequently enlarged, with Japan joining this exercise in 2015. The Indian Armed Forces too conducts and participates in various bilateral and trilateral military exercises with the US, Australia and Japan.[23] Moreover, cooperation between India, the US, Australia and Japan in the field of civilian use of nuclear technology has leapt forward. Therefore, complemented by bilateral and trilateral dialogues between the US, Japan, Australia and India, the Quad is more than just a simple autonomy–security trade-off model of alliance.[24] To begin with, it seeks to make a mark in the Indo-Pacific region which by 2030 is expected to account for '21 of the top 25 sea and air trade routes, around two-thirds of global oil shipments and one-third of the world's bulk cargo movements.'[25] Effectively, the Quad members are eager to protect the future. Individually, each of the four countries has a great deal at stake.

In Search of Partnerships: The US

As a 'preponderant power',[26] the United States has shaped international agenda, but it has faced criticism too. In the face of an adverse anti-American global order, the United States now seems to be a 'reluctant internationalist', especially with the advent of Donald Trump, who focused on policies such as 'Make America Great Again' and 'America First'.[27] American 'exceptionalism'[28] is increasingly being challenged and subtle changes in the world order are now growing visible. Russia's invasion of Ukraine continues to test the West's forbearance, and China's eagerness to engage with the Taliban in Afghanistan demonstrates that 'revisionist powers'[29] are no longer going to accept the US-led liberal order readily.

In 2017, at the Asia-Pacific Economic Cooperation (APEC) Summit in Vietnam, President Trump remarked that, as a Pacific nation, its vision is to have a 'free and open Indo-Pacific'.[30] The 2019 Indo-Pacific Strategy Report points towards 'the linkages between economics, governance, and security' of the region, and also suggests that 'economic security is national security.'[31] The report also states, 'As China continues its economic and military ascendance, it seeks Indo-Pacific regional hegemony in the near-term and, ultimately global preeminence in the long-term.'[32] This invariably leads to the question 'whether China and the United States can escape Thucydides's Trap'.[33] However, political rhetoric during the Trump–Xi era reached a new level with the United States standing at the forefront of a new group of countries that is now resisting China's rise in the name of safeguarding the 'liberal world order'.[34] In the meanwhile, China has raised the ante in the Indo-Pacific region. Beijing has been extremely critical of the US Navy's 'freedom of navigation' patrols and wants to create a 'veto-zone' near the Chinese border to curtail activities of the US military and navy in the region.[35] Importantly, since the conflict in Ukraine, tensions between Washington and Beijing have escalated, significantly impacting global supply chains and leading to significant repercussions for security in the Indo-Pacific region.[36] There is a growing realisation that even the largest country cannot achieve the outcomes it wants without the help of others.[37] Therefore, countries such as India, Australia and Japan can play major roles in helping the US retain its 'strategic outreach' in the Indo-Pacific. M. S. Pardesi notes that while the United States remains the most important strategic player in Asia in the foreseeable future, it cannot define the strategic contours of Asia all by itself.[38] The ensuing strategic environment makes it imperative for the US to seek some form of alliance or partnership to retain its edge in world politics, more so in the Indo-Pacific region. The Quad is a major step forward in facing a common adversary such as the revisionist state of China.[39]

The Resurgent Power: Japan

In the past, Japan's foreign policy has been largely regarded as 'passive, risk-avoiding, ineffective and flexible diplomacy'.[40] Over the years, Japan has been at the forefront when it comes to adherence to multilateral treaties.[41] But the major predicament it finds itself in is that it continues to be seen as a US protectorate[42] or its 'junior partner',[43] an image which it wants to shake off. Officially the US–Japan relations seem to be on solid footing.[44] However, in the age of 'parabellum',[45] Japan has sought to diversify and strengthen its basket of relations, especially with countries like India. Japan is increasingly concerned about countries like China as 'changes in the balance of power are accelerating and becoming more complex, thereby increasing uncertainty over the existing order.'[46] Prime Minister Abe has formulated and pushed forward three specific Indo-Pacific frameworks: the 'Confluence of the Two Seas' (*futatsu no umi no majiwari*) in 2007, the 'Security Diamond'[47] in 2012 and the 'Free and Open Indo-Pacific' (FOIP) (*jiyudeopun'na indo-taiheiyo*) in 2016.[48] Different commentators have noted that through the FOIP strategy, Japan not only seeks to defend the rules-based order established by the United States,[49] but also hopes to diplomatically dissuade China from carrying out activities which undermine stability in the Indo-Pacific.[50] While Sino-Japanese trade continues to be robust, the Chinese persist in contesting the Senkaku/Diaoyu Islands in the East China Sea. This has surely led to further tensions in Sino-Japanese relations.

The problem is that the 'cost–benefit bilateralism'[51] pushed forward by the Trump administration has left US allies worried. The Japanese are beginning to question Washington's credible commitment to Japan's defence and regional stability.[52] Japan has adopted 'tactical hedging',[53] a strategy 'which is located between balancing and bandwagoning',[54] which enables it to flexibly incorporate other regional states' preferences into its FOIP policy to cope with challenges from China. However, the key problem for Japan that often goes unnoticed in these strategic games is that, very often, its domestic structures are not strong enough to support its foreign policy goals. Essentially, then, Japan's base for a belligerent foreign policy seems weak. Therefore, given the fickle nature of US support, Japan has to invest more resources in a complex web of alliances to offset any kind of disturbance in the Indo-Pacific region and in East China Sea in particular. While it may be too early to claim that 'Japanese pacifism is dead'[55], Japan surely has realised that alliances and partnerships with other like-minded countries can help contain China in its backyard. For Japan, the Quad symbolises the convergence of values, policies, goals and the need to address threats to strategic commons. Japan is now increasingly concerned by the deepening of strategic alliances between Russia and China, as well as China's unilateral efforts to alter the existing state of affairs in the East and South China Seas.[56] The Kishida administration has pointed out that Japan is committed to the 'four pillars of cooperation for the FOIP'[57] and given the challenges at its doorstep, it needs partnerships that can promote stability in the Indo-Pacific. Japan's military budget is also expected to grow in the near future. According to reports, 'Japan's defence acquisition expenditure will reach a value of $83.4 billion by 2028, with a compound annual growth rate of 5.9 per cent during 2023–28'.[58]

The Cautious Member: India

For a country that espouses to be the next great power, India has adopted a rather ambivalent position when it comes to cooperation through multilateral institutions, more specifically the Quad. Such an approach however is not surprising, given that Indian foreign policy principles stress on non-interference, peaceful settlement of disputes and non-alignment. Over the years, India has adopted a three-fold approach to achieving its foreign policy goals which involve: first, 'traditional multilateralism in global forums'; second, 'bilateralism in the region with selected strategic partners'; and third, 'increasing involvement in clubs (such as BRICS)'.[59] While there has been an incremental positive change in the global community's view of India and its contributions to greater causes, policy makers are growing to realise that India needs to be more proactive in protecting its interests in its immediate vicinity as well as in the 'extended neighbourhood'.

While the 'Look East Policy' sought to enhance India's engagement with ASEAN countries, the 'Act East' Policy sought 'to foster closer cooperation with Asian economies to its east, [and further,] India's approach to the

Indo-Pacific is much more directly designed to counter China's growing power and expansion into South Asia and the Indian Ocean'.[60] Prime Minister Narendra Modi, at the 2018 Shangri La Dialogue, put forth India's views on the Indo-Pacific, wherein he saw the region as 'free, open, inclusive'. Furthermore, he argued the need for a 'common rules-based order for the region', wherein all nations would have 'equal access as a right under international law to the use of common spaces on sea and in the air that would require freedom of navigation, unimpeded commerce and peaceful settlement of disputes in accordance with international law'.[61] However, the vastness of the concept of the Indo-Pacific and the number of states it encompasses, makes it impossible for a country like India to comprehensively practice a uniform policy for the region. Therefore, in practice, the government has adopted a multitude of policies and treaties to address the concerns emanating from this vast region, particularly with respect to the ASEAN countries and the South China and East China Seas.

The growing Chinese influence in the South China Sea and the ASEAN region has certainly hastened the process of deepening of ties between India and the other democratic powers in the Indo-Pacific region. While China continues to downplay the 'string of pearls' theory,[62] it cannot be easily washed away. According to the Government of India, the Quad dialogue continues to be a consultative process with focus 'on cooperation in areas such as connectivity, sustainable development, counter-terrorism, non-proliferation and maritime and cyber security, with a view to promoting peace, stability and prosperity in an increasingly inter-connected Indo-Pacific region that the four countries share with each other and with other partners.'[63] India's need for the Quad stems from its insecurities, but it does not want to portray itself as a desperate alliance-seeker. India's hesitance to publicly denounce Russia's invasion of Ukraine, its emphasis on 'strategic autonomy', and participation in non-Western multilateral frameworks like the BRICS and the SCO have all contributed to the country's reputation as a cautious participant. Derek Grossman points out that India is the 'weakest link'[64] in the Quad.

While New Delhi may have reservations about the West, it definitely is not comfortable with Beijing increasing its footprint in Southeast Asia and the larger Indo-Pacific region. Again, albeit through a partnership, the Quad is an adequate platform for India to move up the hierarchical world order. A forum like the Quad provides hope for India; it is expected that this quadrilateral forum would help protect its 'core' strategic interests, i.e., 'contain' China's expansion into India's extended neighbourhood. Furthermore, by stressing on cooperation between members based on the virtues of electoral democracy and civil liberties, it helps reconfirm the deficiencies in the Chinese political system. However, New Delhi is unlikely to commit to any formal alliance, particularly at a time when the United States is emphasising the principle of 'burden sharing'.[65]

Dilemmas of a Middle Power: Australia

Countries like Australia have adopted a 'constructivist approach' to the maintenance of its status as a middle power, wherein it plays the role of an 'advocator' in case of regional issues and in multilateral institutions though means such as issue-based coalition, regional diplomacy and stress in agreements and protocols.[66] Australia has always advocated a 'rules-based order'[67] in the Asia Pacific region. According to Gyngell and Wesley, Australia has played an important part in several global frameworks and discussions as a middle power.[68] Despite frequent changes in political leadership, the post-war evolution of Australian diplomacy produced a number of recurring patterns of foreign policy consistent with middle power behaviour, such as independence of action within alliance responsibilities; pragmatic approaches to regional engagement with Asia; and a focus on pursuing political outcomes that benefit the international community as a whole.[69] As Australia seeks to flex its middle power muscles, it realises that it still may not have enough power to tackle the impending challenges in its neighbourhood alone; and thus, it needs partnerships with other like-minded states.

By 2050, almost half of the world's economic output is expected to come from the Indo-Pacific.[70] This presents opportunities to increase Australia's economy and security as the Indo-Pacific region grows in economic and strategic weight.[71] The key problem is that a 'liminal'[72] Australia is stuck between the 'past', i.e., its strong historical linkages with the Commonwealth and the US-led democratic liberal order, and the 'present', i.e., its changing role in the context of Asia Pacific region and its growing economic dependence on China. It is running out of time and choices. In 2019, China emerged as Australia's largest trading partner, constituting 32.7 per cent (USD 89.2 billion) of its total exports.[73] Meanwhile, Australian foreign policy—especially in the security arena—has again been seen as 'an adjunct of, and supplement to, the foreign policy of the United States';[74] and its role has been mockingly hailed as the 'deputy sheriff' of the United States in Southeast Asia.[75] Though China has recently emerged as Australia's biggest trading partner, political relations between Australia and China have been rather chequered. It must be recalled that just like the United States, Australia too had strongly condemned China's human rights record in the wake of the June 4th incident of 1989.[76]

For Australia, China is thus a 'complex partner'[77], one who has practised 'economic realism'[78] to an unprecedented extent. In 2018, the then Foreign Minister Julie Bishop publicly expressed concern that BRI investments in the South Pacific would be 'detrimental to [these countries'] long-term sovereignty'.[79] More importantly, Australia is again very concerned that the liberal order established by the US, which has benefitted Australia immensely, is now being challenged by China. Ideally, Australia would like to 'credibly provide for its own defence' which would 'at least substantially raise the risks and costs to an aggressor',[80] but if it can deter China's growing ambitions in its neighbourhood through collaboration with other 'like-minded' nations,[81] then the latter would be more preferable. As things stand, Australia is the big blue whale in the Pacific region, which although not predatory is too large to be ignored. As a middle power, Australia is big enough to enable its choice of advocating multilateralism and norm-rule setting behaviour or regional exertions to have greater impact than would be the case for smaller powers.[82] Present settings pose risks of policy incoherence and Australia's stance may potentially be interpreted as 'choosing sides' between the region's great powers.[83]

Challenges Ahead

The relationship between a hegemon in decline and a rising power is bound to generate considerable amount of friction in economic and strategic areas as well as value systems. Invariably, in the era of strategic competition, states will undertake both internal and external balancing to help increase their own power within the international system while preventing the rising influence of others.[84] Scholars like J. Shifrinson have argued that 'Chinese predation is overstated.'[85] But actions on the ground reveal that China is not only establishing a strong foothold in key maritime routes but it also plays a critical role in emerging markets.

Furthermore, by setting up new military bases and initiating grand connectivity projects across continents, rising powers like China are not only making the existing hegemon uncomfortable but also generating insecurity amongst its neighbours. While the issues of security and stability continue to remain contested, what is clear is that the Quad will seek to contain a rising China. But this task will be far from easy. The failure to add a collective military dimension to the Quad also reflects the existing contradictions between the member nations.

Quad: United and Divided

The Quad countries are tied to each other bilaterally through a variety of strategic partnerships, trade and monetary institutions, and values which are espoused as being democratic. Democratic alliances do appear distinctively durable when measured against the background of the constantly shifting international environment.[86] The problem is that decoupling of ties with China has been difficult for member states. Individually, the Quad members continue to have robust relations with China in different ways in spite of the growing strategic challenges in the Indo-Pacific. According to Ambassador Gurjit Singh, in 2022, US-China trade set a new record at USD 691 billion, and 'Japanese imports from China grew by 21.8% to $190 billion while export growth crawled by 5.7% to $145 billion'.[87] Furthermore, China remains Australia's largest bilateral trading partner and despite tensions at the border, 'India-China trade in 2022 touched a record $135.98 billion'.[88] Despite the growing institutionalisation of the Quad, it is evident that the member nations still exhibit disparities in terms of 'threat perception, risk tolerance, military capacity, strategic culture, and collaboration'.[89] However, given the contrasts in perceptions of the Indo-Pacific between India and other members of the Quad, it is evident that this multilateral framework is unlikely to take on a militarised character.

On the positive side, high levels of bilateral trade between members of the Quad and China have ensured that the chances of overt hostility are minimised to a large extent. On its part, through 'complex patchworks',[90] Beijing too has become involved with the Quad members by way of mechanisms like the East Asia Summit, ASEAN+3 and BRICS, which has ensured that the applecart is not upset and the situation in the Indo-Pacific region continues to remain stable.

ASEAN: The Pivot of the Indo-Pacific

G. John Ikenberry and Daniel H. Nexon have noted that the next few decades will likely see continued contestation, adjustment, negotiation and even conflict over international order.[91] In this contested period, regions will become 'substantially more important' sites of conflict and cooperation and also acquire '"substantial" autonomy from the system-level interactions of the global powers'.[92] One of the most intriguing questions that will trouble all parties is not what the Quad offers to the Indo-Pacific region (more specifically the ASEAN members) but rather, what do the ASEAN members expect from the Quad? Under these circumstances, ASEAN will probably become the 'pivot' of the Indo-Pacific region. It has been projected that the total regional GDP will increase from USD 3.2 trillion in 2019 to around USD 7.6 trillion by 2030, and the ASEAN region will be one of the key drivers of global economy.[93] In 2019, China's trade volume with ASEAN climbed by 14 per cent to 4.43 trillion yuan.[94] However, the ASEAN region is not a homogenous entity and splits are clearly visible between the members of the ASEAN. Territorial disputes exist amongst the members of the ASEAN and also with China. No clear roadmap exists regarding resolution of territorial claims in the ASEAN region.[95] Furthermore, there is no unanimous view amongst the members of ASEAN regarding the Indo-Pacific region and what they expect from the Quad. There are growing murmurs about the need for the Quad to adopt a Quad Plus mechanism which would include the ASEAN members. In addition, while there are platforms like the ASEAN Regional Forum and the East Asia Summit (EAS) which seek to address maritime concerns of the ASEAN members, they continue to remain slightly reserved when it comes to choosing a particular strategy or policy proposed by the Quad collectively, or by a member of the Quad individually or by China. Nevertheless, what it provides ASEAN with is an opportunity to extract benefits from the major powers.

Role of the Hegemon

The United States, which has largely helped create the liberal order, is now undergoing a crisis as other countries are seeking to alter the status quo. Zbigniew Brzezinski has argued that 'the United States must realise that stability in Asia can no longer be imposed by a non-Asian power, least of all by the direct application of US military power'.[96] But the US does realise that it can be the 'pivot' of the region and through its system of alliance/ partnership/dialogue amongst the middle powers, it can ensure that its position and its ideas remain supreme in the Indo-Pacific region. While the Quad is an informal strategic dialogue between four major democratic countries, its success hinges on the role of the US. The economies of Japan, Australia and India are not only very integrated to that of the US, but the latter has also been the dominant player in the bilateral and trilateral defence relations amongst the Quad members. Strengthening diplomatic relations with the US is beneficial for all parties since it will increase power and, to some degree, alleviate regional security concerns. Likewise, given that the US is involved in numerous combat zones, Washington would expect stronger help from Quad members, particularly in terms of logistical and information sharing, as well as diplomatic support in international forums.

The Trump administration often emphasised that the US cannot be held solely accountable when it comes to addressing challenges posed by combat zones.[97] In contrast, the Biden administration is committed to ensuring that the US's foreign policy remains fruitful through fostering partnerships.[98] Therefore, the US continues to diplomatically invest in India. However, within the context of a dynamic global system, where the pursuit of national interests remains of utmost importance, it is probable that interactions between nations will increasingly adopt a contractual framework. Scholars like Ikenberry have argued that 'the way in which liberal order evolves will hinge in important respects on the United States and its willingness and ability to make new commitments to rules and institutions while simultaneously reducing its rights and privileges within the order'.[99] As American prestige and the capacity to shape events plummets,[100] the Quad gives an opportunity to the US to reassert its credentials as the foremost power in world politics and President Joe Biden's stating that the Quad in 20–30 years will change the world dynamics[101] clearly signifies the growing strategic focus of the Biden administration on the Quad. The failure of the Quad to achieve its goal—stability in the Indo-Pacific and contain China—will have major implications for the US and for the liberal democratic world. It will firstly devour the argument that democratic nations are like magnets or natural allies; secondly, it will imply the gradual demise of multinational defence organisations; and thirdly, in the absence of commitment, hedging[102] will become the new normal for nation states. Under these circumstances, the role of the US in shaping and giving momentum to the Quad is anyone's guess. The 'democracy magnet' does not serve as a guarantee of commitment towards collective security by member states of Quad. The differences between the US, Japan, Australia and India become too stark when it comes to reaching a consensus on measures needed for containment of China. The growing bilateral as well as trilateral relations have certainly helped generate a certain degree of confidence amongst the members, but the contours of response to a 'rising China' continue to remain undefined. The aberrant behaviour of the Quad states reflects that in an anarchical world, hedging by member countries will remain the best bet to address China's boisterous behaviour in world politics.

Conclusion

The problems of 'chain-ganging' and 'buck-passing'[103] will test the resilience of any alliance. The Quad, if it is seen as a loose alliance among the US, Japan, Australia and India, will invariably face these problems. The decline of the hegemon has quickened as well as deepened strategic relations between the members of the 'democratic security diamond'. Therefore, it is not surprising that the fear of a rising China, which is challenging the liberal order and the growth of bilateral partnership between the Quad members, cannot be delinked. The presence of US naval forces in the Indo-Pacific region serves as an 'insurance policy' for Japan and Australia. In the coming years, India, which seeks to maintain its strategic autonomy, will soon need to make certain hard decisions regarding alliances and partnerships in order to secure its core interests.

Studies reveal that while the economic interdependence does not alone prevent the outbreak of international conflicts, it does play a major role in influencing the nature and intensity of conflict.[104] The Janus-faced relations between the members of the Quad and China implies that there is not only a lack of trust but also that the stakes are too high for any kind of direct confrontation. Essentially, the US, Japan, Australia and India would not like to cede ground to China any more. The countries in the Indo-Pacific region, particularly the ASEAN nations, are diverse politically as well as in foreign policy goals, and partnerships of ASEAN member countries are at times contradictory to each other. For instance, China's relations with Cambodia and US's relations with Vietnam have reached new levels of cooperation. All parties are keeping all their options open in spite of identifying their own adversaries.

At the heart of the strategic competition between the Quad and China is the clash between the democratic worldview of the former and the authoritarian ethos advocated by the latter.[105] What serves as a major irritant to China is not the 'ganging up' of democratic countries against its rise, but the reiteration to the global community of the superiority of liberal democratic values by the US and other rising democratic powers. This is in direct contrast to the Chinese model of development and governance where the thrust is on outcomes and not the process.[106] Just as the US has begun to consolidate its relationship with other rising democracies, China's support for non-liberal regimes continues to be unwavering. Tarun Chhabra opines that 'as China's relative power increases, the US and allied planners should prepare for a global environment that grows increasingly hostile to democracy and liberal values.'[107]

China has now emerged as Washington's most credible competitor. So it becomes imperative for the US to seek alliances in the form of dyads, triads and quads to counter the challenging force. Meanwhile, the middle-power democratic countries like India, Japan and Australia stand to substantially gain by being united, but differing perceptions about national security and defence threaten to make this multilateral framework rather 'toothless'. Although the classical balance-of-power theory would have argued that countries in such a situation would seek to balance the hegemon, in the present time, when strategic interests are well identified and similarity of value systems becomes preponderant, the members of the Quad would rather seek to maintain the status quo in the Indo-Pacific region. The challenges of burden-sharing, lack of well-defined principles of collective security and a multifaceted relationship with a common adversary will invariably mean that the Quad is more akin to a 'democratic entente' rather than being a democratic alliance or partnership. Currently, the Quad remains a superficial dialogue process; whether it can overcome its inherent contradictions is debatable.

Notes and References

1. Joseph M. Grieco, 'Anarchy and the limits of cooperation: A realist critique of the newest liberal institutionalism', *International Organization*, vol. 42, no. 3 (1988), pp. 485–507.

2. The White House, 'Quad Leaders' Joint Statement', 20 May 2023, available at https://www.whitehouse.gov/briefing-room/statements-releases/2023/05/20/quad-leaders-joint-statement/, accessed on 9 October 2023.

3. Ministry of External Affairs, Government of India, 'India-Australia-Japan-U.S. Consultations on Indo-Pacific' ,November 12, 2017, available at https://mea.gov.in/press-releases.htm?dtl/29110/IndiaAustraliaJapanUS_Consultations_on_IndoPacific_November_12_2017, accessed on 1 September 2023.

4. John J. Mearsheimer, 'Bound to Fail: The Rise and Fall of the Liberal International Order', *International Security*, vol. 43, no. 4 (Spring 2019), p. 44.

5. Mark Beeson and Richard Higgott, 'The changing architecture of politics in the Asia-Pacific: Australia's middle power moment?' *International Relations of the Asia-Pacific*, vol. 14 (2014), p. 217.

6. Australian Government, '2017 Foreign Policy White Paper', p. 25, available at https://www.globalsecurity.org/military/library/report/2017/australia_2017_foreign_policy_white_paper.pdf, accessed on 1 September 2023.

7. David Scott, 'Australia's embrace of the 'Indo-Pacific': New term, new region, new strategy?' *International Relations of the Asia-Pacific*, vol. 13, no. 3 (2013), p. 17, available at https://theasiadialogue.com/wp-content/uploads/2018/01/australia-indo-pacific.pdf, accessed on 16 April 2020.

8. David Scott, 'India and the Allure of the "Indo-Pacific"', *International Studies*, vol. 49, no. 3–4 (2012), p. 166.

9. K. He, 'Three Faces of the Indo-Pacific: Understanding the "Indo-Pacific" from an IR Theory Perspective', *East Asia,* vol. 35, no. 2 (2018), p. 150.

10. Prime Minister of Australia, 'Quad Leaders' Vision Statement - Enduring Partners for the Indo-Pacific', 20 May 2023, available at https://www.pm.gov.au/media/quad-leaders-vision-statement-enduring-partners-indo-pacific, accessed on 9 October 2023.

11. Leigh Hartman, 'What is the U.S. Indo-Pacific strategy?', *Share America*, 23 September 2019, available at https://share.america.gov/what-is-u-s-indo-pacific-strategy/, accessed on 3 April 2020.

12. Ministry of External Affairs, Government of India, 'Prime Minister's Keynote Address at Shangri La Dialogue', 1 June 2018, available at https://www.mea.gov.in/Speeches-Statements.htm?dtl/29943/Prime+Ministers+Keynote+Address+at+Shangri+La+Dialogue+June+01+2018, accessed on 3 April 2020.

13. 'China mocks Australia over "Indo-Pacific" concept it says will "dissipate"', 8 March 2018, available at https://www.abc.net.au/news/2018-03-08/china-mocks-australia-over-indo-pacific-concept/9529548, accessed on 23 April 2020.

14. M. Beeson, 'Alternative realities: Explaining security in the Asia-Pacific', *Review of International Studies,* vol. 43, no. 3 (2017), p. 13.

15. Benjamin Fordham and Paul Poast, 'All Alliances Are Multilateral: Rethinking Alliance Formation', *Journal of Conflict Resolution*, vol. 60, no. 5 (2014), p. 6; Hans Morgenthau, *Politics Among Nations* (New York: McGraw Hill, 1948).

16. Daniel Y. Chiu, 'International Alliances in the Power Cycle Theory of State Behavior', *International Political Science Review*, vol. 24, no. 1 (2003), p. 124; S. M. Walt, *The Origins of Alliances* (Ithaca, NY: Cornell University Press, 1987).

17. James D. Morrow, 'Alliances and Asymmetry: An Alternative to the Capability Aggregation Model of Alliances', *American Journal of Political Science*, vol. 35, no. 4 (November 1991), p. 906.

18. Michael R. Kenwick, John A. Vasquez, and Matthew A. Powers, 'Do Alliances Really Deter?' *The Journal of Politics*, vol. 77, no. 4 (July 2015), p. 934.

19. For more details, see Andriy Tyushka and Lucyna Czechowska, *Strategic Partnerships, International Politics and IR Theory* (Edward Elgar Publishing Ltd, 2019).

20. 'Joint Statement - Australia—Japan—United States Defence Ministers Meeting', Department of Defence, Australian Government, 3 June 2018, available at https://www.minister.defence.gov.au/minister/marise-payne/statements/joint-statement-australia-japan-united-states-defence-ministers, accessed on 11 April 2020.

21. Dhruva Jaishankar, 'The Real Significance of the Quad', *The Strategist*, 24 October 2018, available at https://www.aspistrategist.org.au/the-real-significance-of-the-quad/, accessed on 10 April 2020.

22. N. D. Anderson and V. D. Cha, 'The Case of the Pivot to Asia: System Effects and the Origins of Strategy', *Political Science Quarterly*, vol. 132, no. 4 (2017), p. 598.

23. Press Information Bureau, Government of India, Ministry of Defence, 'Military Exercises', available at https://pib.gov.in/newsite/PrintRelease.aspx?relid=199791, accessed on 6 April 2020.

24. James D. Morrow, 'Alliances and Asymmetry: An Alternative to the Capability Aggregation Model of Alliances', *American Journal of Political Science*, vol. 35, no. 4 (November 1991), p. 930.

25. Kevin Andrews, 'India is a key partner in Indo-Pacific region', *The Hindu*, 1 September 2015, available at https://www.thehindu.com/opinion/op-ed/india-is-a-key-partner-in-indopacific-region/article7600487.ece, accessed on 6 April 2020.

26. J. S. Nye, 'Redefining the National Interest', *Foreign Affairs*, vol. 78, no. 4 (1999), p. 30.

27. Fraser Cameron, *US Foreign Policy after the Cold War: Global Hegemon or Reluctant Sheriff?* (Routledge: London, 2002), p. 3.

28. For more details, see Joseph S. Nye, Jr, 'The rise and fall of American hegemony from Wilson to Trump', *International Affairs*, vol. 95, no. 1 (January 2019), pp. 63–80.

29. Angela Stent, 'Russia and China: Axis of Revisionists?', *Brookings*, February 2020, available at https://www.brookings.edu/articles/russia-and-china-axis-of-revisionists/, accessed on 9 October 2023.

30. Department of State, United States of America, *A Free and Open Indo-Pacific: Advancing a Shared Vision*, 4 November 2019, available at https://www.

state.gov/wp-content/uploads/2019/11/Free-and-Open-Indo-Pacific-4Nov2019.pdf, accessed on 9 October 2023.

31. Department of Defense, USA, 'Indo-Pacific Strategy Report: Preparedness, Partnerships, and Promoting a Networked Region', 1 June 2019, p. 4, available at https://media.defense.gov/2019/Jul/01/2002152311/-1/-1/1/DEPARTMENT-OF-DEFENSE-INDO-PACIFIC-STRATEGY-REPORT-2019.PDF, accessed on 10 April 2020.

32. Ibid., p. 8.

33. Graham Allison, 'The Thucydides Trap', *Foreign Policy*, 9 June 2017, available at https://foreignpolicy.com/2017/06/09/the-thucydides-trap/, accessed on 9 October 2023.

34. Sanja Arežina, 'U.S.-China Relations Under the Trump Administration Changes and Challenges', *China Quarterly of International Strategic Studies*, vol. 5, no. 3, p. 313; also refer to Gideon Rose, 'The Fourth Founding: The United States and the Liberal Order', *Foreign Affairs* (May/June 2020), available at https://www.foreignaffairs.com/articles/united-states/2018-12-11/fourth-founding, accessed on 12 May 2020.

35. D. Roy, 'Assertive China: Irredentism or Expansionism?" *Survival*, vol. 61, no. 1 (2019), p. 57.

36. David Gura, 'How high tensions between China and the U.S. are impacting American companies', *NPR*, 26 August 2023, available at https://www.npr.org/2023/08/26/1195711197/china-us-trade-tensions-commerce-secretary-gina-raimondo, accessed on 9 October 2023.

37. Joseph S. Nye, Jr, 'The Future of American Power: Dominance and Decline in Perspective', *Foreign Affairs*, vol. 89, no. 6, The World Ahead (November/December 2010), p. 12.

38. M. S. Pardesi, 'The Indo-Pacific: A "new" region or the return of history?' *Australian Journal of International Affairs*, vol. 74, no. 2 (November 2019), p. 15.

39. G. John Ikenberry and Daniel H. Nexon, 'Hegemony Studies 3.0: The Dynamics of Hegemonic Orders', *Security Studies*, vol. 28, no. 3 (2019), p. 414; also refer to Daniel W. Drezner, 'Counter-Hegemonic Strategies in the Global Economy', *Security Studies*, vol. 28, no. 3 (June–July 2019), pp. 505–31.

40. L. L. I. Vidal, 'Beyond the *Gaiatsu* Model: Japan's Asia-Pacific Policy and Neoclassical Realism', *Journal of Asian Security and International Affairs*, vol. 9, no. 1, pp. 26–49, available at https://doi.org/10.1177/23477970221076641, accessed on 15 January 2024.

41. T. Inoguchi, 'A call for a new Japanese foreign policy: The dilemmas of a stakeholder state', *International Affairs*, vol. 90, no. 4 (2014), p. 957.

42. Ibid., p. 956.

43. Richard Holbrooke, 'Japan and the United States: Ending the Unequal Partnership', *Foreign Affairs*, vol. 70, no. 5, America and the Pacific, 1941–1991 (Winter, 1991), p. 52.

44. The White House, 'Statement from the President on the 60th Anniversary of the United States–Japan Treaty of Mutual Cooperation and Security', available at https://trumpwhitehouse.archives.gov/briefings-statements/statement-president-60th-anniversary-united-states-japan-treaty-mutual-cooperation-security/, accessed on 1 September 2023.

45. The Latin phrase '*si vis pacem, para bellum*' stands for 'if you want peace, prepare for war'.

46. Ministry of Foreign Affairs, Japan, *Diplomatic Bluebook 2019*, available at https://www.mofa.go.jp/policy/other/bluebook/2019/html/chapter1/c0101.html, accessed on 1 September 2023.

47. Shinzo Abe, proposed his famous 'democratic security diamond', consisting of Australia, India, Japan and the United States (the members of the original 2007 Quadrilateral Security Dialogue, or 'Quad'), in 2012. For more details, see Kai He and Mingjiang Li, 'Understanding the dynamics of the Indo-Pacific: US–China strategic competition, regional actors, and beyond', *International Affairs*, vol. 96, no. 1 (January 2020), p. 3; also refer to Shinzo Abe, 'Asia's Democratic Security Diamond', Project Syndicate, 27 December 2012, available at https://www.project-syndicate.org/commentary/a-strategic-alliance-for-japan-and-india-by-shinzo-abe?barrier=accesspaylog, accessed on 13 April 2020.

48. David Scott, 'The Geoeconomics and Geopolitics of Japan's "Indo-Pacific" Strategy', *Journal of Asian Security and International Affairs*, vol. 6, no. 2 (2019), p. 138.

49. Kei Koga, 'Japan's "Indo-Pacific" Question: Countering China or Shaping a New Regional Order?' *International Affairs*, vol. 96, no. 1 (2020), p. 50.

50. William Choong, 'The Return of the Indo-Pacific Strategy: An Assessment', *Australian Journal of International Affairs,* vol. 73 (2019), p. 3.

51. Doug Stokes, 'Trump, American Hegemony and the Future of the Liberal International Order', *International Affairs*, vol. 94, no. 1 (2018), p. 149.

52. Richard Samuels and Corey Wallace, 'Introduction: Japan's Pivot in Asia', *International Affairs,* vol. 94, no. 4 (2018), p. 703.

53. Kai He and Mingjiang Li, 'Understanding the dynamics of the Indo-Pacific-China strategic competition, regional actors, and beyond,' *International Affairs*, vol. 96, no. 1 (January 2020), pp. 3–4.

54. Kei Koga, 'The Concept of "Hedging" Revisited: The Case of Japan's Foreign Policy Strategy in East Asia's Power Shift', *International Studies Review*, vol. 20, no. 4 (December 2018), p. 633.

55. Karl Gustafsson, L. Hagström and U. Hanssen, 'Japan's Pacifism Is Dead', *Survival*, vol. 60, no. 6 (2018), p. 152.

56. Cabinet Secretariat of Japan, 'National Security Strategy of Japan', December 2022, available at https://www.cas.go.jp/jp/siryou/221216anzenhoshou/nss-e.pdf, accessed on 9 October 2023.

57. Government of Japan, 'New Plan for a "Free and Open Indo-Pacific": Policy Speech by PM Kishida', 20 March 2023, available at https://www.japan.

go.jp/kizuna/2023/05/new_plan_for_free_and_open_indo-pacific.html, accessed on 9 October 2023.

58. Mike Yeo, 'Japan increases defence spending', Australian Defence Magazine, 25 August 2023, available at https://www.australiandefence.com.au/defence/budget-policy/japan-increases-defence-spending, accessed on 9 October 2023.

59. Herbert Wulf and Tobias Debiel, 'India's "Strategic Autonomy" and the Club Model of Global Governance: Why the Indian BRICS Engagement Warrants a Less Ambiguous Foreign Policy Doctrine', *Strategic Analysis*, vol. 39, no. 1 (2015), p. 27.

60. Rajesh Rajagopalan, 'Evasive Balancing: India's Unviable Indo-Pacific Strategy', *International Affairs*, vol. 96, no. 1 (January 2020), p. 79.

61. Ministry of External Affairs, Government of India, 'Prime Minister's Keynote Address at Shangri La Dialogue (June 01, 2018)', available at https://www.mea.gov.in/Speeches-Statements.htm?dtl/29943/Prime+Ministers+Keynote+Address+at+Shangri+La+Dialogue+June+01+2018, accessed on 13 April 2020.

62. Junaid Ashraf, 'String of Pearls and China's Emerging Strategic Culture', *Strategic Studies*, vol. 37, no. 4 (2017), pp. 166–81, available at https://www.jstor.org/stable/48537578, accessed 8 October 2023.

63. Ministry of External Affairs, Government of India, 'Question No. 2411 Features of Quadrilateral Security Dialogue', 3 January 2019, available at https://mea.gov.in/rajya-sabha.htm?dtl/30869/question+no2411+features+of+quadrilateral+security+dialogue, accessed on 22 April 2020.

64. Derek Grossman, 'India Is the Weakest Link in the Quad', *Foreign Policy*, 23 July 2018, available at https://foreignpolicy.com/2018/07/23/india-is-the-weakest-link-in-the-quad/, accessed on 9 October 2023.

65. Department of State, United States of America, 'Integrated Country Strategy', 27 May 2022, available at https://www.state.gov/wp-content/uploads/2022/07/ICS_SCA_India_Public.pdf, accessed on 9 October 2023.

66. Nur Luthfi Hidayatullah, 'Classifying Middle Powers based on their Regional and Multilateral Roles: Differentiating Middle Power Enforcers, Assemblers and Advocators', *Advances in Social Science, Education and Humanities Research* (ASSEHR), vol. 143, p. 2.

67. B. Reilly, 'The return of values in Australian foreign policy', *Australian Journal of International Affairs* (November 2019), p. 3.

68. Allan Gyngell and Michael Wesley, *Making Australian Foreign Policy* (UK: Cambridge University Press, 2003), p. 226.

69. Carl Ungerer, 'The "Middle Power" Concept in Australian Foreign Policy', *Australian Journal of Politics and History*, vol. 53, no. 4 (2007), p. 550.

70. The Government of UK , *Global Trade Outlook*, February 2023, available at https://assets.publishing.service.gov.uk/government/uploads/system/uploads/

attachment_data/file/1139093/global-trade-outlook-february-2023.pdf, accessed on 9 October 2023.

71. Government of Australia, '2016 Defence White Paper', p. 14, available at https://www.defence.gov.au/whitepaper/Docs/2016-Defence-White-Paper.pdf, accessed on 19 April 2020.

72. R. A. Higgott and K. R. Nossal, 'The International Politics of Liminality: Relocating Australia in the Asia Pacific', *Australian Journal of Political Science*, vol. 32, no. 2 (1997), p. 171; also refer to Allan Patience, *Australian Foreign Policy in Asia: Middle Power or Awkward Partner?* (Palgrave Macmilan, 2018).

73. Daniel Workman, 'Australia's Top Trading Partners', World's Top Exports, available at http://www.worldstopexports.com/australias-top-import-partners/, accessed on 10 April 2020.

74. Beeson and Higgott, 'The changing architecture of politics in the Asia-Pacific', p. 225.

75. Ralf Emmers, 'The Role of Middle Powers in Asian Multilateralism', *Asia Policy*, vol. 13, no. 4 (October 2018), p. 46.

76. Yi Wang, *Australia–China Relations post 1949: Sixty Years of Trade and Politics* (UK: Ashgate, 2012), p. 4.

77. Fabrice Argounès, 'L'Australie : la tentation de la puissance régionale' [Australia: the Temptation of Regional Power], *Pouvoirs*, vol. 141, no. 2 (2012), p. 103–116, available at https://www.cairn-int.info/article-E_POUV_141_0103--australia-the-temptation-of-regionalpow.htm, accessed on 16 April 2020.

78. Maaike Okano-Heijmans, 'Power Shift: Economic Realism and Economic Diplomacy on the Rise', in Enrico Fels, Jan-Frederik Kremer and Katharina Kronenberg (eds), *Power in the 21st Century: International Security and International Political Economy in a Changing World* (NY: Springer, 2012), p. 272.

79. J. Wilson, 'Diversifying Australia's Indo-Pacific Infrastructure Diplomacy', 16 April 2019, Australian Institute of International Affairs, available at http://www.internationalaffairs.org.au/australianoutlook/diversifying-australias-indo-pacific-infrastructure-diplomacy/, accessed on 14 April 2020.

80. Andrew Carr, 'Is Australia a middle power? A systemic impact approach', *Australian Journal of International Affairs*, vol. 68, no. 1 (2014), p. 81.

81. Brendan Taylor, 'Is Australia's Indo-Pacific strategy an illusion?', *International Affairs*, vol. 96, no. 1 (January 2020), p. 101.

82. David Scott, 'Australia as a Middle Power: Ambiguities of Role and Identity', *Seton Hall Journal of Diplomacy and International Relations* (Summer/Fall 2013), p. 112.

83. Wilson, 'Diversifying Australia's Indo-Pacific Infrastructure Diplomacy'.

84. B. D. Blankenship and B. Denison, 'Is America Prepared for Great-power Competition?' *Survival*, vol. 61, no. 5 (2019), p. 45.

85. For more details, see Joshua Shifrinson, 'The rise of China, balance of power theory and US national security: Reasons for optimism?' *Journal of Strategic Studies*, vol. 43, no. 2 (2020), pp. 175–216.

86. Kurt Taylor Gaubatz, 'Democratic states and commitment in international relations', *International Organization,* vol. 50, no. 1 (Winter 1996), p.137.

87. Gurjit Singh, 'Is the Quad Decoupling from China?', Gateway House, 18 February 2023, available at https://www.gatewayhouse.in/is-the-quad-decoupling-from-china/, accessed on 9 October 2023.

88. Ibid.

89. Lavina Lee, 'Assessing the Quad: Prospects and Limitations of Quadrilateral Cooperation for Advancing Australia's Interests,' Lowy Institute, 20 May 2020, available at https://www.lowyinstitute.org/publications/assessing-quad-prospects-limitations-quadrilateral-cooperation-advancing-australia-s, accessed on 9 October 2023.

90. F. Zhang, 'China's Curious Nonchalance Towards the Indo-Pacific', *Survival*, vol. 61, no. 3 (2019), p. 204; also refer to Victor D. Cha, 'Complex Patchworks: U.S. Alliances as Part of Asia's Regional Architecture', *Asia Policy,* no. 11 (January 2011), pp. 27–50.

91. Ikenberry and Nexon, 'Hegemony Studies 3.0: The Dynamics of Hegemonic Orders', pp. 419–420.

92. A. Acharya, 'The Emerging Regional Architecture of World Politics', *World Politics*, vol. 59, no. 4 (2007), p. 629; also refer to Barry Buzan and Ole Wasver, *Regions and Powers: The Structure of International Security* (Cambridge: Cambridge University Press, 2003), p. 564; also see Peter J. Katzenstein, *A World of Regions: Asia and Europe in the American Imperium* (Ithaca, N.Y.: Cornell University Press, 2005), pp. 297.

93. Rajiv Biswas, 'Trade with China driving ASEAN's growth', *China Daily*, 7 January 2020, available at https://www.chinadaily.com.cn/a/202001/07/WS5e13e802a310cf3e35582e22.html, accessed on 5 April 2020.

94. Ji Xianbai, 'The rise of China-ASEAN trade amid trans-Pacific decoupling', CGTN, 19 March 2020, available at https://news.cgtn.com/news/2020-03-19/The-rise-of-China-ASEAN-trade-amid-trans-Pacific-decoupling-OXZHjem1c4/index.html, accessed on 5 April 2020.

95. For more details, see Nicole Jenne, 'Managing Territorial Disputes in Southeast Asia: Is There More than the South China Sea?', *Journal of Current Southeast Asian Affairs*, vol. 36, no. 3 (2017), pp. 35–61.

96. Beeson and Higgott, 'The changing architecture of politics in the Asia-Pacific', p.b227; also see Z. Brzezinski, 'Balancing the East, upgrading the west: US grand strategy in an age of upheaval', *Foreign Affairs*, vol. 9, no. 1 (2012), pp. 97–104.

97. The White House, 'Remarks by President Trump and NATO Secretary General Jens Stoltenberg Before Bilateral Meeting', 2 April 2019, available at

https://trumpwhitehouse.archives.gov/briefings-statements/remarks-president-trump-nato-secretary-general-jens-stoltenberg-bilateral-meeting/, accessed on 6 September 2023.

98. Christopher Preble, Andrew Hyde, Emma Ashford, et al., 'Experts React: Biden Administration's National Security Strategy', Stimson, 14 October 2022, available at https://www.stimson.org/2022/experts-react-biden-administrations-national-security-strategy/, accessed on 9 October 2023.

99. G. John Ikenberry, 'Liberal Internationalism 3.0: America and the Dilemmas of Liberal World Order', *Perspectives on Politics*, vol. 7, no. 1 (March 2009), p. 84.

100. Hillel Fradkin and Lewis Libby, 'Erdogan's Grand Vision: Rise and Decline', *World Affairs*, vol. 175, no. 6 (March/April 2013), p. 50.

101. 'US President Joe Biden underlines Quad's vision, says, "in 20-30 years it will change world dynamics"', *Livemint*, 20 May 2023, available at https://www.livemint.com/news/world/us-president-joe-biden-underlines-quads-vision-says-in-20-30-years-it-will-change-world-dynamics-11684595196815.html, accessed on 13 February 2024.

102. For more details, see J. D. Ciorciari and J. Haacke, 'Hedging in international relations: An introduction', *International Relations of the Asia-Pacific,* vol. 19, no. 3 (2019), pp. 367–374, available at https://academic.oup.com/irap/article-abstract/19/3/367/5563899?redirectedFrom=fulltext, accessed on 6 September 2023.

103. Thomas J. Christensen and Jack Snyder, 'Chain gangs and passed bucks: Predicting alliance patterns in multipolarity', *International Organization*, vol. 44, no. 2 (Spring 1990), p. 140; see also Rohan Mukherjee, 'Japan's strategic outreach to India and the prospects of a Japan–India alliance', *International Affairs*, vol. 94, no. 4 (2018), p. 854.

104. Mina E. Tanious, 'The impact of economic interdependence on the probability of conflict between states: The case of "American–Chinese relationship on Taiwan since 1995"', *Review of Economics and Political Science*, vol. 4, no. 1 (2019), p. 52.

105. H. Brands, 'Democracy vs Authoritarianism: How Ideology Shapes Great-Power Conflict', *Survival,* vol. 60, no. 5 (2018), p. 67.

106. For more details, see He Li, 'The Chinese Discourse on Good Governance: Content and Implications', *Journal of Contemporary China* (March 2020), available at https://www.tandfonline.com/doi/abs/10.1080/10670564.2020.1744376?journalCode=cjcc20, pp.1–14.

107. Tarun Chhabra, 'The China challenge, democracy, and U.S. grand strategy', Foreign Policy at Brookings, p. 5, available at https://www.brookings.edu/wp-content/uploads/2019/02/FP_20190227_us_grand_strategy_chhabra.pdf, accessed on 5 April 2020.

seven

Securing the Indo-Pacific

Cooperation of Two Maritime Resident Powers

JOSHY M. PAUL

The emergence of nomenclature about regional dynamism can be attributed to the growing importance of a rising state beyond its periphery. The rising state can demonstrate its ability to transcend its influence to distant locations based on its burgeoning regional interests and material capabilities. Ever since the economic boom occurred in Japan during the 1980s, the nation became the engine of growth for most of the economies in East Asia, which led to attracting the attention of economic experts around the world to the economic dynamism of East Asia, and that in turn culminated in popularising the regional nomenclature called 'Asia-Pacific'. The concept of Asia-Pacific was rooted in commerce, finance and politics; it lacked the security orientation to address many challenging issues. The regional dynamism later transformed into security and strategy with the rise of China and US–China rivalry. As a result, the issue of security of the Asia-Pacific maritime domain gained traction by the beginning of the 21st century, and so the idea of regional space evolved into the maritime domain called 'Indo-Pacific', which comprises the maritime security of the Western Pacific and the Indian Ocean Region (IOR).[1] The reasons for this shift are many, including the need to protect the sea lines of communication (SLOCs), the rise of China as a great maritime power, the relative decline of US preponderance, new and emerging threats in the Indian Ocean, and most importantly the rise of India as a dominant naval power in the IOR and its increasing cooperation with the US and its allies in Asia, particularly Japan.

The Indo-Pacific is indeed a new strategic theatre in international politics. It is a confluence of an existing power, a rising power, and a few secondary powers, and is also home to the world's fastest-growing economies. It has emerged in the 21st century as a new strategic domain when two major democracies—India and Japan—began to cooperate for the protection of sea lines of communication connecting the Indian Ocean and the Western Pacific.[2] India was excluded in the Asia-Pacific construct but has now become a crucial player in the security of the Indo-Pacific. Given the importance of the Indo-Pacific, the US renamed its Pacific Command (PACOM) as Indo-Pacific Command (INDOPACOM). Similarly, the Chinese military modernisation programme launched in the 1990s has made China a preeminent regional power, and its Anti-Access/Area Denial strategy has enabled Beijing to challenge US supremacy in the Western Pacific. As a result, the US is not only seeking more strategic partnerships with like-minded countries but is also expecting Asian countries to contribute more towards regional peace and stability.[3] The Indo-Pacific, thus, is going to be the most contested place in the 21st century, with competition not only between the US and China but between China and other regional powers as well. China, the rising power in Asia, is trying to establish its order in the Western Pacific by marginalising the US and has also launched expansionist policies towards the IOR. The Indo-Pacific, which became a part of the official lexicon of Australian white paper[4] and the US security strategy for Asia,[5] thus holds the key to global security and a new world order.

The terminology 'maritime security' is different from 'maritime interests'; the latter is more generic, referring normally to economic interests, while the former falls in the category of 'high politics' in international relations (IR) theory nexused with the grand strategy of states.[6] In maritime security cooperation, countries tend to focus on politico-security matters and practice hard-power methods such as naval cooperation, joint exercises, mutual visits of high dignitaries, and so on. Two countries join together only when they see a synergy of interests between them, which are inherently connected with their geostrategic interests. As a major power in the Western Pacific, Japan seeks to expand its presence in the Indian Ocean through cooperation with India, and India in turn looks for the same with respect to the Western Pacific. In addition, both consider the rise of China as potentially dangerous for their security interests.

The maritime security cooperation between India and Japan can be seen as two secondary states in the Indo-Pacific joining together to prevent one country from getting a dominant position in order to preserve a free and open Indo-Pacific.[7] The rise of a new hegemon is a threat to both the existing hegemon and the local powers, that is, the secondary states in the region. Secondary powers are the states who 'can disrupt the system, but not change it, through unilateral action'.[8] Secondary states come below the great powers but ahead of the middle powers in the hierarchy of states in the international system.[9] The behaviour of secondary states is largely influenced by their regional security environment.[10] If regional security dynamics are going in the direction of unipolarity, then the secondary states come together and contest the dominance of a new hegemon. In this process, they adopt hard balancing, soft balancing, blackmail and leash slipping to oppose and limit the rising hegemon's power.[11] To counter the Chinese hegemony, India and Japan prefer soft balancing rather than hard balancing or forming a coalition with the US. In case of hard balancing, states usually focus on the overall balance of power and seek to assemble a countervailing coalition that will be strong enough to keep the dominant power in check, no matter what policies it decides to pursue.[12] By contrast, soft balancing opposes a potential threat without a formal military alliance.[13] Soft balancing accepts the current balance of power but seeks to obtain better outcomes within it, by assembling available resources designed to thwart or impede specific policies of the hegemon. India–Japan maritime security cooperation is the best example of how secondary states come together against a potential hegemon and marshal their capabilities and strategies in a synergised manner.

India and Japan, standing at important locations in the Indo-Pacific, are regional heavyweights in terms of military postures, although they vary in their defence strategy. Japan's defence is allied with the US security umbrella system, while India's security arrangement is independent, that is, it has 'strategic autonomy'. Till the beginning of the 21st century, Japan had not recognised India as a regional player as Tokyo looked at Asian security through the prism of the erstwhile Cold War rhetoric. However, because of India's economic progress and its naval prowess in the IOR, Tokyo gradually began considering India as an important regional power and recognised that cooperation with India would serve its interests well. India's naval capability is well-appreciated across the globe both in terms of humanitarian operations, such as the 2004 tsunami rescue efforts and antipiracy operations in the IOR, and its resilience against any major crisis.[14] India's emerging naval prowess was recognised by Japan for the first time when the Japanese merchant ship MV *Alondra Rainbow* was rescued by Indian naval forces in 1999.[15] This rescue operation manifested a closer maritime security cooperation between India and Japan that heralded a new beginning in the India–Japan relationship.[16] Since then Japan began to consider India as an important strategic partner and New Delhi has been increasingly depicted in Japan's strategic formulations.[17] From 2007 onwards Japan has begun to feature South Asia, predominantly India, in its annual white paper *Defence of Japan* published by the Ministry of Defence, and the 2011 issue stated that, because of its location, India is an 'extremely important country in a geopolitical sense for Japan'.[18]

The regional security situations in East Asia and Japan's own security calculations have also contributed to strengthening India–Japan maritime security cooperation. China's economic rise and its quantum leap in defence spending raised Japan's suspicions about China's military posture. From the late 1990s, China has had a focused naval modernisation programme to be able to push back the United States from the Western Pacific in order to become a preeminent naval power in the region.[19] Tokyo perceived that the crisis in the Taiwan Strait and the related implications of China's military presence in the region would become a major threat for Japan in the long term.[20] For instance, Japan's Defence Ministry's 'National Defense Program Guideline for FY 2005' expressed concern that 'China, which has a strong influence on the security in this region, has been modernizing its nuclear and missile capabilities as well as naval and air forces, and expanding its area of operation at sea. We have to remain attentive to its future course.'[21] So Japan sought to widen its strategic partnership, by not just depending on the US alliance system to counter China but enhancing its cooperation with fellow countries in Asia. Another reason for the India–Japan strategic cooperation has been Japan's own effort to become a 'normal' military power in the new century.[22] By the end of the Cold War, Japan's security calculus began to change profoundly, forcing it to formulate new strategies to face a 'multiplicity of challenges', which include the nuclear crisis in the Korean peninsula, China's rapid military modernisation programme, the relative strategic decline of the US in the Asia-Pacific region, and the criticism of Tokyo's 'cheque-book' diplomacy.[23] This raised a debate in Japan about its future strategies to preserve security and sovereignty.[24] Subsequently, Japan pursued a 'proactive' diplomacy with a view to widening the circle of free societies in Asia to include

'India and Australia as well as [...] the 10 members of the Association of Southeast Asian Nations'.[25]

The importance of the coming together of Japan and India for maritime security objectives is evident in the statements by the Japanese leaders. The 'Confluence of the Two Seas'[26] which was promulgated by Prime Minister Shinzo Abe in 2007 at the Indian Parliament, and his Foreign Minister Taro Aso's 'Arc of Freedom and Prosperity' initiative, which he proposed in his address at the Japan Institute of International Affairs in November 2006,[27] are noteworthy examples of the two countries beginning to view the Pacific and the Indian Ocean as a single entity for security aspects. This became the basis for conceptualising the Indo-Pacific as a new strategic theatre in the subsequent period. Widening the scope of the strategic cooperation, Japanese Prime Minister Abe further proposed multilateral security frameworks in the Indo-Pacific comprising Japan, India, US, and Australia such as the 'alliance of democracies and security architecture for the Asia Pacific region';[28] 'Democratic Security Diamond' of 2012,[29] and 'Quadrilateral Security Dialogue' (Quad) in 2017.[30] In all these cooperative mechanisms, Japan considers India as an equal partner along with its traditional allies—the US and Australia. This is a major shift in Japan's approach towards India, especially because erstwhile India–Japan relations were marred by a nuclear stalemate.[31]

Japan's Maritime Security Strategy

As an island nation, maritime security is vital to Japan's overall security and economic growth. The southwest trade route (composed of several interlinking sea lines passing through the Indian Ocean) connecting Japan with Europe, Middle East and Southeast Asia is critical to Japan's economy.[32] Other trade routes connecting continental Asia, Australasia and trans-Pacific are less vulnerable and traverse through the ocean or sparsely populated areas. But the southwest stream is potentially vulnerable, even during peacetime, because it passes through various chokepoints such as the Malacca, Sunda and Lombok Straits, and also through the piracy-prone area of the Gulf of Aden in the Indian Ocean. It must be noted that oil remains Japan's most important strategic commodity and 80 per cent of it comes from the Middle East. So any instability in the region or disruption in the supply route will immensely affect Japan's security calculations.[33]

Importantly, Japan doesn't have military partnership with any of the littoral countries along the southwest route, while China continues to aggressively establish its dominance in this route, especially in the South China Sea. As a result, the SLOCs traversing the Indian Ocean assume particular importance in Japan's energy security strategy.

Japan's current security strategy focuses principally, if not exclusively, on East Asian issues. Although the end of the Cold War has brought new security concepts to East Asia, the essence of the Japanese naval strategy remains intact: it seeks to contain the naval reach of hostile Asian land powers within the marginal waters along the Japanese archipelago, thereby restricting their access to the open ocean.[34] To ensure its territorial freedom and sovereignty, Tokyo has gradually strengthened its defence forces, particularly naval systems, including submarines and helicopter carriers, and has introduced a new concept of 'dynamic defense' in Japan's Self Defence Force's operational strategy.[35] Still, Japan, with only modest power projection capabilities of its own, is significantly constrained by the ability to move maritime resources away from this primary theatre.[36] Both the East China Sea and the South China Sea are critical for Japan, the former being the home to its territorial integrity and the latter the lifeline for Japan's energy consumption. This has caused Japan a major geostrategic dilemma about allocating its naval assets: it needs assets for both territorial security and protection of the SLOCs. So Japan's 'southern' strategy is to maintain close economic and security cooperation with powerful countries in the region that can withstand Chinese assertiveness.[37]

China's assertive maritime activities around the Senkaku Islands in the East China Sea caused Japan to believe that the Chinese grand strategy is by and large focused on attaining regional hegemony and extra-regional power projection.[38] China has shown further assertiveness in expanding towards the South China Sea by creating artificial islands and claiming almost 90 per cent of the water body as its sovereign territory.[39] China, with its expanding diplomatic, economic and military reach, is thus incrementally imposing its will on the region. Chinese dominance in the South China Sea and its capability to interdict Japan-bound shipping vessels is considered one of the major maritime security concerns for Japan.[40] In this context, the Japanese government has shifted its strategic focus from the Cold War-centric north to the south of Japan to meet the challenges emanating from the rise of China, especially its growing naval power. At the same time, there is a growing realisation among the strategic community and policymakers in Japan that its complete dependence on the US for security would not sustain for long and thus Japan's security policy must look beyond the US-centric strategy.[41] Japan cannot be sure that the United States would see the same level of threat in China's rise as Japan does. As a precaution, Japan has started diversifying its strategic relationships with other regional countries and is exploring pathways towards greater strategic independence.[42] Importantly, concerns with Chinese assertiveness in the maritime domain have replaced the (already softening) traditional distrust of Japan's security role among the ASEAN countries.[43] This has made Japan enhance cooperation with other countries, as indicated in the 2011 National Defense Program Guidelines, which states that

> Japan will also maintain and enhance security cooperation with the Association of Southeast Asian Nations (ASEAN) countries, which are its traditional partners. Moreover, Japan will enhance cooperation with India and other countries that share common interests in ensuring the security of maritime navigation from Africa and the Middle East to East Asia.[44]

When Shinzo Abe came back to power in 2012, he sought to replace Japan's dependent foreign policy by adopting an 'activist international role' for Japan.[45] Along with multilateral mechanisms, Abe proposed the 'Free and Open Indo-Pacific Strategy' which emphasised the importance of the rule of law and an open economy free from coercion as well as freedom and prosperity from Asia to Africa through the Indian Ocean and the Pacific Ocean.[46] In this effort, it is important for Japan to 'strengthen strategic collaboration with India, which has a historical relationship with East Africa, as well as the US and Australia.'[47] Tokyo believes that since India is the largest resident power in the Indian Ocean, it would be beneficial for Japan to expand cooperation to other regions, including the African coast. Moreover, the proposed Asia-Africa Growth Corridor (AAGC) mooted by India and Japan could counter the Chinese 'debt-trap' model of soft power influence under the Belt and Road Initiative (BRI).[48] Tokyo wants to send a clear message to the international community that a possible Chinese order in the Indo-Pacific created through the BRI will not be accepted by Japan. Japan believes in a regional order that is based on the rule of law including high-quality rules for trade, investment and infrastructure; transparency and openness; freedom of navigation; and the prevention of coercive actions against smaller states.[49] Along with the US–Japan alliance, strengthening the partnership with India would protect Japan's interests, and together India and Japan will be able to counter China's hegemonic ambition in the Indo-Pacific.

India and the Indo-Pacific

India's primary focus is the Indian Ocean Region, a large water body with high-profile chokepoints over which the major powers compete for domination. The Indian Navy's 'Maritime Doctrine 2009' clearly stipulates the objective that whatever happens in the IOR can affect India's national security, and so 'maintaining stability, security, and safety at sea, particularly in the IOR' becomes the primary area of interest for the Indian Navy.[50] India's power and prestige at the global level will surely determine how India can cope with the emerging security challenges, both traditional and non-traditional, in the IOR. With a robust naval force in its arsenal, India is looking to emerge as a 'credible and relevant' naval power in the IOR and is also ready to provide assistance to other countries. At the same time, India is looking to cooperate with all the major powers to avoid rivalry over the region. As the 2007 *Maritime Military Strategy* of the Indian Navy says, a credible and relevant naval power such as India 'can act as a strong deterrent to prevent conflict, or to respond, should it become inevitable' in the IOR.[51] The Indian Navy has planned to become a 200-ship navy by the next decade, including in its fleet three aircraft carriers, next-generation frigates, destroyers, corvettes, missile vessels, and conventional as well as nuclear submarines.[52] This will not only help India become a dominant resident power in the IOR but also prop up India's power and prestige in other parts of the Indo-Pacific.

Starting with the Look East policy in the 1990s followed by the Act East Policy under the current Prime Minister, Narendra Modi, India has steadily expanded its presence in the east of the IOR. Although it initially focused on economic cooperation with the nations of Southeast Asia, India's policy towards the east has now expanded into a full-spectrum engagement with the major powers of East Asia, including Japan.[53] Maritime cooperation with the Western-Pacific littoral countries has emboldened India's presence in the Western Pacific as well. Undoubtedly, India is apprehensive of China's assertiveness in both East and South China Seas because if China gets a dominant position in the Western Pacific, thereby marginalising the US, Beijing will try to apply the same tactics towards the IOR. To counter this possibility, India is increasingly expanding its strategic presence in the Western Pacific including the South China Sea in collaboration with friendly regional countries.[54] India wants to signal to Beijing that it will not remain passive to China's intervention in the IOR.[55] India has shown this through maritime exercises (navy and coast guard) and naval ship port calls as well as regular top-level visits by both civilian and military leaders to various East Asian countries. The annual Malabar naval exercise is now a quadrilateral one comprising India, the US, Japan and Australia and it takes place alternatingly in the Western Pacific and the Bay of Bengal. India is a regular participant in the Rim of Pacific (RIMPAC) Exercise, a US-led initiative of 25 countries to enhance maritime security operations in the region. India is also an observer to the Western Pacific Naval Symposium (WPNS) comprising navies of countries that border the Pacific Ocean. Besides, India conducts bilateral naval exercises with Japan, South Korea, Singapore and Indonesia as well. The regional countries see India as a counterweight to China's possible dominance in the water body. India's continuous naval presence in the South China Sea littorals through maritime exercises with and port visits to friendly countries has indeed irked China.[56] For instance, when the 2017 edition of SIMBEX (Singapore-India Maritime Bilateral Exercises) was conducted in the South China Sea, China protested by saying that such activities should not hurt the 'interests of other countries'.[57] In the next section we will discuss how India's maritime pivot to the east and Japan's southern strategy converges and becomes a deterrent factor against Chinese supremacy in the Indo-Pacific.

India–Japan Maritime Security Cooperation

India–Japan maritime security cooperation began at the dawn of the 21st century. It is Japan's growing realisation of India's naval prowess in the IOR that has brought Tokyo to build a stable and closer partnership with India for its security imperatives in the IOR. Since 80 per cent of the oil and 20 per cent of the ships bound for Japan pass through the Indian Ocean, protection in the IOR is a matter of major concern for Japan in its security calculations. Japan initially looked upon the bilateral cooperation mainly to protect the SLOCs and have India's security assistance for Japan-bound ships in the Indian Ocean after the MV *Alondra Rainbow* fiasco.[58] This led to close defence cooperation between the two countries which became one of the defining instances of security cooperation in the 21st century in the international relations of the Asia-Pacific region.

Following the then Indian Defence Minister George Fernandes' visit to Japan in 2000, India and Japan decided to hold annual security dialogues and military-to-military talks as well as joint naval exercises, search and rescue missions, and cooperation in anti-piracy measures in the Malacca Strait.[59] Subsequently, the two countries held their first ever defence ministerial-level meeting in 2001. At that time there were many terrorists and criminal organisations involved in arms smuggling, drug trafficking and piracy in the region, such as the Abu Sayyaf Group in the Philippines, various crime syndicates in Indonesia and Malaysia, the Liberation Tigers of Tamil Eelam (LTTE) in Sri Lanka and Al Qaeda and its affiliates in the Persian Gulf.[60] The geostrategic importance of India for Japanese maritime security had by then emerged as one of the critical components in Japan's strategy of importing a steady and uninterrupted supply of energy from the Middle East. As a major power with considerable naval prowess, Japan realised that India could assume a high-profile role in patrolling and safeguarding the busiest sea lane in the Indian Ocean. Close cooperation with India would therefore guarantee the safe passage of Japan-bound oil and merchandise ships. To enhance maritime cooperation, Japan participated in the International Fleet Review held in Mumbai in February 2001. This was followed by the visit of a Maritime Self Defense Force (MSDF) squadron to Chennai in May 2001, and similar friendly visits have continued since then. To commemorate the 1999 *Alondra Rainbow* incident, a joint Coast Guard exercise on search and rescue operations has also been launched.[61] During the then Japanese Foreign Minister Kawaguchi Yoriko's visit to Delhi in 2003, she stated that

> cooperative maintenance of the security of maritime traffic in the sea lanes that stretch across the Indian Ocean and the Strait of Malacca [is] among the security and defence issues that deserve our increased attention. Both countries share common interest and concerns regarding the issues.[62]

The India–Japan relationship, which started with Japan's concern for SLOC protection in the Indian Ocean, then progressed to the next level with the new aim of balancing China. It is Japan's willingness to enhance its security cooperation with India to counter China that has brought both countries closer than ever before. When former Prime Minister Junichiro Koizumi visited New Delhi in 2005 he advocated the creation of a 'new Asian era' in partnership with India, signed the Japan-India Global Partnership with an eight-point plan and launched a High Level Strategic Dialogue on security matters.[63] The 2008 Joint Declaration on Security further strengthened the bilateral defence cooperation and emphasised regular strategic dialogues including periodic staff talks between navies to enhance cooperation and build a 'core ability'[64] for maritime operation and disaster relief. Japan's first ever doctrine on national security, titled 'National Security Strategy', published in 2013 highlights the importance of strengthening maritime security cooperation with India by stating that 'India is also geopolitically important for Japan, as it is positioned in the centre of sea lines of communication. Japan will strengthen bilateral relations in a broad range of areas, including maritime security, based on the bilateral Strategic and Global Partnership'.[65]

Maritime security cooperation with Japan has not only enhanced India's presence in the Western Pacific but has helped India play a crucial role in the United States' strategic policy choices towards the Indo-Pacific. The US was widening its strategic partnership beyond the traditional alliance system in Asia and the Indo-Japanese strategic cooperation became a perfect part of Washington's changing Asia policy. Since Japan is an ally of the US, the 2005 Indo-US civil nuclear deal and the subsequent strategic cooperation partnership agreements between India and the US have also contributed towards strengthening India–Japan security cooperation because the veil of the nuclear shadow has now been lifted. Japan became keen to include the US in the Indo-Pacific security mechanism and expressed its interest in participating in the Indo-US Malabar exercise as well. In April 2007, for the first time, Japan participated in a trilateral naval exercise called TRILATEX-07 with India and the US navy. It was held near the Boso Peninsula in central Japan and saw the participation of four destroyers from Japan's Maritime Self-Defence Force and three warships from the Indian Navy in a six hour drill.[66] Another exercise was conducted in August 2008 near Mumbai, in which the training ship MSDF *Kashima*, two frontline guided missile destroyers *Asagiri* and *Umigiri*, and one Delhi class and one Corvette class ship from the Indian side also participated.[67] Taking the maritime cooperation a step further, the Japanese MSDF participated along with the US, Australia and Singapore navies in the Malabar exercise held in the Bay of Bengal in September 2007, which focused on anti-submarine warfare, maritime interdiction and anti-piracy search and seizure operations.[68] However, the quadrilateral maritime initiative had to be abandoned prematurely because it received sharp criticism from China. Chinese officials dubbed the cooperation as a security alliance against China, touting the naval exercise as the 'resurrection of Cold War mentality' in Asia and 'the formation of small NATO to resist China'.[69] At the same time, the Quadrilateral Initiative was not well received among the regional powers in Southeast Asia who perceived that if such a mechanism became an institutional one, their voices would never be heard and the security of Southeast Asia would become a part of the major power struggle. Subsequently, the multilateral maritime security mechanisms involving Japan, India and the United States had to be quietly shelved.

Although the multilateral naval exercise was abandoned, Japan was keen to continue formal cooperation with the Indian Navy. During the Indian Defence Minister A. K. Antony's visit to Tokyo in November 2011, the two countries decided to conduct bilateral naval exercises, and the first official bilateral naval exercise JIMEX was subsequently launched off Sagami Bay in Japan in June 2012. In the first JIMEX, two Japanese destroyers, one maritime patrol aircraft and a helicopter participated while the Indian Navy was represented by INS *Rana*, INS *Shivalik*, INS *Karmukh* and INS *Shakti*.[70] From then onwards, India and Japan have conducted this regular bilateral exercise annually on both the Indian Ocean and the Western Pacific alternatingly. Also, JMSDF and the Indian Navy enhanced their cooperation in the anti-piracy operation in the Gulf of Aden and exchanged schedules for escort of civilian vessels.[71] Japan wanted to join in the Malabar exercise along with the US but New Delhi was anxious about how China would react to the efforts to expand the bilateral exercise into a trilateral one, considering China's earlier accusations. Because of this fear, India was even hesitant to become a member of any formal multilateral mechanism and did not endorse Abe's proposal of the security diamond architecture. However, maritime security cooperation with Japan is something that India cannot afford to ignore since it provides a good platform for reaching out to the Western Pacific. India eventually found a way to include Japan in the Malabar exercise. It was decided that when the exercise was being held in the Pacific, it would be trilateral with Japan's participation, but when it was being held in the Indian Ocean it would remain purely bilateral. Accordingly, the 2014 edition of the Malabar exercise held at Sasebo near Nagasaki was converted into a trilateral one.[72] Earlier in 2009 and 2011, Japan had a modest representation in the Malabar exercise when it was held in the Western Pacific.

As stated earlier, the United States was keen for a firm contribution from both India and Japan to ensure freedom of navigation in the Indo-Pacific. The US pushed for a strong India–Japan partnership because it could be a regional-level counter-mechanism against China which would be beneficial to safeguard the US's interest in the Indo-Pacific. Indeed, the prevailing great power's support is necessary for soft balancing in the Indo-Pacific. When the Indian Prime Minister met the US President Barack Obama in September 2014, both countries 'agreed to upgrade their existing bilateral exercise MALABAR',[73] arguably to include Japan as a regular participant. Subsequently, Japan was officially invited to participate in the 2015 edition of the Malabar exercise held in the Bay of Bengal from 15 to 19 October. The Indian Navy was represented by INS *Sindhuraj* (a diesel-electric submarine), INS *Ranvijay* (a guided missile destroyer), INS *Shivalik* (a stealth frigate), INS *Betwa* (a guided-missile frigate) and INS *Shakti* (a fleet tanker), while the Japanese Navy sent the destroyer JS *Fuyuzuki*, and the US Navy sent the nuclear aircraft carriers USS *Theodore Roosevelt* and USS *Normandy*, the Freedom-class littoral combat ship USS *Fort Worth* and the Los Angeles-class submarine USS *City of Corpus Christi*.[74] This was the first time Japan participated in the Malabar exercise held in the Indian Ocean after the 2007 fiasco. The 2016 edition of Malabar held near Okinawa was the largest ever naval exercise with over 100 assets including warships, fighters and surveillance aircraft. The US brought its supercarrier Nimitz-class ship USS *John C Stennis*; Japan fielded JS *Hyuga*, a helicopter carrier and destroyer, the largest warship in the stable of the JMSDF; and India was represented by two stealth frigates: INS *Sahyadri* and INS *Satpura*, a fleet tanker called INS *Shakti* and a missile corvette called INS *Kirch*. Malabar 2016 was not just a multilateral naval exercise, but a combined show of the strength of the three navies to China as it was held about 400 kilometres from the contested Senkaku Islands in the East China Sea. From 2020 onwards, Malabar became a quadrilateral naval exercise, bringing Australia into the grouping, and the first ever formal quadrilateral naval exercise took place in two phases: Phase I from 3 to 6 November near the coast of Visakhapatnam in the Bay of Bengal, and Phase II from 17 to 20 November in the Arabian Sea.[75]

Of late, Japan has been more interested in strengthening the maritime security cooperation in a multilateral way involving the US and other security partners. Tokyo is enthusiastic about including India in such a multilateral mechanism, including the latest Quadrilateral Security Dialogue (Quad/QSD) mechanism mooted by the Abe administration in 2017. For Japan, India's involvement in the multilateral groupings in the Indo-Pacific is the best hedge against China. Unlike the other three members, India had been endorsing the Quad as a quiet partner but following the Galwan fiasco, it has begun actively engaging with the other Quad members.[76] However, India still prefers a strong bilateral mechanism with Japan, while keeping a low profile on the multilateral one. This is because active engagement with the Quad would be construed as a hard balancing mechanism that India does not want to engage in as of now. For New Delhi, a strong maritime security cooperation with Japan is not only to enhance India's primacy in the Indian Ocean but also to establish its strategic presence in both Southeast Asia and the Western Pacific. On the other hand, for Japan, a robust regional security network with India and other friendly countries in the region would not just protect its interests but also deter China from using its military for coercive purposes in the future. Such a partnership will also enhance Japan's ambition of being a 'normal' military power with a good relationship with major countries in the international system.

In fact, the cooperation of defence forces at various levels will enhance the effectiveness of the balancing strategy. Both India and Japan are now gradually stepping up their naval cooperation to make the balancing process more fruitful. When the Indian Defence Minister Rajnath Singh visited Japan in September 2019, both countries decided to strengthen maritime security cooperation to further promote the idea of a 'free and open Indo-Pacific', with an eye on countering China's creeping assertiveness over the water body.[77] In the 11th Annual Summit Meeting between Narendra Modi, and Shinzo Abe, held in October 2018, India and Japan decided to begin negotiations for the Acquisition and Cross-Servicing Agreement (ACSA) on the lines of India–US Logistics Exchange Memorandum of Agreement (LEMOA) inked in 2016.[78] The ACSA, signed in September 2020, facilitates the navies of both countries to use each other's bases, either at home or overseas, thereby fundamentally increasing each country's ability to sustain its presence in an expanded region.[79] Through this agreement, Indian warships operating in the

Western Pacific can refuel and replenish supplies at Japanese military bases, and Japanese ships in the Indian Ocean at Indian bases. This will ensure both navies broaden their scope of interaction and there will be greater synergy between the two which in turn will foster an understanding of each other's operational strategies. The agreement also allows India to use Japan's recently set-up military base in Djibouti, on the other side of the Indian Ocean. With Japanese support, the Indian Navy can conduct enhanced operations and frequent deployment of its naval ships in the Western Pacific akin to what the Chinese navy does in the IOR.

India and Japan have not yet been able to utilise the economic potential of maritime security cooperation in its fullest sense. The sustainability of security cooperation is also dependent on economic dividends which can accrue through trade in defence products, joint development of systems and technology transfers. On the one hand, Japan is not aggressive in searching for the right market for its defense products, while for India Japanese systems are too expensive. For instance, India has not been able to successfully purchase the Japanese US-2 ShinMaywa amphibious aircraft. If both countries work together to find a way out in this area, it would not only be beneficial for them but also for the region as a whole, and especially for Southeast Asian states that are enhancing their defence preparedness.

Conclusion

India–Japan maritime security cooperation has now become a determining factor in the security dynamics of the Indo-Pacific. As the Indian strategist Brahma Chellaney points out, the India–Japan partnership 'serves as the [linchpin] for establishing an Indo-Pacific order based on the principles of the rule of law, free trade, freedom of navigation and peaceful resolution of disputes'.[80] Unlike China, India and Japan are democratic states which pursue similar policies of transparency and openness, and prefer a rules-based order in the Indo-Pacific. Both countries oppose a single hegemonic dominance in Asia, while at the same time, want the US to remain committed to ensuring the security of the Indo-Pacific with a strong naval presence in the region. As India and Japan are secondary powers in Asia, their security and sovereignty would be heavily affected if China establishes hegemony in the Indo-Pacific region because hegemons would not allow peer competitors to challenge their position in the same region. In this regard, it is imperative for the secondary states to come together and ensure that China does not occupy a hegemonic position in the Indo-Pacific, and in a way, contain China's rise. Their synchronised voice should have significant weightage in defining and establishing the rules of the Indo-Pacific region, and shaping the evolving geostrategic landscape over the coming decades.

At the same time, a hard balancing in the form of a military alliance is unlikely to take place because the defence policies of the two countries are different from each other; Japan's defence policy is allied with the US security alliance system, while India follows a 'strategic autonomy' in its security strategy. Also, a hard balancing would provoke China which would affect the bilateral relationship with Beijing, something both countries want to avoid. At the same time, establishing a rules-based order in the Indo-Pacific is important for both India and Japan as their trade and security are inextricably linked with the developments in the maritime domain.

India and Japan need to strengthen their resources so that they remain the most powerful states in their own backyard, that is, the Indo-Pacific, and become a potential challenge for any power trying to assert dominance in the region. Instead of seeking for a coalition against China, the US can help enhance the capacity of India and Japan who can then be the first line of defence against China's ambitious expansionist strategy. If China were to implement its order in the Indo-Pacific, then it is India and Japan that are going to be affected the most as they are the nearest rivals of Beijing. The Chinese strategy is to ensure that there is no resistance from the regional countries so that it can marshal all its capabilities against the US. By becoming a strong deterrent against China individually as well as in a combined manner, India and Japan can bring about peace and security in the Indo-Pacific.

Notes and References

1. Gurpreet S. Khurana, 'Security of Sea Lines: Prospects for India–Japan Cooperation', *Strategic Analysis*, vol. 31, no. 1 (2007), pp. 139–153.
2. Ibid.
3. Zalmay Khalilzad, David T. Orletsky et al., 'The United States and Asia: Toward a New U.S. Strategy and Force Posture' (Santa Monica, CA: RAND

Corporation, 2001), available at https://www.rand.org/pubs/monograph_reports/MR1315.html, accessed on 8 September 2023.

4. Australian Government, *2017 Foreign Policy White Paper*, available at https://www.dfat.gov.au/sites/default/files/minisite/static/4ca0813c-585e-4fe1-86eb-de665e65001a/fpwhitepaper/foreign-policy-white-paper/prime-ministers-introduction.html, accessed 20 December 2020.

5. Department of Defense, USA, 'Indo-Pacific Strategy Report: Preparedness, Partnerships, and Promoting a Networked Region', 1 June 2019, available at https://media.defense.gov/2019/Jul/01/2002152311/-1/-1/1/DEPARTMENT-OF-DEFENSE-INDO-PACIFIC-STRATEGY-REPORT-2019.PDF, accessed on 30 November 2020.

6. You Ji, 'Deciphering Beijing's Maritime Security Policy and Strategy in Managing Sovereignty Disputes in the China Seas', *RSIS Policy Brief*, October 2013, available at https://www.rsis.edu.sg/rsis-publication/rsis/216-deciphering-beijings-maritime/#.XcFDxNR97Gg, accessed on 25 November 2020.

7. Joshy M. Paul, 'India–Japan maritime security cooperation: Secondary states' soft balancing in the Indo-Pacific', *Maritime Affairs*, vol. 15, no. 2 (2019), pp. 59–77.

8. Steven E. Lobell, Neal G. Jesse and Kristen P. Williams, 'Why do secondary states choose to support, follow or challenge?' *International Politics*, vol. 52, no. 2 (2015), p.148.

9. David R. Mares, 'Middle powers under hegemony: To challenge or acquiesce in hegemonic enforcement,' *International Studies Quarterly*, vol. 32, no. 4 (1988), pp. 453–471.

10. Daniel Flemesa and Leslie Wehner, 'Drivers of strategic contestation: The case of South America,' *International Politics*, vol. 52, no. 2 (2015), pp. 163–177.

11. Neal G. Jesse, Steven E. Lobell, Galia Press-Barnathan and Kristen P. Williams, 'The Leader Can't Lead When the Followers Won't Follow: The Limitations of Hegemony', in Kristen P. Williams, Steven E. Lobell and Neal G. Jesse, eds, *Beyond Great Powers and Hegemons: Why Secondary States Support, Follow or Challenge* (Stanford, CA: Stanford University Press, 2012), pp. 1–31.

12. Stephen M. Walt, 'Alliances in a Unipolar World', *World Politics*, vol. 61, no. 1 (2009), pp. 86–120.

13. T. V. Paul, 'Introduction: The enduring axioms of balance of power theory and their contemporary relevance', in T. V. Paul, James J. Wirtz and Michel Fortmann, eds, *Balance of Power: Theory and Practice in the 21st Century* (California: Stanford University Press, 2004), pp. 1–25.

14. Don Berlin, 'The rise of India and the Indian Ocean', *Journal of the Indian Ocean Region*, vol. 7, no. 1 (2011), pp. 1–31.

15. Vijay Sakhuja, 'Indo-Japanese Maritime Security Cooperation', *Strategic Analysis*, vol. 24, no. 1 (2000), pp. 187–89.

16. Ibid; Khurana, 'Security of Sea Lines'.

17. Joshy M. Paul, 'India–Japan Security Cooperation: A New Era of Partnership in Asia', *Maritime Affairs*, vol. 8, no. 1 (2012), pp. 31–50.

18. Ministry of Defence, Japan, *Defence of Japan 2011*, Annual White Paper (Tokyo: Government of Japan, 2011), p. 335.

19. Richard Bitzinger, 'Modernising China's Military, 1997-2012', *China Perspective*, vol. 4, no. 88 (2011), pp. 7–15.

20. Christopher W. Hughes, 'Japan's Re-emergence as a "Normal" Military Power', Adelphi Paper 368–9 (London: International Institute of Strategic Studies, 2004).

21. Ministry of Defence, Japan, 'National Defense Program Guideline, FY 2005-', 10 December 2004, p. 2–3, available at https://japan.kantei.go.jp/policy/2004/1210taikou_e.html, accessed on 8 September 2023.

22. Christopher W. Hughes, 'Japanese Military Modernization: In Search of a "Normal" Security Role', in Ashley J. Tellis and Michael Wills, eds, *Strategic Asia 2005-06: Military Modernization in an Era of Uncertainty* (Washington DC: The National Bureau of Asian Research, 2005), pp. 105–134.

23. Ibid.

24. Michael J. Green, *Japan's Reluctant Realism: Foreign Policy Challenges in an Era of Uncertain Power* (New York: Palgrave, 2001).

25. 'Mr. Abe's Pitch to the Diet', *The Japan Times*, 28 January 2007, p. 12.

26. Ministry of Foreign Affairs, Government of Japan, 'Confluence of the Two Seas: Speech by H.E. Mr. Shinzo Abe, Prime Minister of Japan at the Parliament of the Republic of India', 22 August 2007, available at http://www.mofa.go.jp/region/asia-paci/pmv0708/speech-2.html, accessed on 20 December 2020.

27. 'Arc of Freedom and Prosperity: Japan's Expanding Diplomatic Horizons, Speech by Mr. Taro Aso, Minister for Foreign Affairs on the Occasion of the Japan Institute of International Affairs Seminar', 30 November 2006, available at http://www.mofa.go.jp/announce/fm/aso/speech0611.html, accessed on 20 December 2020.

28. Thomas S. Wilkins, 'Japan's alliance diversification: A comparative analysis of the Indian and Australian strategic partnerships', *International Relations of the Asia-Pacific*, vol. 11, no. 1 (2011), pp. 115–155.

29. Shinzo Abe, 'Asia's Democratic Security Diamond', *Project Syndicate*, 27 December 2012, available at https://www.project-syndicate.org/magazine/a-strategic-alliance-for-japan-and-india-by-shinzo-abe?barrier=accesspaylog, accessed on 11 September 2023.

30. Saki Hayashi and Yosuke Onchi, 'Japan to propose dialogue with US, India and Australia', *Nikkei Asian Review*, 26 October 2017, available at https://asia.nikkei.com/Politics/Japan-to-propose-dialogue-with-US-India-and-Australia2, accessed on 15 October 2020.

31. Purnendra Jain, 'Japan–India Relations: Peaks and Troughs', *The Round Table*, vol. 99, no. 409 (2010), pp. 403–412.

32. Euan Graham, *Japan's Sea Lane Security, 1940–2004: A Matter of Life and Death* (London: Nissan Institute/Routledge, 2006), p. 24.

33. Raquel Shaoul, 'Japan's Changing Defense Policy: Military Deployment in the Persian Gulf', *Japanese Studies*, vol. 27, no. 3 (2007), pp. 231–246.

34. Tetsuo Kotani, 'Reluctant Seapower: Geopolitics in Asia and Japan's Maritime Strategy', in Peter Dutton, Robert Ross and Øystein Tunsjø, eds, *Twenty-First Century Seapower: Cooperation and Conflict at Sea* (London: Routledge, 2012), pp. 136–153.

35. Ministry of Defense, Japan, *National Defense Program Guidelines for FY 2011 and beyond*, 17 December 2010, available at https://japan.kantei.go.jp/kakugikettei/2010/ndpg.pdf, accessed on 11 September 2023.

36. Corey Wallace and Shogo Suzuki, 'Explaining Japan's response to geopolitical vulnerability', *International Affairs*, vol. 94, no. 4 (2018), pp. 711–734.

37. Corey Wallace, 'Leaving (north-east) Asia? Japan's southern strategy', *International Affairs*, vol. 94, no. 4 (2018), pp. 883–904.

38. Yasuhiro Matsuda, 'How to understand China's assertiveness since 2009: Hypotheses and policy implications', in Michael J. Green and Zack Cooper, eds, *Strategic Japan: New Approaches to Foreign Policy and the U.S.-Japan Alliance* (Maryland: Rowman & Littlefield, 2015), pp. 7–33.

39. Richard Q. Turcsányi, *Chinese Assertiveness in the South China Sea: Power Sources, Domestic Politics, and Reactive Foreign Policy* (Heidelberg: Springer, 2018).

40. Brahma Chellaney, 'Japan's Pivotal Role in the Emerging Indo-Pacific Order', *Asia-Pacific Review*, vol. 25, no. 1 (2018), pp. 38–51.

41. Laura Rosenberger, 'Can the U.S.-Japan Alliance Survive Trump?' *Foreign Policy*, 9 February 2017, available at https://foreignpolicy.com/2017/02/09/can-the-u-s-japan-alliance-survive-trump/, accessed on 15 June 2020.

42. Richard J. Samuels and Corey Wallace, 'Introduction: Japan's Pivot in Asia', *International Affairs*, vol. 94, no. 4 (2018), pp. 703–710.

43. Corey Wallace, 'Japan's strategic pivot south: Diversifying the dual hedge', *International Relations of the Asia-Pacific*, vol. 13, no. 3 (2013), pp. 479–517.

44. Ministry of Defense, Japan, *National Defense Program Guidelines for FY 2011*, p. 9.

45. Kenneth B. Pyle, 'Japan's Return to Great Power Politics: Abe's Restoration', *Asia Policy*, vol. 13, no. 2 (April 2018), pp. 69–90.

46. Prime Minister of Japan and His Cabinet, 'Address by Prime Minister Shinzo Abe at the Opening Session of the Sixth Tokyo International Conference on African Development (TICAD VI)', 27 August 2016, available at https://japan.kantei.go.jp/97_abe/statement/201608/1218850_11013.html, accessed on 15 November 2020.

47. Ministry of Foreign Affairs, Japan, 'Priority Policy for Development Cooperation FY2017' (Tokyo: Government of Japan, 2017), available at https://www.mofa.go.jp/files/000259285.pdf, accessed on 25 June 2020.

48. Frank-Jurgen Richter, 'The alternative to Chinese debt for Africa from Japan and India', *Nikkei Asia*, 23 November 2018, available at https://asia.nikkei.com/Opinion/The-alternative-to-Chinese-debt-for-Africa-from-Japan-and-India, accessed on 15 June 2020.

49. Michael J. Green, 'Japan's "Free and Open Indo-Pacific Strategy" as Grand Strategy', *We are Tomodachi*, Spring 2018, pp. 28–29, available at https://www.japan.go.jp/letters/ebook72/book.pdf, accessed on 15 May 2020.

50. Indian Navy, *Indian Maritime Doctrine* (Integrated Headquarters, Ministry of Defence [Navy], New Delhi: 2009), p. 62.

51. Indian Navy, *Freedom to Use the Seas: India's Maritime Military Strategy* (Integrated Headquarters, Ministry of Defence [Navy], New Delhi: 2007), p. iv.

52. R. Prasannan, 'We aim to be a 200-ship navy in a decade: Interview/ Admiral Sunil Lanba, Chief of Naval Staff', *The Week*, 17 December 2017, available at https://www.theweek.in/theweek/current/we-aim-to-be-a-200-ship-navy-in-a-decade.html, accessed on 11 November 2020.

53. Walter C. Ladwig III, 'Delhi's Pacific Ambition: Naval Power, "Look East", and India's Emerging Influence in the Asia-Pacific', *Asian Security*, vol. 5, no. 2 (2009), pp. 87–113.

54. C. Raja Mohan, *Samudra Manthan: Sino-Indian Rivalry in the Indo-Pacific* (Washington D.C.: Carnegie Endowment for International Peace, 2012).

55. Joshy M. Paul, 'India's Maritime Pivot to the East', *The Diplomat*, 8 March 2018, available at https://thediplomat.com/2018/03/indias-maritime-pivot-to-the-east/, accessed on 15 June 2020.

56. Dipanjan Roy Chaudhury, 'China objects to the presence of Indian ships in South China Sea', *The Economic Times*, 13 July 2018, available at https://economictimes.indiatimes.com/articleshow/52369749.cms?utm_source=contentofinterest&utm_medium=text&utm_campaign=cppst, accessed on 27 December 2020.

57. Ananth Krishnan, 'China says India-Singapore South China Sea drills "should not hurt interests of other countries"', *India Today*, 19 May 2017, available at https://www.indiatoday.in/world/story/south-china-sea-india-singaporemilitary-sea-drills-977985-2017-05-19, accessed on 15 June 2020.

58. In October 1999, a Japanese merchant ship MV *Alondra Rainbow* was hijacked in the Malacca Strait, and in November, the same year, it was recovered off the coast of Goa in a joint operation by the Indian Navy and the Coast Guard.

59. Ministry of Foreign Affairs of Japan, 'Details of the meetings held between Minister of Defence George Fernandes of the Republic of India and Chief Cabinet

Mikio Aoki and Director-General Tsutomu Kawara of the Defense Agency', Press Conference by the Press Secretary, 12 January 2000, available at https://www.mofa.go.jp/announce/press/2000/1/112.html,accessed on 15 December 2020.

60. Paul, 'India–Japan Security Cooperation'.

61. 'Coast Guards of India, Japan hold joint naval exercise', *The Economic Times*, 17 January 2018, available at https://economictimes.indiatimes.com/news/defence/coast-guards-of-india-japan-hold-joint-navalexercise/articleshow/62541689.cms, accessed on 18 December 2020.

62. Kawaguchi Yoriko, cited in Madhuchanda Ghosh, 'India and Japan's Growing Synergy', *Asian Survey*, vol. 48, no. 2 (2008), pp. 287–88.

63. Ministry of Foreign Affairs, Tokyo, 'Japan-India Partnership in a New Asian Era: Strategic Orientation of Japan-India Global Partnership', 29 April 2005, available at https://www.mofa.go.jp/region/asia-paci/india/partner0504.html#:~:text=Japan%20and%20India%20share%20a,partnership%20between%20the%20two%20countries., accessed on 12 September 2023.

64. Ministry of Foreign Affairs, Tokyo, 'Action Plan to advance Security Cooperation based on the Joint Declaration on Security Cooperation between Japan and India', 29 December 2009, available at https://www.mofa.go.jp/region/asia-paci/india/pmv0912/action.html, accessed on 15 December 2020.

65. Prime Minister's Office, Government of Japan, 'National Security Strategy', 17 December 2013, p. 24, available at http://japan.kantei.go.jp/96_abe/documents/2013/__icsFiles/afieldfile/2013/12/17/NSS.pdf, accessed on 16 December 2020.

66. Prakash Panneerselvam, 'India-Japan Maritime Security Cooperation (1999–2009): A Report', *JMSDF Staff College Review*, vol. 2 (2013), pp. 67–112, available at https://www.mod.go.jp/msdf/navcol/assets/pdf/ssg2013_06_00.en.pdf, accessed on 15 December 2020.

67. 'Japanese Naval Ships to Visit India from Aug. 23-26', *One India*, 20 August 2008, available at https://www.oneindia.com/2008/08/20/japanese-naval-ships-aug-23-26-1219241100.html accessed on 12 September 2023.

68. Wallace, 'Japan's strategic pivot south'.

69. Sun Cheng, 'A Comparative Analysis of Abe's and Fukuda's Asia Diplomacy', *China International Studies*, no. 10 (Spring 2008), pp. 58–72.

70. Press Information Bureau, 'First Bilateral Maritime Exercise between India and Japan "Jimex 12" to Commence on 09 Jun 12', 8 June 2012, available at http://pib.gov.in/newsite/PrintRelease.aspx?relid=84780, accessed on 12 September 2023.

71. *East Asian Strategic Review 2013*, National Institute for Defense Studies (Tokyo, Japan: *The Japan Times*, 2013), p. 57, available at https://www.nids.mod.go.jp/english/publication/east-asian/e2013.html, accessed on 22 February 2024.

72. Indian Navy, 'Malabar 2014: A Multilateral Naval Exercise Starts', available at https://www.indiannavy.nic.in/content/malabar-2014-multilateral-naval-exercise-starts, accessed on 15 December 2020.

73. The White House, 'U.S.-India Joint Statement', 30 September 2014, available at https://obamawhitehouse.archives.gov/the-press-office/2014/09/30/us-india-joint-statement, accessed on 25 December 2020.

74. Indian Navy, 'Indo-US Exercise - Malabar 15', available at https://www.indiannavy.nic.in/content/indo-us-exercise-malabar-15-0, accessed on 25 December 2020.

75. 'Malabar Exercise 2020: India joins the US, Japan, Australia for Quad's naval war game; Check details', *Financial Express*, 3 November 2020, available at https://www.financialexpress.com/defence/malabar-exercise-2020-india-joins-the-us-japan-australia-for-quads-naval-war-game-check-details/2120055/, accessed on 25 December 2020.

76. Aditi Malhotra, 'Engagement, not Entanglement: India's Relationship with the Quad', *Georgetown Journal of International Affairs*, 1 May 2023, available at https://gjia.georgetown.edu/2023/05/01/engagement-not-entanglement-indias-relationship-with-the-quad/, accessed on 1 October 2023.

77. *The Japan Times*, 'Japan and India defense chiefs seeking to boost cooperation, says Defense Minister Takeshi Iwaya after meet', 3 September 2019, available at https://www.japantimes.co.jp/news/2019/09/03/national/politics-diplomacy/japan-india-defense-chiefs-seek-boost-cooperation/#.XW3nYLhGTRw, accessed on 25 December 2020.

78. Ajai Shukla, 'PM Modi, Shinzo Abe summit could kick off defence logistic support pact', *Business Standard*, 23 October 2018, available at https://www.business-standard.com/article/current-affairs/pm-modi-shinzo-abe-summit-could-kick-off-defence-logistic-support-pact-118102300047_1.html#:~:text=PM%20Modi%2C%20Shinzo%20Abe%20summit%20could%20kick%20off%20defence%20logistic%20support%20pact,-Ajai%20Shukla%20%7C%20New&text=ACSA%20is%20the%20traditional%20term,supplies%20from%20Japanese%20military%20bases, accessed on 22 December 2020.

79. Rezaul H. Laskar, 'India, Japan ink pact to bolster defence forces', *Hindustan Times*, 10 September 2020, available at https://www.hindustantimes.com/india-news/india-japan-ink-pact-to-bolster-defence-forces/story-xOCacyTP5OIADoqruteQBI.html, accessed on 25 December 2020.

80. Brahma Chellaney, 'The linchpins for a rules-based Indo-Pacific', *The Japan Times*, 25 October 2018, available at https://www.japantimes.co.jp/opinion/2018/10/25/commentary/japan-commentary/linchpins-rules-based-indo-pacific/, accessed on 25 December 2020.

eight

India, Japan and the US

Shaping Strategic Discourse in the Indo-Pacific

SAYANTAN HALDAR

The unprecedented rise of the Indo-Pacific narrative has been a major development in contemporary geopolitics. In this rubric, the emergence of an assertive China has been at the heart of the geostrategic cooperation between India, Japan and the US. This chapter argues that despite India and Japan having major stakes in the Indo-Pacific by virtue of their geographical rationale, their proactive role within Asia, especially in light of China's rise, can be traced back to the 'Pivot to Asia' doctrine. This chapter will look at the 'rise and return' of the Indo-Pacific and argue that the strategic partnership between New Delhi, Tokyo and Washington has so far been based purely on their felt need to securitise the region, manifested in terms of the Quadrilateral Security Dialogue (Quad/QSD) and the Malabar Exercise. There is yet much to do on the economic front. This can be explained by the absence of India and the US in the Regional Comprehensive Economic Partnership (RCEP), despite Japan's core position in the partnership. Even though there have been various bilateral economic engagements among India, Japan and the US, there needs to be a more robust trilateral economic partnership between them, which can result in a cemented strategic convergence to take on China's mighty rise.

The rise of the concept of the 'Indo-Pacific' has been one of the most dynamic developments in contemporary global politics. The relevance of this emergent development can be mapped by taking cognisance of the variety of pressing issues that have overlapped to form its manifestation. As the world turns towards Asia to map its instrumental role in shaping the overall geopolitical discourse, the Indo-Pacific has stood out as one of the key areas that are likely to heavily inform the debate. Firstly, let us look at the players involved in the region. Sitting at the heart of Asia, by virtue of geographical rationale, it is obvious that the region will involve major players which in turn shape a majority of Asian geopolitics. The Indo-Pacific has seen active engagement from Asian countries like Japan and India, as well as countries such as the US and Australia which contribute significantly to the geopolitical profile of the region. China has been another major player that has guided the geopolitical relevance of the Indo-Pacific. As President Xi Jinping has articulated, China has laid out its aim to emerge as the Asian giant with intentions to become a global leader. In this pursuit, China has actively engaged in expanding its remit of influence in the region which has caused a new wave of geopolitical and geostrategic tension among the leading Asian players. In a similar vein, the felt need of securitisation of the region has increasingly gained momentum in the strategic calculus among the leading regional players.[1]

With the gradually increasing relevance of maritime security, the geopolitical theatre of maritime Asia has witnessed an escalation of strategic importance. India, the US and Japan have been staunch advocates of a 'norm-based' Indo-Pacific which is free, open and fair.[2] Contrary to this, China has been engaged in the act of claiming major parts of the region as its own, citing its historical roots. In order to have a deeper understanding of this, the Indo-Pacific must foremost be located in its geographical as well as historical context. Geographically speaking, the Indo-Pacific is largely understood as a net manifestation of the 'confluence' of the Indian Ocean Region and the Asia Pacific. This was first prompted in 2007, by Japan's then Prime Minister Shinzo Abe, during his speech 'Confluence of the Two Seas' in the Indian Parliament.[3] Rahul Roy-Chaudhury and Kate Sullivan de Estrada describe the contours of the Indo-Pacific as a 'vital and contiguous strategic arena' between the Indian and Pacific oceans.[4] The idea and relevance of the Indo-Pacific gained prominence gradually since the end of the Cold War. However, Manjeet S. Pardesi reveals in his influential work on the Indo-Pacific that there is nothing new or unnatural about the concept of Indo-Pacific; in fact, he characterises the regained prominence of the region as a 'return of history'.[5] In India's strategic circles, Gurpreet S. Khurana's seminal work on the 'rise and return' of the Indo-Pacific has guided a significant body of literature on the concept.[6] According to Khurana, Indo-Pacific found its early articulation as representing the 'non-Atlantic view of the world'.[7] However, security became the 'contemporary driver' of the concept. In a world order characterised by the US's leading role, the concept of the

Indo-Pacific also gained ground due to Washington's strategy for Asia. With President Barack Obama's articulation of 'Pivot to Asia' in 2011, its Asian allies, namely Japan and India among others, gained strategic prominence, especially in light of an ever-assertive China. This chapter argues that even though the concept of the Indo-Pacific figured in the strategic circles of India and Japan, the contemporary geopolitical developments in the region can be largely traced back to the pivot strategy which encouraged a robust engagement of major players in Asia. As a result of this, countries like India and Japan have also articulated their strategic interests in the region in a reinvigorated manner. Both New Delhi and Tokyo have high stakes in the region by virtue of their geographical centrality. India, Japan and the United States have found common ground to forge a strong strategic partnership in the face of a rising China. Towards this end, the Indo-Pacific has emerged as the hot bed of geopolitical competition and contestation. This has also led to an intensive geostrategic cooperation between the US and its Asian allies to securitise the region. Various initiatives like the Quad and the Malabar Exercise have been undertaken to give shape to security cooperation between the three countries. The following sections will demonstrate that even though the US's pivot strategy has been instrumental in initiating cooperation with local players in Asia, it is now important and essential for Asian powers like Japan and India to sustain this cooperation in order to contain China. Even though the US is a major player in the region, the contours of contemporary Asian geopolitics will be inevitably shaped by Asian powers such as India and Japan, among others. However, first, it is important to contextualise the problem against the backdrop of 'Pivot to Asia'.

Pivot to Asia: Contemporary Discourse

The critical role played by the US and its Asian allies, including India and Japan, can be traced back to Barack Obama's flagship foreign policy initiative, the 'pivot to Asia'. This strategy gained a lot of attention as it aimed at establishing the contours of interaction, both political and diplomatic, of the US, which is the world's largest economy, with Asia, which has long been projected as the focal point of geopolitics in the 21st century. However, it is also important to reflect on why there was a need to design such a strategy. Here, it must be noted that, with the increasing difficulties fuelled by the financial crises in the preceding decade and the military over-stretch, the US's strategy to maintain its looming presence in Asia, without having an explicitly proactive role, was given shape with its 'pivot'.[8] Even though the strategy involved interaction with China, Washington's foreign policy towards Asia has been largely premised on countering Beijing's overtures. As a part of Washington's strategy to sustain a world order led by the US, containing China has been one of its foremost priorities in recent times. In the face of an assertive China, India and Japan have emerged as 'pivotal' players as a part of the US's vision for Asia.

Beijing's rise as a major player has been catalysed by its prolific economic growth. In 2010, China surpassed Japan to become the second largest economy in the world.[9] This rise is also marked by a shift in China's foreign policy. China's foreign policy under President Xi Jinping has emphasised his Chinese dream which is guided by the need for a 'national rejuvenation'. Beijing has focused on characterising Asia, and especially its neighbouring regions—both territorial and maritime—as contours of its geopolitical preponderance. China's increasing assertiveness in the South China Sea and East Asia is premised on the belief that increased Chinese power should translate into increased control, even at the expense of its neighbours' sovereignty.[10] Therefore, China's view of the extensive engagement of the US in the Indo-Pacific has predominantly been marked by a threat perception. This has prompted a Sino-US geostrategic competition for primacy in the region. In this context, the US's pivot strategy of privileging a proactive role of its allies in the region is strategically crucial. Firstly, China's claim of preponderance in the Indo-Pacific is largely driven by its historical stake in the region. In this context, to have a robust network of local allies would be strategically beneficial for the US. Secondly, it is important for the US to ensure that local players in Asia establish a strong opposition to Chinese rise, which would in turn also shape how other smaller countries in the region, who may otherwise be susceptible to China, react to its rise. Thirdly, the US's current leadership has been characterised primarily by its reluctance to proactively engage with geopolitical issues in Asia. This can be seen in the US's growing apathy to sustain its security arrangements with Japan and the Korean peninsula without a burden-sharing model. Going back to the origins of the pivot strategy, one of the key issues that the leadership in Washington has prioritised is the US's need to involve its partners in its foreign policy vision. Similarly, from Washington's perspective, having a more involved and invested India and Japan would result in a win-win situation for itself. However, this should not be misunderstood as the US's reluctance to engage in the Indo-Pacific. Washington has repeatedly exhibited its willingness to counter China's rise, albeit for its own geopolitical interests. But how does the concept of the Indo-Pacific and involvement of India and Japan fit into the US's foreign policy vision? In this light, Joshy M. Paul highlights that strong cooperation between India and Japan would prompt the US to focus on China while not having to worry about sustaining its own security alliances.[11] According to Timothy Doyle and Dennis Rumley, the US has constructed the Indo-Pacific in a 'geo-political sense' which is instrumental in serving the 'economic, military and national interests' of Trump's '"America first" promise'.[12]

However, before looking further into the USA's strategy to counter China using the 'pivot', it is important to critically examine the very idea of 'Pivot to Asia' as a concept as well as a policy. Even though strategic circles in India have largely been positively inclined towards India assuming a leading role in the region, there has been some scepticism about the concept of the pivot. India's own geopolitical ambition of being a regional leader has been guided by its robust economy as well as a more concerted effort undertaken by the leadership in New Delhi to proactively engage in its neighbourhood. In this context, New Delhi's enthusiasm with the US's Asia Policy can be well understood. Similarly, Japan's enthusiasm regarding the Indo-Pacific has been unprecedented and the US's strategy aligns with its own geopolitical interests and its perceived security dilemma. As China articulates its assertions in its neighbourhood, the regional players have increasingly felt the need to have a robust security engagement among themselves. However, scholars have also critically reflected on Obama's handling of his own strategy. While there was general agreement on the legitimacy of such a design, his record of translating rhetoric into practice remained poor. This legacy has been carried forward by his successor, Donald Trump. Michal Kolmaš and Šárka Kolmašová observe that there has been no tangible development on this front in the Trump era.[13] These fundamental questions regarding the pivot strategy have cast a shadow on its future. What will be the US's role in Asia? What will strategic cooperation between India, Japan and the US look like? These are the central questions that dominate the discourse on the future of Asia. In this light, the Indo-Pacific has emerged as an important site of contestation, which, in ways, will be instrumental in shaping the larger discourse of Asian geopolitics in the times to come. Building on this analysis, this chapter will argue that even though the pivot strategy was largely instrumental in shaping India and Japan as counteractive forces to China in the region, the US's growing reluctance to solely engage in Asia as well as the emergence of the Asian powers have now made it inevitable for New Delhi and Tokyo to lead the efforts in containing China. India and Japan's extensive engagement in the region has been increasingly driven by their respective strategic interests in the Indo-Pacific. Therefore, while the US remains an important force in Asia, it alone cannot articulate the geopolitical trajectory of the region without active engagement from its Asian partners and allies. This, coupled with the US's inward turn with its 'America First' policy, has posited India, Japan and the US at a unique situation where the regional powers have emerged as important players, especially in the context of the Indo-Pacific. The privileging of the regional players has in turn prompted a geopolitical competition within Asia. India and Japan have emerged as two crucial players, opposing China's rise. Apart from occupying a crucial place in the US's pivot design, India and Japan have their respective historical engagements with China which has further shaped their foreign policies towards Beijing. The historical linkages have also informed the contemporary geostrategic competition between the different Asian countries in the Indo-Pacific.

Maritime Asia: Site of Contestation

This chapter is premised on the understanding of an increasing strategic relevance of Asia, especially in the maritime space. With Asian countries rising to prominence in the global network of trade, the regional maritime linkages of connectivity have gained renewed importance. For instance, the IOR has been at the centre of India's geopolitical imagination as it forges trade, connectivity and security ties with Southeast Asia, East Asia as well as Africa. Similarly for Japan and China, the maritime domain has been the focus of their geopolitical strategy to build on their respective connectivity linkages to facilitate trade and cultural exchanges. In a similar vein, the idea of the Indo-Pacific has drawn humungous attention in recent times. With the blooming of centres for economic engagement in Asia, the regional maritime space has gained significant prominence.

The Indo-Pacific Region houses crucial networks of maritime trade and connectivity which makes it an important area that will shape the great regional game. China's attempts to make use of the maritime space in order to transcend some of its major territorial long routes demonstrate its vision for the region. As China gears up to expand volumes of its trade, security and cultural exchanges with its partners in the neighbouring regions as well as Africa, it has emphasised on escalating its assertiveness in the regional maritime space. Similarly, India, Japan and the US have increasingly articulated their maritime engagement strategy. Trade and commerce have emerged as the primary area in which the maritime domain has opened new routes for these countries. The US has been one of the oldest players in the region and holds a pivotal place in the larger geostrategic architecture of the Indo-Pacific. However, with the onset of a more proactive engagement by both India and Japan, the regional maritime space has become a site for converging trade routes and maritime networks. India, for example, has found new rigour in articulating its maritime strategy in the IOR. This has also been prompted by the USA's concerted effort to 'de-centre' China and to privilege India in an American world order.[14] According to Sumit Ganguly, New Delhi will only occasionally exhibit keen interest in endowing itself with the 'responsibility to protect' in the Indian Ocean, subject to the confluence of capabilities, self-interest and normative concerns.[15] However, in the context of the Indo-Pacific, Pooja Bhatt argues that India should play the role of a 'consensus builder' in building unity before exhibiting the 'responsibility to protect'.[16] In this light, the rhetoric of the 'Indian Ocean as India's ocean' has gained significant momentum. New Delhi's articulation of this new strategy has been observed by many in the strategic circles as a part of its ambition to evolve from being just a 'balancer' in the region to a leading player. Similarly, Japan's foreign policy, especially under its former Prime Minister, Shinzo Abe, has been guided by its economic rationale. This shows that Tokyo has reinvigorated its focus on its maritime vision. Trade routes through the seas have been one of the most characteristic features of the emergent centrality of the Asian players. Here, it must also be taken into cognisance that most of the countries involved in the region are littoral states, which makes them relevant stakeholders in the great maritime game.

Despite the economic and commercial rationale forming the primary basis for the Asian countries' heightened engagement in the seas, the contesting claims and strategies have necessitated a more securitised outlook in their respective maritime strategies. This can be understood by focusing on the nature of engagement between the major players in the region. The following sections of the chapter will argue that despite there being an economic basis to these countries' interests in the Indo-Pacific, it is in fact the geostrategic competition between the US and China that has shaped a majority of their internal engagement.

With maritime space being a crucial site for geopolitical contestation, China's 'expansive' intention has led to major claim disputes in the Pacific and the Indian oceans.[17] A number of countries including India, Japan as well as member countries of the Association of the South East Asian Nations (ASEAN) like Philippines and Indonesia have been at the receiving end of China's encroachment practices.[18] Before discussing the maritime geostrategic competition in the Pacific and Indian oceans due to the varied geopolitical interests in the region between China, India, Japan, the US and others, it is important to reflect on the rationale that is guiding China's behaviour in the region. China has charted a path of unprecedented economic development over the years that can be traced back to the end of the 1970s. China's growing economic profile has necessitated that it broaden its horizon of commercial engagement with its partner countries not just in its neighbourhood, but also beyond. Establishing a strong network of connectivity routes has therefore become a fundamental geostrategic imperative guiding Beijing's foreign policy objective. In this context, the Chinese, under President Xi Jinping, have designed their pet globalisation project: the Belt and Road Initiative. Through this initiative, China intends to retrace its historical trade linkages spread across the world, across continents, from Asia to Europe and Africa. Ever since this plan was announced in 2013, China has significantly invested towards its implementation which has involved a great deal of emphasis on trade and connectivity through sea routes. Maritime connectivity has thus been an integral part of China's grand strategy. China's economic growth has also in turn led to a renewed focus on expanding its trade ties in volume. To this end, Beijing has shifted its development focus towards the domain of connectivity. Maritime connectivity in particular has seen a sharp rise in engagement from Beijing as well as other rising powers. As mentioned earlier, China's maritime imagination has been centred on its historical claims in its littoral sphere. However, most of China's claims have been met with contestation from its neighbouring countries. But what is unique in contemporary Chinese assertiveness is its military might. China, under Xi Jinping, has seen the manifestation of a prolonged process of military modernisation. Therefore, Beijing's expansive economic ambitions, coupled with its military assertiveness, have led to China emerging as a country with a strong military presence, especially in the maritime space. This has inevitably complicated the on-going geostrategic competition in the region. The economic nature of the competition has evolved into a geostrategic competition for primacy with the addition of military dynamics. This has also cautioned the other players in the region, for whom securitisation has become one of the primary areas of engagement in order to counter China. The US and its Asian allies have been at the forefront to tackle this military assertiveness.

Mapping the US–India–Japan Partnership in the Indo-Pacific

Washington's strategy in the Indo-Pacific, especially under Donald Trump, has been premised on the need to balance China's military assertiveness in the region. US's counter-balancing efforts vis-à-vis China are based on certain elements in the larger political structure that guide the discourse of global politics. A majority of analysts in Washington, New Delhi and Tokyo have pointed out certain fundamental differences between China and themselves based on their political orientation. Beijing's assertiveness is largely seen as a part of its larger effort to fortify its military positions in the maritime sphere in the Indo-Pacific region, with the ultimate aim to establish itself as the leading player in the region. This coupled with a coercive attitude that is based on Beijing's alleged encroachment efforts and misappropriation of others' territories, manifested in terms of territorial disputes, have projected Beijing as a coercive rising power with no respect for norms, which are the backbone of global order. Contrary to this, the US and its allies, India and Japan, have been viewed as the harbingers of an orderly arrangement in the Indo-Pacific. Their engagement has been portrayed as a coming together of robust democracies in the face of an authoritarian China. Therefore, it can be seen as a contest of political values that has manifested in this geopolitical competition. The US, India and Japan have articulated their vision for the region which is based on freedom of navigation as well as mutual respect for each other's territories, which has been spelt out at a rhetorical level through the concept of a 'free and open Indo-Pacific'. One of the binding factors for the US and its allies has been the need to create a 'rules-based order' in the region that would facilitate greater trade and connectivity engagements. This comes in contrast to the coercive assertiveness of China in the region. The US, hailed as the leader of the liberal world order, has emphasised the need for a rules-based and open Indo-Pacific as it best represents its regional strategic interests. Similarly, Japan's idea of maritime navigation has also been guided by its persistence of a rules-based order which would secure its maritime space in the face of an encroaching China. India too has now shed light on its maritime vision which follows the rules-based order. According to Ian Hall, one of the most significant changes brought by the Narendra Modi government in 2014 was the 'adoption of the language' of a rules-based order.[19] The US has been trying to consolidate its allies based on the commonality in their visions of a norms-based region without any sort of coercive aggression akin to what China practises.

Let us now focus on India and Japan, two of the US's central allies in its vision for Asia. Both India and Japan have a significant stake in the Indo-Pacific and they have accordingly articulated their vision for the region. Here, at the outset, it must be understood that Japan has been one of the first countries to have explicitly pushed for an Indo-Pacific 'narrative'. Japan, under Shinzo Abe, has seen tremendous economic growth which has made it an important stakeholder in the future of the region. Because of its longstanding territorial disputes, Japan positions itself crucially to ensure that the region is adequately securitised to avoid any kind of unprecedented Chinese aggression. US–Japan ties have long dominated Tokyo's vision for its security architecture. In the case of the Indo-Pacific too, Japan has advocated for a strong strategic partnership among regional countries with aligning interests to protect their freedom of navigation in the face of an aggressive and assertive China. The 'free and open Indo-Pacific' doctrine has since Abe's time been at the heart of Japan's regional geopolitical vision. However, with the change in Tokyo's leadership, it is important to keep an eye on how Japan continues to articulate its strategic vision for the Indo-Pacific. One of the key concerns dominating Tokyo's strategic thinking has been its economic engagement with partner countries. Like most of the US's allies, Japan too has been heavily invested in reimagining its economic and strategic partnerships with Washington's 'inward' turn to domestic politics. Shinzo Abe has been a key figure in charting a new economic trajectory for Tokyo. Abe's leadership in matters of Japan's economic and strategic choices have been exemplary in shaping its contemporary geopolitical profile. The term 'Abenomics' has been used to define his economic vision for Japan. However, it must be understood that much of Japan's strategic choices are still premised on its partnership with the US, which in a sense has been the leading player in Japan's security architecture. However, with the rise of China and in the face of Donald Trump's reluctance to be a leading player in managing the security framework in Japan as well as in the Korean peninsula, Tokyo has found itself in a unique position with the responsibility to make critical choices that would shape its future economic and security profile in the region. Additionally, Japan has made consistent efforts in expanding its trade networks to ensure greater engagement with India and Africa.

One of the most significant turns in Japan's strategic thinking has been its reorientation with regards to its security policy. Traditionally, the US–Japan relationship has defined the contours of Japan's security policy. However, with the onset of the Trump administration and Washington being vocal about Japan's over-dependence on the US, Tokyo has had to reimagine its security framework. This can be substantiated by looking at Japan's steady increase in its defence budget over the years, especially in the air and maritime arenas. Some scholars have noted that this might well be considered as the watershed moment in Japanese security framework.[20] This is also in line with Japan's strategic vision for economic development. Considering Japan's economic engagement with Southeast Asia, India and Africa, the Indo-Pacific is a crucial area which Tokyo should secure in order to successfully carry out its trade and connectivity initiatives.

Let us now turn to another important player, India. According to many strategic thinkers, India has a prime role in giving shape to the idea of an 'Asian century'.[21] New Delhi's geopolitical ambitions have seen a steady rise with the turn of the century. According to Harsh V. Pant, India's strategic thinking has seen a shift in wanting to become a leading power in its region rather than a mere balancer to great power politics.[22] Under Prime Minister Modi, India has been engaged in articulating its robust foreign policy vision within its neighbourhood as well as within the extended remit of its influence. This can be understood as not just a result of New Delhi's shift in strategic thinking, but also as a response to China's growing presence in the region. India continues to view South Asia as its 'sphere of influence', often emphasising the 'India-centric' character of the region.[23] With China's robust engagement with countries in South Asia, like Pakistan, Sri Lanka and Nepal, India has found it imperative to design its own network of trade, connectivity and security initiatives to assert its regional dominance. This has manifested through several initiatives undertaken by New Delhi aimed at highlighting India's preponderance in the region. The 'Neighbourhood First' policy is one such initiative, which intends to privilege India's neighbouring countries in its foreign policy vision. Other such initiatives include the rejuvenation of the Bay of Bengal Initiative for Multi-Sectoral Technical and Economic Cooperation (BIMSTEC) as well as the Act East Policy that prioritises India's engagement with Southeast Asia. Several scholars have pointed out that these initiatives can be seen as a response to China's extensive engagement with India's 'sphere of influence'.[24] In this context, the maritime space has been one of the prime areas of focus for New Delhi. Historically, the IOR has been at the heart of India's maritime vision as India is uniquely placed at the centre of the region. Much of New Delhi's new calibrated efforts of establishing itself as a regional leader are premised on the maritime domain. These include initiatives such as Project Mausam which aimed to revive the historical 'spice route' and the Chabahar Port project. India's strategic partnerships are also heavily based on the adjoining maritime space in the Indian Ocean and beyond. One significant instance is that of the Asia-Africa Growth Corridor (AAGC) project with Japan, which entails a sea corridor linking Africa with India and other countries of South-East Asia and Oceania. India has envisioned similar engagements with other countries such as Australia, Malaysia and Indonesia. The Indo-Pacific has thus emerged as a potential opportunity for New Delhi to coordinate with partner countries in the region with aligning interests. Former Indian Foreign Secretary Harsh V. Shringla posited that 'an Indo-Pacific guided by norms and governed by rules, with freedom of navigation, open connectivity, and respect for territorial integrity and sovereignty of all states, is an article of faith for India'.[25] While historically, India has been ambiguous in terms of addressing the China question, the recent confrontations between the two neighbouring giants have been instrumental in India's unprecedented articulation of its Indo-Pacific vision. In 2018, Narendra Modi advocated for a 'free and open Indo-Pacific', asserting its objection to China's coercive attitude in the region.[26] However, there has been an interesting development in the region at the 35th ASEAN summit, held in Bangkok in 2019, where India withdrew from the RCEP, which was designed as a Free Trade Agreement (FTA) and considered the economic cornerstone of the Indo-Pacific narrative. This then bears the question: What is the reason behind this divergence in New Delhi's engagement amidst the confluence of alignments?

Security and Economy: Stock-Taking Strategic Divergences

It is important to look at the economic and security considerations of the leading players in the Indo-Pacific domain. A coherent vision and policy would entail common ground between the two domains of economic and security policy. However, what is visible in India's engagement in the region is that New Delhi's vision for the Indo-Pacific as a geoeconomic theatre and a security landscape are different. However, this is not true for its partners, the US and Japan. Let us now analyse this argument by looking at New Delhi's foreign policy towards the region. The looming threat of China in the region necessitates that stakeholder countries like India, Japan and the US have a holistic approach in combating Beijing's assertiveness. This would entail a robust strategic partnership among the allies. However, New Delhi's approach towards the Indo-Pacific appears to be fragmented and non-uniform based on the domain of engagement in question. This can be understood by New Delhi's simultaneous reluctance to participate in the RCEP, which is the single-largest FTA programme binding the major players in the Indo-Pacific, and eager enthusiasm for the Quad, a security arrangement between India, Japan, the US and Australia.

The Quad has emerged as one of the most important developments instrumental in shaping the Indo-Pacific discourse. Following the need to have a security arrangement in place, India, Japan, the US and Australia developed this mechanism to facilitate joint cooperation to securitise the region. This quadrilateral security dialogue is considered by many as the cornerstone of the Indo-Pacific, developed to combat an assertive China. Even though the Quad is not a new formulation, it was revived in 2017 on the sidelines of the ASEAN summit in Manila. Since then the Quad arrangement has received a lot of attention, not just from its participant countries, but also globally, from external players in Europe and Africa.

China's response to the Quad has been significant in terms of shaping the related geopolitical discourse. Beijing views the Quad as a potential hindrance to its expanding footprint in Asia. The anxiety with the security arrangement envisioned through Quad has been articulated by the Chinese who suspect it to be an 'Asian NATO'.[27] But what does the Quad truly entail? The mechanism should be seen as an attempt to consolidate security of the region. This necessitates further scrutiny of the nature of emergent discourse on the Indo-Pacific. The contemporary discourse on the Indo-Pacific is premised on the heightened security architecture that is shaping up owing to the active engagement of the central players in the region. Japan took the lead in framing the security architecture in the region, and Prime Minister Shinzo Abe has been instrumental in breathing life to the Quad. The coming together of the four major democracies of the region has attracted a lot of attention in strategic circles. India, Japan, the US and Australia have revived the conversation about securitising the region in order to combat China's heavy military and infrastructure deployment. However, it is also important to focus on the ideological opposition offered by the Quad countries to China. While Beijing is largely viewed as a unilateral coercive power with an aggressive attitude to expand its realm of influence, the Quad countries have emphasised their democratic value system. Therefore, China's opposition by the Quad countries has been posited as an attempt by democratic countries to resist Beijing's coercive behaviour. This has reiterated the notion that the Quad is a coming together of four democracies which advocate for an open and rules-based order in the region. The importance of having a norms-based Indo-Pacific, which is free and open, lies at the heart of the Quad's imagination of the region. A similar vein of thought can be found in Prime Minister Shinzo Abe's path-breaking speech, 'Confluence of the Two Seas', where he made a case for friendship among citizens of the democracies that lie on the opposite edges of the seas as an imperative to guide his vision for the future of Asia.[28] This has led to another major development among the member countries of the Quad: the initiation of the Malabar Exercise. The Malabar Exercise is a naval exercise which began in 1992 between India and the US and was later joined by Japan in 2007. However, Japan became a regular member of the exercise only since 2014. One of the most relevant developments of the Malabar Exercise which has received a lot of attention has been the addition of Australia to this joint naval exercise in 2020, which was held in the Bay of Bengal and the Arabian Sea. The addition of Australia to the drill marks the joint collaboration of the four countries for the first time in 13 years. Because of this, the discourse surrounding the Quad and the potential for a joint security architecture has gained a lot of steam. It can be argued that the Malabar Exercise could potentially be the building block for the institutionalisation of the Quad. Many scholars have argued that the Malabar Exercise, especially after the addition of Australia, can be seen as instrumental in fuelling the Quad narrative.[29]

However, despite there being enough ground of active engagement among India, Japan and the US, there have been significant divergences which merit further analysis. Firstly, it must be understood that the contemporary narrative about the Indo-Pacific region has a lot to do with cartographic imagination. Here it is important to see whether all the three nations are in agreement over defining the contours and scope of the Indo-Pacific. While Japan, under Shinzo Abe, took the lead in articulating the vision and scope of shaping the 'broader Asia', it is necessary to locate the divergences that have remained in the strategic thinking of the leading players. Tokyo has been one of the strongest advocates of the Indo-Pacific in explicit terms. As a part of Shinzo Abe's foreign policy vision, Japan has actively invoked the narrative. However, that is not true for the other partner countries. One of the primary reasons for the reluctance of the other countries to explicitly indulge in the Indo-Pacific narrative is the China factor. Engagement with China still remains an important and necessary element of the emergent maritime politics in the region. Therefore, India's stance on this issue has been tactical and calibrated. Rajesh Rajagopalan posits that India's strategy in the Indo-Pacific can be seen as 'evasive balancing'.[30] However, India's increasing contestation with China has had an effect on India's foreign policy vision for the Indo-Pacific. Since 2017, India and China have been directly engaged in border stand-offs and diplomatic disagreements. Even though both Narendra Modi and Xi Jinping have hosted each other for informal summits, scholars have argued that it has not been effective in facilitating amelioration of relations between the two neighbours.[31] The border stand-offs at Doklam and Ladakh in 2017 and 2020 respectively, coupled with China's disagreement with India over terrorist outfits at multilateral forums as well as increasing geopolitical competition in India's neighbouring countries of Nepal and Sri Lanka have all added to this dynamic. This has resulted in India's relatively stern approach towards China, shedding its past ambiguity over addressing the China question regionally or globally. This shift in India's approach has resulted in speculation over India's domestic measures to 'disengage' with China.[32] One of the most important developments in this regard has been Prime Minister Modi's address at the Shangri La conference at Singapore. Modi clearly enunciated his vision for the Indo-Pacific, calling it a 'free, open and inclusive' region, and stressed that all players should have 'equal access as a right under international law to use the common spaces on sea and in the air that would require freedom of navigation'.[33] This has been observed as India's response to China's coercive assertion and exclusive claim on the South China Sea region, and beyond. Therefore, despite there being mechanisms of cooperation in place between India and China, there have been disagreements between the two giants.[34] This has further culminated into an even more stressful relationship in the aftermath of the 2020 border disputes. This could be seen as India's opportunity to break away from the shackles of its dilemma in positing itself vis-à-vis China.

Secondly, another major development that has caused divergence among players in the region has been India's decision to withdraw from the RCEP. The RCEP is a free trade agreement put together by the East Asian and Southeast Asian countries by combining two earlier proposals of FTAs: the East Asia Free Trade Area led by China and the Comprehensive Economic Partnership in East Asia led by Japan. The RCEP was conceptualised as an ASEAN-led initiative which aimed to 'multilateralise the regional trade system'.[35] Prime Minister Modi reflected on the RCEP as an 'important initiative' that will integrate the region.[36] However, in November 2019, India announced its withdrawal from the RCEP citing some 'significant core issues that remained unresolved'.[37] Although many were surprised by India's decision to leave the RCEP, it was largely understood as India's attempt to check the trade deficit it has with China. Many have advocated for India to reconsider its decision in order to make the Indian market more competitive and realise Prime Minister Modi's USD 5 trillion economy mark.[38] However, it has also been speculated that India's reluctance to proceed in the RCEP has been prompted primarily by the fact that the RCEP is largely seen as a Chinese effort to consolidate regional trade arrangements. The RCEP has indeed received a lot of attention from Beijing since, for China, it is an opportunity to 'marginalise' the US and create a regional commercial integration. The focus on RCEP has been to create a free trade agreement that has an 'Asian shape'.[39] Therefore, it would not be in India's strategic interest to actively pursue a free trade agreement primarily designed by China. This also falls in line with India's decision to not be a part of China's BRI. However, Japan is an active member and advocate of the RCEP. India's exit from the partnership has prompted Japan to reach out to New Delhi and ask India to reconsider their decision.[40] The then Japanese Chief Cabinet Secretary Yoshihide Suga reiterated the belief that Japan would play a leading role to take the RCEP forward with all players including India. However, in spite of Japan's insistence, India has not changed its decision regarding the RCEP. This has manifested as a major divergence between India and Japan in terms of their regional economic strategy. While many could argue that China's overwhelming presence has rightly prompted India to leave the RCEP, it may also be posited that Japan's leading role in giving shape to the RCEP was a strong ground and a good opportunity for India to consolidate its ties with Japan and project a combined front as the leading force in the region. This has also brought to light India and Japan's difference in approach towards the Indo-Pacific in terms of looking at it as security architecture and a way of economic integration. While it appears that for Japan, the Indo-Pacific is a holistic amalgamation where it seeks active engagement, for India the economic and security rationales for the Indo-Pacific are still decoupled. This merits further scrutiny into and discussion on the way forward for India and Japan as well as the US in order to better understand the emergent strategic discourse of the Indo-Pacific.

What Does the Future Hold?

The 21st century has majorly recalibrated strategic equations in Asia. After Prime Minister Abe's visit to India in 2007, New Delhi and Tokyo have pursued an impressive strategic cooperation. According to Madhuchanda Ghosh, this 'saga of mutual intransigence and psychological distance' between New Delhi and Tokyo was amended with the end of the Cold War.[41] The increasing 'synergy' between the two countries have deepened further owing to their common strategic interests and objectives in the face of China's rise. Both Japan and India continue to pose major challenges to China's attempt at a hegemonic rise in Asia and its assertion of a sphere of influence in the Indo-Pacific. Additionally, India and Japan have shared a strategic proximity with the US, which has been a major player in the region. The 'pivot to Asia' doctrine gave shape to the India–Japan–US trilateral alliance, which has since come a long way. Maritime Asia has been at the heart of the three countries' shared interests. The convergence of these leading players has also strengthened the 'anti-China' narrative in Asia. While China intends to expand its sphere of influence in its neighbourhood by deploying military and infrastructure initiatives in the region, the formidable strategic partnership between New Delhi, Tokyo and Washington has made it their priority to counter China's might. The Quadrilateral Security Dialogue has similarly prompted a strong counter to China. Roy-Chaudhury and de Estrada note that despite no clear enunciation of intent to contain China's growing infrastructure and military deployment in the region, it is clear that the concept of the Indo-Pacific has been devised as a response to China's rise.[42] This response has been largely shaped by the (re)formulation of the Quad, with active participation of the member countries. All the participating countries in the Quad are strategically placed to counter China's expanse. In this way, the Quad has been the driver of securitisation of the Indo-Pacific. The Malabar Exercise, which became a quadrilateral exercise in 2020, has been another building block towards establishing a concerted opposition to China's rise.

However, it is important to take stock of the divergences that lie within these groupings. Japan's leadership change, with Prime Minister Yoshihide Suga taking charge, had caused some speculation over the handling of the Indo-Pacific question. This mainly stemmed from his predecessor Abe's excessive optimism regarding the Indo-Pacific. According to Jagannath P. Panda, it is important for India and Japan to sustain the synergy that Abe brought to India–Japan ties, as well as make use of the new global power dynamics.[43] Suga had indeed been quite perceptive of Abe's Indo-Pacific vision. The change in leadership in the US, with Joe Biden's victory in the elections, has also resulted in a lot of speculation about his foreign policy vision. In this context, Harsh Pant however points out that the Indo-Pacific is 'all a-churn' at the moment and is not in a position to wait for Washington to articulate its strategy for the region.[44] Therefore, it is important for all the three countries to engage in a way that would better facilitate their joint cooperation to resist an assertive China. Even though Asia and the Indo-Pacific have been at the heart of this contestation, there has been a growing realisation that strategic developments in the region will not just have regional implications, but also global ones.

Conclusion

It may be argued in conclusion that contemporary developments in the Indo-Pacific narrative will have crucial implications for the world in the coming days. The geostrategic power play in the region will influence the totality of world politics as the players poised to shape the future world order have begun engaging in the region. It can be rightly said that the Indo-Pacific is a building block for the future. Even though the US has not been a local player, it has always been an instrumental force in shaping the geopolitics of Asia. This chapter has argued that the contemporary churnings in the Indo-Pacific may be traced back to Barack Obama's 'Pivot to Asia' strategy. Even though it was understood as the US's attempt to operationalise a burden-sharing model in Asia, it did empower India and Japan, among other countries, to pursue their own strategic interests towards a common goal. For instance, China's assertive rise in the neighbourhood has been at the core of the partnership between India, Japan and the US. China is a common threat to all the three, considering Beijing's attempt to assert its unilateral dominance in territorial as well as maritime Asia. The trilateral cooperation between India, Japan and the US has significantly raised the stakes of maritime geopolitics. The rise of Asia is now being mapped with the rise of the Indo-Pacific. While a large body of literature shows that the Indo-Pacific is not a new concept, its rejuvenation in strategic circles and calculations after the Cold War has been unprecedented.

It is imperative to point out that the geostrategic contestation between China and India, Japan and the US can be seen as a clash of two ideas. On the one hand there is China, which is pursuing a coercive line of foreign policy as evident through its assertiveness in the South China Sea as well as the various border disputes that have taken place in the recent past. On the other hand is the trilateral cooperation between India, Japan and the US representing a 'rules-based' global partnership. This partnership has also been seen as the coming together of robust democracies to assert democratic and inclusive values in the Indo-Pacific region. This is clear from the 'fair and open Indo-Pacific' rhetoric pushed by these countries.

However, there have been internal divergences among the three partner countries. While the security rationale has been the chief driving force of this trilateral cooperation—the Quadrilateral Security

Dialogue and the Malabar Exercise being significant developments in this regard—there have been divergences on economic policies. In terms of security, the military exercises in the IOR have been understood by many as a strategic response to China, making Beijing cautious of a potential 'Asian NATO'. But on the economic front, things have not been as positive. India's exit from the RCEP in 2019 has revealed the need to have a more robust economic engagement among the three countries. Despite there being multiple bilateral economic engagements among the three countries, a joint trilateral cooperation that would match the scale of their security nexus is still absent. Even though the RCEP has Japan as one of its core visionary members, India's decision of leaving the FTA has been a significant setback for the 'anti-China' mobilisation of the three countries. With the US not being a part of RCEP, and India's recent decision to exit, strategic circles have speculated that China might be one of the primary reasons for the absence of these two countries. It may then be argued that Japan despite being a core advocate of the RCEP has not been able to mobilise its other partners to join the economic platform, thereby conceding the central space in the RCEP to China. While there has been tacit exhibition of apprehensions about a China-driven FTA, disengaging from the RCEP altogether may be seen as aiding and cementing China's centrality in the grouping. However, one of the positive outcomes from this has been the fact that India, Japan and the US have been able to maintain their strategic autonomy. Besides their robust engagement in the security domain, they have simultaneously been able to protect their own interests in matters that the others do not necessarily align with. Although at a conceptual level, this essence of autonomy and equality sounds good and represents a healthy environment of strategic alliance, in the specific context of the Indo-Pacific, it is nevertheless imperative for the three countries to align their security, economic and political interests in order to counter the mammoth rise of China. Beijing will be prompt in pointing out the absence of a holistic solidarity and cooperation framework between India, Japan and the US in order to further strengthen its own position. Therefore, it may not be wise for the three allies to decouple the domains of cooperation. Having a holistic approach with entwining scopes of engagement in terms of security, the economic and the political will go a long way in cementing the strategic cooperation between the three and establish them as the drivers of the strategic discourse of the Indo-Pacific.

Notes and References

1. Gurpreet S. Khurana, 'The "Indo-Pacific" Idea: Origins, Conceptualizations and the Way Ahead', *Journal of Indian Ocean Rim Studies*, vol. 2, no. 2 (June 2019).

2. Kei Koga, 'Japan's "Indo-Pacific" question: Countering China or shaping a new regional order?', *International Affairs*, vol. 96, no. 1 (January 2020), available at https://doi.org/10.1093/ia/iiz241, accessed on 13 September 2023.

3. Ministry of Foreign Affairs, Japan, 'Confluence of the Two Seas', 22 August 2007, available at https://www.mofa.go.jp/region/asia-paci/pmv0708/speech-2.html, accessed on 7 September 2020.

4. Rahul Roy-Chaudhury and Kate Sullivan de Estrada, 'India, the Indo-Pacific and the Quad', *Survival: Global Politics and Strategy*, vol. 60, no. 3 (June 2018), p. 182, available at https://doi.org/10.1080/00396338.2018.1470773, accessed on 13 September 2023.

5. Manjeet S. Pardesi, 'The Indo-Pacific: A "new" region or the return of history?', *Australian Journal of International Affairs*, vol. 74, no. 2 (November 2019), p. 14, available at https://doi.org/10.1080/10357718.2019.1693496, accessed on 13 September 2023.

6. Khurana, 'The "Indo-Pacific" Idea'.

7. Ibid., p. 3.

8. Yogesh Joshi, 'Between "Concern" and "Opportunity": US Pivot to Asia and Foreign Policy Debate in India', *Journal of Asian Security and International Affairs*, vol. 2, no. 3 (December 2015), pp. 314–315, available at https://www.jstor.org/stable/48602325, accessed on 13 September 2023.

9. Aileen Wang and Alan Wheatley, 'China overtakes Japan as No. 2 economy: FX chief', *Reuters*, 30 July 2010, available at https://www.reuters.com/article/us-china-economy-safe-idUSTRE66T1HT20100730, accessed on 29 September 2023.

10. Taehwa Hong, 'Free and Open Indo-Pacific Strategy: Accurate Diagnosis, Imperfect Prescription', *SNU Journal of International Affairs*, vol. 3, no. 1 (January 2018), p. 34.

11. Joshy M. Paul, 'India–Japan maritime security cooperation: Secondary states' soft balancing in the Indo-Pacific', *Maritime Affairs: Journal of the National Maritime Foundation of India*, vol. 15, no. 2 (January 2020), p. 14, available at https://doi.org/10.1080/09733159.2019.1710384, accessed on 13 September 2023.

12. Timothy Doyle and Dennis Rumley, *The Rise and Return of the Indo-Pacific* (London: Oxford University Press, 2019), p. 83.

13. Michal Kolmaš and Šárka Kolmašová, 'A "pivot" that never existed: America's Asian strategy under Obama and Trump', *Cambridge Review of International Affairs*, vol. 32, no. 1 (January 2019), pp. 75–76, available at https://doi.org/10.1080/09557571.2018.1553936, accessed on 13 September 2023.

14. Pardesi, 'The Indo-Pacific: A "new" region', pp. 16–17.

15. Sumit Ganguly, 'India and the Responsibility to Protect', *International Relations*, vol. 30, no. 3 (July 2016), p. 10, available at https://doi.org/10.1177/0047117816659593, accessed on 14 September 2023.

16. Pooja Bhatt, 'A Pivot in Asia', *The Hindu*, 30 January 2018, available at https://www.thehindu.com/opinion/op-ed/a-pivot-in-asia/article22567706.ece, accessed on 14 November 2020.

17. Yoginder Kandhari, 'China's Expansionism: A Strategic Perspective', *Indian Defence Review*, 10 July 2020, available at http://www.indiandefencereview.com/news/chinas-expansionism-a-strategic-perspective/, accessed on 26 November 2020.

18. C. Raja Mohan, 'China now has the power to alter territorial status quo', *The Indian Express*, 9 June 2020, available at https://indianexpress.com/article/opinion/columns/india-china-ladakh-lac-border-dispute-c-raja-mohan-6449294/, accessed on 17 November 2020.

19. Ian Hall, 'India and a Regional Rules-Based Order: Equity and Inclusion', *Security Challenges*, vol. 16, no. 3 (August 2020), p. 27, available at https://www.jstor.org/stable/10.2307/26924336, accessed on 14 September 2023.

20. Koga, 'Japan's "Indo-Pacific" question', p. 71.

21. David Scott, 'The 21st Century as Whose Century?', *Journal of World-Systems Research*, vol. 13, no. 2 (August 2007), pp. 106–108, available at https://doi.org/10.5195/jwsr.2007.350, accessed on 14 September 2023.

22. Harsh V. Pant, *Indian Foreign Policy: The Modi Era* (New Delhi: Har-Anand Publishers, 2019).

23. S. D. Muni, 'South Asia', in Md. Ayoob, ed., *Conflict and Intervention in the Third World* (Canberra: Australian National University Press, 1980), p. 39.

24. Vivek Mishra and Sayantan Haldar, 'Emerging Contours of Asian Maritime Connectivity: Economic and Strategic Objectives', *India Quarterly*, vol. 76, no. 3 (July 2020), p. 475, available at https://doi.org/10.1177/0974928420936136, accessed on 29 September 2023.

25. Harsh V. Shringla, 'More and more countries now share India's view for the region', *The Indian Express*, 7 November 2020, available at https://indianexpress.com/article/opinion/columns/india-pacific-relations-quad-exercise-6982086/, accessed on 1 December 2020.

26. Ministry of External Affairs, Government of India, 'Prime Minister's Keynote Address at Shangri La Dialogue', 1 June 2018, available at https://mea.gov.in/Speeches-Statements.htm?dtl/29943/Prime_Ministers_Keynote_Address_at_Shangri_La_Dialogue_June_01_2018, accessed on 15 September 2020.

27. Abhijnan Rej, 'China and the Quad: From Sea Foam to Indo-Pacific NATO', *The Diplomat*, 15 October 2020, available at https://thediplomat.com/2020/10/china-and-the-quad-from-sea-foam-to-asian-nato/, accessed on 19 November 2020.

28. Ministry of Foreign Affairs, Japan, 'Confluence of the Two Seas'.

29. Dinkar Peri, 'Malabar 2020: The coming together of the QUAD in the seas', *The Hindu*, 31 October 2020, available at https://www.thehindu.com/news/national/malabar-2020-the-coming-together-of-the-quad-in-the-seas/article61734428.ece, accessed on 29 September 2023.

30. Rajesh Rajagopalan, 'Evasive balancing: India's unviable Indo-Pacific strategy', *International Affairs*, vol. 96, no. 1 (January 2020), pp. 81–83, available at https://doi.org/10.1093/ia/iiz224, accessed on 14 September 2023.

31. Ipsita Chakravarty, 'Beyond Modi-Xi summits: To avoid military escalation, what are India's options?' *Scroll*, 5 September 2020, available at https://scroll.in/article/972235/beyond-modi-xi-summits-to-avoid-military-escalation-what-are-indias-options, accessed on 12 November 2020.

32. Sanjib Pohit, 'How to disengage Indian economy smartly from China', *The Hindu Business Line*, 15 July 2020, available at https://www.thehindubusinessline.com/opinion/disengaging-the-indian-economy-from-china/article32082237.ece, accessed on 21 November 2020.

33. Ministry of External Affairs, Government of India, 'Prime Minister's Keynote Address at Shangri La Dialogue'.

34. Harsh V. Pant, 'Sino-Indian Maritime Ambitions Collide in the Indian Ocean', *Journal of Asian Security and International Affairs*, vol. 1, no. 2 (August 2014), p. 199, available at https://doi.org/10.1177%2F2347797014536640, accessed on 14 September 2023.

35. Jeffrey D. Wilson, 'Mega-Regional Trade Deals in the Asia-Pacific: Choosing Between the TPP and RCEP?', *Journal of Contemporary Asia*, vol. 45, no. 2 (September 2014), p. 349, available at https://doi.org/10.1080/00472336.2014.956138, accessed on 14 September 2023.

36. Ministry of External Affairs, Government of India, 'Prime Minister's Keynote Address at Shangri La Dialogue'.

37. V. S. Seshadri, 'RCEP and India: What Next?', *Indian Foreign Affairs Journal*, vol. 14, no. 2 (April 2019), p. 88.

38. Raj Verma, 'The Regional Comprehensive Economic Partnership and India: A test case of Narendra Modi's statesmanship', *Australian Journal of International Affairs*, vol. 74, no. 5 (February 2020), p. 6, available at https://doi.org/10.1080/10357718.2020.1725425, accessed on 14 September 2023.

39. Matteo Dian and Silvia Menegazzi, *New Regional Initiatives in China's Foreign Policy* (Cham: Palgrave Macmillan, 2018), p. 112.

40. 'India's exit from RCEP leaves Japan and China unsure about future direction of free trade pact', *The Japan Times*, 5 November 2019, available at https://www.japantimes.co.jp/news/2019/11/05/asia-pacific/asian-rcep-nations-effectively-give-year-end-goal-free-trade-deal/, accessed on 25 November 2020.

41. Madhuchanda Ghosh, 'India and Japan's Growing Synergy: From a Political to a Strategic Focus', *Asian Survey*, vol. 48, no. 2 (April 2008), p. 301, available at https://doi.org/10.1525/as.2008.48.2.282, accessed on 14 September 2023.

42. Roy-Chaudhury and de Estrada, 'India, the Indo-Pacific and the Quad', p. 182.

43. Jagannath P. Panda, 'Suga, India-Japan Ties and the Domestic Drawing', *Japan Forward*, 1 October 2020, available at https://japan-forward.com/asias-next-page-suga-india-japan-ties-and-the-domestic-drawing/, accessed on 1 December 2020.

44. Harsh V. Pant, 'The Indo-Pacific is all a-churn in response to Joe Biden's victory', *ORF Commentaries*, 26 November 2020, available at https://www.orfonline.org/research/the-indo-pacific-is-all-a-churn-in-response-to-joe-bidens-victory/, accessed on 1 December 2020.

PART II

PERSPECTIVES FROM JAPAN

nine

Japan–India Security Cooperation amidst Regional Flux

Satoru Nagao

Since the 2000s, furthering cooperation in security between Japan and India has become more and more plausible. The two countries began the Japan–India–US–Australia quadrilateral dialogue, the Japan–India–US and Japan–India–Australia trilateral dialogues and the Japan–India foreign and defence 2+2 bilateral dialogue. Since 2012, Japan has participated in the Indian Ocean Naval Symposium (IONS).[1] The two countries also began joint naval exercises as an annual bilateral exercise, called Japan-India Maritime Exercise (JIMEX) in 2012. The India–US Malabar exercises decided to include Japan as a regular member since 2016.[2] And since 2019, annual ground and air joint exercises, 'Dharma Guardian' and 'Shinyuu Maitri', have started.[3] Bilaterally, India and Japan signed a General Security of Military Information Agreement (GSOMIA) in 2015 and an Acquisition and Cross-Servicing Agreement (ACSA) in 2020.[4] These exercises and agreements have strengthened the security ties between Japan and India and furthered the 'Free and Open Indo-Pacific Strategy'.

But why does Japan seek security cooperation with India? The following sections will analyse two questions: 1) Why has Japan tried to share more security burden? 2) What can Japan–India cooperation do?

Why has Japan tried to share more security burden?

It is important for Japan to enhance its security cooperation with US allies such as Australia, UK, France and Germany as well as other friendly countries. Japan cooperates actively with these countries by sharing information, holding joint exercises and developing and producing defense equipment jointly. For example, between 2017 and 2018, Japan signed Acquisition and Cross-Servicing Agreements with Australia, the UK and France, to facilitate exchange of mutual logistical support including materials and ammunition for joint exercises, UN Peacekeeping Operations (UNPKO) and other initiatives. In 2016, Japan and the UK held joint air combat exercises for the first time. Japan and France also held joint exercises in 2017.[5] Negotiations are also underway between these countries to start joint arms development projects.

Moreover, Japan is working towards building the capacities of various defence forces in Southeast Asia. For instance, Japan is planning to donate used P-3C patrol planes to Malaysia, Vietnam and Sri Lanka. Japan will supply warning and control radar systems to Philippines too.[6] Donating and exporting equipment can be an effective way to promote long-term relations because the recipients would need training to use the equipment and regular maintenance of supplies.

Why has Japan tried to share a greater security burden? One can argue that it is because the changing security situation has pushed Japan to do so. For a long time, bilateral alliances led by the US, such as the US–Japan, US–Australia, US–Philippines and US–South Korea partnerships have maintained order in the Indo-Pacific, upholding the 'old' security framework which resembles a 'hub-and-spoke system'. In this system, there is a lack of depth in the defence relations among the different allies. For example, both Japan and Australia are US allies, but they share no close security relations with each other. Under this system, the US allies and friendly countries are heavily dependent on US military power.

A salient feature of the recent security situation is the changing US–China military balance. For example, between 2000 and 2021, the US commissioned 24 new submarines; during the same period, China commissioned at least 59 submarines.[7] Although it is still expected that the US would prevail if war should break out, it is also true that US military influence in the Indo-Pacific region has been declining gradually. This is evident from the fact that the US has not been able to dissuade China from building artificial islands in the South China Sea.[8] And if US influence is declining, the 'old' security framework no longer remains reliable. This has resulted in the US allies and friendly countries in the Indo-Pacific viewing the future with anxiety.

In light of this, a new security framework is gradually emerging. This framework is a security network of numerous bilateral, trilateral, quadrilateral and other multilateral cooperative relationships among the US allies and friendly countries. This cooperation includes not only US-led Japan–US–Australia, Japan–India–US and Japan–India–US–Australia partnerships, but also trilateral relations such as Japan–India–Australia and India–Australia–Indonesia, which do not include the US.

This new security framework presents several strong points of marked benefit. First, because this system is not heavily dependent on US influence, the adverse impact of the US's declining influence in the region will be minimal. Secondly, because this system includes India and Southeast Asian countries that are gradually growing in influence, this multilateral security framework can maintain sufficient power for a long time, especially through the adoption of a rules-based approach.

What can Japan–India cooperation do?

In this context, it is important to discuss Japan's strategic cooperation with India and what role this cooperation plays. There are three ways in which the Japan–India security cooperation can contribute towards maintaining a military balance with China and supporting the new security framework. The India–Japan security partnership facilitates Japan's support to India during India–China conflicts, lowers the heavy security burden of Japan and US in the Indian Ocean and supports countries around South China Sea.

India–China Conflict and Japan's Support

With China's rapid military modernisation, the extent of Chinese military activities has been widening and has now spread to the Indo-China border areas. In addition, China is deploying troops in Pakistan-administered Kashmir as well as in parts of the China-Pakistan Economic Corridor (CPEC). Beijing is also developing infrastructure projects to connect China to Nepal. Further, China has been involved in disputes over areas like Doklam, claimed by both China and Bhutan, where it insists on building new roads to deploy more military forces.

In 2020, the situation escalated further. China entered Indian territory, causing a clash between the two sides in June. At least 20 Indian soldiers sacrificed their lives (the Chinese fatalities are unknown).[9] Following this clash, China continued to redeploy fighter jets and missiles from other areas of China. For example, China moved H-6 bombers that can employ cruise missiles from Wugong to Golmud and Kashgar. China also deployed DF-21 missiles, which use new types of warheads that the US and Japan cannot intercept through missile defense systems, to Kailash Mansarovar. At the Hotan airbase, China has been increasing heavy fighters and bombers such as the J-11 and J-16 as well as other types of military aircraft such as the Y-8G electronic reconnaissance aircraft, the KJ-500 early warning aircraft and the CH-4 drone. The latest J-20 stealth fighter jets have also been deployed. To protect these airfields and missiles, China is now deploying S-300 surface-to-air missiles. In an attempt to match China's build-up, India has repeatedly conducted missile tests. In six weeks between September and October 2020, India conducted more than 12 missile tests.[10]

What role should Japan–India cooperation play in face of these challenges with China? To analyse that, one must ask the following two questions: First, what kind of a war scenario can we foresee if the Indo-China border stand-off escalates? And second, what are the options available to Japan and India that they can collaborate on?

If the Indo-China Conflict Escalates

From a military balance perspective, China has an advantage because geographically, China operates from higher ground. Their ground forces can identify from above where they should aim and fire guns. It is also easier for China to transport heavy cargo downhill whereas India needs to transport its cargo uphill. China can also easily overcome the effects of altitude sickness before an operation starts while Indian soldiers moving to a higher altitude will only be able to overcome altitude sickness after any operation starts. China has an advantage in terms of infrastructure as well. Within two days, Chinese armed forces can be ready for battle in a border area whereas India needs a week's preparation due to a lack of infrastructure on the Indian side.[11]

However, India has the upper hand in a few other areas and it is expected that India's reaction will make China restrain the size of their operation. Firstly, from an air operation perspective, China is at a disadvantage. Their airports are located on high ground, which means that the air is thin and fighter jets therefore operate with insufficient lifting power. Chinese fighter jets can carry only about half of their payload in such thin air.[12] If the ground battle escalated to an air battle, it would be a more advantageous scenario for India. Secondly, if the international community including the US think that the Indo-China military conflict might escalate to a nuclear war, they will intervene to prevent this. In such a scenario, it is expected that the US will support India, and not China. In addition, if the purpose of China's incursive military operations is to provide a warning to India and other countries and showcase China's power, even a small 'victory' would be sufficient. Since a massive-scale military operation is not necessary to achieve this 'victory', it might convince China to restrain the size of the operation.

India and Japan's Options and Possible Areas of Cooperation

The Japan–India security cooperation can have a significant role to play in the face of China's aggression. Dissuading China from starting a military operation should be Japan and India's primary policy goal. To this end, Japan and India can make effective use of their respective geographical locations. Because the two countries are located at opposite sides of China, Japan–India cooperation can strengthen each country and help them overcome their respective inferiority in terms of size. For example, if India and Japan work together, India would not need to deal with all the Chinese fighters at the same time as China would be likely to want to keep some of its fighters to its east against Japan, and vice versa.

For this purpose, Japan's infrastructure projects in Northeast India can prove to be very effective. The main objective of such projects is to increase trade between India and Southeast Asia. However, this road can also be used by the Indian Army to deploy more forces and send supplies to the border area. Japan's support is also necessary to bolster India's efforts to modernise defence in the Indo-China border area. For example, because India's air defence system is obsolete, importing Japan's radar system to strengthen India's air defence and air control capabilities in the Indo-China border area would be an effective measure.

A Japan–India cooperation can have a considerable effect in the event of an Indo-China crisis. Two instances of Japan's support towards India, namely the dispatch of an Izumo-class helicopter carrier with a US aircraft carrier during the Malabar Exercise in 2017, and the statement of support for India from the Japanese ambassador, had a significant impact on the Indo-China stand-off at Doklam in 2017. A similar situation occurred in 2020 during the Galwan crisis. Japan too can use India's support in a similar way in the event of a future conflict with China.

Another good means to dissuade China would be to draw China's attention toward Japan and away from India. For example, if Japan deployed its Self-Defense Forces (SDF) in the Senkaku Islands, China would as a countermeasure deploy more forces in that direction rather than toward India. If the Japanese SDF conducts a Freedom of Navigation operation with the US Navy in the South China Sea or the Taiwan Strait, China would no longer be able to concentrate its military forces at the Indo-China border area. And if China cannot concentrate its forces at the Indo-China border, it would not be able to commence offensive military operations against India.

To improve security strategy and to contain China's aggression, recently, Japan decided to purchase limited offensive capabilities, including small aircraft carriers, F-35 stealth fighter jets and standoff weapons.[13] Similarly, India is procuring airlift equipment such as heavy and middle transport planes, heavy transport helicopters and air-liftable howitzers in order to establish air-mobile offensive capability against China. Australia has also announced plans to possess long-range strike capabilities.[14] These offensive capabilities will give these countries more flexible choices when they need to deal with China.

Lowering the Security Burden in the Indian Ocean

An effective India–Japan partnership can also lead toward lowering the heavy security burden of Japan and the US in the Indian Ocean with India's gradual rise to prominence in the region. With China's growing influence in the Indian Ocean Region (IOR), it is essential for Japan and India, as well as the US, to work together to strengthen each other's defences, especially in terms of naval power. Since India already occupies a key position in the IOR geographically, cooperation among the friendly countries would lessen the security burden of Japan and the US when it comes to maritime security in the Indian Ocean.

Increased Military Presence of China in the Indian Ocean

Since the mid-2000s, China's military activities in the Indian Ocean have been rising as the changing geopolitical scenario has threatened its sea lines of communication (SLOCs) through the Strait of Malacca, thereby posing a risk to China's imports from the Middle East. In order to lessen its dependence on the Malacca Strait, China is trying to make alternative trade routes through Pakistan and Myanmar as part of the 'One Belt One Road' initiative, later renamed the Belt and Road Initiative (BRI).

According to Admiral Sunil Lanba, Chief of the Naval Staff of the Indian Navy, at least six to eight Chinese warships can always be found in the Indian Ocean.[15] In addition, China exports submarines to countries around India. Bangladesh received two submarines from China in 2016 and Pakistan imported eight Chinese submarines for their navy.[16] The Indian Navy will need to have enough ships to keep a regular watch over the location and movement of these foreign 'Chinese' submarines as they can potentially attack India's nuclear ballistic missile submarines and disrupt SLOCs. This implies that these submarines deployed by China will, to a great extent, regulate India's naval activities.

However, China's strategic weakness is that it does not have a naval port in the region. To resolve this, China is setting up a base in Djibouti. In addition, under the 'String of Pearl Strategy', China is investing to develop several ports in the Indian Ocean such as Gwadar in Pakistan, Hambantota in Sri Lanka, Chittagong in Bangladesh and Kyaukphyu in Myanmar. Currently, China is planning to deploy two marine brigades to defend their bases in Djibouti and Gwadar.[17] If the Chinese navy also uses civil-purpose ports as naval supply bases, China could successfully tackle their weakness of not having a naval port in the region.

India's Key Role in the Indian Ocean

It is the changing US–China military balance that has most likely caused China's heightened assertiveness the Indian Ocean of late. The US influence in the IOR was considerable in the 1970s. However, with the decline of US naval power after the Cold War, the military balance has been upset and the IOR has seen an increase in Chinese naval activities, especially in the East China Sea and South China Sea. To restore balance, a third country must fill the potential power vacuum in this region.

There is a high possibility that, in the near future, India will become the most influential sea power in the IOR. There are six factors that Alfred Thayer Mahan, who analysed why Britain had been a sea power, pointed out.[18] According to him, the core factors of a sea power are as follows:

1) geographical position
2) physical conformation (especially, the length of coast lines)
3) extent of territory (especially the balance between the extent of coastal line and military defence resources)
4) size of population (for working at sea)
5) character of the people
6) character of the government.

Taking these factors into account, we shall try to see if India is indeed an influential sea power.

First of all, India has an advantageous 'geographical position' because the Indian subcontinent is separated from the Eurasian continent by high mountains. This advantage has historically proven to be significant. Some of the major empires which dominated most of the subcontinent in Indian history were the Mauryan Empire, the Mughal Empire and the British Raj. The territories of these three empires were very similar and were determined by the mountain range to the north. In a way, the Indian subcontinent is a kind of island.

Besides the three aforementioned empires, the history of Cholas too indicates another geographical advantage for India. Representatives of the Chola Empire, which was located in southern India, made an expedition to Southeast Asia in the 11th century. The sphere of the empire's influence had expanded along the coastal area off the Bay of Bengal. Since India is located at the northern centre of the Indian Ocean, it is not only able to access Southeast Asia, but also all sides of the Indian Ocean, including the Middle East and East Africa.

Second, India also has the right 'physical conformation' because it has 7,517 km of coastline (of which 6,100 km is of the mainland). As a coastal country in the IOR, India has enough 'extent of territory', the third of Mahan's criteria, as well as a strong navy. To further strengthen its navy, India is trying to acquire more than 100 warships. By 2030, India plans to increase its number of warships from 139 to 212.[19]

As of 2017, India had the third largest number of seafarers with about 150,000 sailors employed around the world.[20] Thus, India also satisfies the condition of 'size of population' working at sea. Based on the history of the Chola Empire, there is also a possibility that the 'character of the people' in India could be sea-power oriented. The Indian government is definitely interested in expanding its sea power, proving that the 'character of government' is also sea-power oriented. This is evident from the fact that in India's defence budget, the navy's share has increased from 12.7 per cent in 1990 to 14.7 per cent in 2019.[21]

Thus, according to Mahan's theory, India has sufficient potential to become a sea power and thereby establish itself as an influential country in the IOR. If India has the required will and develops sufficient capabilities, Japan could gain a lot from its cooperation with India. If India can ensure maritime security in the Indian Ocean, its allies Japan and the US will be relieved from the heavy burden to safeguard security in the Indian Ocean and can instead deploy more military force in the East China Sea and West China Sea to maintain the military balance in Asia.

Contribution of Japan–India Defence Cooperation

If India becomes a sea power, how can a Japan–India defence cooperation be beneficial? Firstly, India can use Japan's technology to strengthen India's naval power. For example, similar to the infrastructural support in the Indo-China border area, Japan is also planning to assist India's airport project in the Andaman and Nicobar Islands. If India could strengthen its bases in the IOR, it would be relatively easy to project power over the Malacca Strait. Japan can also contribute to India's shipbuilding capabilities to build warships including aircraft carriers and submarines. Japan already possesses sophisticated helicopter carriers, cruisers, destroyers, frigates and conventional submarines, which can also prove to be useful to India.

Further, according to the 'Joint Press Statement on the India-Japan Annual Defence Ministerial Dialogue' published in September 2017, the two governments, during this ministerial dialogue, 'welcomed the constructive engagement between Acquisition, Technology and Logistic Agency (ATLA) and Defence Research and Development Organisation (DRDO) and agreed to commence the technical discussions for research collaboration in the areas of Unmanned Ground Vehicles and Robotics.'[22] The ministers also commended the 'conduct of the first-ever meeting on defence industry cooperation held by ATLA and Department of Defence Production (DDP) in Tokyo'.[23] In 2018, India and Japan started the joint development of unmanned ground vehicles, which can be very useful along the India–China border where conditions are too harsh for people to stay through the winter. During the 2017 dialogue, the ministers also took note of 'the ongoing close cooperation between the Japan Maritime Self-Defence Force (JMSDF) and the Indian Navy in various specialised areas of mutual interest, including anti-submarine aspects'.[24]

In the future, the two countries can take this cooperation further to a higher level by collaborating on projects such as a sea-based missile defence system and mine-sweeping, to name a few. Arms trade can be another important part of Japan–India strategic cooperation. Currently, Japan and India are negotiating the UNICORN antenna for an indigenous naval ship of India.[25] Therefore, to deal with China's naval activities in the Indian Ocean, Japan–India strategic cooperation could be very effective.

Cooperation to Support Coastal Countries in the IOR

China has invested heavily to build infrastructure in the coastal countries along the Indian Ocean and has been trying to expand its influence in the region. If India does not acquire enough technology and power, China will further increase their influence in the IOR, which can hurt India's image of being a 'great power'. For example, Sri Lanka is situated at an important location and safeguards several SLOCs. To take advantage of this, China is building ports in Colombo and Hambantota. Along with lending economic support to Sri Lanka, China has also sent submarines to Sri Lanka.

In this context, an India–Japan infrastructure cooperation can be a useful method to neutralise China's influence in the IOR. Sri Lanka had no alternative to the 'debt diplomacy' offer from China: the threat of sanctions and war crimes charges in the wake of Sri Lanka's civil war meant that China was the only country willing to provide it with massive investment. Beijing thus created a huge debt for Sri Lanka, which enabled China to negotiate the 99-year lease of the Hambantota port. In a scenario like this, India and Japan can offer alternatives. For example, Japan offered to finance Bangladesh's Matarbari port project and Bangladesh chose to go ahead with Japan's initiative instead of China's Sonadia project. India and Japan can use a similar tactic in other cases too. Currently, India and Japan are collaborating to improve the Colombo port and Trincomalee port in Sri Lanka. If China starts using the Hambantota port as a naval supply base, Sri Lanka can suggest that India and Japan (and the US) use Trincomalee, which is a suitable naval port. Sri Lanka can thus remain neutral, and India and Japan can neutralise China's influence in the region. It is also possible that the Chabahar port project in Iran will successfully challenge the importance of China's Gwadar port in Pakistan, since Central Asian countries could use both the Chinese route and the India–Japan route to export their natural resources instead of depending on just one route. The Asia-Africa Growth Corridor (AAGC) and other Japan-India joint infrastructure projects in Africa will further affect China's growing influence in the IOR.

Lending Support to Countries around South China Sea

Because China's military power is far more than other countries in the region, the Southeast Asian countries around South China Sea need to amalgamate their leaderships into one integrated front and beef up their military power with the help of trustworthy partners who can provide these coastal countries with adequate military support. In this context, a Japan–India strategic cooperation can be very useful.

According to Pankaj Jha, 'With increasing Chinese assertion in the South China Sea since 2001, many countries like Vietnam, Philippines and Singapore want India's increased presence in the Southeast Asia'.[26] And by now, India has already started to support armed forces in Southeast Asia as a part of its 'Look East Policy' and its updated version, the 'Act East Policy'. India has also trained personnel such as the crew of aircraft carriers in Thailand, and pilots and land crew of fighter airplanes in Malaysia, and has agreed to train the pilots and provide maintenance to the fighter airplanes in the Indonesian Air Force. Meanwhile Singapore is using India's land and air base for their training. Philippines will purchase the BrahMos cruise missile from India. The development of India–Vietnam security cooperation has led to India training Vietnamese submarine crew and fighter pilots, and plans are underway to export the BrahMos cruise missile and the Akash surface-to-air missile to Vietnam as well as to donate four patrol vessels to Vietnam.[27]

Japan, unlike India, has not supported armed forces in Southeast Asia in a very long time, but has supported other systems indirectly related with maritime security in the South China Sea. These include anti-piracy systems, Tsunami warning systems, cyber defence systems and infrastructure like air and sea ports. Under Prime Minister Shinzo Abe, Japan also started arms donation to these countries.

If Japan and India collaborate with each other, countries around South China Sea can receive more effective support. For instance, when a

Malaysian airplane was lost in 2014, coastal countries including Vietnam could not trace the plane's whereabouts because they had insufficient radar systems to detect it. In a scenario like this, if Japan lent its support to build a radar and communication network in Vietnam and the Indian Air Force trained Vietnam People's Air Force to use the network system, Vietnam could have effectively handled the crisis.

As mentioned earlier, Japan has invested in India's strategic road project in Northeast India. If road connections are made to increase India–Southeast Asia trade, it is possible that this trade would significantly reduce China's influence in Southeast Asia. Currently, Japan is building an East–West Economic Corridor (EWEC) from Vietnam to Myanmar, which will also connect to roads in Northeast India. The 'Japan-India Joint Statement: Toward a Free, Open and Prosperous Indo-Pacific' mentioned that 'The two Prime Ministers welcomed the Japan-India cooperation on development of India's North Eastern Region (NER) as a concrete symbol of developing synergies between India's Act East Policy and Japan's Free and Open Indo-Pacific Strategy'.[28]

Japan has plans of supporting infrastructure projects in the Andaman and Nicobar Islands near the Malacca Strait and SLOCs in the Indian Ocean. In 2001, India set up the Andaman and Nicobar Command, with integrated headquarters for the Army, Navy and Air Force. Furthermore, India is modernising its security infrastructure to deploy larger warships, patrol planes and transport planes.[29] Some media reports indicate that Japan has decided to support radar facilities and power plants in the Andaman and Nicobar Islands as well as build a fibre cable connection between mainland India and the islands.[30] Although these are civil projects to resolve electric power shortage, it is highly probable that the project will have a strategic effect on China, whose submarines often venture into the Indian Ocean. These submarines sail from Hainan island through South China Sea and the Malacca Strait. Therefore, to track China's submarine activities, the Andaman and Nicobar archipelago is an excellent location. Recent media reports indicate that Japan, India and the US are planning to install a submarine detecting sensor system along the coastline of the Bay of Bengal.[31] Furthermore, India and the US are negotiating an information-sharing system to track when Chinese submarines leave from Hainan. If Japan invests in infrastructure projects in the Andaman and Nicobar Islands, it will further enhance India's naval capability to detect Chinese submarine activities.

India has several other defence cooperations with countries around the South China Sea. Since 1993, India has engaged in joint exercises with Singapore. In 2002, India started a coordinated patrol with Indonesia. The India–Thailand joint patrol started in 2005.[32] Now, India is set to join the Malacca Strait Patrol Group, which comprises forces from Singapore, Indonesia, Thailand and Malaysia.[33] In March 2017, the Japan-India Dialogue on ASEAN was launched. One can hope that such dialogue will promote more practical trilateral strategic dialogues between India and Japan and Southeast Asian countries such as Vietnam, Philippines, Singapore, Indonesia, and Malaysia. Through such trilateral dialogues, Japan and India would be able to share information, better identify the needs of these Southeast Asian countries and decide how to cooperate and support these countries.

Conclusion

Even though Japan is geographically far from India, furthering cooperation in security between Japan and India has become more and more plausible in recent times because of the changing US–China power balance. US allies and friendly countries now require a new security framework to adjust to the changed geopolitical situation. In the new security system that has emerged, Japan–India cooperation has an important role to play. To maintain balance in the Indo-Pacific region, Japan and India can cooperate by supporting each other during conflicts such as the India–China conflict, sharing the security burden in the Indian Ocean and collaborating to support countries around China in the South China Sea. The time has come to proactively further the Japan–India cooperation to ensure prosperous stability in the Indo-Pacific region.

Notes and References

1. Indian Ocean Naval Symposium, Homepage, available at https://www.ions.global/ions-working-groups, accessed on 5 December 2023.

2. Franz-Stefan Gady, 'Confirmed: Japan Will Permanently Join US-India Naval Exercises', *The Diplomat*, 13 October 2015, available at https://thediplomat.

com/2015/10/confirmed-japan-will-permanently-join-us-india-naval-exercises/ accessed on 5 December 2023.

3. Press Information Bureau, Government of India, 'Curtain Raiser: Indo-Japan Joint Military Exercise DHARMA GUARDIAN – 2019', 12 October 2019, available at https://pib.gov.in/newsite/PrintRelease.aspx?relid=193756, accessed 16 January 2024; Pranav Kulkarni, 'Indian and Japanese air forces to kick start exercise Shinyuu Maitri today', *Times Now News*, 17 October 2019, available at https://www.timesnownews.com/india/article/indian-and-japanese-air-forces-to-kick-start-exercise-shinyuu-maitri-today/504769, accessed 16 January 2024.

4. Ministry of Defence, Government of Japan, 'Defense of Japan (Annual White Paper)', available at https://www.mod.go.jp/en/publ/w_paper/index.html, accessed on 5 December 2023.

5. Ibid.

6. 'Japan may help SL buy P-3C maritime surveillance aircraft', *Daily Mirror*, 21 April 2017, available at https://www.dailymirror.lk/article/Japan-may-help-SL-buy-P-C-maritime-surveillance-aircraft-127555.html, accessed on 5 December 2023.

7. The International Institute for Strategic Studies, *The Military Balance 2023* (UK: Taylor and Francis, 2023).

8. 'China has fully militarized three islands in South China Sea, US admiral says', *Associated Press*, 21 March 2022, available at https://www.theguardian.com/world/2022/mar/21/china-has-fully-militarized-three-islands-in-south-china-sea-us-admiral-says, accessed 22 January 2024.

9. Soutik Biswas, 'India-China clash: 20 Indian troops killed in Ladakh fighting', BBC News, 16 June 2020, available at https://www.bbc.com/news/world-asia-53061476, accessed on 19 September 2023.

10. "India test fires 12 missiles in 45 days, sends strong message to China, Pakistan," *The Economic Times*, October 23, 2020, available at https://economictimes.indiatimes.com/news/defence/india-test-fires-12-missiles-in-45-days-sends-strong-message-to-china-pakistan/videoshow/78828501.cms?from=mdr accessed on December 5, 2023.

11. Deeptiman Tiwary, 'Chinese clearing forest cover to grab border land', *The Economic Times*, 26 August 2013, available at http://articles.timesofindia.indiatimes.com/2013-08-26/india/41453967_1_chinese-troops-incursion-sino-indian-border, accessed on 20 September 2023.

12. Vishnu Som, 'Exclusive: Why Indian Air Force May Best Chinese Jets In An Air Battle Over Tibet', NDTV, 9 August 2017, available at https://www.ndtv.com/india-news/exclusive-why-indian-air-force-may-best-chinese-jets-in-an-air-battle-over-tibet-1735052, accessed on 26 November 2017.

13. 'Japan Prepares For F-35B Carrier Operations', *Naval News*, 3 October 2023, available at https://www.navalnews.com/naval-news/2023/10/japan-prepares-for-f-35b-carrier-operations/ accessed on 5 December 2023.

14. Scott Morrison, Prime Minister of Australia, 'Long Range Strike Capabilities to Maintain Regional Security', 1 July 2020, available at https://www.minister.defence.gov.au/media-releases/2020-07-01/long-range-strike-capabilities-maintain-regional-security, accessed on 20 September 2023.

15. Anirban Bhaumik, '6-8 Chinese Navy ships always in Indian Ocean', *Deccan Herald*, 10 January 2019, available at https://www.deccanherald.com/india/6-8-chinese-navy-ships-always-712273.html, accessed on 20 September 2023.

16. 'Bangladesh Navy gets 2 submarines', *The Daily Star*, 14 November 2016, available at https://www.thedailystar.net/country/bangladesh-navy-gets-2-chinese-submarines-1314553, accessed on 5 December 2023; Usman Ansari, 'Pakistan To Buy 8 Submarines From China', *Defense News*, 3 April 2015, available at https://www.defensenews.com/naval/2015/04/03/pakistan-to-buy-8-submarines-from-china/, accessed on 5 December 2023.

17. Ananth Krishnan, 'China may station Marines in Gwadar, say PLA insiders', *India Today*, 13 March 2017, available at https://www.indiatoday.in/world/asia/story/pla-navy-plans-china-navy-marine-corps-gwadar-djibouti-965353-2017-03-13, accessed on 20 September 2023.

18. Alfred Thayer Mahan, *The Influence of Sea Power upon History: 1660–1783* (United States: Little, Brown and Co., 1890).

19. K. S. Subramanian, 'Bridge the Gap between Plan and Execution: What Ails Warship Building in India', *Indian Military Review*, vol. 7 (December 2016), pp.10–12; 'Indian Navy to have 200 warships in next 10 years', *The Times of India*, 13 November 2013, available at http://articles.timesofindia.indiatimes.com/2013-11-13/india/44028232_1_ins-vikramaditya-navy-day-ins-khukri, accessed on 26 November 2017.

20. Homepage of the Directorate General Shipping, Ministry of Ports, Shipping, and Waterways, Government of India, available at https://www.dgshipping.gov.in/Content/OurStrength.aspx#:~:text=The%20seafarers%20employed%20on%20ships,to%20the%20world%20maritime%20industry, accessed on 7 January 2021.

21. Ministry of Defence, Government of India, 'Annual Report 2021-22', available at https://mod.gov.in/sites/default/files/AR_0.pdf, accessed on 22 January 2024.

22. Press Information Bureau, Government of India, Ministry of Defence, 'Joint Press Statement on the India-Japan Annual Defence Ministerial Dialogue', 6 September 2017, available at https://pib.gov.in/newsite/PrintRelease.aspx?relid=170560 , accessed on 20 September 2023.

23. Ibid.

24. Ministry of Foreign Affairs, Government of Japan, 'Japan-India Joint Statement: Toward a Free, Open and Prosperous Indo-Pacific', 14 September 2017, available at http://www.mofa.go.jp/mofaj/files/000289999.pdf, accessed on 26 November 2017.

25. 'Japan to Export to India Stealthy UNICORN NORA-50 Integration Mast', 16 October 2022, IndraStra Global News, available at https://www.indrastra.com/2022/10/japan-to-export-to-india-stealthy.html, accessed on 16 January 2024.

26. Pankaj K. Jha, *India and China in Southeast Asia: Competition or Cooperation?* (Manas Publications, 2013), p.132.

27. Premesha Saha, 'India's growing strategic footprint in the Indo-Pacific', Observer Research Foundation, 15 August 2023, available at https://www.orfonline.org/expert-speak/indias-growing-strategic-footprint-in-the-indo-pacific, accessed on 16 January 2024.

28. Ministry of Foreign Affairs, Government of Japan, 'Japan-India Joint Statement: Toward a Free, Open and Prosperous Indo-Pacific'.

29. Ministry of Defence, Government of India, 'Annual Report 2021-22'.

30. 'NEC completes submarine cable system for BSNL connecting Chennai, India and the Andaman & Nicobar Islands', NEC, 18 December 2020, available at https://www.nec.com/en/press/202012/global_20201218_01.html, accessed on 5 December 2023.

31. Abhijit Singh, 'India's "Undersea Wall" in the Eastern Indian Ocean', *Asia Maritime Transparency Initiative*, 15 June 2016, available at http://amti.csis.org/indias-undersea-wall-eastern-indian-ocean/, accessed on 8 October 2017.

32. Saha, 'India's growing strategic footprint in the Indo-Pacific'.

33. Ajay Banerjee, 'India set to join Malacca patrol group', *The Tribune*, 9 April 2017, available at http://www.tribuneindia.com/news/nation/india-set-to-join-malacca-patrol-group/389602.html , accessed on 26 November 2017.

ten

Japan–India Economic Partnership in an Evolving Strategic Context

Makoto Kojima

Japan and India have a long history of economic interaction. They are natural partners, with an economic complementarity that is potentially quite high. Being burdened with a mature economy, an ageing population and a low birth rate, Japan is in need of a growth scenario. To plan the development of such a scenario, it is quite natural for Japan to expand its relationship with India. India also has high expectations of Japan as a development partner. India has become the largest recipient of Japanese official development assistance (ODA) since 2004[1] and Japan's foreign direct investment (FDI) in India has shown a dynamic trend since 2008. However, bilateral trade between the two countries has been sluggish, lagging far behind India's trade with the Association of Southeast Asian Nations (ASEAN), China and other trading partners, even though the Japan-India Comprehensive Economic Partnership Agreement (CEPA) came into effect in 2011 (Figure 10.1).

Meanwhile, keeping an eye on the strategic importance of a tie-up with each other, Japan and India entered into a Strategic and Global Partnership in 2006 against the backdrop of geopolitical change triggered by China's emergence, which provided a framework for long-term cooperation in both economic and security-related fields. The Indo-Japan annual summit meeting has been instrumental in implementing bilateral collaboration in Indian infrastructure through ODA. The Delhi–Mumbai Industrial Corridor (DMIC) project, with the Western Dedicated Freight Corridor (DFC) as its backbone, serves as an important symbol of the advanced bilateral collaboration related to Indian infrastructure development. The Modi government has provided new momentum to bolstering the

Japan–India relations: in 2014, this relationship was elevated to a Special Strategic and Global Partnership.

A growing Chinese assertive behaviour, the US–China conflict and an outbreak of COVID-19 in 2020 have combined to press for a reorganisation of the current Sino-centric global supply chain and give impetus to strengthen solidarity among the four members of the Quadrilateral Security Dialogue (Quad). This chapter discusses the latest trends in security relations and the multi-faceted aspects of Japan–India bilateral relations under a growing convergence of security and economic aspects brought about by recent global disruptive movements.

Japan–India Strategic Linkages

Formation of a Strategic and Global Partnership

What makes Japan–India relations figure prominently among other bilateral relations in the Asian region is that the two countries have gradually and steadily consolidated a bilateral framework for economic as well as security cooperation. As policymakers appear to be convinced, a bilateral relationship cannot be endured unless it is underpinned by strategic ties.[2] Both Japan and India share the common interest: how to deal with China, which has made rapid strides towards becoming the major power under the banner of 'the great rejuvenation of the Chinese nation'.

In the past, Japan–India relations had temporarily soured when India conducted nuclear tests in 1998, followed by Japan's freezing of grant aid for new projects (except for emergency and humanitarian assistance as well as grassroots cooperation) and suspending yen loans for new projects. It was Prime Minister Yoshiro Mori's visit to India in August 2000 that marked a starting point for the subsequent improvement of bilateral relations. The 'Global Partnership between Japan and India in the 21st Century' was launched,[3] which confirmed that the two countries would work together by pooling their strengths and expertise not only for their mutual benefit, but for the rest of the world as well.

Prime Minister Junichiro Koizumi's visit to India in April 2005 marked the launch of the 'Japan–India Partnership in a New Asian Era',[4] which was aimed at reinforcing strategic emphasis on the global partnership between the two countries against the background of geopolitical change in Asia triggered by China's assertive emergence. Japan succeeded in inviting India along with Australia and New Zealand to be the founding members of the East Asia Summit (EAS) which was inaugurated in December 2005. With a view to check a growing Chinese ascendancy in the EAS, Japan assigned more weight to the 'ASEAN+6' (China, Japan, Korea, India, Australia and New Zealand) framework rather than the 'ASEAN+3' (Japan, China and Korea) framework as promulgated by China.

At the India–Japan summit meeting held in Tokyo in December 2006, Prime Ministers Manmohan Singh and Shinzo Abe announced the 'Joint Statement towards Japan–India Strategic and Global Partnership'. The Joint Statement held great importance because it confirmed that both prime ministers would meet every year. India was the first country to which Japan made an official promise of mutual visitation. For India, Japan was the second country after Russia to have such an arrangement with. Since then, besides the prime ministers' mutual visitation, annual ministerial dialogues between their foreign ministries, defence ministries and ministers dealing with finance, economy, trade, and energy have also been institutionalised.

The 'Joint Declaration on Security Cooperation between Japan–India' signed at the annual summit meeting in October 2008[5] is noteworthy because it provided a comprehensive framework for enhanced security cooperation between the two countries. For India, this was the second security agreement, following one signed with Australia in March 2007. The 2008 Joint Declaration was followed up by the Action Plan in December 2009, which outlined a more detailed strategic and defence cooperation,[6] including an annual strategic dialogue between foreign ministers, an annual subcabinet/senior official 2+2 dialogue and bilateral naval exercises.

The Japan–India annual summit meeting has been decisively important in implementing bilateral collaboration in Indian infrastructure. It is no exaggeration to say that such a gigantic project as the Delhi–Mumbai Industrial Corridor or the Dedicated Freight Corridor could not have taken shape or the decision to introduce the Shinkansen system to the Mumbai–Ahmedabad bullet train project could not have been finalised without the Strategic and Global Partnership framework.

Bilateral Relations, Keeping an Eye on the Indo-Pacific

Prime Minister Narendra Modi attaches no less importance to relations with Japan than his predecessor Manmohan Singh. Modi has a close personal bond with Prime Minister Shinzo Abe, viewing Japan as an 'all-weather' friend strategically committed to India's economic modernisation.[7] Abe and Modi adopted the 'Tokyo Declaration for Japan–India Special Strategic and Global Partnership' in September 2014,[8] elevating Japan and India's bilateral relationship to the Special Strategic and Global Partnership and stressing further progress in bilateral security and further expansion of Japanese investment into India. Both Japan and India set a target of doubling Japanese FDI and the number of Japanese companies in India. Japan expressed its intention to provide 3.3 trillion yen in public and private financing to India over the next five years.[9] As for the security partnership, both countries affirmed the importance of regular bilateral maritime exercises and Japan's continued participation in the India–US Malabar exercise series. They also decided to discuss elevation of the official trilateral dialogue between Japan, India and the US to a dialogue among their respective foreign ministers.

The 'Japan and India Vision 2025 Special Strategic and Global Partnership' was announced at the Delhi summit meeting in December 2015,[10] which showed further deepening of bilateral relations in the field of economic and security cooperation. Prime Ministers Abe and Modi welcomed the conclusion of two security-related agreements: one related to the transfer of defence equipment and technology, and the other related to security measures for the protection of classified military information. These agreements would make way for future projects on defence equipment and technology cooperation, including India's acquisition of the Japanese US-2 amphibious aircraft, and would deepen bilateral cooperation for the defence of the sea lines of communication (SLOCs) in the Indo-Pacific region.

Regarding bilateral collaboration in infrastructure development, the two prime ministers confirmed that, in addition to the ongoing DMIC project, the Chennai–Bengaluru Industrial Corridor (CBIC) project would be implemented using ODA loan schemes. It is noteworthy that in the field of railway, besides the abovementioned introduction of the Japanese bullet train (*Shinkansen*) system to the Mumbai–Ahmedabad route, the two prime ministers have confirmed the signing of a memorandum of comprehensive technical cooperation including railway safety, rolling stock manufacturing, and station re-development, which would broaden commercial opportunities for Japanese companies.

At the summit meeting held in Tokyo in November 2016, the Agreement for Cooperation in the Peaceful Use of Nuclear Energy was signed,[11] which would enable Japanese companies, including their subsidiaries in the US, to export their nuclear plants to India. The two prime ministers decided to seek synergy between India's 'Act East Policy' and Japan's 'Free and Open Indo-Pacific (FOIP) Strategy' for better regional integration and improved connectivity through industrial networks. Enhancing road connectivity in North East India and cooperation in the development of infrastructure and connectivity for the Iranian port of Chabahar were also mentioned. At the summit meeting held in Gandhinagar in September 2017, the two prime ministers reiterated their strong commitment to work together and with other countries in the Indo-Pacific region including Africa.

It was at the 2015 Delhi meeting that the Indo-Pacific concept was introduced for the first time at the summit level. The term Indo-Pacific is a geographical concept of a 'broader Asia', which originated in a speech made by Prime Minister Abe in the Indian Parliament in 2007, titled 'Confluence of the Two Seas'.[12] Subsequently, the then US Secretary of State, Hillary Clinton, noted the importance of translating the growing connection between the Indian and Pacific Oceans into an operational concept, indicating that the 'stretch of sea from the Indian Ocean through the Strait of Malacca to the Pacific contains the world's most vibrant trade and energy routes'.[13] The Indo-Pacific concept reflects the fact that the accelerating economic and security connections between the Western Pacific and the Indian Ocean Region are creating a single strategic system against the background of the geographically expanding interests of China and India.[14] Recognising that peace, stability and development in the Indo-Pacific are indispensable to national security and prosperity, the forementioned 'Japan and India Vision 2025' emphasised the importance of close cooperation between Japan and India. The Indo-Pacific concept has also gained currency in the US, which is exemplified by the fact that President Donald Trump used the term 'Indo-Pacific', instead of 'Asia Pacific' in his remarks at the Asia-Pacific Economic Cooperation (APEC) Summit held in Da Nang in November 2017.[15]

At a time when India was preoccupied in dealing with the COVID-19 pandemic in June 2020, the India–China border clash took place in eastern Ladakh, claiming the largest number of victims among Indian soldiers since the 1962 Sino-Indian border war. Anti-China feelings flared up in India after the incident, with India accelerating its decoupling from China in trade and investment as it felt that its efforts towards confidence-building after the stand-off at Doklam plateau in 2017 were crushed by China. Under the guiding principle of strategic autonomy, and following its erstwhile nonaligned foreign policy, India had for long been pursuing an omnidirectional diplomacy. The latest border clash, however, resulted in India increasingly shifting toward strengthening bilateral and multilateral security cooperation with Japan, the US and Australia under the FOIP framework, with the revived Quad at its core.

Trends in Bilateral Trade and FDI

Sluggish Japan–India Trade

Before World War II, India had been Japan's major trade partner, accounting for 10–15 per cent of Japan's foreign trade up until 1937.[16] Major imported products from India were cotton and pig iron. Japan and India were mutual competitors in textile and steel industries. After World War II, India remained an important trade partner of Japan, accounting for 2–4 per cent of trade until around 1965.[17] Iron ore replaced pig iron as the major imported product from India. Iron ore from India played a crucial role in the remarkable post-war development of the Japanese steel industry until Japan started to import iron ore on a large scale from Australia and Brazil. Since the mid-1960s, under its closed inward-looking regime, India has struggled with industrial stagnation and has been left behind by the global tide of rapid economic development. Japan, in contrast, joined the Organization for Economic Co-operation and Development (OECD) in 1964 and has since pursued high-speed economic growth, quickly becoming an economic superpower. Japan's economic relations with Asian countries increasingly emphasised East Asian countries, and Japan and India have gradually become economically estranged from each other.

Along with the introduction of economic reforms in 1991, India adopted an outward-looking policy to stimulate its economy by riding the wave of globalisation. Japan–India economic relations showed signs of expansion in the 1990s, which were again set back in 1998 because

Figure 10.1 India's Trade with East Asia (2000–01 to 2022–23)

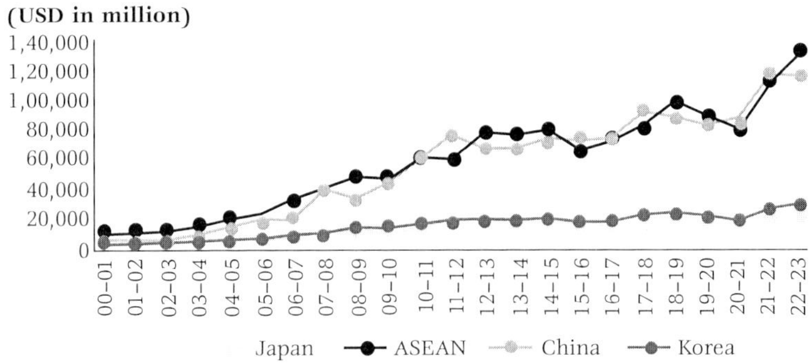

Source: Graph prepared by the author with data taken from Export Import Data Bank, Ministry of Commerce and Industry, Government of India.

of Japan's sanctions against India in the aftermath of India's nuclear tests. It was only in 2003–04 that bilateral trade started to present an upward trend, increasing from USD 5.36 billion to USD 18.51 billion in 2011–12. Improved bilateral trade, however, has stagnated since then and has been largely overshadowed by India's other bilateral trading relations such as those with ASEAN, China and Korea. In fact, Japan–India bilateral trade was surpassed by India–China trade in 2002–03 and by India–Korea trade in 2005–06 (Figure 10.1). Under the 'Look East Policy', India–China and India–ASEAN trade had quadrupled relative to Japan. Japan's share in all Indian trade declined from 5.9 per cent in 1997–98 to 2.2 per cent in 2019–20, with Japan's rank declining from third biggest trading partner in the mid-1990s to below fifteenth. India's share in Japan's trade was only 1.1 per cent, with India's rank as Japan's largest trading partner stagnating below twentieth (Figure 10.1).[18]

The Japan–India Comprehensive Economic Partnership Agreement (CEPA) came into effect in August 2011.[19] Under the CEPA, tariffs on 90 per cent of Indian goods and 97 per cent of Japanese goods were scheduled for elimination over the course of 10 years. Japan–India bilateral trade jumped from USD 13.72 billion in 2010–11 to USD 18.51 billion in 2011–12 and to USD 18.52 billion in 2012–13. Since then, however, it has decreased to USD 13.60 billion in 2016–17, failing to rise again to USD 18 billion afterward (Figure 10.1). Given that India's total trade has also been shrinking since 2011–12, it might be too early to appraise the effects of the CEPA on the status of Japan–India trade, but its impact has not been discouraging so far.

To explain the currently sluggish Japan–India bilateral trade, we can point out the following three challenges. First, Japanese exports to India have been overwhelmed by a sweeping expansion of Chinese exports to India. China has successfully penetrated the Indian market with low-priced goods even without enjoying any benefits such as those enjoyed by Japan under the CEPA. One example is Japanese exports of steel products to India. Hot and cold rolled steel plates, alloy steel and galvanised steel sheets have been scheduled for exemption from 5 per cent tariffs within five years from 2011–12. Japanese exports of steel products increased from USD 1.37 billion in 2010–11 to USD 2.08 billion in 2012–13, but thereafter decreased to USD 0.93 billion in 2016–17. By contrast, Chinese steel products exports to India increased from USD 2.98 billion to USD 3.55 billion during the same period.[20]

Second, horizontal trade has not developed between Japan and India as it has in the trade of industrial products and parts between Japan and East Asian countries. Petroleum products, notably naphtha, accounted for almost 15 per cent of India's exports to Japan in 2018–19, followed by organic chemicals, precious stones and marine products.[21] The expansion of Japanese FDI into India holds the key for India to be incorporated into the existing East Asian production network, thereby building horizontal trade between the two countries.

Third, there are obstacles to Japan's import of Indian pharmaceutical products. India is a country that has a strong advantage in manufacturing pharmaceutical products, especially generic medicines, which constitute India's second most important export items to the US, following precious stones.[22] The Japan–India CEPA allows the countries to accord 'national treatment' for the registration of generic medicines and related applications. But even then, there are still many hurdles for Japan to overcome to expand the import of pharmaceutical products from India. India's export of pharmaceutical products to Japan increased from USD 13.8 million in 2010–11 to USD 67 million in 2012–13, but it stagnated thereafter. While India exported USD 6.3 billion in pharmaceuticals to the United States, corresponding exports to Japan were only USD 62.4 million. Considering that the Japanese government intends to increase the share of generic medicine from 56.2 per cent in 2015–16 to more than 80 per cent by 2020–21[23] to check ballooning medical expenditures, there should be much room for the expansion of imports of generic medicines from India under the Japan–India CEPA framework.

Active FDI from Japan

In contrast to trade, FDI has been experiencing a more dynamic trend. According to the FDI data compiled by the Indian Ministry of Commerce and Industry,[24] Japan is a major investor in India, with Japanese FDI, as of 2020, closely comparable to that of the Netherlands, and exceeded only by Mauritius and Singapore, which provide special tax benefits for investors. Japan accounted for 7 per cent of the total cumulative FDI inflows into India during the period April 2000 to March 2020.[25] According to the net flow-based FDI data provided by the Japanese government,[26] Japan's FDI in India grew sharply in the years since 2007, increasing from the USD 500 million level in 2006 to the USD 1,500 million level in 2007. The purchase of Ranbaxy Laboratories, India's largest pharmaceutical company, by Daiichi Sankyo, and NTT Docomo's equity participation in Tata Teleservices caused Japan's FDI in India to surge to USD 5,551

Figure 10.2 Japan's FDI in India (2003–22)

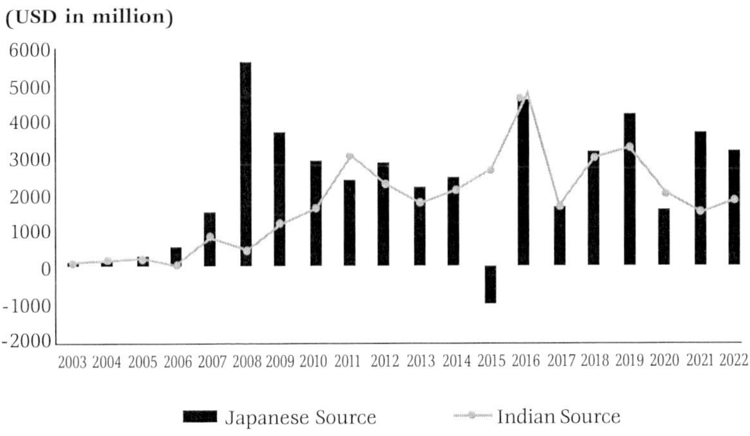

Source: Data calculated from Balance of Payments statistics published by the Ministry of Finance, Japan and Japan External Trade Organization (JETRO); Fact Sheet on Foreign Direct Investment (FDI) published by the Ministry of Commerce and Industry, India.

million in 2008 and USD 3,664 million in 2009, which are comparable to the levels of Japan's FDI in ASEAN and China. Subsequently, with the two abovementioned companies withdrawing from the Indian market,[27] Japan's FDI in India slowed down and turned negative in 2015, but it rose again thereafter (Figure 10.2).

The data provided by the Indian government, as mentioned above, indicates that Japan's FDI in India increased after 2008, reaching a peak in 2016. A wide discrepancy in statistical data between Japanese and Indian sources can be traced to the following reasons: India's FDI data do not include re-invested earnings, and the investment made by NTT Docomo and Daiichi Sankyo in 2008 was rolled over to be posted on the FDI data of 2016–17.

An increase in Japanese FDI into India is also reflected in the number of Japanese companies operating in India. From October 2008 to October 2019, the number of Japanese companies increased from 550 to 1454, with the bases of operation increasing from 838 to 5022 (Figure 10.3).[28]

Figure 10.3: Japanese Companies Establishing a Presence in India (October 2008 to October 2022)

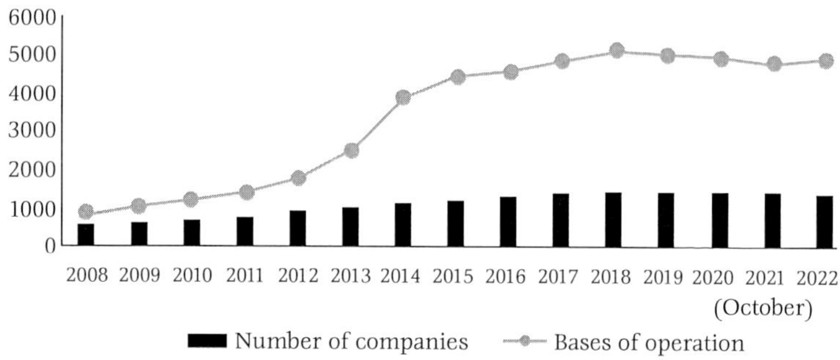

Source: Embassy of Japan in India and JETRO.

In the past, Japanese FDI into India had been geared toward the manufacturing sector, attracting 76 per cent of the total Japanese FDI stocks into India as of 2016. Looking at the subsector level, transport machinery—mostly automobiles and automobile parts—accounted for 42 per cent of the total Japanese FDI into India. Major Japanese assemblers including Suzuki, Nissan, Toyota and Honda have marked

India as a strongpoint for the production of small cars and sport utility vehicles (SUVs) in their global strategy. As indicated by Suzuki's success in India, Japanese automakers' advance into the market has contributed greatly to raising Indian manufacturing industry standards, mainly by increasing workers' skill and improving quality control. It is noteworthy that a growing number of Indian manufacturers have been awarded the prestigious Japanese Deming Prize for their contributions to the field of total quality management (TQM).[29]

The strong presence of Japanese automobile assemblers and auto part manufacturers induces other companies involved in steel, machines, power plants and logistics to come to India. In the air conditioner sector, Daikin has maintained its position as the top brand in India. The advance of Japanese companies into India is increasing in a wide range of areas such as pharmaceuticals, foods, retails, stationery, cosmetics and sanitary goods. In the retail sector, Muji of Ryohin Keikaku opened its first Indian outlet in Mumbai in August 2016, and Fast Retailing opened its first Uniqlo store in New Delhi in October 2019. SoftBank is already one of the largest investors in India's e-commerce market. Japanese financial institutions including insurance companies are also making their presence felt in the Indian financial market.

A 2019 survey, conducted by Japan Bank for International Cooperation (JBIC),[30] of Japanese manufacturers with oversea subsidiaries revealed that India ranked as the most desirable place to do business in the long term (the next 10 years) as well as in the medium term (the next three years). The most frequently given reason for India's attractiveness was the future prospect of the domestic market. Expectations toward India stood out compared to other regions. On the other hand, India ranked lower than many other geographic regions in the degree of satisfaction with sales and earnings, a measure of business performance, and in this metric India was placed at the same level as Brazil and Russia. According to the survey, some of the issues hindering investments were a lack of infrastructure, severe competition with other countries and a lack of transparency in the execution of laws.

As of 2021, as many as 12 Japan Industrial Townships (JITs) are being set up in nine states of India, with a view to addressing the various issues confronting Japanese investors in India, such as problems related to underdeveloped infrastructure, land acquisition and complicated clearances.[31] Clearing these issues might be extremely helpful for Japanese

SMEs wanting to invest in India. Following Prime Minister Narendra Modi's visit to Japan in September 2014, a special cell known as 'Japan Plus' was set up under the Government of India to facilitate and fast-track investment proposals from Japan.[32] The cell is placed under the Department of Industrial Policy and Promotion (DIPP), Ministry of Commerce and Industry. The team comprises six members: four from the Government of India and two from Japan's Ministry of Economy, Trade and Industry (METI). The decision to place members of a foreign government within a unit under the Government of India is unusual, and it further indicates that both governments are engaged in close cooperation for facilitating Japan's investment in India.

Apart from issues concerning the investment climate in India, the divergence in corporate culture between the two countries poses another challenge for Japan's FDI in India. From the Indian viewpoint, Japanese companies tend to be risk-averse and are shy about committing themselves deeply to local Indian businesses from a long-term perspective. The difference of style in negotiation sometimes becomes an obstacle to reaching an agreement between the two sides. When starting a negotiation, Indians tend to prioritise the establishment of a basic agreement and discuss details only after a deal is completed, whereas the Japanese side is more likely to be perfectionist, and insists on discussing details from the start. Furthermore, unlike in Japan, the current management in most Indian companies comprises a younger generation, with managers who are culturally more in tune with Western styles of management.[33]

Infrastructure Development through Japanese ODA

Japan has played a significant role in the development of India's infrastructure. India was the first recipient of international yen loans that Japan began to provide in 1958. Since 2004–05, India has been the largest recipient of Japan's ODA. As of fiscal year 2018, Japan pledged yen loans worth 534.7 billion yen to India, 68 per cent of which was intended for transportation (metro 31 per cent, freight railway 15 per cent, high-speed railway 9 per cent, and others 13 per cent), followed by energy 11 per cent, water supply and sewage 9 per cent, agriculture and forestry 6 per cent, and others 6 per cent.[34] Japanese ODA not only had a significant impact on infrastructure development in India in the fields of power sector, transportation, and water supply and sewerage, but it has also been instrumental in encouraging Japanese companies to invest in infrastructure-related areas.

The following five factors are the reasons behind the conspicuous expansion of yen loans to India: 1) Large-scale projects such as the metro railway and Dedicated Freight Corridor (DFC) are on the rise; 2) there is a strong request from the Indian government for the provision of yen loans; 3) there has been no delay in repayment of yen loans thanks to the proper management of debt services; 4) capital requirements are huge in India, reflecting an enormous demand for development; and 5) India's competent authorities have exhibited a high ability to effectively implement projects.[35]

A large share of yen loans went toward the construction of subway systems. The Delhi Metro that began operating in 2002 is a successful example of the transfer of Japan's operation systems, construction culture and safety technology to India. Japan's support of subway systems has spread from New Delhi to Ahmedabad, Mumbai, Kolkata and Chennai. More Japan–India collaboration can be expected in future projects because 50 large cities in India with populations of more than two million are expected to receive metro rail systems.

Currently, the Indian government is focusing on the development and connectivity of the Northeast region. The region is connected with the main part of India through the Siliguri Corridor, a narrow stretch of land of about 22 km wide sandwiched between Nepal and Bangladesh, which is known also as the Chicken's Neck. The Northeast region, which is desperately in need of development, is being paid attention for its geopolitical importance as it connects India with Myanmar, Bangladesh and Bhutan. Through the India–Japan Act East Forum set up in 2017, Japan has deeply committed to the improvement of the region's infrastructure, including the 19 km-long bridge on Brahmaputra in Assam and Meghalaya.[36]

Japan–India collaboration has been indispensable to the enhancement of transport connectivity in India, as is evident from the numerous metro rail projects, the Mumbai Trans-Harbour Link Project, the North East Road Connectivity Improvement Project, and the three major projects discussed in further detail below: the DMIC, the Western DFC, and the Mumbai–Ahmedabad High-Speed Railway (HSR).

The Delhi–Mumbai Industrial Corridor

India is developing plans for five industrial corridors:[37] Delhi–Mumbai, Amritsar–Delhi–Kolkata, Chennai–Bengaluru, Bengaluru–Mumbai and Visakhapatnam–Chennai. Of these five, it is the Delhi–Mumbai Industrial Corridor (DMIC), a joint Japan–India project with an estimated investment between USD 90 billion and USD 100 billion, that is drawing the most attention as the flagship project of India–Japan collaboration.

With the Western DFC—a dedicated freight railway—serving as the backbone, the DMIC plans to construct 24 Industrial Nodes with world-class infrastructure across six states in western India by 2040.[38] Currently, eight of them are underway in Phase 1. The six states are India's important commercial and industrial areas, accounting for 58 per cent of total industrial production, 45 per cent of total employment, and 57 per cent of total exports as of 2010.[39]

The idea of promoting the DMIC was endorsed at the Japan–India summit meeting in December 2006. The DMIC Development Corporation (DMICDC) was established under the Indian government in 2008. The Japanese government has taken a 26 per cent equity interest in the DMICDC since 2013,[40] sending two Japanese officers as board members. The DMICDC was renamed National Industrial Corridor Development Corporation (NICDC) to control all the five corridors.

Some claim that Japanese enthusiasm and participation in the DMIC project is waning.[41] At the annual Japan–India summit meeting in December 2011, Japan pledged a USD 4.5 billion loan to the DMIC project, and the 19 prospective projects proposed by the Japanese side for constructing environmentally friendly smart communities—including projects for power supply, metro railway and water supply—were formerly endorsed by the two countries in November 2012.[42] Of these projects, the only successful case is the Logistics Data Bank (LDB) project, an IT-driven logistics visualisation services project. The LDB project started in 2016 as a joint venture between Japan's NEC Corp. and DMICDC to visualise international marine container delivery by affixing radio frequency identification (RFID) tags, which has seen success in shortening transportation lead time and bringing efficiency in logistics and supply chain. It can be said that the list of 19 prospective projects was presented by the Japanese side without conducting a scrupulous feasibility analysis, and therefore these projects have fallen short of gaining a strong commitment from Japanese companies.

The Western DFC

As early as April 2005, the prime ministers of Japan and India made a joint declaration at the summit meeting on the feasibility and possible funding of dedicated rail freight corridors, with a view to provide a safe and efficient transportation system, running at the speed of 100 km/h. The Dedicated Freight Corridor Corporation of India Limited (DFCCIL) was established as a 'special purpose vehicle' in 2006 to construct and operate the two freight corridors: The Western DFC connecting the states between Haryana and Maharashtra to be financed using a soft loan provided by the Japan International Cooperation Agency (JICA), and the Eastern DFC connecting the states between Punjab and West Bengal to be financed by the World Bank and public–private partnership (PPP). At the summit meeting in October 2008, Prime Minister Taro Aso promised a USD 450 billion ODA loan for the construction of Phase 1 of the Western DFC project.[43]

The Western DFC will extend 1,504 km from Dadri in the Delhi National Capital Region to the Jawaharlal Nehru Port (JNPT). Electric locomotives will transport double-stack containers on a double-track railroad. Freight that took two to three days to travel from Delhi to Mumbai through conventional railways will now be able to complete the trip in a single day and freight capacity will increase 2.4 times per day.[44]

The Western DFC project was provided with a 731.5 billion yen loan for Phases 1 and 2. At the summit meeting in April 2005, it was decided that the funding offered by Japan would be made under the Special Terms for Economic Partnership (STEP) loan, which means that more than 30 per cent of the materials used is to be supplied by Japan,[45] and the Japanese are required to be the main contractors for each railway contract package.

There has been criticism that these STEP loans—tied loans in favour of Japanese companies—have contributed to the delay of the Western DFC. The participation of major Japanese construction companies was presumed in the field of civil engineering work, but no major companies dared to participate in the DFC project due to their risk-averse behaviour. Eventually, after a long period of preparation, civil engineering work for the Phase 1 section (Rewari to Vadodara) started in September 2013, with Larsen & Toubro taking charge of it in tie-up with the Japanese trading company Sojitz Corporation as the prime contractor. As for the electric locomotive project of the Western DFC, India's Ministry of Railways is set to handle it since cost factors made Japanese companies reluctant to participate. As of October 2019, the construction of the Western DFC is 63 per cent complete for the Phase 1 section and 31 per cent complete for the Phase 2 section (Dadri to Rewari and Vadodara to JNPT). Rail services on this route are scheduled to begin by the end of 2024. Meanwhile, the Dadri-Sanand route became operational in October 2023, even though the whole line is not open yet.[46]

Mumbai–Ahmedabad High-Speed Railway

The construction of the Mumbai–Ahmedabad High-Speed Railway (MAHSR) is attracting considerable interest as the new symbol of joint Japan–India projects. Japan has faced stiff competition from other countries in bidding for this project. For instance, a pre-feasibility study was conducted by a French company. The Indian government however placed high confidence on the safety and punctuality of Japan's HSR technologies, and following the summit meeting held in May 2013 between Prime Ministers Shinzo Abe and Manmohan Singh, a Memorandum of Understanding (MOU) was signed between Indian Railway and Japan International Cooperation Agency to conduct a joint feasibility study of the Ahmadabad–Mumbai route.[47]

It was at the summit meeting held in Delhi in December 2015 that Prime Ministers Modi and Abe confirmed that the Shinkansen system would be introduced to the HSR on the Mumbai–Ahmedabad route.[48] The Shinkansen system will sharply reduce the transportation time between Mumbai and Ahmedabad, an extent of 509 km, from eight hours to two hours and 30 minutes. During the summit meeting held in Gandhinagar in September 2017, the cornerstone for this project was laid. According to the Ministry of Railways' Vision 2020,[49] India has a plan to introduce high-speed trains providing services at 250–350 km/h along six routes: Delhi–Amritsar, Pune–Mumbai–Ahmedabad, Hyderabad–Chennai, Howrah–Haldia, Chennai–Trivandrum and Delhi–Patna. Of these six routes, the Mumbai–Ahmedabad route within the DMIC is the most promising from the standpoint of marketability, considering its high population density across the high-income regions.

The total project cost for the Mumbai–Ahmedabad route is estimated to be INR 790 billion, and approximately 81 per cent of the total cost is to be covered by Japanese ODA.[50] The terms and conditions of the loan are quite favourable for the Indian side: 0.1 per cent interest rate with a repayment period of 50 years (including 15 years of grace period). It is rather unusual that India is receiving this Japanese ODA on such a large scale under such favourable terms and conditions as indicated above. The financing is on the basis of a bilateral tied loan, which means that only Japanese or Indian companies are entitled to play the role of prime contractors for each contract package. Unlike the STEP loan, there is no mandatory requirement for procurement from Japan, except for those specifically important areas such as electric works and rolling stock.

East Japan Railway is responsible for the transfer of Shinkansen technology in areas such as rolling stock, operations, and the training of Indian personnel. Human resources development for operation, maintenance and management of the HSR is indispensable to the success of the Shinkansen system in India. The planned production of 160 units of Shinkansen rolling stock will take place in Japan and this rolling stock will be widely used not only on the Ahmedabad–Mumbai route but also on other railway routes.

While construction has been planned to take place from 2018 to the end of 2023, there is still much uncertainty about costs and expropriation of land. Indian Railways has already acquired 80 per cent of the land needed for the construction of the high-speed railway as of October 2021.[51] However, in the October 2019 election of the Maharashtra Legislative Assembly, the ruling Bhartiya Janata Party (BJP) did not win a majority, and a coalition government led by the regional party of Shiv Sena—which is sceptical about the high-speed project—took power. Considering the tardy progress of land acquisition in Maharashtra, the inauguration date for the MAHSR was revised from December 2023 to October 2028. Meanwhile, even before the whole line opens, following trial runs on a 47-km stretch connecting Surat to Bilimore, the Indian government has come up with a plan to commence operation on the 352-km section in Gujarat in 2027.[52]

New Horizons in Japan–India Relations

Coordinated Efforts to Reduce Reliance on China

The outbreak of COVID-19 taught both Japan and India a lesson about the dangers of heavy reliance on Sino-centred supply chains for movement of their strategic materials. In the early spring of 2020, Japan suddenly faced an acute shortage of masks even though Japanese companies were producing a large volume of masks in China, only because China stopped shipping these masks to Japan during the COVID-19 pandemic. In response to this, in April 2020, Japan announced an emergency economic package of 243.5 billion yen to encourage the transfer and diversification of production locations away from China to Japan and ASEAN countries (220 billion yen for transfer to Japan, and 23.5 billion yen for transfer to ASEAN countries).[53] Shortly thereafter, the Japanese government announced that the above supplementary budget earmarked for transfer to ASEAN nations would be available also if the production location is shifted to India or Bangladesh. In September 2020, the economic ministers of Japan, India and Australia made a joint statement[54] announcing that the three countries have recognised the pressing need for regional cooperation on supply chain resilience and shared their intention to work together toward a new initiative. Meanwhile, although a broad consensus has been reached regarding the necessity of reorganising supply chains, there is still a tendency among Japanese companies to maintain and expand their business in China, lured by the huge and expanding markets there.

India is currently at the forefront of reorganising supply chains in the region. At the end of March 2020, the Modi government launched a national lockdown for two months to contain the spread of the COVID-19 virus. During this very period when the lockdown disrupted economic activities and imposed great pains on the population, the Indian government launched an economic package in May 2020 under the Atmanirbhar Bharat (Self-Reliant India) Mission, worth USD 280 billion, which was equivalent to around 10 per cent of its GDP.[55] The mission was noteworthy not only for its large-scale relief measures but for initiating a slew of multi-sectoral supply-side structural reforms to lend flexibility and resilience to supply chains. As a part of Atmanirbhar Bharat Mission, the Production-Linked Incentive (PLI) scheme was launched in April 2020 to make India a manufacturing hub. The scheme has an outlay of almost INR 3 trillion over five years, covering 14 sectors including mobile phones, pharma products and medical devices.[56] According to the scheme, incentives of 4–6 per cent are given on incremental sales of the registered companies which include not only domestic firms but global companies like Samsung, Foxcon and Wistron. In tandem with the PLI scheme, the Indian government launched other successive measures to decouple from

China. Since April 2020, government approval has been made mandatory for all FDI from China. After the border clash broke out in Ladakh in June 2020, India took steps to ban Chinese-owned smartphone apps and tighten import restriction measures against China.

Due to the impact of COVID-19, India saw its GDP shrink by almost 8 per cent and global FDI inflow fell by 42 per cent in 2020, but FDI rose by 13 per cent to USD 57 billion.[57] What contributed most to the expansion of India's FDI inflow were the fresh investments made by the US global companies including Apple, Google and Amazon against the backdrop of a growing US–China conflict. Thus, FDI from the US to India increased from USD 4.2 in 2019–20 to USD 13.8 billion in 2020–21.[58]

Here, we should like to highlight the new surge of Taiwanese investment into India. Taiwan is the hometown of the world's largest electronic manufacturing services (EMS) companies. It is well-known that a huge inflow of Taiwanese FDI contributed greatly to China becoming a global electronic manufacturing centre. Meanwhile, reacting against the 'One China' policy vehemently promoted by the People's Republic of China (PRC), the current Tsai Ing-wen government has taken up the banner of 'de-Sinicisation' and has adopted the New Southbound Policy, providing preferential treatment to encourage Taiwanese companies to relocate their production base away from China. In addition to that, the US–China conflict gave an impetus for Taiwanese companies to expand their investment in India. Following the announcement by Apple in February 2020 to begin direct and online selling in India,[59] Taiwanese companies such as Foxcon and Wistron decided to expand their plants in India. These activities are expected to contribute to India becoming a major manufacturing power in the imminent future. The Taiwanese firm TSMC, the world's most valuable semiconductor company, is set to start up its R&D centre in Japan, and has already set up its office in India. We can expect that the tripartite relationship between Japan, India and Taiwan will constitute a powerful combination of hardware and software in supply chain.

Difference in Stance over the RCEP

Japan has the track record of taking leadership in formalising a large free trade pact: The Comprehensive and Progressive Agreement for Trans-Pacific Partnership (CPTPP), also known as TPP11. The CPTPP came into effect in March 2018, in the aftermath of the withdrawal of the US from the Trans-Pacific Partnership (TPP), under President Donald Trump. Dreaming of the emergence of a mega free trade pact covering 48 per cent of the world's population and 32 per cent of the global GDP, Japan had been strongly supportive of India's membership in the Regional Comprehensive Economic Partnership (RCEP).[60] When the summit meeting of 16 Asian countries, comprising the 10 members of ASEAN and six other countries, namely China, India, Japan, Korea, Australia and New Zealand, was held in November 2019, all the RCEP participating countries were expected to ink the pact, but India held back citing the reason of 'significant outstanding issues, which remain unresolved'.[61] Because of Japan's insistence that it is better not to start the RCEP without India, the formal deal which was to be signed at the 2019 Bangkok summit meeting was postponed to 2020.

In November 2020, an online ministerial meeting of the countries concerned was held, and a final agreement was reached to start the RCEP without India. Before the 2019 Bangkok summit meeting, there was heavy indication that India would finally sign the deal. Indeed, a government-appointed high-level advisory group (HLAG) published a report[62] just 10 days before the Bangkok summit meeting, advocating that it might not be an option for India to keep out of the RCEP because it would exclude India from a large regional market and thereby prevent it from achieving the target of doubling its exports to USD 1 trillion (including services exports) by 2025. Just few days before the Bangkok summit meeting, India's Commerce and Industry Minister Piyush Goyal cautioned against unwarranted and unfair fear psychosis against free trade agreements created by a few people.[63] After arriving in Bangkok, Prime Minister Narendra Modi said that India would like a win-win outcome, while addressing concerns over unsustainable trade deficits. All of this suggests that India put off making its final decision till the very last moment, trying to explore the various possibilities of signing the deal.

Under its outward-oriented policy, India already concluded 12 Free Trade Agreements (FTAs)/Economic Partnership Agreements (EPAs) and five Preferential Trade Agreements (PTAs).[64] However, India has yet to enjoy expected benefits under the current FTAs/EPAs, as it has growing trade deficits with the current FTA/EPA partners including Japan, Korea and ASEAN countries. India has a grievance that its export of goods like pharmaceuticals, steel and tires has been prevented from expanding due to non-tariff barriers, while India provides preferential access to its expanding market. The most dreadful matter for India is its trade deficits with China. Although India has not concluded a formal FTA with Beijing, it already accounted for 29 per cent of the India's total trade deficits in 2018–19.[65]

Under the Atmanirbhar Bharat Mission, India aims to be self-reliant as a nation, but at the same time, it wants to become a global manufacturing hub by linking up with the global supply chain. As a matter of fact, since the 'Make in India' initiative was launched in 2014, a rather protectionist policy has been adopted, with the average tariff increasing from 13 per cent in 2014 to 18 per cent in 2020.[66] At the same time, some noteworthy reforms have also been implemented, including the introduction of the Goods and Services Tax (GST) and the Insolvency and Bankruptcy Code (IBC). The 2020 border clash in Ladakh in the middle of the COVID-19 pandemic impelled India to reduce its dependence on China for its imports. India needs import substitution vis-à-vis China and a free trade policy vis-à-vis the rest of the world, according to economic advisor Arvind Virmani.[67] Given that India needs to strengthen its economic competitiveness before it can do away with its protectionist policies, it may be hard for India to join the RCEP in the near future.

Strengthening Bilateral Collaboration in Information and Communication Technology (ICT)

Accounting for 55 per cent of global IT offshoring, the Indian IT industry has maintained its status as a leading industry, with its revenue size reaching about USD 177 billion in fiscal year 2018 and exports accounting for about 83 per cent of its revenues.[68] The US accounts for 62 per cent of the Indian IT export markets, followed by the UK (17 per cent), and the EU (11 per cent). Japan's share is only about 1 per cent of the total Indian IT exports.[69] Considering that Japan is globally ranked as the third largest IT services market and yet faces an acute shortage of IT engineers, IT collaboration between Japan and India has great potential that is yet unrealised. Despite the fact that India is held in high esteem with regard to high-quality control/management capability and a wide scope of IT skills, when looking offshore, Japanese companies prefer to turn to China, where they can find many IT engineers with good Japanese language skills.

The main reasons for Japan not using India's IT capabilities fully include language barriers and cultural misunderstanding, scarcity of Indian residents or Indian students in Japan, lack of globalised human resources in Japan and different software development styles. The Japanese style is characterised by an integral approach, accompanied by ambiguity in requirement specifications. When IT vendors fail to understand the precise requirements of customers, e.g., whether it is cost reduction or something else, customer satisfaction remains low and business cannot be expected to expand.

Meanwhile, considering that both Japan and India are natural partners based on mutual respect and reliance, a new trend of bilateral collaboration has emerged in the area of information and communication technology—that of cyber security. In terms of deepening bilateral collaboration over information-sharing and strategy for cyber security, the First Japan–India Cyber Dialogue was held in 2017, which was followed by the Second and Third Dialogues in 2017 and 2019 respectively.

In October 2018, a Memorandum of Cooperation (MoC) on Japan–India Digital Partnership was signed between Japan's Ministry of Economy, Trade and Industry (METI) and India's Ministry of Electronics and Information Technology (MeitY).[70] Recognising that Japan and India would be able to build a distinguished partnership by leveraging advantages of each other toward the era of next generation technologies when integration of hardware and software will be increasingly required, the scope of cooperation was confirmed to include the following items: 1) supporting Indian startups; 2) promoting digital corporate partnerships; 3) establishing a partnership mechanism to manufacture and design electronics ecosystems; 4) utilising Indian IT talent in Japanese companies; 5) promoting R&D cooperation in artificial intelligence; and 6) promoting cooperation in areas such as cyber security and security of digital infrastructure of future networks as well as the development of submarine cable projects.

As recently as January 2021, another MoC was signed between Japan's Ministry of Internal Affairs and Communications and India's Ministry of Communications and IT to step up cooperation[71] in the field of ICT, including areas such as 5G technology, telecom security, submarine optical fibre cable to Indian islands, spectrum management, smart cities, high-altitude platform for broadband in unconnected areas, disaster management, and public safety, among others. The agreement is intended also as a countermove to China's growing influence in telecommunications and digital infrastructure. The Japanese company NEC has already laid a 2,312 km-long submarine fibre cable connecting Chennai with the

Andaman and Nicobar Islands in August 2020.[72] As a next step, the Indian government is planning to connect Lakshadweep Islands to the mainland with submarine optical fibre cable, and NEC may be the preferred choice of the Indian government to carry out this project.

Having established the Unique Identification Authority of India (UIDAI) in 2009, India has launched the world's largest national identification system, with over 1.3 billion enrollments almost completed.[73] The system assigns a unique 12-digit identification number or 'Aadhaar' number which is based on multiple biometrics such as fingerprints, face images and iris images. It was the Japanese company NEC which made an indispensable contribution to the development of the abovementioned biometrics system. On the other hand, Japan had launched its 'My Number' system in 2016, but the spread of the system has been significantly delayed. With an aim to accelerate the process, Japan has established the Digital Agency in September 2021, which is intended to oversee Japan's catchup on digitalisation and to boldly promote digital transformation among its population. There is a growing consensus among the Japanese that Japan should learn from the Indian experience with regard to the promotion of its digital transformation. According to the METI, the shortage of IT personnel in Japan has been forecast to expand from 300,000 in 2020 to 450,000 by 2030.[74] Faced with such an acute shortage of IT personnel, it seems unavoidable for Japan to strengthen its ties with India.

Conclusions

Japan and India have established a framework for long-term economic and security cooperation under the Strategic and Global Partnership. A synergy of security and economic relations has helped to consolidate bilateral Japan–India relations as a whole. As Asia's leading democracies, both Japan and India share the belief that they will serve as key anchors for advancing peace, stability and prosperity in the region. As a mature economy with declining birth rates, Japan regards its strong partnership with India as important for its own growth scenario. India in turn regards Japan as a key partner to upgrade its manufacturing and infrastructure. Japan has played a leading role in building industrial corridors, high-speed railway and freight corridors, urban metro systems as well as in furthering connectivity in India's Northeast. The integration of external and domestic corridors will engender the creation of a dynamic international production network linking South Asia to ASEAN and East Asia, with India at the centre.

Both Japan and India have a mutual interest in dealing with an assertive China that has become the most important trading partner for both countries. The outbreak of COVID-19 taught both Japan and India a lesson as to the danger of heavy reliance on Sino-centred supply chains for transport of strategic materials. During the lockdown in 2020, India launched a comprehensive economic package to lend flexibility and resilience to supply chains, and the Sino-Indian border clash in the same year compelled India to introduce further measures to decouple from China. In September 2020, the economic ministers of Japan, India and Australia recognised the pressing need for regional cooperation on supply chain resilience and shared their intention to work together toward a new initiative. Although, given that currently India's stance is to strengthen its economic competitiveness, it is still a long way from giving up its protectionist policies, which makes it hard for India to join the RCEP.

Amid the impact of COVID-19, India saw FDI rising by 13 per cent to USD 57 billion in 2020, due to the increase in inflow of FDI from the US against the backdrop of a growing US–China conflict,[75] which in turn gave Taiwanese companies an impetus to expand their investment in India. The tripartite relationship between Japan, India and Taiwan—which has the world's largest electronic manufacturing services (EMS) companies—can be expected to constitute a powerful combination of hardware and software in supply chain.

Japan–India bilateral trade is still sluggish, and collaboration in ICT too has been far below the potential level. However, a new trend of bilateral collaboration has emerged in ICT areas associated with trust and security which has resulted in a series of productive Cyber Dialogues and two Memorandums of Cooperation have been signed to enhance digital partnership and increase cooperation in advanced fields such as 5G technology. The Japanese company NEC, which had contributed greatly to the development of the Aadhaar biometrics system, completed a project to install submarine fibre cables connecting the Indian mainland with the Andaman and Nicobar Islands in August 2020. Japan however continues to struggle in promoting its digital transformation. Considering the acute shortage of IT personnel in Japan, Japan is ever-eager to strengthen its relations with India.

Notes and References

1. JICA India Office, 'Tai-Indo-kyouryoku no Genjou [The Current Situation of Cooperation for India]', August 2018, available at https://www.jica.go.jp/Resource/india/office/others/ku57pq000020wb9a-att/outline_201808.pdf, accessed on 25 October 2023.

2. G. V. K. Naidu, 'Whither the Look East Policy: India and Southeast Asia', *Strategic Analysis*, vol. 28, no. 2 (April–Jun 2004).

3. Ministry of Foreign Affairs, Government of Japan, 'Global Partnership between Japan and India in the 21st Century', 23 August 2000), available at https://www.mofa.go.jp/region/asia-paci/pmv0008/india_s.html, accessed on 7 October 2023.

4. Ministry of Foreign Affairs, Government of Japan, 'Japan-India Partnership in a New Asian Era: Strategic Orientation of Japan-India Global Partnership', 29 April 2005, available at https://www.mofa.go.jp/region/asia-paci/india/partner0504.html, accessed on 7 October 2023.

5. Ministry of Foreign Affairs, Government of Japan, 'Joint Declaration on Security Cooperation between Japan-India', 22 October 2008, available at https://www.mofa.go.jp/region/asia-paci/india/pmv0810/joint-d.html, accessed on 7 October 2023.

6. Ministry of Foreign Affairs, Government of Japan, 'Action Plan to advance Security Cooperation based on the Joint Declaration on Security Cooperation between Japan and India', 29 December 2009, available at https://www.mofa.go.jp/region/asia.paci/india/pmv0912/action.html, accessed on 7 October 2023.

7. Sanjaya Baru, 'Two Years of the Narendra Modi Government in India—A View from India', *Contemporary India Forum Quarterly Journal*, vol. 30 (2016).

8. Ministry of Foreign Affairs, Government of Japan, 'Tokyo Declaration for Japan-India Special Strategic and Global Partnership', 1 September 2014), available at https://www.mofa.go.jp/files/000050532.pdf#:~:text=Meeting%20in%20Tokyo%20on%201%20September%202014%2C%20Prime,stability%20and%20prosperity%20in%20Asia%20and%20the%20world, accessed on 7 October 2023.

9. Ibid.

10. Ministry of Foreign Affairs, Government of Japan, 'Japan and India Vision 2015 Special Global Partnership', 12 December 2015, available at https://www.mofa.go.jp/s_sa/sw/in/page3e_000432.html, accessed on 7 October 2023.

11. Ministry of Foreign Affairs, Government of Japan, 'Agreement between the Government of Japan and the Government of the Republic of India for Cooperation in the Peaceful Uses of Nuclear Energy', 11 November 2016, available at https://www.mofa.go.jp/files/000241570.pdf, accessed on 7 October 2023.

12. Shinzo Abe, 'Confluence of the Two Seas', Speech at the Parliament of the Republic of India, 22 August 2007, available at http://www.mofa.go.jp/region/asia-paci/pmv0708/speech-2.html, accessed on 22 September 2023.

13. Hillary Clinton, 'America's Pacific Century', *Foreign Policy*, 11 October 2011, available at https://foreignpolicy.com/2011/10/11/americas-pacific-century/, accessed on 22 September 2023.

14. Rory Medcalf, 'Australia's New Strategic Geography', in Priya Chacko, ed., *New Regional Geopolitics in the Indo-Pacific: Drivers, Dynamics and Consequences* (London and New York: Routledge, 2016).

15. The White House, 'Remarks by President Trump at APEC CEO Summit | Da Nang, Vietnam', 10 November 2017, available at https://trumpwhitehouse.archives.gov/briefings-statements/remarks-president-trump-apec-ceo-summit-da-nang-vietnam/, accessed on 25 October 2023.

16. Makoto Kojima, *Indo-keizai ga Ajia o Kaeru* [The Indian Economy Making Change in Asia] (Tokyo and Kyoto: PHP Institute, 1995).

17. Ibid.

18. Based on the data provided by Ministry of Commerce and Industry, Government of India, 'Export Import Data Bank', available at https://tradestat.commerce.gov.in/ sp, accessed on 16 October 2023.

19. Comprehensive Economic Partnership Agreement between Japan and the Republic of India, available at https://www.mofa.go.jp/region/asia-paci/india/epa201102/pdfs/ijcepa_ba_e.pdf, accessed on 22 September 2023.

20. Ministry of Commerce and Industry, Government of India, 'Export Import Data Bank'.

21. Ibid.

22. Ibid.

23. Ministry of Health, Labor and Welfare, Government of Japan, 'Kohatsu-Iyakuhin no Suryo-shea no Suii to Mokuhyou [The Quantity Trend and Goal of the Share of Generics]', 14 June 2017, available at https://www.mhlw.go.jp/content/12404000/000493982.pdf, accessed on 16 October 2023.

24. Ministry of Commerce and Industry, Government of India, 'Fact Sheet on FDI Statistics', available at https://dpiit.gov.in/publications/fdi-statistics, accessed on 16 October 2023.

25. Ministry of Commerce and Industry, Government of India, 'Fact Sheet on Foreign Direct Investment (FDI)from April, 2000 to March, 2020', available at https://dpiit.gov.in/sites/default/files/FDI_Factsheet_March20_28May_2020.pdf, accessed on 17 January 2024.

26. JETRO, 'Nihon no Chokusetsu-Toshi [Direct Investment of Japan]', available at https://www.jetro.go.jp/world/japan/stats/fdi.html, accessed on 16 October 2023.

27. Skand Tayal, 'Japan's investments in India have not been without pitfalls', *The Asian Age*, 16 April 2019, available at https://www.asianage.com/india/all-india/150419/japans-investments-in-india-have-not-been-without-pitfalls.html, accessed on 22 September 2023.

28. Embassy of Japan in India and JETRO, 'Japanese Business Establishments in India', August 2020, available at https://www.in.emb-japan.go.jp/PDF/2019_co_list_en.pdf, accessed on 22 January 2024.

29. The Deming Prize, among the highest awards for TQM in the world, was established in 1951 by the Union of Japanese Scientists and Engineers (JUSE) in commemoration of the late Dr William Edwards Deming who contributed greatly to Japan's proliferation of statistical quality control after World War II. The total number of companies awarded the Deming Prize was nearly 257 during the period 1951 to 2019, most of which were Japanese companies. However, looking at the recent period of 2001–2019, of the total 75 awarded companies, as many as 35 were Indian companies.

30. JBIC, 'FY2019 JBIC Survey (the 31st) Report on Overseas Business Operations by Japanese Manufacturing Companies', available at https://www.jbic.go.jp/en/information/press/press-2019/1127-012855.html, assessed on 21 October 2023.

31. Department For Promotion of Industry & Internal Trade, Ministry of Commerce and Industry, India, 'Update on Japan Industrial Townships (JITs) in India', available at https://www.meti.go.jp/press/2021/02/20220228004/20220228004-b.pdf, accessed on 22 January 2024.

32. 'Inside DIPP, Japan Plus gets going on $33.5-bn dream', *Business Standard*, 19 February 2015, available at https://www.business-standard.com/article/economy-policy/inside-dipp-japan-plus-gets-going-on-33-5-bn-dream-115021800931_1.html, accessed on 17 January 2024.

33. India is ranked third in the world with more than 4,200 start-ups. India is the youngest start-up nation in the world, with 72 per cent of the founders being younger than 35 years old. See NASSCOM, *The IT-BPM Sector in India: Strategic Review 2016* (NASSCOM, 2016).

34. Katsuo Matsumoto, 'Japan-India Economic Cooperation through Official Development Assistance-Current Status and Future Outlook', *Contemporary India Forum Quarterly Journal*, vol. 44 (2020).

35. Ibid.

36. The Embassy of Japan in India, 'Foundation Laying Ceremony for the Dhubri-Phulbhari Bridge, supported by Japanese ODA loan', 18 February 2021, available at https://www.in.emb-japan.go.jp/itpr_en/11_000001_00117.html, assessed on 21 October 2023.

37. If one connects these five industrial corridors, they almost overlap with the highway network of the Golden Quadrilateral.

38. Ministry of Commerce and Industry, Government of India, 'Concept Paper: Delhi-Mumbai Industrial Corridor', August 2007, available at https://dmaicindia.files.wordpress.com/2013/07/concept-paper-of-dmic-2007.pdf, accessed on 22 September 2023.

39. DMICDC, 'The DMIC Corridor', 14 June 2014.

40. Katsuhiko Murayama (JICA expert), 'DMIC Koso ni-tsui-te (On the DMIC Plan)', DMICDC, 17 April 2014.

41. Based on my interview with a senior JICA officer, 21 August 2018, Delhi.

42. Murayama, op. cit.

43. Ministry of Land, Infrastructure, Transport and Tourism, Government of Japan, 'Kamotsu-Senyo-Testudo-Keikaku (DFC) (The Plan of Dedicated Freight Corridor)', document accessed during my interview with an officer–in-charge, 11 November 2012.

44. Based on the table (Basic Design Features) included in the presentation by Ashutosh Rankawat (Executive Director/WDFC, DFCCI), 'Western Dedicated Corridor: Project outlines, Features, Current status and its impact on logistics service improvement,' delivered at the seminar held by DMICDC, JBIC and JICA on 15 October 2019 in Delhi.

45. JICA, 'Operational Rules of Special Terms for Economic Partnership (STEP) of Japanese ODA Loans', 9 May 2013, available at https://www.jica.go.jp/Resource/english/our_work/types_of_assistance/oda_loans/step/c8h0vm000053zae9-att/operational_rules_2013.pdf, accessed on 21 October 2023.

46. DFCCIL, PROJECT MAO OF DFCCIL, 1 July 2023, available at https://dfccil.com, accessed on 21 October 2023.

47. Raghav Thakur, 'India establishes High-Speed Rail Corporation', *IRJ* (*International Railway Journal*), 31 October 2013, available at https://www.railjournal.com/regions/asia/india-establishes-high-speed-rail-corporation/, accessed on 23 October 2023.

48. Japan was all the more anxious to reach an agreement on the Mumbai–Ahmedabad route because Japan lost to China in the bidding for the HSR in Indonesia in September 2015, just three months before the summit meeting with India.

49. Ministry of Railways, Government of India, 'India Railways VISION 2020', December 2009, available at https://indianrailways.gov.in/railwayboard/uploads/directorate/infra/downloads/VISION_2020_Eng_SUBMITTED_TO_PARLIAMENT.pdf, accessed on 23 October 2023.

50. The Japanese ODA (yen loan) will not cover import taxes, land acquisition costs and administration costs, or other ineligible costs and fees, as mutually agreed.

51. Avinash Nair, 'Mumbai-Ahmedabad bullet train project: NHSRCL says 80% acquired, Rs 7,027 crore compensation paid', *The Indian Express*, 16 October 2021, available at https://indianexpress.com/article/cities/ahmedabad/mumbai-ahmedabad-bullet-train-project-nhsrcl-land-acquisition-7574053/, accessed on 17 January 2024.

52. Based on my interview with Osamu Murata, Executive Officer, MAHSR Headquarters, Japan International Consultants for Transportation Co., Ltd. (JIC), on 10 March 2022.

53. Isabel Raynolds and Emi Urabe, 'Japan to Fund Firms to Shift Production Out of China,' *Bloomberg*, 9 April 2020, available at https://www.bloomberg.com/news/articles/2020-04-08/japan-to-fund-firms-to-shift-production-out-of-china#xj4y7vzkg, accessed on 23 October 2023.

54. Ministry of Economy, Trade and Industry, Government of Japan, 'Australia-India-Japan Economic Ministers' Joint Statement on Supply Chain Resilience', 1 September 2020, available at https://www.meti.go.jp/press/2020/09/20200901008/20200901008-1.pdf, accessed on 24 September 2023.

55. Ministry of finance, Government of India, 'Aatma Nirbhar Bharat Package – Progress So Far,' 1 October 2020, available at https://pib.gov.in/PressReleasePage.aspx?PRID=1660691, accessed on 23 October 2023.

56. ClearIAS, 'PLI Scheme: All About Production Linked Incentive,' 23 November 2022, available at https://www.clearias.com/pli-scheme/, accessed on 24 October 2023.

57. UNCTAD, *Investment Trends Monitor*, no. 36 (October 2020).

58. Ministry of Commerce and Industry, Government of India, 'Fact Sheet on Foreign Direct Investment (FDI) Inflow', various issues, available at https://dpiit.gov.in/publications/fdi-statistics, accessed on 24 October 2023.

59. 'Apple to start selling online in India this year, first retail store in 2021: Tim Cook', 27 February 2020, *The Week*, available at https://www.theweek.in/news/biz-tech/2020/02/27/apple-to-start-selling-online-in-india-this-year-first-retail-store-only-by-2021-tim-cook.html, accessed on 24 September 2023.

60. 'Japan indicates efforts on to address India's concerns over RCEP', *The Economic Times*, 1 December 2019, available at https://economictimes.indiatimes.com/news/economy/foreign-trade/japan-indicates-efforts-on-to-address-indias-concerns-over-rcep/articleshow/72318409.cms, accessed on 17 January 2024.

61. Ibid.

62. Ministry of Commerce and industry, Government of India, 'Report of the High-level Advisory Group', 12 September 2023, available at https://qcin.org/public/uploads/ck-docs/1610088582.HLAG%20Report%20(Flyers%20Included)_Oct%2025,%202019.pdf, accessed on 24 October 2023.

63. 'Piyush Goyal on free trade agreements: Don't create fear psychosis', 31 October 2019, *The Indian Express*, available at https://indianexpress.com/article/business/economy/piyush-goyal-on-free-trade-agreements-dont-create-fear-psychosis-6095382/, accessed on 24 September 2023.

64. Ministry of Commerce and Industry, Government of India, 'Trade Agreements', available at https://commerce.gov.in/international-trade/trade-agreements/, accessed on 24 October 2023.

65. Ministry of Commerce and Industry, Government of India, 'Export Import Data Bank', available at https://tradestat.commerce.gov.in/eidb/default.asp, accessed on 16 October 2023.

66. Arvind Subramanian and Shoumitro Chatterjee, 'India's export opportunities could be significant even in a post-COVID world', *The Indian Express*, 14 October 2020.

67. 'Indian economy will see double-digit growth next fiscal: Former CEA Arvind Virmani', 18 November 2020, *The Economic Times*, available at https://economictimes.indiatimes.com/news/economy/finance/indian-economy-will-see-double-digit-growth-next-fiscal-former-cea-arvind-virmani/articleshow/79285032.cms?utm_source=contentofinterest&utm_medium=text&utm_campaign=cppst, accessed on 24 September 2023.

68. The composition of the Indian IT industry is as follows: IT services constituted 51.2 per cent of the total revenues in fiscal year 2018, followed by business process management (BPM) (19.7 per cent), software products and engineering services (20.6 per cent), and hardware (8.5 per cent). See Ministry of Finance, Government of India, *Economic Survey 2019-20*, vol. 2, chapter 9 (2020).

69. Ministry of Finance, Government of India, *Economic Survey 2019-20*.

70. Ministry of Electronics and Information Technology, 'Bilateral Cooperation', available at https://www.meity.gov.in/content/country-wise-status, accessed on 24 October 2023.

71. Ministry of Internal Affairs and Communications, 'Signing of the First Comprehensive Memorandum of Cooperation in the Field of Information and Communications Technology with the Ministry of Communications of the Republic of India', 15 January 2021, available at https://www.soumu.go.jp/main_sosiki/joho_tsusin/eng/pressrelease/2021/1/15_07.html#:~:text=The%20Ministry%20of%20Internal%20Affairs%20and%20Communications%20and,industries%20in%20both%20countries%2C%20including%20topics%20on%20startups, accessed on 25 October 2023.

72. NEC, 'NEC, Inndo Chennai to Anndaman-Nikobaru Shotou o Musubu 2,300 km no Hikari-Kaitei-Keiburu no Kennsetsu o Kannryou [NEC has completed the construction of laying optical submarine cables between Chennai and Andaman Nicobar Islands]', 15 January 2020, available at https://jpn.nec.com/press/202012/20201218_01.html, accessed on 25 October 2023.

73. 'India uses digital banking and biometrics to organize its 1.3 billion population', *The Economic Times*, 13 March 2021, available at https://economictimes.indiatimes.com/news/economy/policy/india-uses-digital-banking-and-biometrics-to-organize-its-1-3-billion-population/articleshow/81478987.cms?from=mdr, accessed on 17 January 2024.

74. Ministry of Economy and Industry, Government of Japan, 'IT-Jinzai-Jukyu ni-kansuru Chousa [Research on the Supply and Demand of IT Personel]', April 2019, available at https://www.meti.go.jp/policy/it_policy/jinzai/gaiyou.pdf., accessed on 25 October 2023.

75. Durgesh K. Rai, 'DPG POLICY BRIEF, FDI Flows to India: Recent Trends, Challenges and Way Forward', 28 February 2021, available at https://www.delhipolicygroup.org/publication/policy-briefs/fdi-flows-to-india-recent-trends-challenges-and-way-forward-2225.html#:~:text=While%20FDI%20flows%20to%20India,France%2C%20the%20UK%20and%20Brazil., accessed on 22 January 2024.

eleven

Institutionalising the Indo-Pacific

Japan–India Cooperation over Regional Multilateralism

KEI KOGA

The relation between Japan and India is one of the bilateral relations that is indispensable in shaping a regional order in the Indo-Pacific region. While India as a regional major power is located in the centre of the Indian Ocean, Japan is a staunch ally of the United States, whose strategic horizon currently expands from the Western Pacific to the Indian Ocean. The bilateral strategic ties between Japan and India have steadily grown since 2000, when Prime Minister Yoshiro Mori came on an official trip to India for the promotion of socio-economic and political cooperation and aimed to nurture a 'global partnership'. The relationship between the two countries then upgraded to a 'Global and Strategic Partnership' in 2006 and to a 'Special Strategic and Global Partnership' in 2016. Japan–India functional and institutional cooperation has also been strengthened, through military agreements, such as the Acquisition and Cross-Servicing Agreement (ACSA); economic agreements, such as the Comprehensive Economic Partnership Agreement (CEPA); and policy coordination mechanisms, such as the 2+2 Foreign and Defense Ministerial Meeting.

Empirically, such development of bilateral cooperation would lead partners to create policy coordination mechanisms to facilitate multilateralism. This is particularly so when the partner states share the same political values and views on democracy and human rights, and when they are treaty allies. For instance, Japan and the United States have begun to coordinate their policies toward global and regional multilateralism, particularly since the 1996 Joint Declaration on Security.[1] Japan and Australia became strategic partners after the 2006 joint declaration on security, aiming to coordinate their policy towards regional multilateralism, with the formation of mechanisms such as the ASEAN Regional Forum (ARF) and the East Asia Summit (EAS).[2] But India is neither a treaty ally with Japan nor a US ally, and thus it is not clear the extent to which Japan and India cooperate with each other toward regional multilateralism, particularly in the Indo-Pacific region.

The existing literature on this subject, while insightful, does not sufficiently tackle this question. Most focus on Japan's or India's individual foreign policy strategy, but even those who focus on Japan–India relations do not have a consensual view on policy coordination for multilateralism.[3] In fact, while some assume that the expansion of Japan's strategic scope to the Indo-Pacific region naturally leads Japan and India to have greater cooperation in both bilateral and multilateral settings, others argue that India's traditional foreign policy orientation, leaning toward 'strategic autonomy' or 'non-alignment', becomes an obstacle for bilateral cooperation.[4]

In this context, this chapter explores convergence and divergence in strategic posture and policy priorities between Japan and India in regional multilateralism, focusing on the Quadrilateral Security Dialogue (QSD) or Quad—the informal grouping of Australia, India, Japan and the United States. This idea of the Quad was proposed by Prime Minister Shinzo Abe in 2007. However, it soon dissipated since China raised its concern about the QSD's strategic intention, and Australia and India were too hesitant to consolidate a grouping that would excessively provoke China. As China became more assertive in the 2010s, this idea was resurrected in 2017, when the United States began to launch its Free and Open Indo-Pacific (FOIP) strategy and explicitly take a firmer foreign policy stance against China as one of the 'revisionist states'.[5]

The Quad is a particularly important multilateral grouping in the Indo-Pacific region because it enjoys relative diplomatic autonomy, free from dominant regional rules and norms of other institutions, mainly ASEAN and ASEAN-led institutions.[6] Also, the Quad's members are major democratic powers and have a certain diplomatic influence in their respective subregions. Further, it has an important strategic potential to deter China—be it in areas of military, economy, or diplomacy—if the members agree to coordinate their policies for such a purpose. So the question arises: Is the Japan–India enhanced bilateral cooperation any indication of the great promise of a successful institutionalisation of the Quad in the future?

I argue that despite the diplomatic momentum to institutionalise the Quad, the enhancement of Japan–India bilateral cooperation does not necessarily translate into their policy coordination for the purpose of institutionalising the Quad as a strategic tool to counter China. This is mainly because, unlike the relationships between the United States and its allies, the strategic objectives and approaches of India and Japan are often different—while Japan expanded its strategic horizon to engage with India and maintain the rules-based international order in the Indo-Pacific, India's enhancement of the bilateral cooperation with Japan essentially stems from the need to maintain its 'strategic autonomy' to prioritise its own national security, not from its strong diplomatic will to maintain and enhance the existing international order. These divergent perspectives limit Japan–India policy coordination to multilateralism while a structural change, particularly the rise of an assertive China in the 2010s, explains the formation and consolidation of the Quad.

To illustrate this point, I will examine the development of Japan–India bilateral relations since the turn of the millennium and then discuss the affinity of policy and strategic posture toward regional institutions, particularly the Quad. For this purpose, I employ the statements made in official documents, mainly from the Ministry of Foreign Affairs of Japan and the Ministry of External Affairs of India, as well as media reports on Japan–India bilateral cooperation and policy coordination toward the Quad. While it is difficult to find concrete evidence of bilateral policy coordination toward multilateralism, these statements and reports help us identify the converging and diverging points of the policies of the two countries.

This chapter is structured in four parts. The first part discusses the evolution of Japan–India bilateral cooperation since 2000. The second part discusses Japan–India cooperation toward regional multilateralism, and the third examines the affinity of Japan and India's strategic posture toward the Quad. The fourth part discusses the potentials and challenges of Japan–India bilateral cooperation toward regional multilateralism, particularly the Quad, in the Indo-Pacific region.

Japan–India Bilateral Cooperation in the 21st Century

Japan–India relations have become one of the most important strategic partnerships in the Indo-Pacific region. However, the development of this bilateral relation was not always straightforward in the post-Cold War era. Japan's Official Development Assistance (ODA) to India was relatively large during the 1990s (Figure 11.1), but when India conducted nuclear tests twice in 1998, Japan decided to stop providing new yen loans and grants. This economic sanction was lifted in 2001, when Japan was convinced that India's nuclear posture had significantly improved, as evident from India's declaration of a voluntary nuclear test moratorium. Subsequently, the amount of Japan's ODA to India gradually increased, except during the 2010 global financial crisis and a temporary reduction of loan assistance in 2014.

In terms of political relations, Japan began to show its willingness to improving its relationship with India since around 2000 with the hope to seize the economic opportunities that India's vast market would provide. In the 21st century, the bilateral relations have developed through three phases: 1) the 2000–04 economic cooperation; 2) the 2005–14 political and security cooperation; and 3) the 2015–20 strategic cooperation.

In the first phase, Japan and India started to focus on improving their relations since the beginning of the new millennium, mainly through economic cooperation. Despite the economic sanctions that Japan imposed

Figure 11.1 Japan's ODA to India (1990–2018)

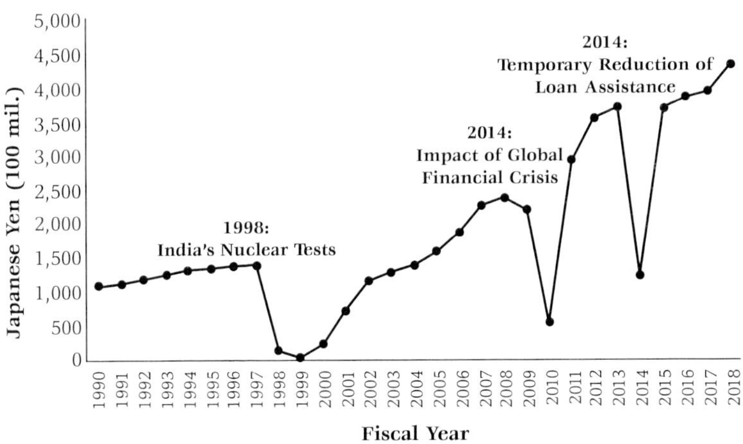

Source: Ministry of Foreign Affairs of Japan

on India for its 1998 nuclear tests, Prime Minister Yoshiro Mori made an official visit to India in August 2000 and agreed to establish a 'Global Partnership in the 21st Century'.[7] In his speech, Mori emphasised the fact that the two countries shared the same democratic principles and were gradually becoming economically important in the world. Mori's speech focused on the enhancement of bilateral cooperation on economy, information and communication technology; the significance of the Group of Four (G4) for the United Nations Security Council reforms; and the promotion of democratic values. Japan lifted its economic sanction on India in October 2001, and soon after, Prime Minister Junichiro Koizumi and Prime Minister Atal Bihari Vajpayee signed the Japan-India Joint Declaration, which institutionalised the annual meeting of foreign ministers.[8] As India underwent economic reforms, Japan continued to provide yen loans as part of its ODA, and became the number one loan provider to India in 2004.[9]

The early 2000s therefore saw bilateral efforts to strengthen Japan–India economic cooperation, but this trend slightly shifted to include strategic functionality in November 2004, when the Japan–India summit was held. The two countries attempted to focus on the global arena, particularly on preventing the 'arc of instability' and advancing Manmohan Singh's idea of an 'arc of advantage', a regional economic community including ASEAN, China, Japan, Korea, and India, which would have large resources and could promote regional prosperity.[10] The summit agendas such as bilateral economic cooperation and development assistance were however not new, and even later in 2005, Prime Minister Koizumi mentioned that the core challenge of the bilateral global partnership remained economic cooperation.[11] But the 2004 summit did create an opportunity to expand the scope of the bilateral cooperation to areas beyond economic ties.

The second phase, the period of 2005–14, saw a significant development of the Japan–India bilateral relationships in terms of its scope of agendas and institutionalisation of dialogues. This was clearly indicated in the 2005 bilateral summit, which stated that both Japan and India would 'expand their traditional bilateral cooperation to cooperation in Asia and beyond'.[12] Previously, Japan–India relations focused on bilateral economic cooperation while touching on certain global non-traditional security issues, such as counter-terrorism and nuclear non-proliferation. This focus now shifted to the strategic elements in the region and beyond, and to this end, both states aimed to strengthen their bilateral ties comprehensively and promote democracy and new regional architectures in Asia. With this aim, they concluded the 'Eight-fold Initiative for Strengthening Japan-India Global Partnership', which included: 1) enhanced dialogues and exchanges; 2) comprehensive economic engagement; 3) enhanced security dialogue and cooperation; 4) science and technology initiatives; 5) cultural and academic initiatives and strengthening of people-to-people contacts; 6) cooperation in ushering a new Asian era; 7) cooperation in UN and other international organisations; and 8) responding to international challenges.[13]

The two countries also decided to hold an annual summit meeting to promote maritime cooperation through naval and coast-guard exchange, and to work together in facilitating regional community-building, including an East Asian Community and an Asian Economic Community—an 'Arc of Advantage and Prosperity'—by including India in the East Asia Summit. The bilateral relationship soon upgraded to the 'Japan–India Strategic and Global Partnership' in 2006, comprehending political security and economic cooperation as well as people-to-people exchange.[14] Yet, while the bilateral relations were institutionalised, India and Japan's policy coordination toward regional institutions remained unclear.

In 2007, Foreign Minister Taro Aso proposed the synthesis of his value-based 'Arc of Freedom and Prosperity' and Prime Minister Manmohan Singh's economic idea of the 'Arc of Advantages and Prosperity' as an extension of Japan's value-oriented diplomacy. Further, Prime Minister Shinzo Abe's speech at the Indian Parliament in 2007, 'Confluence of the Two Seas', envisioned the elevation of the bilateral cooperation to encompass a broader Asia with other regional democratic partners, namely the United States and Australia, with the aim that 'the seas of freedom and prosperity... will be open and transparent to all'.[15] As such, Abe and Aso pushed their value-oriented diplomacy by attempting to create the Quad with the United States, India and Australia, which showed Japan's eagerness to facilitate bilateral and multilateral strategic cooperation with India and Australia. Nevertheless, such efforts were not successful because of India as well as Australia's hesitance and fear to provoke China, coupled with Abe's sudden resignation from his prime ministership in 2007.[16]

On the other hand, the bilateral strategic dialogues were reinforced. The new mechanisms included the establishment of the Foreign Ministers' Strategic Dialogue and the Vice Minister/Defense Secretary-level regular Defense Policy Dialogue, beginning from 2007, the biannual Foreign Secretary/Vice Minister-level 2+2 dialogue from 2010, and the Japan–India Maritime Affairs Dialogue from 2013, besides regular consultations between the Secretary-General of the National Security Secretariat of Japan and India's National Security Advisor.[17] While political-security dialogues deepened and became multi-layered, the dialogues to further economic cooperation continued since 2006, eventually resulting in the Comprehensive Economic Partnership Agreement (CEPA) in February 2010.[18]

These culminated in the upgrade of Japan–India bilateral relations to the 'Japan–India *Special* Strategic and Global Partnership' in 2014.[19] The relationship was no longer confined to socio-economic cooperation but included political security cooperation as a core aspect of the bilateral relations as illustrated in the signing of a Memorandum of Cooperation and Exchanges in the Field of Defense, relating to the collaboration in defense technology and equipment.[20] In November 2014, both Abe and Modi agreed to enhance strategic bilateral cooperation to improve the 'stability and development of "Indo-Pacific"' with the two regional frameworks, namely Japan–US–India and Japan–Australia–India cooperation.[21]

In the third phase, between 2015–20, Japan and India further consolidated their strategic partnership. This was partly because China's geostrategic influence—through its increasing military and economic capabilities, China's 'Belt and Road Initiative' (BRI) and assertive diplomacies in the maritime domain—became more apparent, and partly because Japan under the Abe administration took a more active diplomatic stance toward India and other regional powers, namely Australia and the United States. In this context, the erstwhile bilateral dialogues now extended to include a third party, formulating the Japan–Australia–India Vice Ministers' Meeting and the Japan–India–US Trilateral Ministerial in 2015.[22] Also, the sensitive agendas, such as the South China Sea issue, were discussed more explicitly as Japan began to openly address these issues. For example, in the 2015 bilateral summit meeting, Prime Minister Abe emphasised the importance of the rule of law in the maritime domain, touching upon the South China Sea disputes, a view which Prime Minister Modi shared.[23] The most notable outcome of the 2015 summit meeting was the 'Japan and India Vision 2025 Special Strategic and Global Partnership'.[24] This statement was the landmark document which became the basis of Japan's FOIP in 2016, setting detailed guidelines in bilateral cooperation in the Indo-Pacific region.

Diplomatically, therefore, Japan and India expanded their bilateral relations to cover the Indo-Pacific region. Both agreed to commit to realise 'a peaceful, open, equitable, stable and rules-based order in the Indo-Pacific region and beyond' through close bilateral consultations and dialogues with partners.[25] To this end, the two particularly emphasised the importance of cooperation in infrastructure development, manufacturing and high technology, and global commons, particularly, maritime, space and cyber domains. Defense technology cooperation such as co-development and co-production, including future projects such as the US-2 amphibian aircraft, was also discussed. Consequently, four important bilateral agreements were concluded: the transfer of defense equipment and technology; security measures for the protection of classified military information; cooperation in the peaceful uses of nuclear energy; and the 400 billion yen ODA to India.[26] Furthermore, India invited Japan to be a permanent participant of the US–India joint military exercise, Malabar, in 2015.[27]

Since then, the bilateral and trilateral dialogues that included Japan and India constantly discussed regional strategic issues, such as the South China Sea and the peace and stability of the Indo-Pacific region. After Japan launched its new strategic vision, FOIP, Prime Minister Abe stated that India was the 'most important country in terms of linking Asia and Africa' and expressed Japan's willingness to continuously further the bilateral cooperation.[28] In response, Prime Minister Modi put emphasis on the 'Act East Policy' (AEP) as a primary objective in the Indo-Pacific and both countries promised to explore the possible synergy between the FOIP and the AEP.[29] By 2018, Japan and India shared the same Indo-Pacific vision that the region should be

> a rules-based order that respects sovereignty and territorial integrity of nations, ensures freedom of navigation and overflight as well as unimpeded lawful commerce, and seeks peaceful resolution of disputes with full respect for legal and diplomatic processes in accordance with the universally recognised principles of international law, including those reflected in the UNCLOS, without resorting to threat or use of force.[30]

This bilateral strategic convergence also enabled both states to hold the very first 2+2 Ministerial Meeting in November 2019 and conclude the ACSA.[31]

In sum, the past three decades of Japan–India relations illustrate the gradual consolidation of strategic cooperation in the Indo-Pacific region, over three phases of development, from 2000–04 to 2005–14 to 2015–20. Although the COVID-19 pandemic in 2020–21 slowed down the bilateral cooperation and dialogues, the India–Japan relationship has remained positive, and their cooperation with other regional partners, particularly the United States and Australia has been strengthened. However, Japan and India's political intention to bilaterally cooperate in the Indo-Pacific region does not guarantee a successful policy coordination to create tangible projects. In comparison with Japan–US and Japan–Australia relations, Japan–India regional cooperative schemes have remained low-key or unclear.

The next section examines Japan–India cooperation to bolster multilateralism in the Indo-Pacific region, particularly the Quad.

Bilateral Cooperation toward Multilateralism: Regional Organisations and the Quad 2.0

Japan and India have several overlapping memberships in regional multilateral institutions in Asia. There are three characteristics that define these memberships. First, as Table 11.1 shows, all overlapping memberships are within Southeast Asia-led institutions, namely the ASEAN Regional Forum (ARF), Asian Cooperation Dialogue (ACD), ASEAN Defense Ministers' Meeting Plus (ADMM-Plus) and East Asia Summit (EAS). Second, these multilateral regional organisations are relatively new, and before 2002, there was only ARF, where Japan and India's memberships overlapped. Third, there are several regional organisations, such as the South Asian Association for Regional Cooperation (SAARC) and the Indian Ocean Rim Association (IORA), that include both Japan and India, but either as an observer or a dialogue partner. In that sense, there was no significant diplomatic opportunity for Japan and India to cooperate in regional multilateralism in the past.

That said, EAS has been generally considered to be potentially the most important platform in the region for Japan and India. This is simply because while ARF, ACD and ADMM-Plus are based on Foreign Ministers-led meetings, EAS is the leaders' meeting. Furthermore, when the membership expansion of EAS was discussed among the ASEAN+3 members in the early 2000s, Japan pushed for membership of India as

Table 11.1 Japan and India's Membership in the Major Indo-Pacific Regional Institutions

Major Regional Institutions in the Indo-Pacific	Japan	India
ASEAN Regional Forum (1994–)	Y	Y
Asian Cooperation Dialogue (2002–)	Y	Y
East Asia Summit (2005–)	Y	Y
ASEAN Defense Ministers' Meeting Plus (2010–)	Y	Y
Asia-Europe Meeting (1996–)	Y	O
South Asian Association for Regional Cooperation (1985–)	O	Y
Indian Ocean Rim Association (1997–)	O	Y
Asia Pacific Economic Cooperation (1989–)	Y	N
ASEAN+3 (1997–)	Y	N
Shanghai Cooperation Organisation (2001–)	N	Y
Conference on Interaction and Confidence-Building Measures in Asia (1999–)	N	Y

Y: Member
N: Non-Member
O: Observer or Dialogue Partner
Source: Data compiled by the author from various sources.

one of the foremost regional democracies, aiming to prevent China from being the most influential power in EAS.[32]

It is EAS for which Japan and India often declared their intention to coordinate their policies.[33] Also, since 2006, Japan and India have emphasised on the importance of close consultation with India in community-building efforts in East Asia.[34] Although this diplomatic momentum dissipated with Abe's resignation in 2007, Japan's commitment to pursuing policy coordination for EAS in terms of non-traditional security cooperation and regional cooperation, such as climate change and an East Asian community-building, continued.[35] With growing concerns about the rise of assertive China, Japan and India declared to strengthen the EAS as a prime political, security and strategic framework led by regional leaders. In this context, Japan and India decided to create a bilateral dialogue on ASEAN affairs in 2014, although such an initiative was realised only later in 2017.[36]

In the 2010s, Japan and India emphasised the importance of multilateral or minilateral policy coordination. In addition to EAS, the trilateral cooperation with the United States was being consolidated, and together the countries aimed to create 'concrete and demonstrable projects to their shared interests and those of other partners'.[37] Since then, Japan and India's diplomatic emphasis on the importance of EAS and attempts to shape EAS as 'the premier leaders-led forum' have continued, although the two countries have been increasingly frustrated by the slow process of the institutional development of EAS.[38]

At the same time, India and Japan have also been cautious about their policy toward multilateralism with ASEAN, since ASEAN has been traditionally anxious about its diplomatic marginalisation by regional great powers in the post-Cold War era.[39] Thus, in 2015, Japan and India, along with the United States, explicitly reiterated their strong 'support for ASEAN centrality in the multilateral political and security architecture in the Asia-Pacific region' and the importance of EAS.[40] Also, to enhance India–Japan connections with ASEAN and alleviate India's concern about China's infrastructure development in South Asia through BRI, Foreign Minister Fumio Kishida resurrected the idea of Japan's cooperation with SAARC and proposed the enhancement of connectivity between SAARC and ASEAN, although India's response to this was rather muted.[41]

Nevertheless, this diplomatic momentum to jointly buttress ASEAN-led institutions, particularly EAS, gradually weakened because ASEAN's institutional progress was significantly slow. This was mainly caused by ASEAN's strict institutional norms, such as a non-interference principle, requirement of consensus in decision-making, and the idea of ASEAN centrality, as well as by the fact that both Japan and India's influence on ASEAN-led institutions has been quite limited. After the emergence of the Indo-Pacific as a new geographical scope, Japan and India started to quietly invest in a new grouping, the Quad, although they continued to emphasise their strong support for ASEAN's institutional norms and principles, particularly ASEAN centrality.

From Quad 2.0 to 3.0: Affinity of Japan and India's Strategic Posture

Japan and India, along with the United States and Australia, have their own regional strategic grouping, the so-called 'Quad 2.0'.[42] Although Prime Minister Abe's idea of establishing 'Quad 1.0' around 2007 dissipated because of Australia and India's hesitance, the grouping resurrected in 2017, when the United States launched its FOIP strategy. Although it is still an informal group yet to be fully institutionalised as an official regional institution, the group has been holding regular consultations and has more pre-set agendas.

As Table 11.2 shows, there have been two significant institutional developments in the Quad. One is that the level of the meetings was steadily elevated from the senior official level to the foreign minister level to the summit level. The other is that while the initial meetings were organised back-to-back with other international meetings, namely, the Shangri-La Dialogue, EAS and UN General Assembly, after 2020, the meetings tend to be organised independently. The COVID-19 pandemic changed the format of the meeting to online and accelerated this trend of the meeting being a standalone one, as evident from the second foreign ministers' meeting in October 2020 and the summit meeting in March 2021.

The institutionalisation of the grouping, however, does not indicate the congruence of national interests, and on the contrary, there are divergent national interests and strategic postures toward the Indo-Pacific region among the Quad member states. But there has been growing strategic convergence since 2017, developed through four phases: 1) the kick-off meeting in 2017 (the 1st meeting); 2) the converging of principles between 2018 and 2019 (the 2nd, 3rd and 4th meetings); 3) the promotion of functional cooperation and group expansion since 2019 (the 5th, 6th, 7th, 8th and 9th meetings); and 4) the further institutionalisation of Quad 2.0 in 2021 (the 10th and 11th meetings).

The first phase was the kick-off meeting among senior officials of Japan, India, Australia and the United States. This meeting was held after the United States under the Trump administration started to use the term 'FOIP' in November 2017, and it was only an informal consultation between the four to share their strategic perspectives, and thus it did not produce any joint statement. Furthermore, there were divergences in their perspectives, particularly between India and the three other states. More specifically, the United States, Japan and Australia shared their regional visions, emphasising the importance of a 'free and open Indo-Pacific' and 'the rules-based order', and they expressed their desire for continuing the discussion among the four.[43] On the other hand, India did not quite share the same view and emphasised inclusiveness by using the phrase, 'free, open, prosperous and inclusive Indo-Pacific region' instead of FOIP.[44] In

Table 11.2 Quad Meetings from 2017 to 2023

No.	Date	Venue	Level	Back-to-Back With
1	12 Nov. 2017	Philippines	Senior Official	East Asia Summit (SOM)
2	7 June 2018	Singapore	Senior Official	Shangri-La Dialogue
3	15 Nov. 2018	Singapore	Senior Official	East Asia Summit (SOM)
4	31 May 2019	Thailand	Senior Official	East Asia Summit (SOM)
5	26 Sep. 2019	The United States	Foreign Ministers	UN General Assembly
6	4 Nov. 2019	Thailand	Senior Official	East Asia Summit (SOM)
7	25 Sep. 2020	Virtual	Senior Official	-
8	6 Oct. 2020	Japan	Foreign Ministers	-
9	18 Dec. 2020	Virtual	Senior Official	-
10	18 Feb. 2021	Virtual	Foreign Ministers	-
11	12 Mar. 2021	Virtual	Summit	-
12	24 Sep. 2021	The United States	Summit	-
13	11 Feb. 2022	Australia	Foreign Ministers	-
14	3 Mar. 2022	Virtual	Summit	-
15	24 May 2022	Japan	Summit	-
16	23 Sep. 2022	The United States	Foreign Ministers	UN General Assembly
17	20 May 2023	Japan	Summit	-
18	22 Sep. 2023	The United States	Foreign Ministers	UN General Assembly

Source: Ministry of Foreign Affairs of Japan

addition, India did not explicitly indicate a political desire for continuous discussion and instead insisted on the importance of its 'Act East Policy' as the 'cornerstone' of the engagement to the region.[45]

Despite the enhancement of bilateral relations, India was hesitant to share Japan's concerns. This is understandable because Japan and Australia are two important regional treaty allies of the United States, who share similar concerns about China's behaviour, and their strategic cooperation and institutional ties are much stronger than among other states. Further, although it was not explicitly discussed in the first meeting, India had a stake in engaging with Southeast Asia and ASEAN, which tended to see China as an economic opportunity rather than a security threat, and did not show a strong counter-China posture.[46] Unless the concept of the FOIP was clarified, it was difficult for India to fully incorporate the FOIP narratives into its own strategic vision.[47] However, despite these divergences, it is also true that the Quad consultation became possible because of the increasing strategic uncertainty caused by regional strategic changes as well as the United States' changing policies under the Trump administration.[48] These structural changes thus created a momentum for the quadrilateral consultation.

The second phase entails the second, third and fourth meetings between 2018 and 2019, when the strategic objectives of the four converged. There are three points that the four members made adjustments on in their Indo-Pacific principles. First, they agreed with India's emphasis on 'inclusivity' in indicating their Indo-Pacific vision in the Quad meeting. Although their diplomatic rhetoric and actions were different, Japan, Australia and the United States all referred to an 'inclusive' Indo-Pacific region in their media release.[49] Second, all the members explicitly emphasised their strong support for ASEAN centrality and ASEAN-led institutions. This was entirely missing in the member states' media statement from the first meeting. In fact, these two points, inclusivity and ASEAN centrality, were made clear in Modi's keynote speech at the 2018 Shangri-La Dialogue, just before the second Quad meeting was held, and its influence was reflected in the Quad meeting.[50] Third, every state agreed to maintain a 'rules-based order' in the Indo-Pacific region. India was not indicating any willingness in the beginning, but it gradually started to use the same terminologies as the other three members. This trend continued in the third and fourth meetings, and thus, the four states came to share the basic objectives for the Indo-Pacific region.[51]

However, some differences remained. The member states' focuses were not narrowed, and the issues that each was willing to tackle and promote through functional cooperation ranged from sustainable development to maritime security to good governance to infrastructure development to connectivity to counter-terrorism to humanitarian assistance/disaster relief (HA/DR). Interestingly, although bilateral and trilateral cooperation among the members had long discussed these areas of cooperation, it did not immediately translate into a quadrilateral cooperation. This divergence was often explained by many analysts as India's 'strategic autonomy', which lay in contrast to the US's willingness to make the democratic coalition of Quad the core institution in the Indo-Pacific region.[52]

The third phase began from the fifth meeting—the very first ministerial meeting—in 2019 and lasted till the ninth meeting in 2020. Given that the four members had reached a certain agreement on the Indo-Pacific vision, they now attempted to coordinate their national policies to address particular issue areas. The fifth, sixth and seventh meetings indicated that consensual areas of cooperation were counter-terrorism, cyber security, HA/DR and quality infrastructure/connectivity.[53] Among them, infrastructure development, which covered development finance, connectivity and quality infrastructure, gained particular focus because of the increasing influence of China's new development practice through the BRI.[54] During this period, the COVID-19 pandemic broke out, which also made the Quad further narrow its focus of functional cooperation to the resilience of supply chain, the COVID-19 counter-measures and critical infrastructure, such as digital connectivity and 5G.[55]

However, these efforts to promote functional cooperation did not completely converge the Quad members' strategic postures toward the Indo-Pacific region. This is well illustrated by the non-issuance of a joint statement of the Foreign Ministers' meetings in 2019 and 2020. During these meetings, the United States became increasingly vocal about China's assertive behaviour. In 2020, the US Secretary of State Mike Pompeo explicitly accused the Chinese Communist Party of being an authoritarian regime violating international rules and norms and challenging the current international order.[56] Also, the United States highlighted the importance of 'result-oriented multilateralism' in the Indo-Pacific, which implicitly showed its frustration about ASEAN.[57]

The other three states were not as explicit as the United States, although they were also more or less concerned about China's behaviour. Australia was inclined to share the US's strategic posture, considering its strong support for the Quad's functional cooperation on the areas that China had strong influence over, such as a global supply chain and critical infrastructure; but all three besides the US—Australia, India, and Japan—were still wary about adopting a naming and shaming tactic.[58] In fact, India held a back-to-back meeting with BRICS in September 2019 and stated that it was searching for a new multilateral platform to effectively pursue its own interests, indicating that the Quad was not the only strategic forum for India.[59] Japan under the Suga administration also showed its intention in 2020 to engage with China by organising the Japan–China summit.[60] In a way, each of the four states took an approach to identify functional cooperation that they can pursue, which implicitly had strategic implications toward China, namely in relation to supply chain, critical infrastructure, and COVID-19 vaccine diplomacy, while considering additional members in the future.[61]

The fourth phase started from 2021, representing the rapid institutionalisation of the Quad under the new leadership of US President Joseph Biden, transforming Quad 2.0 into 'Quad 3.0', which laid a more rigid institutional foundation for cooperation.[62] The Biden administration, in accordance with its predecessor Trump's China policy, considered the Quad an important grouping to maintain a rules-based order in the Indo-Pacific region, and aimed to further consolidate the grouping. Although there are still divergences in the members' strategic approaches to achieve the Indo-Pacific vision, the Biden administration took the initiative to hold the first Quad summit in March 2021. This was a small but significant progress in two ways: first, the Quad was able to issue a joint statement for the first time, which indicates soft consensus on the issues of COVID-19, climate change, critical technologies, maritime security, North Korea's denuclearisation, and the restoration of democracy in Myanmar;[63] and second, the regular meetings at senior official and foreign ministerial level were confirmed, and three working groups, namely the Quad Vaccine Experts Group, the Quad Climate Working Group and the Quad Critical and Emerging Technology Working Group, were established.[64]

During this phase, the Quad members discussed China, and each member had individual concerns about Beijing's assertive behaviour in many domains, ranging from the East and South China Seas, human rights situations in Xinjian and development finance.[65] However, given their diverging strategic postures and the more immediate global issues, namely COVID-19, the Quad focused their policy coordination on the COVID-19 countermeasures, critical and emerging technology, and climate change. India emphasised these issues as 'positive agenda[s]' because they did not target any third country but facilitated cooperation for international security and welfare.[66] Nevertheless, these abovementioned issues—except for climate change—have consistently been focused on to check China's vaccine and digital diplomacy, thereby preventing developing states from being vulnerable to China's influence.[67]

In sum, it is clear that throughout the development of Quad 2.0 into Quad 3.0 the member states successfully facilitated cooperation in the Indo-Pacific region, striking a fine balance between their individual strategic posture toward China and their shared interests in tackling non-traditional security agendas. However, it is unclear whether Japan–India bilateral ties helped shape Japan or India's policies toward the Quad. For example, as indicated above, even though the Japan–US–India framework in 2015 provided the basic principles of FOIP, such as respect for ASEAN centrality, it was not reflected in the first Quad meeting.[68] This shows that Japan–India cooperation was not fully utilised to incorporate their shared principles into the Quad, despite the fact that the prime ministers in Japan and India remained the same unlike the change in the US presidency during this period.

Ultimately, Japan has closer security relations with the United States through the US–Japan alliance, and India is the only non-US security ally in the Quad grouping. Although there is a certain strategic affinity between Japan and India, their perspectives are fundamentally shaped by Japan and India's own interests, and their enhanced bilateral relations do not necessarily translate into a discussion in the Quad.

Conclusion: The Future of Japan–India Relations and Indo-Pacific Multilateralism

Japan and India have developed a significant degree of bilateral strategic relations since 2000, expanding their cooperative scope comprehensively from economic to diplomatic to military. However, their policy coordination toward multilateralism has remained weak. While both states viewed the EAS as a potential regional platform for realising a free, open and inclusive Indo-Pacific, there were divergences in the regional visions among the Quad member states, at least in 2017. The Quad was institutionalised rapidly in 2021 under the new US leadership, and now there is a clear, growing convergence in the strategic postures of the four member states. However, as we noted earlier, this convergence was not driven by Japan–India bilateral policy coordination, given that Japan's strategic position was more aligned with the United States and Australia.

Furthermore, the resurrection of the Quad was significantly triggered by a structural factor—China's assertive behaviour in 2010s. Without it, it would have been difficult for the Quad members to hold regular meetings as is evident from Quad 1.0's failure in 2008. This is fundamentally because their strategic postures toward China were not always congruent. But it was the growing concerns about China's increasingly aggressive behaviour in the maritime domain, including its rejection of the 2016 South China Sea Arbitration Tribunal award, and its growing economic and diplomatic influence over developing states in the Indo-Pacific through the BRI that brought the four states together in 2017. It was also China's worsening relations with the individual Quad members—US–China trade and tech war, China's economic coercion and influence operation toward Australia, China's new assertive encroachment near the Senkaku/Diaoyu islands that Japan administers, and India–China border skirmishes in Doklam and Ladakh—that propelled the members to agree with the further institutionalisation of the Quad in 2021.

In this context, Japan–India bilateral relations have not been very impactful in shaping Indo-Pacific multilateralism. India's general hesitance to align itself tightly with other major powers still exists, and such hesitance persists because India aims to ensure its strategic autonomy, preventing itself from getting entrapped in conflicts between other powers, growing China's strategic clout notwithstanding. This posture adopted by India has been consistent since Japan started to improve its relations with India in 2000. The corollary of this is that India's bilateral relations are generally detached from its policy toward multilateralism, and because of this, the creation of a multilateral security framework, such as a collective self-defense mechanism, that can target a third party will be extremely difficult, if not impossible. This is well-illustrated by the fact that India did not align with Japan, the United States and Australia to condemn Russia's aggression toward Ukraine in February 2022 although the Quad held a leaders' meeting in March 2022.[69]

However, there are two interesting observations on the development of Japan–India relations and their policies toward multilateralism. One is that India does not entirely stay away from regional multilateralism, and when strategic interests on a particular issue converge, India is willing to cooperate with other regional states. Despite the Quad's strategic connotation of being counter-China, the grouping was able to agree on the establishment of three working groups in 2021, further expanding its cooperative agendas, and the fact that this manoeuvre was not rejected by India or others indicates that issue-based cooperation is possible. The other is that Japan–India bilateral relations are likely to gradually deepen in the future as they are not tightly linked with regional multilateralism. In this sense, it is entirely possible for both states to continuously examine the issue areas that they are interested in cooperating on and then deepen their functional cooperation accordingly. This can also become a foundation for the two states to expand their cooperation with other regional powers, and not only democratic states.

The nature of Japan–India bilateral cooperation is not the same as that of US allies, such as the US–Japan and Japan–Australia relations, and enhanced India–Japan bilateral relations do not translate into the creation of a stronger policy coordination mechanism toward multilateralism in the Indo-Pacific region. Nevertheless, bilateral cooperation provides an important tool for understanding potential areas of strategic convergence which could nurture a new multilateral coalition for regional peace and stability.

Notes and References

1. Ministry of Foreign Affairs, Japan (MOFA), 'Japan-U.S. Joint Declaration on Security: Alliance for the 21st Century', 17 April 1996, available at https://www.mofa.go.jp/region/n-america/us/security/security.html, accessed on 26 September 2023.

2. MOFA, 'Japan-Australia Joint Declaration on Security Cooperation', 13 March 2007, available at https://www.mofa.go.jp/region/asia-paci/australia/joint0703.html, accessed on 26 September 2023.

3. For example, Teresita Schaffer and Howard Schaffer, *India at the Global High Table: The Quest for Regional Primacy and Strategic Autonomy* (Washington, D.C.: Brookings Institution Press, 2016); Takenori Horimoto, 'Explaining India's Foreign Policy: From Dream to Realization of Major Power', *International Relations of the Asia-Pacific*, vol. 17, no. 3 (2017), pp. 463–496; Harsh Pant and Abhijnan Rej, 'Is India Ready for the Indo-Pacific?' *The Washington Quarterly*, vol. 41, no. 2 (2018), pp. 47–61; Rohan Mukherjee, 'Chaos as opportunity: The United States and world order in India's grand strategy', *Contemporary Politics*, vol. 26, no. 4 (2020), pp. 420–438; Rajesh Rajagopalan, 'Evasive balancing: India's unviable Indo-Pacific strategy', *International Affairs*, vol. 96, no. 1 (2020), pp. 75–93; Ian Hall, 'India and

a Regional Rules-Based Order: Equity and Inclusion', *Security Challenges*, vol. 16, no. 3 (2020), pp. 27–31; Kei Koga, 'Japan's "Indo-Pacific" question: Countering China or shaping a new regional order?', *International Affairs*, vol. 96, no. 1 (2000), pp. 49–73; Aurelio Insisa and Giulio Pugliese, 'The free and open Indo-Pacific versus the belt and road: Spheres of influence and Sino-Japanese relations', *The Pacific Review*, online first (2020); Christopher Huges, Alessio Patalano and Robert Ward, 'Japan's Grand Strategy: The Abe Era and Its Aftermath', *Survival*, vol. 63, no. 1 (2021), pp. 125–160; Tomohiko Satake and Ryo Sahashi, 'The Rise of China and Japan's Vision for Free and Open Indo-Pacific', *Journal of Contemporary China*, vol. 30, no. 127, pp. 18–35; Yuichi Hosoya, 'Helping the US Lead Again: Japan's Vision of a Free and Open Indo-Pacific', *Global Asia*, vol. 16, no. 1 (2021), pp. 52–56; Kei Koga, 'Japan's FOIP under the Suga Administration: Opportunities and Challenges in Southeast Asia', *East Asian Policy*, vol. 13, no. 3 (2021), pp. 84–100.

4. For example, Sunil Khilani, Rajiv Kumar, Pratap Bhanu Mehta, Prakash Menon, Nandan Nilekani, Srinath Raghavan, Shyam Saran and Siddharth Varadarajan, 'Non-Alignment 2.0: A Foreign and Strategic Policy for India in the Twenty First Century', 29 February 2012, available at https://cprindia.org/briefsreports/nonalignment-2-0-a-foreign-and-strategic-policy-for-india-in-the-twenty-first-century/, accessed on 26 September 2023; C. Raja Mohan, 'India: Between "Strategic Autonomy" and "Geopolitical Opportunity"', *Asia Policy*, vol. 15 (2013), pp. 21–25; Harsh Pant and Julie Super, 'India's "non-alignment" conundrum: A twentieth century policy in a changing world', *International Affairs*, vol. 91, no. 4 (2015), pp. 747–764; Walter Ladwig III and Anit Mukherjee, 'India and the United States: The Contours of an Asian Partnership', *Asian Policy*, vol. 14, no. 1 (2019), pp. 3–18; Itty Abraham, 'The End of India's Strategic Autonomy?', *China-India Brief*, no. 169, 22–30 October 2020, available at https://lkyspp.nus.edu.sg/cag/publications/details/china-india-brief-169, accessed on 26 September 2023.

5. 'Remarks by President Trump at APEC CEO Summit', 10 November 2017, available at https://trumpwhitehouse.archives.gov/briefings-statements/remarks-president-trump-apec-ceo-summit-da-nang-vietnam/, accessed on 26 September 2023; The White House, 'National Security Strategy of the United States of America', December 2017, available at https://trumpwhitehouse.archives.gov/wp-content/uploads/2017/12/NSS-Final-12-18-2017-0905.pdf, accessed on 26 September 2023.

6. Kei Koga, 'Quad 3.0: Japan, Indo-Pacific and Minilateralism', *East Asian Policy*, vol. 14, no. 1 (2022), pp. 20–38.

7. MOFA, 'Nichi-In shuno kaidan (gaiyo)' [Japan-India Summit (Summary)], 23 August 2000, available at https://www.mofa.go.jp/mofaj/kaidan/kiroku/s_mori/arc_00/asia4_00/n_i.html, accessed on 26 September 2023; MOFA, 'Mori soridaijin enzetsu: 21seiki ni okeru nichi in gurobaru patonasippu no kochiku' [Prime

Minister Mori's Speech: The establishment of Japan-India Global Partnership in the 21st Century], 24 August 2000, available at https://www.mofa.go.jp/mofaj/press/enzetsu/12/ems_0824.html, accessed on 26 September 2023.

8. MOFA, 'Japan-India Joint Declaration', 10 December 2001, available at https://www.mofa.go.jp/region/asia-paci/india/joint0112.html, accessed on 26 September 2023.

9. MOFA, 'Nichi Indo gaisho kaidan (gaiyo)' [Japan-India Foreign Ministers' Meeting (Summary)], 27 November 2004, available at https://www.mofa.go.jp/mofaj/kaidan/g_machimura/asean_04/j_india_g.html, accessed on 26 September 2023.

10. MOFA, 'Nihon Indo shuno kaidan (kekka gaiyo)' [Japan-India Summit Meeting (Summary)], 29 November 2004, available at https://www.mofa.go.jp/mofaj/kaidan/s_koi/asean3_04/india_g.html, accessed on 26 September 2023; Government of India, 'PM's Address at Third India-Asean Business Summit', 19 October 2004, available at https://archivepmo.nic.in/drmanmohansingh/speech-details.php?nodeid=30, accessed on 26 September 2023.

11. MOFA, 'Prime Minister Koizumi's Speech', 29 April 2005, available at https://www.mofa.go.jp/mofaj/press/enzetsu/17/ekoi_0429.html, accessed on 26 September 2023.

12. MOFA, 'Japan-India Partnership in a New Asian Era: Strategic Orientation of Japan-India Global Partnership', 30 April 2005, available at https://www.mofa.go.jp/region/asia-paci/india/partner0504.html, accessed on 26 September 2023.

13. Ibid.

14. MOFA, 'Joint Statement: Towards Japan-India Strategic Global Partnership', 15 December 2006, available at https://www.mofa.go.jp/region/asia-paci/india/pdfs/joint0612.pdf, accessed on 26 September 2023.

15. MOFA, 'Confluence of the Two Seas', 22 August 2007, available at https://www.mofa.go.jp/region/asia-paci/pmv0708/speech-2.html, accessed on 26 September 2023.

16. Shinzo Abe, '"Jiyu de hirakareta Indo taiheiyo" ni miru senryakuteki shiko' [Strategic thinking on the Free and Open Indo-Pacific], *Gaiko*, no. 65 (2021), p. 95.

17. MOFA, 'Aso gaimu daijin no indo homon nit suite (kekka gaiyo)' [Foreign Minister Aso's Visit to India (Summary)], 18 January 2006, available at https://www.mofa.go.jp/mofaj/kaidan/g_aso/in_paki_05/g_india.html, accessed on 26 September 2023; Fukushiro Nukaga, 'Chi-iki anzenhosho to nichibei kyoryoku ni tsuite' (Regional Security and US-Japan Cooperation), 1 May 2007, available at http://www.ja-nsrg.or.jp/forum2007-9/f9panel2-nukaga.pdf, accessed on 28 October 2023; MOFA, 'Joint Statement on the Roadmap for New Dimensions to the Strategic and Global Partnership between Japan and India', 23 August 2007, available at https://www.mofa.go.jp/region/asia-paci/pmv0708/joint-2.

html, accessed on 26 September 2023; MOFA, 'Daiikkai Nichi Indo jikankyu "2+2" taiwa oyobi Nichi Indo gaimujikankyu seimu kyogi (kekka gaiyo)' [The 1st Japan-India '2+2' vice ministers/foreign secretary and Japan-India foreign vice minister-level political dialogue (summary)], July 2010, available at https://www.mofa.go.jp/mofaj/area/india/2plus2taiwa_2010.html, accessed on 26 September 2023; Ministry of External Affairs (MEA), India, 'First India-Japan Maritime Affairs Dialogue', 29 January 2013, available at https://mea.gov.in/press-releases.htm?dtl/21141/First+IndiaJapan+Maritime+Affairs+Dialogue, accessed on 26 September 2023; MOFA, 'Japan-India Joint Statement: Intensifying the Strategic and Global Partnership', 25 January 2014, available at https://www.mofa.go.jp/files/000025064.pdf, accessed on 26 September 2023.

18. MOFA, 'Nihon Indo shunokaidan (gaiyo)' [Japan-India Summit Meeting (Summary)], 17 July 2006, available at https://www.mofa.go.jp/mofaj/kaidan/s_koi/g8_06/jin_gaiyo.html, accessed on 26 September 2023; MOFA, 'Nihonkoku to Indo kyowakoku tono aida no hokatsuteki Keizai renkei kyotei non shomei oyobi Maehara daijin to sharuma indo shoko daijin tono kaidan' [the Comprehensive Economic Parntership Agreement between Japan and the Republic of India and dialogues between Foreign Minister Seiji Maehara and Minister of Commerce and Industry Anand Sharma], 16 February 2010, available at https://www.mofa.go.jp/mofaj/press/release/23/2/0216_02.html, accessed on 26 September 2023.

19. MOFA, 'Tokyo Declaration for Japan-India Special Strategic and Global Partnership', 1 September 2014, available at https://www.mofa.go.jp/mofaj/files/000050549.pdf, accessed on 26 September 2023.

20. 'India, Japan to "upgrade" defence cooperation', *The Indian Express*, 1 September 2014, available at https://indianexpress.com/article/india/india-others/india-japan-to-upgrade-defence-cooperation/, accessed on 26 September 2023.

21. MOFA, 'Japan-India Summit Meeting', 14 November 2014, available at https://www.mofa.go.jp/s_sa/sw/in/page24e_000065.html, accessed on 26 September 2023.

22. MOFA, 'Eighth Japan-India Foreign Ministers' Strategic Dialogue', 18 January 2015, available at https://www.mofa.go.jp/s_sa/sw/in/page3e_000295.html, accessed on 26 September 2023; MOFA, 'Nichi Go In jikankyogi oyobi Nhichi Indo gaimu jikan taiwa no kaisai' [Japan-Australia-India Vice Ministers Meeting and Japan-India Vice Foreign Ministers Dialogue], 5 June 2015, available at https://www.mofa.go.jp/mofaj/press/release/press4_002192.html, accessed on 26 September 2023.

23. MOFA, 'Japan-India Summit Meeting', 21 November 2015, available at https://www.mofa.go.jp/s_sa/sw/in/page24e_000117.html, accessed on 26 September 2023.

24. MOFA, 'Japan and India Vision 2025 Special Strategic and Global Partnership: Working Together for Peace and Prosperity of the Indo-Pacific Region

and the World', 12 December 2015, available at https://www.mofa.go.jp/s_sa/sw/in/page3e_000432.html, accessed on 26 September 2023.

25. Ibid.

26. Ibid.

27. Vivek Raghuvanshi, 'Japan to Join Malabar as Permanent Participant', 13 October 2015, available at https://www.defensenews.com/naval/2015/10/13/japan-to-join-malabar-as-permanent-participant/, accessed on 26 September 2023.

28. MOFA, 'Japan-India Summit Meeting', 7 September 2016, available at https://www.mofa.go.jp/s_sa/sw/in/page4e_000515.html, accessed on 26 September 2023.

29. MOFA, 'Japan-India Summit Meeting', 11 November 2016, available at https://www.mofa.go.jp/s_sa/sw/in/page3e_000616.html, accessed on 26 September 2023.

30. MOFA, 'Japan-India Vision Statement', 29 October 2018, available at https://www.mofa.go.jp/mofaj/files/000413507.pdf, accessed on 26 September 2023.

31. MOFA, 'Joint Statement: First Japan-India 2+2 Foreign and Defence Ministerial Meeting', 30 November 2019, available at https://www.mofa.go.jp/mofaj/files/000544338.pdf, accessed on 26 September 2023; MOFA, 'Agreement between the Government of Japan and the Government of the Republic of India Concerning Reciprocal Provision of Supplies and Services between the Self-Defense Forces of Japan and the Indian Armed Forces', 10 September 2020, available at https://www.mofa.go.jp/files/100091751.pdf, accessed on 26 September 2023.

32. Kei Koga, 'Wedge Strategy, Japan-ASEAN Cooperation, and the Making of EAS: Implications for Indo-Pacific Institutionalization', in John Ciorciari and Kiyoteru Tsutsui, eds, *The Courteous Power: Japan and Southeast Asia in the Indo-Pacific Era* (Ann Arbor: University of Michigan Press, 2021).

33. There was an attempt to include India in East Asia before the establishment of EAS in 2002, when ASEAN+3 members were eager to discuss an East Asian Community. See MOFA, 'ARF gaisho kaigi ni saishite no Nichi-In gaisho kaidan gaiyo' [Japan-India Foreign Ministers' Meeting at ARF], 1 August 2002, available at https://www.mofa.go.jp/mofaj/kaidan/g_kawaguchi/asean3_02/ji_gaiyo.html, accessed on 26 September 2023.

34. MOFA, 'Aso gaimu daijin no Indo homon (kyodo presuririsu)' [Foreign Minister Aso's visit to India (Joint Press Release)], 4 January 2006, available at https://www.mofa.go.jp/mofaj/kaidan/g_aso/in_paki_05/pr_india.html, accessed on 26 September 2023.

35. MOFA, 'Nichi Indo shuno kaidan (gaiyo)' [Japan-India Summit Meeting (Summary)], 21 November 2009, available at https://www.mofa.go.jp/mofaj/kaidan/s_fukuda/eas_07/jind_gai.html, accessed on 26 September 2023; MOFA, 'Joint Statement by Prime Minister Dr. Yukio Hatoyama and Prime Minister

Dr. Manmohan Singh', 29 December 2009, available at https://www.mofa.go.jp/region/asia-paci/india/pmv0912/joint.html, accessed on 26 September 2023.

36. MOFA, 'Japan-India Joint Statement: Intensifying the Strategic and Global Partnership', 25 January 2014, available at https://www.mofa.go.jp/files/000025064.pdf, accessed on 26 September 2023; MOFA, 'Japan-India Joint Statement: Toward a Free, Open and Prosperous Indo-Pacific', 14 September 2017, available at https://www.mofa.go.jp/mofaj/files/000289999.pdf, accessed on 26 September 2023.

37. Ibid.

38. MOFA, 'Japan-India Summit Meeting', 13 December 2015, available at https://www.mofa.go.jp/s_sa/sw/in/page3e_000436.html, accessed on 26 September 2023; MOFA, 'Japan-India Summit Meeting', 7 September 2016, available at https://www.mofa.go.jp/s_sa/sw/in/page4e_000515.html, accessed on 26 September 2023.

39. Alice Ba, 'Regionalism's multiple negotiations: ASEAN in East Asia', *Cambridge Review of International Affairs*, vol. 22, no. 3 (2009), pp. 345–367; Kei Koga, *Reinventing Regional Security Institutions in Asia and Africa: Power Shifts, Ideas, and Institutional Change* (Oxon and New York: Routledge, 2017). See also Seng Tan, 'Rethinking "ASEAN Centrality" in the Regional Governance of East Asia', *The Singapore Economic Review*, vol. 62, no. 3 (2017), pp. 721–740.

40. MOFA, 'Inaugural U.S.-India-Japan Trilateral Ministerial', 29 September 2015, available at https://www.mofa.go.jp/mofaj/files/000102078.pdf, accessed on 26 September 2023; MOFA, 'Joint Statement: First Japan-India 2+2 Foreign and Defence Ministerial Meeting', 30 November 2019, available at https://www.mofa.go.jp/mofaj/files/000544338.pdf, accessed on 26 September 2023.

41. Earlier in 2007, after Foreign Minister Aso launched the strategic concept, 'Arc of Freedom and Prosperity', Japan started to strengthen its connection with SAARC, through which it attempted to increase its presence in South Asia. See MOFA, 'Joint Press Release: Visit of External Affairs Minister of India to Japan', March 2007, available at https://www.mofa.go.jp/region/asia-paci/india/joint0703.html, accessed on 26 September 2023; MOFA, 'Japan's Support to the SAARC (Priority Areas and Policies)', 3 April 2007, available at https://www.mofa.go.jp/region/asia-paci/saarc/support0704.pdf, accessed on 26 September 2023; MOFA, 'Eighth Japan-India Foreign Ministers' Strategic Dialogue', 18 January 2015, available at https://www.mofa.go.jp/s_sa/sw/in/page3e_000295.html, accessed on 26 September 2023; MOFA, 'Japan-India Joint Statement', 11 November 2016, available at https://www.mofa.go.jp/mofaj/files/000202950.pdf, accessed on 26 September 2023; MOFA, 'Japan-India Joint Statement: Toward a Free, Open and Prosperous Indo-Pacific', 14 September 2017, available at https://www.mofa.go.jp/mofaj/files/000289999.pdf, accessed on 26 September 2023.

42. For example, see Jagannath Panda, 'India's Continental Connect on Indo-Pacific and Quad 2.0', *Asia Pacific Bulletin*, no. 441 (2018).

43. MOFA, 'Australia-India-Japan-U.S. Consultations on the Indo-Pacific', 12 November 2017, available at https://www.mofa.go.jp/press/release/press4e_001789.html, accessed on 26 September 2023; US Department of State, 'Australia-India-Japan-U.S. Consultations on the Indo-Pacific', 12 November 2017, available at https://2017-2021.state.gov/australia-india-japan-u-s-consultations-on-the-indo-pacific/index.html, accessed on 26 September 2023; DFAT, 'Australia-India-Japan-United States consultations on the Indo-Pacific', 12 November 2017, available at https://www.dfat.gov.au/news/media/Pages/aus-india-japan-us-consultations-on-the-indo-pacific, accessed on 26 September 2023.

44. MEA, 'India-Australia-Japan-U.S. Consultations on Indo-Pacific (November 12, 2017)', 12 November 2017, available at https://mea.gov.in/press-releases.htm?dtl/29110/IndiaAustraliaJapanUS_Consultations_on_IndoPacific_November_12_2017, accessed on 26 September 2023.

45. Ibid.

46. Kei Koga, 'Redirecting Strategic Focus in the Age of the Indo-Pacific', *Comparative Connections*, vol. 20, no. 1 (2018), pp. 129–138.

47. Kiran Stacey and Jamie Smyth, 'Diplomatic initiative revived to counter China's growing influence', *Financial Times*, 14 November 2017; 'Quad: It shouldn't be about China, but legit interests', *The Economic Times*, 29 November 2017.

48. Shi Jiangtao and Laura Zhou, 'Wary China on Quad bloc watch after officials from US, Japan, India, and Australia meet on Asean sidelines', *South China Morning Post*, 13 November 2017.

49. MEA, 'India-Australia-Japan-US Consultation', 7 June 2018, available at https://www.mea.gov.in/press-releases.htm?dtl/29961/indiaaustraliajapanus+consultations, accessed on 26 September 2023; MOFA, 'Japan-Australia-India-U.S. Consultation', 7 June 2018, available at https://www.mofa.go.jp/press/release/press4e_002062.html, accessed on 26 September 2023; US Department of State, 'U.S.-Australia-India-Japan Consultations', 7 June 2018, available at https://2017-2021.state.gov/u-s-australia-india-japan-consultations/index.html, accessed on 26 September 2023; DFAT, 'Australia-India-Japan-United States consultation', 7 June 2018, available at https://www.dfat.gov.au/news/media/Pages/australia-india-japan-united-states-consultations, accessed on 26 September 2023.

50. International Institute for Strategic Studies, '17th Asia Security Summit, The IISS Shangri-La Dialogue, Keynote Address: Shri Narendra Modi, Prime Minister of India', 1 June 2018, available at https://www.iiss.org/globalassets/media-library---content--migration/images-delta/dialogues/sld/sld-2018/documents/narendra-modi-sld18.pdf, accessed on 26 September 2023.

51. MOFA, 'Japan-Australia-India-U.S. Consultations', 15 November 2018, available at https://www.mofa.go.jp/press/release/press1e_000099.html, accessed on 26 September 2023; MEA, 'India-Australia-Japan-U.S. Consultations', 15 November 2018, available at https://www.mea.gov.in/press-releases.

htm?dtl/30593/IndiaAustraliaJapanUS_Consultations, accessed on 26 September 2023; US Department of State, 'U.S.-Australia-India-Japan Consultations', 15 November 2018, available at https://2017-2021.state.gov/u-s-australia-india-japan-consultations-2/index.html, accessed on 26 September 2023; DFAT, 'Australia-India-Japan-United States Consultations', 15 November 2018, available at https://www.dfat.gov.au/news/media/Pages/australia-india-japan-united-states-consultations-2018, accessed on 26 September 2023; MOFA, 'Japan-Australia-India-U.S. Consultations', 31 May 2019, available at https://www.mofa.go.jp/press/release/press4e_002464.html, accessed on 26 September 2023; MEA, 'India-Australia-Japan-United States Consultations', 31 May 2019, available at https://www.mea.gov.in/press-releases.htm?dtl/31403/IndiaAustraliaJapanUnited_States_Consultations, accessed on 26 September 2023; U.S. Embassy & Consulates in India, 'U.S.-Australia-India-Japan Consultations ("The Quad")', 31 May 2019, available at https://in.usembassy.gov/u-s-australia-india-japan-consultations-the-quad/, accessed on 26 September 2023; DFAT, 'Australia-India-Japan-United States Consultations', 31 May 2019, available at https://www.dfat.gov.au/news/media/Pages/australia-india-japan-usa-consultations, accessed on 26 September 2023.

52. Bhagyashree Garekar, 'Quad leaders stress Asean's centrality in their Indo-Pacific vision', *The Straits Times*, 17 November 2018; 'Remarks by Secretary Pompeo at the India IDEAS Summit and 44th Annual Meeting of U.S.-India Business Council', *States News Service*, 13 June 2019.

53. MOFA, 'Japan-Australia-India-U.S. Ministerial', 26 September 2019, available at https://www.mofa.go.jp/fp/nsp/page3e_001112.html, accessed on 26 September 2023; US Department of State, 'Readout of U.S.-Australia-India-Japan Ministerial ("The Quad")', 26 September 2019, available at https://2017-2021.state.gov/readout-of-u-s-australia-india-japan-ministerial-the-quad/index.html, accessed on 26 September 2023; MOFA, 'Japan-Australia-India-U.S. Consultations', 4 November 2019, available at https://www.mofa.go.jp/fp/nsp/page4e_001157.html, accessed on 26 September 2023; MEA, 'India-Australia-Japan-United States Consultations', 4 November 2019, available at https://www.mea.gov.in/press-releases.htm?dtl/32006/IndiaAustraliaJapanUnited+States+Consultations, accessed on 26 September 2023; US Department of State, 'U.S.-Australia-India-Japan Consultations ("The Quad")', 4 November 2019, available at https://2017-2021.state.gov/u-s-australia-india-japan-consultations-the-quad-2/index.html, accessed on 26 September 2023; DFAT, 'Australia-India-Japan-United States "Quad" Consultations', 4 November 2019, available at https://www.dfat.gov.au/news/media/Pages/australia-india-japan-united-states-quad-consultations, accessed on 26 September 2023.

54. 'India, Australia, Japan, US discuss digital connectivity, security, supply chain in "Quad" meeting', *Business Line*, 25 September 2020.

55. MOFA, 'Japan-Australia-India-U.S. Consultations', 25 September 2020, available at https://www.mofa.go.jp/press/release/press4e_002912.html, accessed on 26 September 2023; MEA, 'India-Australia-Japan-United States Senior Officials Consultations', 25 September 2020, available at https://mea.gov.in/press-releases.htm?dtl/33059/IndiaAustraliaJapanUnited_States_Senior_Officials_Consultations, accessed on 26 September 2023; US Department of State, 'U.S.-Australia-India-Japan Consultations ("The Quad")', 25 September 2020, available at https://2017-2021-translations.state.gov/2020/09/25/u-s-australia-india-japan-consultations-the-quad/index.html, accessed on 26 September 2023; DFAT, 'Australia-India-Japan-United States Quad Consultations', 25 September 2020, available at https://www.dfat.gov.au/news/media-release/australia-india-japan-united-states-quad-consultations, accessed on 26 September 2023.

56. US State Department, 'Briefing with Senior State Department Officials on Secretary Pompeo's Visit to Japan', 6 October 2020, available at https://2017-2021.state.gov/briefing-with-senior-state-department-officials-on-secretary-pompeos-visit-to-japan/index.html, accessed on 26 September 2023.

57. Abhijnan Rej, 'State Department Officials Clarify Pompeo's Views on the Quad', *The Diplomat*, 7 October 2020, available at https://thediplomat.com/2020/10/state-department-officials-clarify-pompeos-views-on-the-quad/, accessed on 26 September 2023.

58. Minister for Foreign Affairs, Australia, 'Australia-India-Japan-United States Quad Foreign Ministers' Meeting', 6 October 2020, available at https://www.foreignminister.gov.au/minister/marise-payne/media-release/australia-india-japan-united-states-quad-foreign-ministers-meeting, accessed on 26 September 2023.

59. 'Multilateralism for multi-polar opportunities', *India Review & Analysis*, 21 November 2019.

60. 'Jiminto sosaisen no kokaitoron' [Public debate for LDP Presidential Election], *Nihon Keizai Shimbun*, 12 September 2020; 'Kokuminto katariaitai "Ajia ban NATO"' [I am willing to discuss the Japanese public about "Asian NATO"], *Mainichi Shimbun*, 21 July 2018, available at https://mainichi.jp/premier/politics/articles/20180720/pol/00m/010/015000c, accessed on 26 September 2023.

61. Jesse Johnson and Satoshi Sugiyama, '"Quad" meeting in Tokyo prizes symbolism over substance', *The Japan Times*, 7 October 2020.

62. Koga, 'Quad 3.0'.

63. The White House, 'Quad Leaders' Joint Statement: "The Spirit of the Quad"', 12 March 2021, available at https://www.whitehouse.gov/briefing-room/statements-releases/2021/03/12/quad-leaders-joint-statement-the-spirit-of-the-quad/, accessed on 26 September 2023.

64. Ibid.

65. MOFA, 'Japan-Australia-India-U.S. Leaders' Video Conference', 13 March 2021, available at https://www.mofa.go.jp/fp/nsp/page1e_000310.html, accessed on 26 September 2023; US Department of State, 'Press Briefing by Press Secretary Jen Psaki and National Security Advisor Jake Sullivan', 12 March 2021, available at https://www.whitehouse.gov/briefing-room/press-briefings/2021/06/07/press-briefing-by-press-secretary-jen-psaki-and-national-security-advisor-jake-sullivan-june-7-2021/, accessed on 26 September 2023.

66. MEA, 'Transcript of Special Briefing on First Quadrilateral Leaders Virtual Summit by Foreign Secretary (March 12, 2021)', 13 March 2021, available at https://mea.gov.in/media-briefings.htm?dtl/33656/Transcript_of_Special_Briefing_on_First_Quadrilateral_Leaders_Virtual_Summit_by_Foreign_Secretary_March_12_2021, accessed on 26 September 2023.

67. US Department of State, 'Secretary Blinken's Call with Quad Ministers', 18 February 2021, available at https://www.state.gov/secretary-blinkens-call-with-quad-ministers/, accessed on 26 September 2023; Joshua Kurlantzick, 'Assessing China's Digital Silk Road: A Transformative Approach to Technology Financing or a Danger to Freedoms?' Council on Foreign Relations, 18 December 2020, available at https://www.cfr.org/blog/assessing-chinas-digital-silk-road-transformative-approach-technology-financing-or-danger, accessed on 26 September 2023.

68. Kei Koga, 'Institutional Dilemma: Quad and ASEAN in the Indo-Pacific', *Asian Perspective*, vol. 47, no. 1 (2023), pp. 27–48.

69. The White House, 'Quad Joint Leaders' Statement', 24 May 2022, available at https://www.whitehouse.gov/briefing-room/statements-releases/2022/05/24/quad-joint-leaders-statement/, accessed on 27 October 2023.

twelve

Afghanistan after the US Withdrawal
New Avenues for Japan–India Cooperation

Kenta Aoki

On 29 February 2020, Zalmay Khalilzad, US Special Representative for Afghanistan Reconciliation, and Mullah Abdul Ghani Baradar, Deputy Leader of the Taliban[1] and head of Taliban's Qatar office, signed a peace deal in Doha. This deal, hereinafter referred to as the Doha Agreement, guarantees that the Taliban will not allow its members, other individuals or groups, including al-Qa'ida, to use Afghanistan to threaten the security of the US and its allies. Meanwhile, the US will reduce the number of its forces in Afghanistan to 8,600 soldiers within 135 days, and withdraw its remaining forces within 14 months.[2] The international community had expressed concerns that Afghanistan could once again become a safe haven for foreign terrorist organisations through the 'power vacuum' created by the withdrawal of foreign troops. The deal partially addressed these pre-existing concerns. However, the Taliban neither agreed to curb violence nor announce permanent ceasefire, so it is too early to call it a 'peace accord' or something similar.

Following the withdrawal of foreign combat troops at the end of 2014, neighbouring countries such as China, Russia and Iran have been increasing their influence over Afghanistan both economically and strategically. The deal between the US and the Taliban has further shadowed Afghanistan's future prospects. There is also a possibility that the Japanese and Indian investments made so far in Afghanistan could be, in a way, wasted. This chapter will highlight possible areas of cooperation between Japan and India in Afghanistan, in the backdrop of a volatile geopolitical situation. It is imperative to consider how Japan and India can cooperate with Afghanistan to prevent it from becoming a hotbed of terrorism, and transform it into a self-reliant nation rather than a rentier state dependent on foreign aid.

The first section provides an overview of the changing regional dynamics created by the withdrawal of foreign troops and its implications for regional security. The roles of regional countries are also discussed. The second section examines the possible areas of cooperation between Japan and India from the perspective of promoting peace, infrastructure development such as the Chabahar port and connectivity projects, response to the COVID-19 crisis and other strategic areas. The third section will highlight potential implications of Japan–India strategic cooperation for Pakistan's security policy of 'strategic depth' and the US–Iran tension.

On 15 August 2021, the Taliban seized Kabul, and the Islamic Republic of Afghanistan collapsed. At the moment of writing (November 2023), the Taliban is in effective control of almost the entire country. Although the Taliban claims to be working toward achieving Islamic governance as per its own interpretation, there are concerns about the Taliban's monopoly on power and their ties with international terrorist organisations, as well as rampant human rights abuses against women. Japan and India, in coordination with relevant stakeholders, such as the US, the EU, Russia, China, Iran, OIC (Organisation of Islamic Cooperation) members, Pakistan and others, should continue their engagement with Afghanistan to prevent it from becoming a source of instability in the region and beyond.

Changing Dynamics in the Region

'Power Vacuum' after the Withdrawal of Foreign Troops

After the withdrawal of foreign combat troops in 2014, the strength of remaining foreign troops in Afghanistan drastically reduced. At the peak of action, the US and the International Security Assistance Force (ISAF) had deployed approximately 1,40,000 soldiers in Afghanistan.[3] However, there was a gradual realisation that there will be no peace through military solutions in Afghanistan, considering the level of legitimacy the Taliban had[4] and its continued fierce military offensives. Under such circumstances, the International Afghanistan Conference held in Bonn in 2011 set out the 'transformation decade of 2015–2024', during which the Afghan National Security Force (ANSF) assumed full security responsibility, while the international community remained committed to civil assistance to Afghanistan. As of June 2019, the troop strength of the Resolute Support Mission (RSM), which commenced in January 2015 as a successor programme to ISAF, was only 17,148.[5] In addition, RSM's mandate does not include combat, but is limited to training, assisting and advising ANSF.[6] In brief, the troop strength was downsized by seven-eighth and the mandate was modified. This trend continued for some time as the US was obliged to comply with the Doha Agreement. The US reduced its troop strength to 2,500 in January 2021, and eventually completed a total withdrawal on 30 August 2021. This also demonstrated that the balance of power between the Afghan government and the Taliban has changed significantly owing to the security transition.

Over the second half of the Islamic Republic era, the Taliban intensified its military offensive and expanded its influence. According to the United Nations Assistance Mission in Afghanistan (UNAMA), civilian casualties following armed conflicts increased in 2015, reaching 11,452 (3,527 deaths and 7,925 injuries) in 2016, which was the worst since the start of UNAMA's statistics in 2009.[7] The level of violence has remained high since then. For example, civilian casualties accounted for 10,392 (3,403 deaths and 6,989 injuries) in 2019.[8] This is further evidenced by the number of security incidents. According to the Special Inspector General for Afghanistan Reconstruction (SIGAR), the number of security incidents caused by anti-governmental elements (AGEs) totalled 8,204 in the fourth quarter of 2019, which is the worst since the beginning of the statistics in 2010.[9] In terms of stability levels in districts and provinces, as of January 2019, SIGAR estimates that approximately 46 per cent of all districts are either under the control of AGEs or witnessing a conflict between the central government and AGEs.[10] After US President Joe Biden's announcement regarding withdrawal of all US troops from Afghanistan on 14 April 2021, the Taliban intensified its military offensives across Afghanistan, with a particular focus on the northeastern region, which used to be the stronghold of anti-Taliban groups in 1990s, and across the main ring road to cut off supply routes of the ANSF.

The prospect of the Taliban penetrating deeper was supported by the Annex to the Doha Agreement. The US Department of State confirmed that classified annexes to the Doha Agreement exist, which has been seen only by some Taliban members and US high-ranking officials. To summarise the various reports, the Taliban is prohibited from attacking

US troops. However, it is allowed to continue operations against ANSF in rural areas, but not in major cities. Conversely, the US would only be allowed to conduct air strikes within a specific distance of active battlefield operations, but not on Taliban fighters resting in camps or villages. A timeline for events over the next 18 months was also attached.[11] These top-secret annexes to the Doha Agreement severely restricted US ground troop attacks and airstrikes against the Taliban, which allowed the Taliban to gain ground in rural areas.

Increasing Influence of Regional Countries: China, Russia and Iran

1. *China*

After 2014, regional and international powers gradually strengthened their engagements with Afghanistan. The most notable actor in this regard has been China. Afghanistan and China share a 76-km border and have maintained a historical and cultural relationship for a long time. However, China's presence in post-conflict peace-building after 2001 was not very evident. The turning point came in June 2012 when China and Afghanistan decided to upgrade their bilateral relations to the level of a strategic cooperative partnership. It was soon followed by investments in the crude oil basin around the northern Amu River by China National Petroleum Corporation (CNPC) in October 2012, the granting of observer status to Afghanistan in the Shanghai Cooperation Organisation (SCO) in the same year, the establishment of China's post for 'Special Representative for Afghanistan' in July 2014 and the hosting of the Fourth Ministerial Conference of the Heart of Asia–Istanbul Process by China in October 2014. With the gradual withdrawal of foreign combat troops by the end of 2014, China's presence in Afghanistan grew sharply.

The trend continued even after the return of the Taliban. Although no country has recognised the Taliban so far, China announced its official position on the Afghan issue on 12 April 2023. The position consists of 11 points and pledges no interference in Afghanistan's internal affairs, but urges the Taliban to protect the basic rights and interests of the Afghan people including women, children and all ethnic groups. Notably, it urges the US to live up to its commitments and release Afghanistan's frozen overseas assets.[12] Besides, China became the first country to appoint a new Ambassador to Afghanistan, Zhao Xing, who presented his credentials to

Mohammad Hassan Akhund, the acting Prime Minister of the Taliban, on 13 September 2023.[13] In short, China is tactically expanding its influence in Afghanistan after the US withdrawal.

2. *Russia*

Historically, Russia has always paid singular attention to Afghanistan owing to its geographical proximity and strategic interests. During the Cold War, the former Soviet Union started military intervention in Afghanistan, a buffer state between the East and West, in 1979, which lasted for 10 years until 1989. It is difficult to specify reasons for the invasion but it is generally believed that there was a combination of factors. According to Mark Galeotti, some of these were: 1) expansionism, 2) the Brezhnev Doctrine, 3) fear of Americanism, 4) fundamentalism and 5) prancing proconsuls.[14] After the Cold War ended in December 1991, the Soviet Union halted military aid to the Najibullah administration, which gradually resulted in the regime losing ground. Consequently, the Najibullah regime collapsed in April 1992.

Since the establishment of the Hamid Karzai administration in 2001, Russia's presence has remained low-key but with cautious attention. Russia's fear of Afghanistan can be characterised by the following elements: 1) instability in the region, 2) penetration of terrorism and 3) increased smuggling of narcotics. Central Asian Republics (CARs) are backyards for Russia; therefore, from a security perspective, it is important for the country to maintain political stability in Afghanistan and prevent terrorism from crossing borders and entering CARs. This can explain why Russia has shown strategic and political interest in Afghanistan in recent years. For example, in October 2012, Russia extended the lease contract of the 201st Military Base in Tajikistan until 2042.[15] Russia is also concerned about the expansion of the Islamic State Khorasan Province (ISKP) and the Taliban's political move. Russia hosted the intra-Afghan dialogues in November 2018, and again in February and May 2019 to facilitate the peace process between the Afghan government and the Taliban. In addition, counter-narcotics is another factor that makes Russia concerned about the instability in Afghanistan. Soon after the Taliban's return to power, Russia hosted a Moscow Conference on Afghanistan on 20 October 2021, inviting Abdul Salam Hanafi, the acting Prime Minister of the Taliban, to discuss how to engage with the

Taliban. Recognising the Taliban as 'a new reality', Russia continues to be one of its important backers.[16]

3. *Iran*

Iran and Afghanistan share a long border and have historically maintained a deep cultural and religious relationship. Dari, the official language of Afghanistan, is a dialect of Persian, which is an official language of Iran and was the lingua franca in the region in the past. In recent years, the two countries have had a restrained and ambiguous political and economic relationship. The countries enhanced their relationship to the Strategic Cooperation Agreement in August 2013, resulting in a frequent exchange of high-ranking officials. In addition, Iran is currently the number one importer of Afghan goods, replacing Pakistan from the top position.[17] Iran has tried to maintain a constructive relationship with the Taliban as well. This relationship was complicated by the killing of Iranian diplomats in the Consul General of Iran in Mazar-e Sharif in August 1998. However, to counter US influence in the region and to block the infiltration of the Islamic State Khorasan Province (ISKP), Iran maintains strong ties with the Taliban by providing weapons, ammunition and financial resources.[18] It is also worth mentioning that Iran recruited Hazara youth to fight with the Assad regime in Syria to counter the Islamic State.[19] Iran's engagement with Afghanistan is thus different from that of China and Russia.

Peace and Political Process in Afghanistan

In June 2013, the Taliban's Qatar office was inaugurated.[20] Subsequently, the Taliban began to actively participate in meetings held as part of confidence-building measures by Russia, Qatar, Germany and so on. Essentially, the Taliban had not closed their doors to dialogue. The reasons behind the Taliban's active stance towards peace can be attributed to the active peace initiative under Ashraf Ghani's regime and the Trump administration's coming to power in the US.

First, the Ghani administration that assumed office on 29 September 2014 showed strong interest in promoting peace with the Taliban and Hizb-e Islami Gulbuddin (HIG). Consequently, in July 2015, the Afghan government and the Taliban held the first peace negotiations in Murree in Pakistan.[21] However, due to the sudden death of Mullah Omar, the second negotiation was cancelled. The Afghan government subsequently signed a peace deal with HIG, which had fought with the Afghan government as AGE, on 29 September 2016.[22] Although HIG is relatively smaller than the Taliban, this was a significant event that paved the way towards political reconciliation with the Taliban. Finally, President Ghani invited the Taliban for negotiations without any preconditions in the Second Kabul Process Conference on 28 February 2018.[23]

Second, the Trump administration, which assumed office in January 2017, attached great importance to its policy towards Afghanistan in order to end the longest war for the US. The South Asia Strategy, announced on 21 August 2017, outlined the US's continued military engagement to avoid hasty withdrawal.[24] On 16 June 2018, US Secretary of State Mike Pompeo stated that '[t]he United States is prepared to support, facilitate, and participate in these discussions'.[25] This statement showed the gradual softening of US's stance towards Afghanistan. In September 2018, President Trump appointed Zalmay Khalilzad as a Special Representative for Afghanistan Reconciliation and started pushing for peace negotiations between the US and the Taliban.

The two sides had held nine negotiations by September 2019, and Khalilzad stated that a deal has been 'agreed in principle' on 2 September 2019.[26] However, President Trump called off negotiations with the Taliban with immediate effect, after a vehicle-borne improvised explosive device exploded on the foreign troop's convoy in Kabul on 5 September 2019, killing a US soldier.[27] Although this incident cast a shadow on the negotiations, a prisoner exchange in the middle of November 2019 and a surprise visit by President Trump to Bagram Air Base on 28 November paved the way for resuming talks on 7 December. Both sides complied with the pre-agreed reduction in violence for seven days at the end of February 2020,[28] and finally the Doha Agreement was signed on 29 February 2020.

The main components of the Doha Agreement were commitment towards 1) counter-terrorism, 2) withdrawal of US troops, 3) intra-Afghan negotiations and 4) permanent and comprehensive ceasefire. On points 1 and 2, the two sides were in agreement. Under the deal, the Taliban pledged to not allow its members, other individuals, or groups, including al-Qa'ida, to use the soil of Afghanistan to threaten the security of the US and its allies, while the US promised to reduce the number of US forces in Afghanistan to 8,600 within 135 days and ultimately withdraw the remaining forces within 14 months. Regarding the third and fourth points, the Doha Agreement said '[Taliban] will start intra-Afghan negotiations with Afghan sides on March 10, 2020' after up to 5,000 prisoners of the Taliban and up to 1,000 prisoners of the Afghan government are released, and '[a] permanent and comprehensive ceasefire will be an item on the agenda of the intra-Afghan dialogue and negotiations'. From the viewpoint of the Taliban, the US would be gone after 14 months if the Doha Agreement was to be implemented. Overall, the deal was favourable for the Taliban. The fact that the Taliban's fierce military offensives in rural areas started immediately after the Biden's speech in April 2021 demonstrated that the Doha Agreement paved the way for the Taliban's return to power. Ideally, it was hoped that by the time Kabul was besieged, the Islamic Republic would have reached a power-sharing arrangement with the Taliban. Unfortunately, however, President Ghani fled the country with his entourage.

Possible Areas of Cooperation between Japan and India

Civil Assistance over Military Assistance

Under the given circumstances, what should the international community, including Japan and India, do? One must remember that Afghanistan is a sovereign country of Afghans, and therefore, the international community must not place military footprints on Afghan soil. In the past, none of the superpowers, including Britain and the Soviet Union, were able to conquer Afghanistan. The Doha Agreement has also been interpreted as a 'victory' by the Taliban.[29] It would thus be fair to conclude that military intervention can never bring about a positive outcome in Afghanistan.

India's assistance towards Afghanistan dates back to the late 1990s when India armed the Northern Alliance (NA), a united military front that was established in late 1996 after the Taliban took over Kabul. Indian Ambassador Bharath Raj Muthu Kumar, who coordinated military and medical assistance that India covertly provided to Ahmad Shah Massoud and his forces between 1996 and 2000, recalls that India supplied refurbished Kalashnikovs seized in Kashmir, mortars, uniforms, packaged food, medicines, funds and other aid to NA, which needed this help to counter the Taliban, which was supported by the Inter-Services Intelligence

(ISI) of Pakistan.[30] It has been reported that India facilitated the transfer of the wounded to Delhi via Tajikistan by air for medical treatment.[31] Despite all these struggles, Kumar concludes that '[t]he leaders of the present Government and the Taliban are only two major facets of Afghan politics—they have to resolve their differences for that elusive peace and stability'.[32]

Based on the Strategic Partnership Agreement signed in October 2011, India pledged nearly USD 3 billion for civil assistance to Afghanistan.[33] Among other things, such as schools, hospitals and roads, India built a parliament building in Kabul in December 2015, and also constructed the Salma Dam in Herat in June 2016.[34] In February 2021, India pledged to construct the Shah Toot Dam in Kabul. Effectively, India's relationship with Afghanistan is characterised not only by economic but also political and strategic aspects. The two countries maintain and strengthen their ties through regular high-level exchanges. In addition, India's provision of four Mi-25 attack helicopters to ANSF can be seen as a notable gift in terms of strategic ties. India aims to help stabilise Afghanistan in an effort to promote the economic development of Central Asia. Afghanistan is the key to India's 'Connect Central Asia Policy' as Pakistan blocks the flow of goods from India to Central Asia. Conversely, Afghanistan also considers India an important partner, since Pakistan's military establishment covertly supports proxy forces in Afghanistan and Kashmir. From the perspective of Afghanistan, India is thus a balancing actor to Pakistan's influence.

Japan has also upped their civil assistance efforts towards Afghanistan in accordance with the pacifist goals of the Japanese Constitution. The three pillars of Japanese assistance to Afghanistan are: 1) enhancing Afghanistan's capability to maintain security; 2) reintegration of former insurgents into society; and 3) Afghanistan's sustainable and self-reliant development.[35] In the political sphere, Japan hosted key international conferences in 2002 and 2012 to attract pledges by donors in support of Afghanistan. In addition, Japan is one of the biggest donors to the Law and Order Trust Fund (LOTFA) of the United Nations Development Program (UNDP), which supports the salaries of police personnel of the Islamic Republic.[36] In the socio-economic sphere, Japan's assistance varies from constructing schools, clinics, roads, airports to aid in areas such as agriculture, education and public health. Japan's assistance is generally seen as neutral humanitarian assistance by most Afghans. Considering this, Japan and India should respect the sovereignty of Afghanistan and must not intervene in the country's internal affairs. Both countries should continue their engagement with Afghanistan by focusing on civil assistance rather than military assistance.

Supporting the Peace Process

What is most required at this moment is cooperation to support the peace process in Afghanistan. As mentioned earlier, the main stakeholders in the process are the Afghans, namely the Taliban and politically influential leaders living abroad, so outsiders should only aim to support these stakeholders laterally, but effectively. In the past, Qatar, Germany, Russia, France, Japan, Norway and China have facilitated confidence-building meetings, inviting Taliban representatives and government officials in a personal capacity.[37] These meetings were not peace negotiations, but they did contribute to better communication among relevant parties. The Afghan government and the Taliban started a direct negotiation on 12 September 2020 after prisoner exchanges.[38] Although a negotiated settlement was not possible, considering the widespread conflict fatigue caused by protracted clashes in Afghanistan, the two sides agreed to a code of conduct in December 2020. The Taliban has 'diplomatic' relationships with various countries, such as Russia, China, Iran, Uzbekistan, Indonesia, Pakistan, Saudi Arabia and the UAE. There are ways to influence the Taliban through these third parties.

In Afghanistan, third-party interventions are often successful. For example, when Ghani and Abdullah argued about the preliminary results of the presidential election in 2014, John Kerry, the then US Secretary of State, mediated through shuttle diplomacy and settled the dispute by creating the Government of National Unity. Besides, local mechanisms for conflict resolution can also work in the form of third-party interventions. There are unwritten rules in Pashtun society, including a custom called *Jirga/Shura*, which means meeting or gathering, to settle disputes among tribes.

It is important for Japan and India to explore different types of peace efforts in Afghanistan. Doshisha University, Kyoto hosted an international conference on peace in Afghanistan in June 2012, inviting representatives of the Taliban, HIG and the Afghan government. This conference had, at least temporarily, contributed to creating a conducive atmosphere for peace.[39]

Chabahar Port Development and Connectivity Projects

In addition to political engagement, projects leading to improved connectivity can be an option for Japan–India strategic cooperation in Afghanistan. The Chabahar port in Iran, located in Sistan and Balochistan Province, 160 km west of Gwadar port of Pakistan, was developed under a tripartite agreement signed by Afghanistan, India and Iran in May 2016.[40] India provided almost USD 500 million to develop the port and obtained operational rights of the Shaheed Beheshti port in February 2018 for 18 months.[41] This port is expected to contribute to better connectivity in the region, as India will now have easier access to Central Asia and Afghanistan. Iran can also serve as a hub in the region and gain revenue from transiting goods. For land-locked Afghanistan, this is one of the shortest routes to reach the ocean and it has notable strategic significance as it allows Afghanistan to bypass Pakistan. In recent years, the Afghanistan–Pakistan relationship had worsened partly because of Pakistan's covert support for AGEs in Afghanistan. The Afghan government before the Taliban took over blamed Pakistan for providing financial and material support to AGEs. Developing the Chabahar port will benefit Afghanistan from a socio-economic perspective, which will put more pressure on Pakistan by reducing Afghanistan's reliance on Pakistan.

Response to the COVID-19 Crisis

Another area of Japan–India cooperation in Afghanistan was the response to the COVID-19 crisis. The pandemic, which originated in China in the winter of 2019, had become an urgent issue for the entire world. With the support of the international community, Afghanistan had taken measures to prevent the spread of COVID-19, including the establishment of testing centres and the expansion of equipment. In March 2020, a strict lockdown was implemented in the capital city of Kabul, with the closure of schools and borders, and the suspension of international flights. However, the measures to prevent the spread of infection were often taken lightly, and the actual number of infected people might have been much higher due to inadequate testing and statistical systems, as well as the lack of medical personnel and equipment.

During the pandemic, in the arena of international politics, vaccine diplomacy became important. In this respect, the move by the Indian government to hand over 500,000 doses of Bharat Biotech vaccines, the local name for the AstraZeneca vaccine developed in the UK, to Afghanistan was epoch-making, as it was the first vaccine received by the Afghan government.[42] Mass immunisation was critical for the containment of the pandemic, and vaccines played a key role. Although Japan and India faced their own domestic problems, containing a pandemic required mutual cooperation. With this understanding, Japan pledged USD 1.8 million to strengthen response capacity for infectious diseases in Afghanistan in March 2021.[43]

Implications of Japan–India Strategic Cooperation

Pakistan's 'Strategic Depth'

ISI's support for the Taliban is an open secret. Japan–India strategic cooperation in Afghanistan could thus provoke a harsh response from Islamabad. When the Taliban re-captured a truck convoy from warlords in Kandahar in November 1994, then Interior Minister of Pakistan Major General Naseerullah Khan Babar said that the Taliban members are '[their] boys'.[44] In addition, when the US started air bombings in October 2001, Pakistani aircraft transported hundreds of ISI officers, Taliban commanders and foot soldiers belonging to the Islamic Movement of Uzbekistan and al-Qa'ida from Kunduz to Pakistan for their safety.[45] Further, on 1 March 2016, Sartaj Aziz, Advisor to the Pakistan Prime Minister on Foreign Affairs, stated at the Washington's Council on Foreign Relations that '[w] e have some influence over them [the Taliban] because their leadership is in Pakistan and they get some medical facilities. Their families are here'.[46]

Avinash Paliwal advocates that there are three core factors that drive India's Afghanistan policy debates: 1) striking a balance between Afghanistan and Pakistan, 2) the international political environment and 3) the domestic politics of Afghanistan.[47] He uses terms such as 'conciliators' and 'partisans': the former refers to those who believe that India should politically engage with almost every entity including the Afghan Taliban; and the latter refers to those who consider that all factions that are at odds with Pakistan and/or are not under the influence of, or dependent upon,

Islamabad, should be India's natural allies.[48] Based on these diverse ways of thinking, some Indian policymakers advocate a non-military, mostly economic and politically-neutral approach, while others argue in favour of a militarily robust, economically aggressive and politically partisan approach.[49] Considering these aspects, the Japan–India strategic approach towards Afghanistan is likely to affect Japan–Pakistan as well as India–Pakistan relationships to a great extent. This point may be a constraint factor for aggressive cooperation.

The US–Iran Tension and the Middle East

The heightening US–Iran tension has an effect on Japan–India strategic cooperation in Afghanistan. On 3 January 2020, a US drone killed Qasem Sulaimani, Commander of Quds Force of Islamic Revolutionary Guard Corps (IRGC) of Iran, near Baghdad International Airport.[50] Following this incident, the IRGC made retaliatory attacks on US bases in Iraq,[51] although there were no casualties. US President Trump said 'Iran stood off', so apparently the tension was eased, at least temporarily. Subsequently, Iran changed its stance and advocated that the US leave the Middle East. As mentioned previously, the Iran–Taliban relationship has had several ups and downs, but their common goal eventually became the withdrawal of US troops. Iran is now working to strengthen its ties with the Taliban, which also seeks stronger relations with Iran due to its worsening relations with Pakistan. Therefore, Iran's move should be carefully monitored when Japan and India consider how to be committed to Afghanistan.

Conclusion

The situation surrounding Afghanistan is moving quickly. After the signing of the Doha Agreement between the US and the Taliban, the latter's political status improved compared with the past, and it could no longer be characterised as a 'terrorist organisation' or an 'anti-governmental group'. Eventually, the Taliban returned to power in August 2021. There are some anti-Taliban groups, such as the National Resistance Front led by Ahmad Masoud, but there is no momentum toward national reconciliation, and prospects for the future are uncertain. In this context, power-sharing and interpretation of 'Islamic governance' will be the key for establishing the future of Afghanistan.

Japan and India have invested vast resources in Afghanistan for promoting peace, development and unity. However, these efforts should not go in vain. It is necessary for both countries to stand by Afghanistan and make every effort to prevent it from relapsing into civil war again. The form of governance, political system, women's participation and so on, must be decided by the Afghans. In order for that, reconciliation through dialogue is imperative, and this can be supported by the international community, including Japan and India. It is also possible to implement tripartite or multilateral cooperation arrangements, coordinating with other actors, such as the US, EU, Russia, China, Iran, OIC members, Pakistan and so on. It is not easy to bring peace in Afghanistan, where protracted social conflicts have been in place for more than 40 years. However, a peaceful Afghanistan will benefit the entire region. Essentially, the Afghan people deserve a peaceful life. It is imperative for the international community, including Japan and India, to help Afghanistan with cool heads but warm hearts.

Notes and References

1. In Pashtu and Dari, 'Taliban' is the plural form of 'Talib' (which means a 'student' in Arabic). The Taliban does not call itself Taliban but the Islamic Emirate of Afghanistan.

2. US Department of State (DoS), *Agreement for Bringing Peace to Afghanistan between the Islamic Emirate of Afghanistan which is not recognized by the United States as a state and is known as the Taliban and the United States of America*, 29 February 2020, available at https://www.state.gov/wp-content/uploads/2020/02/Agreement-For-Bringing-Peace-to-Afghanistan-02.29.20.pdf, accessed on 13 March 2020.

3. Ian S. Livingston and Michael O'Hanlon, *Afghanistan Index: Also including selected data on Pakistan*, Brookings Institution, 31 March 2016, pp. 4–5, available at https://www.brookings.edu/wp-content/uploads/2016/07/index20160330.pdf, accessed on 31 March 2020.

4. Between 1996 and 2001, the Taliban controlled most of Afghan soil, and the Taliban government was endorsed by three countries: Saudi Arabia, United Arab Emirates and Pakistan.

5. NATO, *Resolute Support Mission (RSM): Key Facts and Figures*, June 2019, available at https://www.nato.int/nato_static_fl2014/assets/pdf/pdf_2019_06/20190625_2019-06-RSM-Placemat.pdf, accessed 10 April 2020.

6. In this chapter, ANSF refers to ANA (Afghan National Army) and AAF (Afghan Air Force) which are under the Ministry of Defense, plus ANP (Afghan National Police) which is under the Ministry of Interior. It does not include NDS (National Directorate of Security) and ALP (Afghan Local Police).

7. UNAMA, *Afghanistan: Protection of Civilians in Armed Conflict 2019*, February 2020, p. 5, available at https://unama.unmissions.org/sites/default/files/afghanistan_protection_of_civilians_annual_report_2019_-_22_february.pdf, accessed 23 February 2020.

8. Ibid.

9. SIGAR, *Quarterly Report to the United States Congress*, 30 January 2020, p. 68, available at https://www.sigar.mil/pdf/quarterlyreports/2020-01-30qr.pdf, accessed 15 March 2020.

10. SIGAR, *Quarterly Report to the United States Congress*, 30 January 2019, p. 70, available at https://www.sigar.mil/pdf/quarterlyreports/2019-01-30qr.pdf, accessed 19 February 2020.

11. Secunder Kermani, 'Taliban peace talks: What to expect from the new round?' *BBC News*, 7 September 2020, available at https://www.bbc.com/news/world-asia-54016760, accessed 13 January 2020; David E. Sanger, Eric Schmitt and Thomas Gibbons-Neff, 'A Secret Accord with the Taliban: When and How the U.S. Would Leave Afghanistan', *The New York Times*, 8 March 2020, available at https://www.nytimes.com/2020/03/08/world/asia/taliban-afghanistan-annexes-peace-agreement.html, accessed 13 January 2021.

12. Ministry of Foreign Affairs of the People's Republic of China, 'China's Position on the Afghan Issue', 12 April 2023, available at https://www.fmprc.gov.cn/mfa_eng/zxxx_662805/202304/t20230412_11057785.html, accessed 25 November 2023.

13. 'China Becomes First Country To Name New Afghanistan Ambassador Under Taliban', *NDTV World*, 13 September 2023, available at https://www.ndtv.com/world-news/china-becomes-first-country-to-name-new-afghanistan-ambassador-under-taliban-4386003, accessed on 18 January 2024.

14. M. Galeotti, *Afghanistan: The Soviet Union's Last War* (London: Frank Cass, 1995), pp. 11–12.

15. 'Russia Signs Deal to Prolong Troop Presence at Tajik Military Base', *Radio Free Europe/Radio Liberty*, 5 October 2012, available at https://www.rferl.org/a/russia-signs-deal-troop-presence-tajikistan-military-base/24730251.html, accessed 31 March 2020.

16. Geeta Mohan, 'Russia hosts talks on Afghanistan, calls on Taliban for an inclusive government', *India Today*, 21 October 2021, available at https://

www.indiatoday.in/world/story/russia-hosts-talks-afghanistan-taliban-inclusive-government-1867248-2021-10-20, accessed on 18 January 2024.

17. CSO, *Statistical Yearbook 2016-2017*, available at http://cso.gov.af/en/page/1500/4722/2016-17, accessed 31 March 2020 (link discontinued).

18. 'Iran Backs Taliban With Cash and Arms', *Wall Street Journal*, 11 June 2015, available at https://www.wsj.com/articles/iran-backs-taliban-with-cash-and-arms-1434065528, accessed 31 March 2020.

19. Amir Toumaj, Candace Rondeaux and Arif Ammar, *Soleimani's Shadow: The Famiyoun Division and Iranian Proxy Warfare Propaganda* (Washington, DC: New America, 2021).

20. When the Taliban's office in Qatar was inaugurated on 18 June 2013, Hamid Karzai, the then President, was furious that a flag of the 'Islamic Emirate of Afghanistan' was hoisted in the office and immediately suspended negotiations with the Taliban.

21. Kenta Aoki, 'Peace Talks between Taliban and the Afghan Government: Repercussions of Mullah Omar's Death', *Journal of Middle Eastern Studies*, vol. 2, no. 524 (September 2015), pp. 95–106.

22. 'Afghanistan: Ghani, Hekmatyar sign peace deal', *Al Jazeera*, 29 September 2016, available at https://www.aljazeera.com/news/2016/9/29/afghanistan-ghani-hekmatyar-sign-peace-deal, accessed on 25 November 2023.

23. 'Afghanistan's Ghani offers talks with Taliban "without preconditions"', *Reuters*, 28 February 2018, available at https://www.reuters.com/article/us-afghanistan-taliban/afghanistans-ghani-offers-talks-with-taliban-without-preconditions-idUSKCN1GC0J0, accessed 31 March 2020.

24. White House Archives, 'Remarks by President Trump on the Strategy in Afghanistan and South Asia', 21 August 2017, available at https://trumpwhitehouse.archives.gov/briefings-statements/remarks-president-trump-strategy-afghanistan-south-asia/#:~:text=We%20are%20not%20nation%2Dbuilding,to%20the%20region%20and%20beyond, accessed 3 October 2023.

25. US DoS, 'On President Ghani's Offer to Extend the Ceasefire and Open Negotiations', 16 June 2018, available at https://2017-2021.state.gov/on-president-ghanis-offer-to-extend-the-ceasefire-and-open-negotiations/, accessed 3 October 2023.

26. 'Exclusive Interview with US Chief Negotiator Zalmay Khalilzad', *Tolo News*, 2 September 2019, available at https://www.youtube.com/watch?v=nb2xQ5liCVI&t=322s, accessed 5 September 2019.

27. 'Taliban suicide bombing kills U.S. soldier, 10 Afghan civilians', *PBS News Hour*, 5 September 2019, available at https://www.pbs.org/newshour/world/taliban-suicide-bombing-kills-u-s-soldier-10-afghan-civilians, accessed on 3 October 2023.

28. 'U.S., Taliban sign deal aimed at ending war in Afghanistan', *CBS News*, 29 February 2020, available at https://www.cbsnews.com/news/us-taliban-peace-deal-leave-afghanistan-2020-02-29/, accessed on 25 November 2023.

29. IEA, 'Payām Za'īm Amārat-Eslāmī-e Afghānestān Amīr-ol-mo'menīn Sheikh Al-hadīs Moulavī Haibatullāh Ākhundzāda Hefzallāh Dar Moured Tavāfoq-e Pāyān-e Eshghāl Bā Ayālāt-e Mottahede Amrīkā', *Sedā-e Jahād*, 29 February 2020, available at http://alemarahdari.com/?p=77053, accessed 13 March 2020 (link discontinued).

30. 'How India secretly armed Afghanistan's Northern Alliance', *The Hindu*, 1 September 2019, available at https://www.thehindu.com/news/national/how-india-secretly-armed-ahmad-shah-massouds-northern-alliance/article29310513.ece, accessed 31 March 2020.

31. Ibid.

32. Ibid.

33. 'Miffed govt lists $3 billion projects as Donald Trump mocks India's Afghanistan aid', *Economic Times*, 4 January 2019, available at https://economictimes.indiatimes.com/news/politics-and-nation/miffed-govt-lists-3-billion-projects-as-donald-trump-mocks-indias-afghanistan-aid/articleshow/67375954.cms?from=mdr, accessed 31 March 2020.

34. Ministry of External Affairs of India, 'Bilateral Brief', December 2018, available at https://www.mea.gov.in/Portal/ForeignRelation/Bilateral_Brief_on_Afghanistan_December_31_2018.pdf, accessed 31 March 2020.

35. Ministry of Foreign Affairs of Japan, 'Japan's Assistance Package to Afghanistan: Japan Has Implemented Approximately USD1.6 billion of Assistance', February 2011, available at https://www.mofa.go.jp/region/middle_e/afghanistan/assist_pac2.html, accessed 31 March 2020.

36. Ministry of Foreign Affairs of Japan, *Nihon no Afghanistan he no shien: Jiritsu shita Afghanistan ni mukete* (Japan's Assistance to Afghanistan: For Self-Reliance of Afghanistan), April 2015, available in Japanese at https://www.mofa.go.jp/mofaj/files/000019265.pdf, accessed 31 March 2020.

37. See Aoki, 'Peace Talks between Taliban and the Afghan Government'.

38. 'Afghanistan Peace Talks Open in Qatar, Seeking End to Decades of War', *The New York Times*, 12 September 2020, available at https://www.nytimes.com/2020/09/12/world/asia/afghanistan-taliban.html, accessed on 25 November 2023.

39. Ko Nakata, *The Truth of the Taliban's Return to Power* (KK Best Sellers, 2021).

40. 'India, Iran and Afghanistan sign trade corridor deal', *Al Jazeera*, 24 May 2016, available at https://www.aljazeera.com/economy/2016/5/24/indian-iran-and-afghanistan-sign-trade-corridor-deal, accessed on 3 October 2023.

41. Press Information Bureau, Government of India, *List of MoUs/Agreements signed during the visit of President of Iran to India*, 17 February 2018, available at https://pib.gov.in/Pressreleaseshare.aspx?PRID=1520839,

42. 'First Shipment of COVID-19 Vaccine Arrives in Kabul from India', *Tolo News*, 7 February 2021, available at https://tolonews.com/health-169832, accessed 14 February 2021.

43. 'Japan pledges US$ 1.8 million to strengthen response capacity for infectious diseases in Afghanistan', 15 March 2021, World Health Organization, available at https://www.emro.who.int/afg/afghanistan-news/japan-pledges-us-18-million-to-strengthen-response-capacity-for-infectious-diseases-in-afghanistan.html, accessed on 3 October 2023.

44. Ahmed Rashid, *Taliban: Militant Islam, Oil and Fundamentalism in Central Asia* (New Haven: Yale University Press, 2000), p. 29.

45. Ahmed Rashid, *Descent into Chaos: How the War against Islamic Extremism is Being Lost in Pakistan, Afghanistan and Central Asia* (London: Penguin Books, 2008), pp. 91–93.

46. 'Aziz admits Pakistan housing Afghan Taliban leaders', *Dawn*, 2 March 2016, available at https://www.dawn.com/news/1243093, accessed 31 March 2020.

47. Avinash Paliwal, *My Enemy's Enemy: India in Afghanistan from the Soviet Invasion to the US Withdrawal* (Uttar Pradesh: Harper Collins, 2017), pp. 13–14.

48. Ibid.

49. Ibid., p. 12.

50. 'US kills Iran's most powerful general in Baghdad airstrike', *The Associated Press*, 3 January 2020, available at https://apnews.com/article/ap-top-news-tehran-international-news-iraq-ali-khamenei-5597ff0f046a67805cc233d5933a53ed, accessed on 25 November 2023.

51. 'Iran launches missile attacks on US facilities in Iraq', *Al Jazeera*, 8 January 2023, available at https://www.aljazeera.com/news/2020/1/8/iran-launches-missile-attacks-on-us-facilities-in-iraq, accessed on 25 November 2023.

thirteen

Remembering the War

Japan's Commemoration of the Battle of Imphal and Kohima

Ryohei Kasai

The year 2019 marked the 75th anniversary of the Battle of Imphal and Kohima, a battle fought between the Japanese Imperial Army and British Indian Army, considered one of the fiercest battles during World War II (WWII). Commemorative events were held in both cities, attended by the Japanese ambassador and the British high commissioner.[1] In June 2019, the Imphal Peace Museum was also inaugurated.[2] Japanese Prime Minister Shinzo Abe had planned a visit to this museum in December, but it was postponed due to issues regarding the security situation in the region. These commemorative events, widely reported in the media, drew considerable attention in Japan. In 2014, similar events were held in Imphal to commemorate the 70th anniversary of the battle with the presence of the Japanese ambassador and British high commissioner as well, but in a low-key way. Before that, the event to commemorate the 60th anniversary in 2004 was even more modest. This brings up the questions: What has made Japan increasingly eager to commemorate the Battle of Imphal and Kohima in recent years? Are there any specific factors that have driven Japan to make this shift, and how have these affected the way Japan commemorates the battle?

To answer these, we must take into consideration two perspectives. First, as the development of India's Northeast is increasingly becoming one of the most important areas of Japan–India bilateral cooperation, it is essential to understand not only the contemporary situation but also what happened in the past and how it affects the present. Second, it should be recalled that most of the theatres where Japan fought WWII fall in the vast area of what we now call the Indo-Pacific. While Japan tries to play a more active role in the fields of politics, economy and security in this emerging region, its memory of the war serves as the backdrop behind its involvement and engagement.

This chapter discusses how Japan has remembered the battle since the end of WWII and how its memory of the battle has changed over the years, focusing especially on the noticeable shift in recent years. The chapter also seeks to identify factors that have brought about such changes and examine if the development of Japan–India relations has any role to play in this shift. Furthermore, it tries to make an assessment of these developments by positioning this topic in the contemporary strategic context.

The Battle of Imphal and Kohima, 1944

Japan started a war against the US, the UK and the Netherlands in December 1941. While the Imperial Navy launched a surprise attack on Pearl Harbor in Hawaii, the Imperial Army attacked British forces in Malaya, swiftly conquering the peninsula and Singapore by mid-February 1942. The Japanese army further advanced to Burma[3] and the British Army was forced to retreat to Northeast India by crossing the mountainous border with thousands of Indian refugees. With this unexpected and swift military success, the plan to attack Northeast India emerged among the Imperial General Headquarters (IGHQ) and the Southern Army that covered the Southeast Asian theatre. Although this plan, Operation 21-Go, was seriously considered, it eventually got shelved because of a number of difficulties including securing a supply source and terrain in the Indo-Burmese border area. There were voices of concern for the operation from the divisional commanders, including Lieutenant General Renya Mutaguchi, who was commanding the 18th Division and would advocate reviving the plan one year later.

In 1943, the plan to attack the British Indian Army in the Northeast made a comeback. The war situation was becoming more difficult for Japan as its Imperial Navy suffered a series of defeats in the Pacific front before the Allies' counterattack. There was no exit possible from the long war against China led by Generalissimo Chiang Kai-shek from Chungking. Germany was also struggling in the war against the Soviet Union. Italy, the other Axis partner, surrendered in September 1943. It was against this backdrop that the Imperial General Headquarters started rethinking the plan. Renamed Operation U-Go, it was an ambitious offensive that aimed to capture Imphal and surrounding areas in order to advance Japan's line of defense westward so as to repel the British Indian Army when they started a reconquest of Burma. It was also expected that a victory would not only cheer up the leadership and the people in Japan but also turn the course of the war in their favour. Furthermore, Subhas Chandra Bose insisted that his Indian National Army (INA) also participate in the operation as a combat force. He speculated that when INA would advance into India, the people in India would join the struggle to drive the British out of their land. The most vocal figure for this operation was Mutaguchi, who was then commanding the 15th Army that covered the central and western parts of Burma. Because of Mutaguchi's strong persistence, Lieutenant General Shozo Kawabe, the commander of the Burma Area Army, accepted the plan, though with several reservations. The plan was eventually approved by the IGHQ in early January 1944.

Operation U-Go started in early March 1944. Mutaguchi's 15th Army launched an attack from three directions: from Homalin to Kohima, from Tamu to Imphal, and from Tedim road to Imphal. In the initial stage, it went as planned: the Japanese army crossed the border and the British Indian Army made a retreat. Japan succeeded in occupying some parts of Kohima and cutting the supply route by blocking the Dimapur–Imphal road. However, this was a tactical withdrawal that Lieutenant General William Slim, the commander of the 14th Army, had planned. It was his intention to bring the Japanese into the Imphal plain and then make a counterattack when they would be short on supply and the situation would become extremely harsh with the onset of the monsoon rain.[4] And this was exactly what happened to the Japanese officers and soldiers on the battlefield: they had to fight the battle with the British Indian Army while struggling with serious hunger and infectious diseases such as malaria and dysentery. A long-awaited withdrawal was finally ordered in early July, but it was not the end of the struggle for the Japanese 15th Army. They still had to walk across the mountains in border areas back to Burma under heavy rains without food supply. It is said that the casualties due to starvation and infectious diseases were higher than that in the actual battle. The withdrawal route was termed '*Hakkotsu kaido*' in Japanese, meaning the Road of White Bones, as most of the bodies of the deceased had to be left behind unburied. The Battle of Imphal and Kohima is considered to be one of the most devastating failures Japan suffered during WWII, which made its defeat in the war more likely than ever. Further, Japan left Burma before its ultimate surrender in August 1945 as it could not repel the Allied forces and reconquer the land.

How Japan Remembered the Battle

Establishment of Monuments

After the surrender, Japan was occupied by the Allied forces until 1951. During the occupation, no explicit activities or events to commemorate the war dead would have been possible. It was on 15 August 1952, a year after Japan regained sovereignty, that the National Memorial Service for War Dead was first held. Since then, this memorial service has been held with the presence of the Japanese Emperor and Empress every year. This service is to commemorate all the war dead—not only the 2.3 million service men, but also the 800 thousand civilians who gave up their lives within and outside Japan. Memorial services have also been held at a local level in places affected by the war, such as, most notably, Hiroshima and Nagasaki, the two cities attacked by the atomic bombs. Yasukuni Shrine in Tokyo also serves as an unofficial place of commemoration of the war dead, although there has been a long dispute over whether it is an appropriate place for remembrance as it enshrines the 'A-class war criminals' of the International Military Tribunal for the Far East, who were convicted for leading the war, including the former Prime Minister General Hideki Tojo, along with millions of war dead.

Memorial visits to the old battlefields across the Pacific and in Northeast and Southeast Asia started gradually as war veterans and bereaved family members travelled to remember the war dead. In the early 1970s, the Japanese government started erecting war memorials in former WWII battlefields. According to Japan's Ministry of Health, Labor and Welfare, by 2001, 15 memorials had been built in Japan (Iwo Jima), the US (Attu Island and Saipan Island), Papua New Guinea, the Philippines, Myanmar, Malaysia, the Republic of Marshall Islands, Palau, Indonesia, India, Russia and Mongolia.[5] Amongst these, 'India Peace Memorial' was established near Imphal by the Japanese government with the cooperation of the Indian government on 25 March 1994. It remains the only Japanese memorial in India as of 2021. The timing of the establishment coincided with the 50th anniversary of the Battle of Imphal and Kohima. The epitaph inscribed on the monument reads:

> THE MONUMENT SHALL STAND AS A PRAYER FOR PEACE AND A SYMBOL OF FRIENDSHIP BETWEEN THE PEOPLES OF JAPAN AND INDIA IN MEMORY OF ALL THOSE WHO LOST THEIR LIVES IN INDIA DURING THE WAR.

There are several characteristics to be noted in this epitaph as well as the memorial. First, while it commemorates all the casualties during the war, regardless of their nationalities, it does not specifically mention the Battle of Imphal and Kohima. It is strange as the memorial stands at the foot of Red Hills, in Maibam Lokpa Ching, Bishnupur district, Manipur, the site of one of the bloodiest combats during the battle. Second, it does not mention the other Allied countries, such as the UK, either. The British memorial in Kohima, Nagaland, has a famous epitaph that reads:

> WHEN YOU GO HOME, TELL THEM OF US AND SAY, FOR YOUR TOMORROW, WE GAVE OUR TODAY.

This memorial, however, stands in the war cemetery for the Allied forces. Third, it is very similar to the peace monument established in Rangoon (today's Yangon), Burma on 28 March 1981. The epitaphs are almost the same except one says 'BURMA' while the other says 'INDIA'. There are differences as well, however. The one in Rangoon stands in the Japanese cemetery, which is also the site of other memorials privately established by *senyukai* or war veterans' groups.[6] In case of the India Peace Memorial, there is a small, private memorial for the Japanese soldiers, but it is located outside the premises of the Peace Memorial.

Bone-collecting Activities

Japan has also worked hard to collect the bones of the war dead for many decades. According to estimates based on official sources, of the 3.1 million Japanese who lost their lives due to the war, the death of 2.4 million took place overseas.[7] In the 1950s, the government began negotiating terms and conditions for dispatching bone-collecting missions with the United States (for Iwo Jima and Okinawa) and other countries across the Pacific as well as Asia. As of July 2021, bones of 1.276 million bodies have been collected and brought home, while bones of 1.124 million remain unrecovered.[8]

Burma and northeastern India have been two of the most important destinations for the dispatch missions as some of the fiercest battles were fought in this theatre during the war and 1,67,000 Japanese are estimated to have died in these two countries. Japan signed a peace treaty and established diplomatic relations with India in 1952 and with Burma in 1954, paving the way for talks on the bone-collecting mission. In February 1956, the mission visited Burma and collected bones in Rangoon, Mandalay, Myitkyina and Lashio.[9] A subgroup comprising three government officials and one representative of bereaved families was dispatched to Tedim, a town close to the Indo-Burmese border, through which the 33rd Division of the Japanese Army had started advancing to Imphal in March 1944. This mission was able to collect bones of some 500 bodies. This subgroup also visited Imphal via Calcutta (now Kolkata) by air. Based on the understanding between the Japanese government and the Indian government, they only held a commemorative ceremony in Imphal with the presence of some officials from the Indian side.[10] There was another mission to India in 1977, but as far as India was concerned, no bone-collecting activity had taken place then. It was only after more than 30 years that the Japanese government restarted the work of bone-collecting. In January 2012, Japan sent a mission including an embassy official to Imphal, with the aim of confirming if the bones of the 11 soldiers buried in the British and Indian cemeteries were Japanese or not.[11] According to the Japanese government, as a result of these activities, bones of 2,545 bodies were collected around Imphal and Kohima by July 2021. Besides the bones of 17,410 bodies brought back right after the war by surviving soldiers, bones of nearly 20,000 bodies were collected later and brought home to Japan.[12] However, bones of about 10,000 Japanese soldiers remain unrecovered in the hills of Manipur and Nagaland.

Reconciliation Efforts with the British

Various efforts for reconciliation between peoples of the countries involved in the Battle of Imphal and Kohima have been conducted privately. In 1983, Masao Hirakubo, a former Japanese army officer who served in the 31st Mountain Artillery Regiment and veteran of the Battle of Kohima, made efforts towards reconciliation between the Japanese and British soldiers who fought one of the fiercest battles in WWII. He later formed the Burma Campaign Society in order to 'nurture friendship by understanding the differences in culture, history, and tradition and continue to pass the veterans' war stories on to younger generations'.[13]

Recent Developments

Shift in 2010s

The various efforts towards remembrance and commemoration of the Battle of Imphal and Kohima made by the government as well as private organisations and individuals remained largely unnoticed by the wider public in post-war Japan for many decades. However, there has been a significant shift since the late 2010s.

An NHK special documentary featuring the Battle of Imphal was broadcasted on 15 August 2017, attracting a renewed interest in the battle. In December 2017, a team from the Japan Association for Recovery and Repatriation of War Casualties visited Manipur in search of bones of Japanese soldiers. A plan to build a memorial museum near Imphal was revealed this year.

Two years later, the 75th anniversary of the battle was commemorated on a much larger scale. Both Japanese and British heads of the mission to India attended the ceremony held in Imphal on 22 June 2019. A commemorative gathering was held in Kohima in early April as well. Japanese Ambassador Kenji Hiramatsu said in his address on the occasion, 'We can truly appreciate the peace we enjoy today only by remembering what we went through. We know that the foundation of our today exists upon the precious and tremendous sacrifices of the past.'[14] He also stressed the importance of people-to-people contact between Japanese and Manipuris, listing a youth exchange programme and a technical training programme. The Imphal Peace Museum was also inaugurated in conjunction with this anniversary. The museum exhibits relics of the soldiers engaged in the battle as well as many accounts of the battle by local people explaining how the war affected their lives. A part of the museum is dedicated to the introduction of rich cultures and traditions of the local people in Manipur and Nagaland. Although this museum was built with assistance of private organisations such as the Nippon Foundation and the Sasakawa Peace Foundation, it seems that the project has been recognised by the Japanese government. This is evident from the presence of Ambassador Hiramatsu at the inauguration ceremony of the museum held on 22 June 2019.[15]

The series of functions held in Imphal and Kohima can be attributed to a growing sense of interest in the battle among Japanese political leadership, the Ministry of Foreign Affairs and media. A joint visit to Imphal and the museum by Prime Ministers Shinzo Abe and Narendra Modi was planned after a summit meeting in Guwahati, Assam, in mid-December 2019. It would have been the first visit by a foreign leader of a major country to Manipur. However, this historic visit did not happen as Abe had to cancel his visit to India due to the unrest over the Citizenship Amendment Bill in Guwahati.[16]

Japan's Growing Involvement in Northeast India

In the 2010s, Japan's focus on India's northeastern region also deepened substantially. It is not a mere coincidence that commemorative activities for the Battle of Imphal and Kohima increased during these years. It showed Japan's eagerness to get involved in this region strategically while also taking into consideration the historical context.

India became the largest recipient of Japan's Official Development Assistance (ODA) in 2003.[17] Japan launched a number of flagship projects related to infrastructure and connectivity such as the Delhi Metro, the Delhi–Mumbai Industrial Corridor (DMIC) and the Dedicated Freight Corridor (DFC). The overall bilateral relationship between Japan and India strengthened rapidly. Japan and India signed the Comprehensive Economic Partnership Agreement in February 2011, boosting bilateral trade and investment. The 'Strategic Global Partnership' was upgraded to '*Special* Strategic Global Partnership' during PM Modi's visit to Japan in September 2014. There have been alternate visits by prime ministers every year until they were paused during the pandemic of COVID-19 in 2020.

India's northeastern region did not appear in the summit-level document until 2014.[18] Prime Ministers Abe and Modi 'placed special emphasis on Japan's cooperation for enhanced connectivity and development in Northeast India and linking the region to other economic corridors in India and to Southeast Asia' in their joint declaration during the latter's visit to Japan in 2014.[19] The Northeast was mentioned in a more specific way in

'Japan-India Vision 2025', a strategic policy document issued during PM Abe's visit to India in December 2015, which listed the improvement of road network connectivity in the region as one of the areas towards which Japan's ODA loans would be directed. Furthermore, the 'Japan-India Coordination Forum for the Development of North Eastern Region' and the 'Act East Forum' were established in 2017, accelerating the development drive for the region and beyond. Through these initiatives, Japan has been working to assist India's effort to turn Northeast from a neglected periphery to the gateway to Southeast Asia. It also matches Japan's own vision for the 'Free and Open Indo-Pacific' as well as India's 'Act East Policy'.

The local government too has shown eagerness towards developing the tourism sector in the region. While the northeastern states have rich tourism resources such as nature, culture and food, visits to the old battlefields and related sites such as war museums, memorials and cemeteries seem to remain one of the biggest motives for Japanese and British tourists who travel in the region. As N. Biren Singh, Chief Minister of Manipur, tweeted in early January 2021: 'Manipur is now on the war tourism map'.[20] The state government too seems to be responding to this growing demand. The Indian government's decision to relax the regulation on visiting the Northeast in 2012 also contributed to the increase of foreign tourists travelling to Manipur and Nagaland.

India's Northeast had been considered as a closed area for decades. Due to this, not only economic activities but also commemorative activities related to the battle of 1944 were limited, if not impossible. But as pointed out above, the fast-growing partnership between Japan and India in the 2010s, coupled with improvement of the security situation in the region, brought about considerable positive repercussions.

Conclusion

Japan has been conducting commemorative activities in India's Northeast in various ways including establishing peace memorials and sending bone-collecting missions since the 1950s. While these are meaningful, due to restrictions in India and indifference in Japan, these efforts remained low-key for a long time. The strategic partnership of Japan and India that began in the 2010s was a game-changer in this regard. It explains why there has been a renewed interest in the Battle of Imphal and Kohima and a series of activities and projects related to it have been held since 2017. One positive effect of these activities might be a growing interest in war-time history both in Japan and India, particularly for younger generations. However, there remain other issues: How can this growing interest in the battle be transformed into a mutual understanding between people in Japan, India and the UK? How should bone-collecting missions be conducted in the region in future? How should interactions and discussions on an intellectual level be pursued? The current situation thus cannot be considered as the end of the process, but only the beginning of a new phase of remembrance of the battle.

Notes and References

1. Major General P. K. Goswami, 'Commemoration 75th Anniversary of the Battle of Kohima and Imphal', United Service Institution of India, 2019, available at https://www.usiofindia.org/events-details/commemoration-75th-anniversary-of-the-battle-of-kohima-and-imphal.html, accessed on 18 January 2024.

2. 'Imphal Peace Museum inaugurated; Platinum Jubilee of Battle of Imphal Commemorated', E-Pao, 22 June 2019, available at https://e-pao.net/GP.asp?src=1..230619.jun19, accessed on 18 January 2024.

3. Burma changed its name to Myanmar in 1989. However, the older name Burma has been used in this chapter as most of the events related to the war and its remembrance took place before the change of name.

4. William Slim, *Defeat Into Victory* (London: Pan Books, 2009).

5. Ministry of Health, Labor and Welfare, Government of Japan, 'Erection of Monuments to War Dead', *Annual Health, Labor and Welfare Report 2020* (provisional English rendering), p. 222, available at https://www.mhlw.go.jp/english/wp/wp-hw13/dl/08e.pdf, accessed on 4 October 2023.

6. Shinzo Hayase, *Senso no kioku wo aruku: tonan ajia no ima* (Tokyo: Iwanami Shoten, 2007), pp. 149–153.

7. Kazufumi Hamai, *Kaigai senbotsusha no sengoshi* (Tokyo: Yoshikawa Kobunkan, 2014), p. 5.

8. Ministry of Health, Labor and Welfare, 'Chiikibetsu senbotsusha ikotsu shuyo gaikenzu', available at https://www.mhlw.go.jp/stf/seisakunitsuite/bunya/0000144250.html, accessed on 1 August 2021.

9. Hamai, *Kaigai senbotsusha no sengoshi*, p. 144.

10. According to Japanese diplomatic cables, Government of India declined to approve the subgroup's visit to Imphal after the mission had left Japan, citing as a reason the worsening of the security situation in the region. After consultations

between diplomatic officials, only a commemorative service was approved. However, bones of some 30 bodies were collected by an official of the Japanese consulate general in Calcutta who had visited Imphal in advance for the ceremony, based on an unofficial permission from the state government. See Hamai, *Kaigai senbotsusha no sengoshi*, pp. 120–121, 144–145.

11. 'Kyunihonhei no ikotsu shushu, 34nen buri saikai Indo hokutobu', *Nihon Keizai Shimbun*, 19 January 2012, available at https://www.nikkei.com/article/DGXNASDG1804C_Z10C12A1CR0000/, accessed on 2 August 2021.

12. Ministry of Health, Labor and Welfare, 'Indo ni okeru ikotsu shuyo jisshi jokyo', available at https://www.mhlw.go.jp/content/12100000/p06.pdf, accessed on 2 August 2021.

13. The Burma Campaign Society, 'About the Burma Campaign Society', available at http://theburmacampaignsociety.org/about-us, accessed on 3 August 2021.

14. Embassy of Japan in India, 'Address by Ambassador Kenji Hiramatsu on the 75th Anniversary of the Battle of Imphal', 4 April 2019, available at https://www.in.emb-japan.go.jp/files/000464856.pdf, accessed on 4 August 2021.

15. Embassy of Japan in India, 'Address by Ambassador Kenji Hiramatsu at the Inauguration Ceremony of the Imphal Peace Museum', available at https://www.in.emb-japan.go.jp/files/000491218.pdf, accessed on 4 August 2021.

16. 'Modi-Abe summit postponed amid protests over citizenship bill', *Nikkei Asia*, 13 December 2019, available at https://asia.nikkei.com/Politics/International-relations/Modi-Abe-summit-postponed-amid-protests-over-citizenship-bill, accessed on 5 August 2021.

17. 'India top recipient of Japanese financial aid since 2003, surpassing China', *The Economic Times*, 26 March 2021, available at https://economictimes.indiatimes.com/news/india/india-top-recipient-of-japanese-financial-aid-since-2003-surpassing-china/articleshow/81710675.cms?utm_source=contentofinterest&utm_medium=text&utm_campaign=cppst, accessed on 18 January 2024.

18. For example, the joint statement issued during Prime Minister Manmohan Singh's visit to Japan in May 2014 did not refer to the Northeast region. See Ministry of Foreign Affairs, 'Joint Statement: Strengthening the Strategic and Global Partnership between Japan and India beyond the 60th Anniversary of Diplomatic Relations', available at https://www.mofa.go.jp/mofaj/files/000005381.pdf, accessed on 10 August 2021.

19. Ministry of Foreign Affairs, 'Tokyo Declaration for Japan-India Special Strategic Global Partnership', 1 September 2014, available at https://www.mofa.go.jp/mofaj/files/000050549.pdf, accessed on 10 August 2021.

20. N. Biren Singh, Twitter Post, 4 January 2021, available at https://twitter.com/nbirensingh/status/1346150828273373185?lang=en, accessed on 10 August 2021.

Notes on the Editors and Contributors

Kenta Aoki is Executive Research Fellow at the Middle East Institute of Japan (MEIJ). His research primarily focuses on contemporary politics in Afghanistan and Iran.

Madhuchanda Ghosh is Assistant Professor at the Department of Political Science, Presidency University, Kolkata. She was a Fulbright Academic and Professional Excellence Fellow at Asia Center of Harvard University (2022).

Sayantan Haldar is a doctoral candidate at the Department of International Relations, South Asian University, New Delhi. He is also Joint Secretary of the Indian Ocean Research Group.

Purnendra Jain is Emeritus Professor at the University of Adelaide. He is also a visiting senior research fellow at the Institute of South Asian Studies, National University of Singapore, and an honorary fellow of the Indo-Pacific Research Centre at Murdoch University. He received the Order of the Rising Sun, Gold Rays with Neck Ribbon in 2021.

Ryohei Kasai is Visiting Associate Professor at Center for South Asian Studies, Gifu Women's University, Japan. He has previously served as a political researcher/advisor at Japanese embassies and is presently a director of the board of the Japan-India Association.

Kei Koga is Associate Professor at the Public Policy and Global Affairs Programme, School of Social Sciences, Nanyang Technological University, Singapore. He is also Non-resident Fellow at The National Bureau of Asia Research, USA.

Makoto Kojima is Professor Emeritus at Takushoku University, Tokyo, where he was earlier a professor of Indian economy for many years. He is also a senior research fellow at the Japan-India Association and was a member of the Japan-India Joint Study Group in 2004–05.

Shubhrajeet Konwer is Associate Professor of Political Science at Gauhati University, Assam. He teaches international relations and comparative politics.

Raj Kumar Kothari is Vice-Chancellor of The Sanskrit College and University, Kolkata and Vice Chancellor (additional charge) of West Bengal State University. He is Professor of Political Science and served as the Head of the Department of Political Science at Diamond Harbour Women's University and Vidyasagar University.

Shashank Mattoo is a New Delhi-based journalist and Foreign Affairs Correspondent with *Mint*. He was previously Junior Fellow at the Observer Research Foundation studying Indo-Pacific and East Asian politics.

Satoru Nagao is Fellow (Non-Resident) at Hudson Institute, Washington D.C. His primary research area is US-Japan-India security cooperation. He holds numerous research positions, including Visiting Fellow at Observer Research Foundation and Director at International Security Industry Council.

Harsh V. Pant is Vice President for Studies and Foreign Policy at Observer Research Foundation, New Delhi. He is Professor of International Relations with King's India Institute at King's College London, and also Director (Honorary) of Delhi School of Transnational Affairs at Delhi University.

Joshy M. Paul is a Research Fellow at Centre for Air Power Studies, New Delhi. He worked as Assistant Professor at the Department of International Studies, School of Law, Christ University, Bangalore, and also with the National Maritime Foundation, New Delhi.

Index